How Cities Won the West

HISTORIES OF THE AMERICAN FRONTIER

Editor:
HOWARD LAMAR, Yale University

Coeditors:
WILLIAM CRONON, University of Wisconsin
MARTHA A. SANDWEISS, Amherst College
DAVID J. WEBER, Southern Methodist University

HOW CITIES WON THE WEST

Four Centuries *of* Urban Change
in Western North America

Carl Abbott

UNIVERSITY OF NEW MEXICO PRESS   ALBUQUERQUE

© 2008 by the University of New Mexico Press
All rights reserved. Published 2008
Printed in the United States of America
13   12   11   10   09   08   1   2   3   4   5   6

Library of Congress Cataloging-in-Publication Data

Abbott, Carl.
How cities won the West : four centuries of urban change
in western North America / Carl Abbott.
p. cm. — (Histories of the American frontier)
Includes bibliographical references and index.
ISBN 978-0-8263-3312-4 (cloth : alk. paper)
    1. Cities and towns—West (U.S.)—History.
    2. Cities and towns—West (U.S.)—Growth.
    3. Cities and towns—Canada, Western—History.
    4. Cities and towns—Canada, Western—Growth.
    5. Metropolitan areas—West (U.S.)—Growth.
    6. Metropolitan areas—Canada, Western—History.
    7. West (U.S.)—Economic conditions.
    8. West (U.S.)—Social life and customs.
    I. Title.
HT123.5.W48A33 2008
307.760978—dc22
                            2008017632

Book design and type composition by Melissa Tandysh
Composed in 10/13 ScalaOT
Display type is ScalaSansOT

CONTENTS

LIST OF FIGURES

LIST OF TABLES

THIS BOOK OWES ITS IMPETUS TO THE LATE MARTIN RIDGE, WHO BUTTON-
holed me at a Western History Association meeting to suggest that I consider
such a project. It owes its title to Richard Wade, who tossed it out as I was
providing a brief tour of Portland, Oregon, and whose intellectual influence is
obvious in my attempts to trace the variety of urban frontiers through which
people with roots in Mexico, East Asia, Europe, eastern Canada, and the eastern United States occupied and changed western North America.

I have incurred a number of debts in researching and writing *How Cities
Won the West*. A short-term fellowship from the Newberry Library gave me
the opportunity to explore unique collections of maps and publications while
enjoying a return to Chicago. Some years ago, a Faculty Enhancement Grant
from the government of Canada allowed me to prepare a course on Canadian
cities, on which I have continued to draw. I have also benefited from the Faculty
Development Fund at Portland State University. Graduate research assistants
in our Urban Studies Program helped to run down stray information and
digest the fast-growing literature on western cities. I particularly appreciate
the help of Lynn Weigand and Joy Margheim. Students in a graduate semi-
nar on cities in the twentieth-century West offered engaging evaluations and
responses to recent scholarship that helped to clarify my own thinking.

A book of this sort, which tries to synthesize and interpret a broad body
of scholarship, is also indebted to hundreds of other scholars: those refer-
enced in the notes, those mentioned in the bibliographical essay, and those
whose names are inadvertently omitted. Fifteen years ago, when I wrote *The
Metropolitan Frontier: Cities in the Modern American West*, I was impressed
by the amount of recent historical writing from the 1980s that made my
work feasible. In writing this new book, I have been impressed two and three
times over by the new and good work on which I have been able to draw. I
thank all these colleagues and trust that I did justice to their own findings
and understandings of western cities.

I have been working on this project, although I did not know it at the time,
since I was hired in fall 1971 as a one-year fill-in to teach western history at the
University of Denver. On the list of my courses were "The Trans-Mississippi
West" and "History of Colorado." Well, I knew from my graduate studies about

the Old Northwest of Ohio, Indiana, Illinois, and Wisconsin (F. J. Turner Country, we might call it), but I had to read very quickly about the Pikes Peak gold rush, Cripple Creek labor strife, Colorado Springs tourism, and the origins and growth of Denver. I have continued to explore these and related topics in other western states and provinces in a book about the rise of Sunbelt cities, the previously mentioned book about western cities since 1940, and several books about my adopted hometown of Portland. As contributors to that work, and to this, I also have to thank various individuals who unwittingly furthered my thinking by inviting me to address specialized conferences or to contribute essays to specialized collections. In alphabetical order, they include Steve Aron, Richard Etulain, Robert Fairbanks, John Findlay, Howard Gillette Jr., Gene Gressley, Arnold Hirsch, Paul Hirt, William Lang, Roger Lotchin, Zane Miller, Ray Mohl, Gerald Nash, William Robbins, and David Wrobel. From our conversations about ways to structure contributions to the Metropolitan Portraits book series, which have affected my treatment of the recent West, I offer the same thanks to Judith Martin, Larry Ford, and Sam Bass Warner Jr.

All Roads Lead to Fresno

They sat against a rock bluff high in the Franklins. . . . To the south the
distant lights of the city lay strewn across the desert floor like a tiara laid
out upon a jeweler's blackcloth.
                    —Cormac McCarthy, *Cities of the Plain* (1998)

All the lights of the city were on now, a vast carpet of them stretching
down the slope to the south and on into the almost infinite distance.
                    —Raymond Chandler, *The Little Sister* (1949)

William Gilpin and William Gibson: The first was a failed politician and
moderately successful land speculator of the mid–nineteenth century. The second is a popular and innovative science fiction writer whose
career took off in the 1980s and was still going strong in the early years of the
twenty-first century.

Apart from their look-alike names, what can they possibly have in com-
mon? The answer is a vision of the future in which the cities of western North
America stand at the center of a global economy. Writing in the 1860s and
1870s, William Gilpin enthusiastically proclaimed that Denver was destined
to grow into the great city of North America and the pivot for trade among
Europe, America, and Asia. Fast-forward more than a century and find William
Gibson constructing a fictional future that revolves around Vancouver, San
Francisco, Los Angeles, Tokyo, and other cities of the Pacific Rim as the sites
of economic and cultural change.

Let's start with Gibson, an American who relocated to Vancouver and helped to launch the "cyberpunk" movement in science fiction. Along with other writers such as Neal Stephenson and Bruce Sterling, he has imagined an information-rich world of intense twenty-first-century capitalism.[1] The "cyber" part of the genre refers to the shared interest in information technology, human–computer interactions, virtual realities, and artificial intelligence. The "punk" part refers to a hard-boiled style adapted from detective stories and noir gangster movies. In the backstory against which these writers draw their neon-buzzing pictures of things soon to come, it's a world that revolves around the Pacific Ocean and assumes the interpenetration of North American and Asian cultures and economies. It's a world in which empire has taken its course westward from continental America to the rim of the Pacific and Seattle and San Francisco stand for the future of the American experiment as the places of economic power and cultural creativity, the pivot points for the twenty-first-century world.

Gibson's novel *Idoru* (1996) typically blends several plot lines. One is the story of Chia Pet McKenzie, a fourteen year old from Seattle whose devotion to an Asian pop music group takes her adventuring to Tokyo to check out troubling rumors. Chia gets pulled into a second high-energy story line about data theft and betrayal among American, Japanese, and Russian criminals. Hovering in the background is a moral tale about the meanings of celebrity, as a computer-generated singer first becomes a popular culture idol (*idoru*) and then takes on a life of her own.

Gibson published *Idoru* fifteen years after he burst onto the science fiction scene with a handful of brilliant short stories, followed by the "Sprawl" series of *Neuromancer* (1984); his work quickly became the public face and epitome of "cyberpunk." Raised in South Carolina, Arizona, and Virginia, he moved to Canada in 1968 with the acquiescence of his draft board and ended up in Vancouver, where he decided to try writing rather than graduate school. He entered the field of science fiction at the same time that Vancouver was turning cosmopolitan: "My wife was born in Vancouver and we moved out here in 1972. . . . At that time Vancouver was a kind of backwater. . . . In the meantime it has become sort of post-modern Pacific-rim and an endlessly expanding urban scene."[2] Vancouver was indeed becoming a multicultural city, where 25,000 Asian immigrants were arriving annually by the early 1990s and only 60 percent of residents used English as a first language by 1991. It was a setting that made Pacific cities and Pacific futures central to Gibson's speculative imagination.

Gibson, himself an expatriate, has made boundary crossing a central feature of his fiction. In *Idoru*, characters come together in Tokyo from Seattle, Tacoma, San Francisco, and Taiwan. Chia encounters a group of Japanese skateboard punks who call themselves the Oakland Overbombers, after a California soccer club. In the sequential *Virtual Light* and *All Tomorrow's*

Parties, the center of action is San Francisco, which attracts its key characters from Los Angeles, Portland, Tokyo, and China. The West Coast city
becomes a metaphor for creativity. The most arresting element of the city is
the San Francisco–Oakland Bay Bridge, where a spontaneous squatter town
has accreted after a quake rendered the bridge unusable. Over the years, the
squatters have built and bolted and glued all sorts of secondary structures to
the frame of the bridge, created their own social rules, and managed their
own barter economy. To a Japanese anthropologist, it is a place of discovery
and magic: "Fairyland. Rain-silvered plywood, broken marble from the walls
of forgotten banks, corrugated plastic, polished brass, sequins, painted can-
vas, mirrors, chrome gone dull and peeling in the salt air." At night the bridge
glows with scrounged and recycled lights and stands as physical expression of
the social variety that fuels creativity:

> Its steel bones, its stranded tendons, were lost within an accretion
> of dreams: tattoo parlors, gaming arcades, dimly lit stalls stacked
> with decaying magazines, sellers of fireworks, of cut bait, betting
> shops, sushi bars, unlicensed pawnbrokers, herbalists, barbers,
> bars. Dreams of commerce, their locations generally corresponding
> with the decks that had once carried vehicular traffic; while above
> them, rising to the very peaks of the cable towers, lifted the intri-
> cately suspended barrio, with its unnumbered population and its
> zones of more private fantasy.[3]

More than a century earlier, William Gilpin offered equally visionary de-
scriptions of the future cities of western North America. He saw himself as
writing scientific forecasts rather than fiction, but he ranged in his imagination just as widely as Gibson. Born in 1822 and a dropout from West Point,
Gilpin had been an explorer and Indian fighter before he settled in Missouri
and began to write about the potential of Kansas City, Missouri. In 1861,
President Lincoln appointed him the first territorial governor of Colorado.
He held the post for only a year but remained a Coloradan until his death in
1894. He speculated in Mexican land grants, unsuccessfully promoted railroads, and sang the praises and prospects of Denver.

In *The Central Gold Region: The Grain, Pastoral and Gold Region of North
America* (1860) and *The Mission of the North American People: Geographical,
Social and Political* (1874), Gilpin developed a geopolitical theory to explain
Denver's anticipated growth. Colorado, of course, encompassed vast mineral
resources and "lands of luxuriant fertility," with the San Luis Valley destined
to emerge as the new Vale of Kashmir. Europe, Asia, and South America
were fragmented continents, divided by their central mountains into small,
isolated maritime pockets. Convexity, isolation, stagnation, and disharmony
went together in the older world. Not so in North America, whose interior

presented toward heaven "an expanded bowl, to receive and fuse into harmony whatsoever enters within its rim." In this "amphitheatre of the world," Denver held a "pre-eminently cosmopolitan" position. Trade between Europe and Asia would flow along the fortieth parallel (the global "axis of intensity"), and Denver was *the* place where "the vast arena of the Pacific" would meet the Atlantic world as "the zodiac of nations closes its circle." Occupying "the focal point of impregnable power in the topographical configuration of the continent," Denver was preordained to be the nation's greatest city.[4]

Gilpin's contemporaries took practical action around the vision of Colorado's centrality. William Byers moved from Omaha to Denver in 1859 to start the *Rocky Mountain News*, which would soon claim by masthead and slogan to speak not for a city but for a future Rocky Mountain Empire. Pamphlets and books extolled the resources of mid-nineteenth-century Colorado and reported on the rapid growth of its biggest city. William Jackson Palmer in 1870 founded the Denver and Rio Grande Railroad to turn Byers's rhetorical empire into fact. His strategy was to construct a line southward from Denver along the base of the Rockies, tapping the mineral regions with spurs up valleys and canyons and looking ultimately toward Mexico. He anchored the railroad in Denver, expanded the industrial base of Pueblo, and built the city of Colorado Springs as a model community for morally sound members of the American and British elite.

Toward the end of his life, as the U.S. railroad system was laying its 150,000th mile of main track and the Canadian system its 15,000th, Gilpin authored yet another book. *The Cosmopolitan Railway: Compacting and Fusing Together All the World's Continents* (1890) still placed Denver squarely in the middle of the future but now as a stop on a grand railroad that was to circle the globe via Colorado, Alaska, and Siberia. The scheme was grandiose, far-fetched, and most unlikely, but this was an era when European and American colonialism, capital, and engineering expertise were opening the resources of Asia, Africa, and the Americas for world markets. The Canadian Pacific had opened the most northerly of transcontinental rail lines in 1885, and Russians would start to build the Trans-Siberian Railroad west from Vladivostok in 1891. Why not go Russia and Canada one better? And why not envision the cities of western America as the linchpins of a global economy?

William Gilpin and William Gibson directly introduce three of the recurring themes for this book about the role of cities in the development of the western half of North America. First, western cities grew as central and centralizing points. They were the places from which Europeans organized trade and commerce, the economic capitals of fast-growing regional economies, and the points of contact between continents. Some nineteenth-century cities were gateways between the West and the world. San Francisco, Portland, and Denver, for example, were places where railroads and shipping lines converged from resource hinterlands on one side and fanned out again

to national and world markets. Other cities lay in the middle of developing regions and provided the range of necessary business services from
bank loans to wholesale supply houses—Salt Lake City, Oklahoma City, Los
Angeles, and Dallas.[5]

Read even briefly in promotional literature or study nineteenth-century
maps and the rhetoric of centrality is inescapable. Was Winnipeg or St. Paul
destined to be the most central and convenient outlet for the northern prairies of the United States and Canada? You took your choice depending
whether you trusted promotional materials from Manitoba or Minnesota.
Was Kansas City or Denver or Chicago or St. Louis to be the nation's great
central city? The answer depended on who you asked. Even in the very middle of the Twin Cities hinterland, Mrs. Linda W. Slaughter could write in 1874
that the new town of Bismarck, strategically placed at the crossing of rail and
river, was "pleasantly situated one mile from the Missouri, about eight hundred miles above Sioux City, and five hundred and fifty miles west of St. Paul,
hence easy of access by both land and water."[6]

In the following decade, the Boise Board of Trade published a map of "the
Inter-Mountain District . . . showing the Present and Prospective Railway
Connections of Boise City." The map spans the vast territory from Denver at
the southeast to Victoria, B.C., to the northwest, with a big star for Boise City
and its radiating railroads. Only on careful inspection can you see that most
of them were "projected" (to California, Spokane, Helena) rather than built
or being built (the Union Pacific from Portland to Salt Lake City) and that
Boise actually needed a twenty-mile "stub" railroad to Nampa to tie into the
main transcontinental line. Nevertheless, the Board of Trade asserted that
Boise soon "will become the commercial and railway capital, as it is now the
political and educational capital, of the inter-mountain district."[7]

But wait, that's also what folks in Spokane believed. That city shows
only as a tiny dot on the Boise map, but in its own mind it was the Rome
of the Greater Northwest. As Katherine Morrissey points out, one need only
inspect the Washington city's own maps and discover that "All Roads Lead
to Spokane."[8] For a reality check, it was indeed Spokane that outgrew Boise
from the 1890s through the early twentieth century. In 1907, the riveting trial
of radical labor activists Big Bill Haywood and Charles Moyer for the murder
of former Idaho governor Frank Steunenberg was held in Boise but directly
involved private detectives from Spokane. The only available rail route from
the trial venue to the Coeur d'Alene mines of northern Idaho, where the "big
trouble" had its roots, went through Spokane.

And where's Fresno? According to the *General Directory of Fresno County,
California, for 1881,* the charming town of 2,000 people had the advantageous
location midway between Stockton and Los Angeles, in the center of a rich
area that might potentially support a city of 40,000. A decade later, readers
of a county history were asked to note that it was in the middle of California's

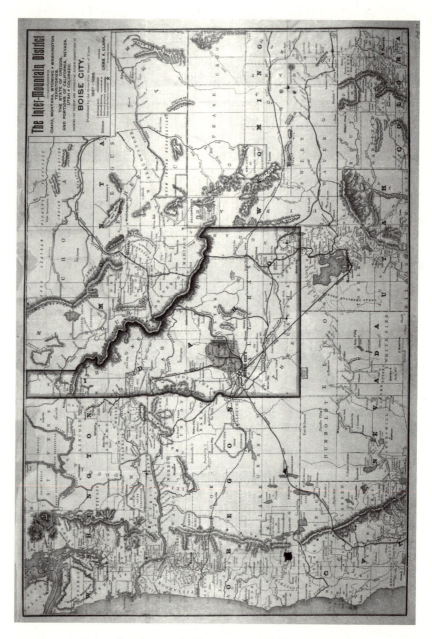

FIGURE 1. Boise's railroad network. The Boise Board of Trade published this map in 1887 in *Boise City and Southwestern Idaho: Resources, Progress, and Prospects.* Like many products of nineteenth-century boosterism, the map mixed existing operational railroads with lines in progress and routes that were still a gleam in their promoters' eyes. (Newberry Library.)

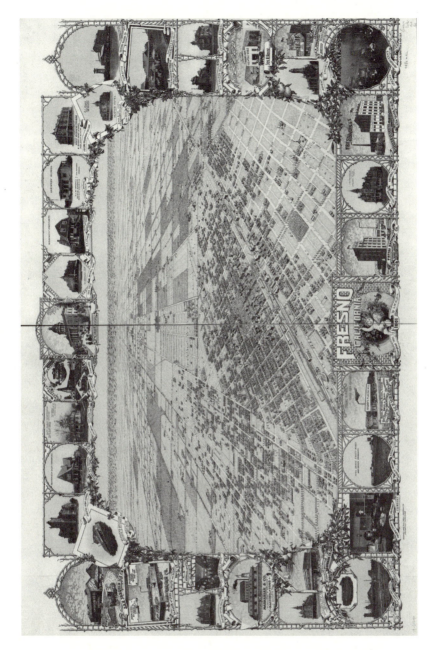

FIGURE 2. Fresno panorama in 1901. As depicted in 1901, roughly a quarter century into its growth, Fresno sits in the midst of farmland where highways and farm roads converge on a railroad. Similarly built cities could be found throughout western North America from California to Texas to Saskatchewan. Insets around the edge of the panorama showed houses, factories, and small commercial buildings—the face of the city before its businessmen built a high-rise downtown in the early twentieth century. (Image from the Library of Congress.)

central valley and the focus of the raisin, wine, wool, and fruit industries. Another booster at the end of the nineteenth century reiterated that "the city of Fresno is the exact geographical center of the State of California, and, what is more to the point, it is the commercial center of the vast and rich valley of the San Joaquin." According to the Fresno County Chamber of Commerce in *Fruitful Fresno: The Superlative County of California* (1917), it had a perfect location, smack in the middle between San Francisco and Los Angeles. All roads lead to Fresno—at least California Routes 41, 99, and 180, if not precisely Interstate 5.[9]

The intent is not to ridicule overblown claims, whether those for Denver, Fresno, or Bismarck. Nor is the purpose to blame boosters for raising false hopes, although Mrs. Slaughter was really stretching to write of blizzard-beset Bismarck that "pioneering in this country is divested of its rougher features. There are no obstacles of nature to overcome."[10] Rather, my intent is to emphasize the ubiquity of the city-building imagination and city-building impulse in shaping western North America. In the nineteenth century this imagination often took the form of bombastic boosterism because that was the rhetorical strategy available. By the later twentieth century, economic development professionals had taken over the job of urban promotion. Their publications now aimed at sophisticated corporations rather than naive land speculators and benefited from training in economics, geography, and regional planning, but their statistical tables and glossy photo spreads are direct descendants of pamphlets cranked out by long-dead newspapers and state immigration offices—down to the maps showing Worldport L.A. or the Dallas/Fort Worth Metroplex or Anchorage airport at the center of everything.

Gibson and Gilpin also direct our attention to a second theme: the cumulative rebalancing of western North America. In 1927 sociologist R. D. McKenzie made the point when he commented: "In the course of time most frontiers grow up. They pass from a pioneer to a settled condition, and in turn become new centers of dominance."[11] Writing from the University of Washington, McKenzie was thinking about the maturing of the United States vis-à-vis England and the emergence of Japan as a rival of Atlantic Europe. His point is equally apt for the contrast between the dependency of the West in the nineteenth century and its maturation as an independent source of economic and cultural change in the later twentieth century.

The eastern United States and Canada developed in the shadow of Europe as parts of an Atlantic system of migrations and economic exchange. Western cities, states, and provinces have been differently placed, looking in four directions: still eastward to be sure but also westward across the Pacific, north to the Arctic, and southward to Hispanic America. This is not a new insight. Writing in the 1880s, Josiah Strong believed that "the West is to dominate the East. With more than twice the room and resources of the East, the West will have probably twice the population and wealth . . . [and]

will determine our national character and, therefore, destiny."[12] California historian and publisher Hubert Howe Bancroft had much the same idea in mind in pointing American attention westward in *The New Pacific* (1899). The idea became a three-dimensional metaphor in journalist Neil Morgan's *Westward Tilt* (1963) and historian Earl Pomeroy's *The Pacific Slope* (1965), both books that have directly influenced my thinking. It appears most recently in Thomas Bender's *A Nation among Nations: America's Place in World History* (2006).[13]

The westward tilt has involved empire, commerce, and people, for the West spins within a distinct set of forces that are manifest in racial and ethnic mix, in economic partners, and in military connections. The United States reached the Pacific in the 1840s by dividing the Oregon country with Britain and seizing California from Mexico. It acquired a transpacific empire a half century later and fought four twentieth-century wars to maintain a position of influence in East Asia.

Flows of people and products followed. After the Immigration Reform Act of 1965 lifted national quotas for entry into the United States, Asian immigration climbed to over two million in the 1970s, 2.8 million in the 1980s, and approximately three million in the 1990s. Migration from Mexico and Central America into the U.S. Southwest grew even more rapidly. The value of U.S. commerce across the Pacific passed that across the Atlantic in the very early 1980s, a milestone that finally realized the boosterish expectations from the Panama Canal, and five of the ten leading U.S. trading partners in 2000 were Asian. Canada's Asian connections also grew in the later twentieth century, resulting in part from changes in Canadian law that replaced a list of "preferred nations" with a system that evaluates all applicants for immigration by a set of individual criteria. In 2001, Statistics Canada recorded that 8.5 percent of the nation's people were Asian Canadian, more than double the U.S. proportion of 3.6 percent.

The results of the continuing rebalancing are apparent in statistics on metropolitan population.[14] In the 2000 census of the United States, western metropolitan areas took eight of the top twenty slots. These eight supercities—Los Angeles, the San Francisco Bay metropolis, Dallas/Fort Worth, Houston, Seattle, Phoenix, San Diego, and Denver—all had more than two million residents and together accounted for 49 percent of the entire regional population. More than 80 percent of the people of California, Washington, Texas, Colorado, Arizona, Nevada, and New Mexico were metropolitan, along with more than 70 percent of those in Utah, Hawaii, and Oregon. The total metropolitan population of all nineteen western states in 2000 was 77,901,000, 28 percent of all Americans. Western cities are continuing to gain on the rest of the United States. If we look only at large metropolitan areas (500,000 people or more), thirteen of the twenty fastest growing were in the West. Las Vegas topped the chart with an astonishing population growth of 83 percent. If we take all metro areas, both small and large, the West accounted for eight of the ten fastest growing and three of the second ten.

The rise of western cities is just as pronounced north of the forty-ninth parallel. In 2001, four of Canada's eight largest Census Metropolitan Areas (CMAs) were western: Vancouver (third), Calgary (fifth), Edmonton (sixth), and Winnipeg (eighth). Along with smaller CMAs like Victoria and Saskatoon, Canada's metropolitan West (with a total of 5,425,000 people in 2001) accounts for 18 percent of all Canadians and 60 percent of the regional population—not quite at the share of the western United States but in the same ballpark (or hockey rink).[15] Calgary at 26 percent and Vancouver at 24 percent were the fastest-growing CMAs between 1991 and 2001.[16]

Gilpin's overblown prose and Gibson's headlong adventure also suggest a third theme: the accelerating transition of western cities from imitators of eastern culture and outposts of eastern capital to innovators that compete with Boston, New York, Washington, Toronto, and Chicago as centers of economic, social, and intellectual change. U.S. cities such as Seattle and Denver struggled mightily in the last decades of the nineteenth century to convince skeptical Easterners that they were sober, safe, and civilized. They staged world's fairs, hosted national political conventions, and promoted railroad tourism. Their civic leaders—usually the postpioneer generation—created public libraries, hired European musicians to lead nascent orchestras, donated the gleanings from European tours to new art museums, and endowed colleges and universities. Vancouver and Victoria meanwhile strove to be sedately British.

Over the course of the twentieth century, however, cultural change has increasingly moved from west to east, and the urban West may well represent a new culture hearth where changing customs and patterns of behavior are forging a new "Middle America" to replace that of the nineteenth and twentieth centuries. Chicagoans invented skyscrapers, but bungalows and suburban ranch houses spread from the West Coast. California suburbs became one of the prototypes for modern communities, with Sun City and Las Vegas following with their own distinct models for decentralized urbanization. The cities of the West were also the originators and field testers for the post–World War II culture of consumption, as well as the popularized locales where Americans could vicariously observe this culture. Much of the cultural capital of North America now comes from the great California cities and western universities. The Bay Area after World War II nurtured and exported a vibrant literature, new lifestyles, and new sets of political issues. Western cities have become centers of popular entertainment ("Hollywood"), multimedia innovation (San Francisco), and technical innovation (Silicon Valley). It is hard to imagine an early-twenty-first-century world without Hewlett-Packard and Intel, Amazon and Microsoft, Pixar

Studios and Industrial Light and Magic. Nor is it easy to imagine a scholarly world without the University of British Columbia, University of Washington, University of Texas, Stanford, Cal Tech, or the half-dozen metropolitan campuses of the University of California.[17]

My title for this book is deliberately provocative, for most historians in the twenty-first century think that the nineteenth-century concept of "winning the West" conceals much more than it illuminates and glosses over a multitude of environmental and societal sins of conquest (Theodore Roosevelt liked the phrase, for goodness sake). If we leave the phrase in semi-ironic quotation marks, however, it reminds us that urban settlements did "win the West" in the seventeenth, eighteenth, and nineteenth centuries as spearheads, anchors, and organizers of conquest and settlement carried out in many European languages. As briefly outlined, they were jumping-off points for exploration and military occupation, entry points for migration, and go-betweens in continental commerce. As western regions developed into components of a global economy—first California, the Northwest Coast, and the Southwest, then the Rocky Mountains and Hawaii, then the northern and southern plains, the Prairie Provinces of Canada, and the Far North—they grew as the organizing centers that assembled and sometimes processed resource exports, distributed eastern and European investment, and served as nodes for radiating railroads and highways.

This short book ranges over a vast territory—from the Gulf of Alaska to the Mississippi River, from the binational metropolis of San Diego/Tijuana to the Prairie Province capitals of Canada. I know that Canada is not the United States and that political institutions and culture have shaped Canadian cities in distinct ways. The two nations, however, passed the symbolic divide from majority rural to majority urban in quick succession: the United States toward the end of the 1910s and Canada in the early 1920s.[18]

At the same time, western Canada and the western United States have shared a long, permeable border and developed in the same eras of global capitalism. In the late nineteenth and early twentieth centuries, the northwestern quadrant of North America was a single arena for resource production from fur trapping to mining to agriculture. The border was open to migratory workers, settlers, and investors who moved easily back and forth in binational transportation corridors and economic regions from the Red River of the North to the great marine highway of Puget Sound and the Strait of Georgia in Washington and British Columbia. Gold rush prospectors from California treated British Columbia as an American annex and got to the mines via the Columbia River. A generation later, Americans got to the Alaskan interior through the Yukon Territory. Aboriginal Canadians provided a migratory labor force for Puget Sound mills. Plains farmers created common borderland farming regions and lifestyles that straddled the official border, as detailed in Wallace Stegner's *Wolf Willow*, a memoir of childhood in the 1910s. The family had already tried Seattle, Bellingham, and Iowa before arriving in Canada and would eventually move on again to Montana. In the summer the family sent its mail orders to Sears. In the winter they moved a few miles north to a small Saskatchewan town, where new school clothes came from the T. Eaton's catalog:

> Our homestead lay south of here, right on the Saskatchewan–
> Montana border—a place so ambiguous in its affiliations that we
> felt as uncertain as the drainage about which way to flow. . . . Our
> lives slopped over the international boundary every summer day.
> Our plowshares bit into Montana sod every time we made the turn
> at the south end of the field. . . . We bought supplies in Harlem or
> Chinook. . . . In the fall we hauled our wheat, if we had made any,
> freely and I suppose illegally across to the Milk River towns and
> sold it where it was handiest to sell it.[19]

These sorts of examples confirm the interpretation outlined more than half a century ago by Marcus Lee Hansen in *The Mingling of the Canadian and American Peoples*.[20] The pioneer of historical study of the Atlantic migrations of the nineteenth century, Hansen noted the openness of the continental border through most of its history. The result is that North America through much of its past has been shaped as a U.S.–Canada borderland just as much as a U.S.–Mexico borderland. In 1950 there were more Canadian-born than Mexican-born residents in all the U.S. cities from San Francisco, Salt Lake City, and Omaha northward. As late as 1980, Canada remained the most important source of immigrants to Bismarck, North Dakota; Billings and Great Falls, Montana; Spokane, Washington; Provo, Utah; Redding, California; and Medford, Oregon.

In broad view, the urban development of Canada from Winnipeg to Victoria is part of the same macro-historical process behind the urbanization of the plains, mountains, and Pacific coast of the United States. The era of settlement and region building started with the European imperial explorations and contests of the seventeenth and eighteenth centuries. It continued through the political assembly of the United States and Canada (recall that 1867 brought both the U.S. purchase of Alaska and the start of a five-year consolidation of separate British colonies into the Dominion of Canada). It stretched into the first decades of the twentieth century as mining towns, logging towns, and agricultural cities filled in the geographic gaps between early leaders such as San Francisco, St. Paul, and San Antonio. Winnipeg is as much a Great Plains gateway as Omaha. Edmonton and Calgary are part of a mid-continent energy empire that reaches south to Houston. Ecological visionaries and urban boosters alike see a single Cascadian region along the Northwest Coast from California redwood country to the Alaska panhandle and centered on Vancouver, Seattle, and Portland.[21] Canada will not get as much attention as the United States because of limits to my expertise and because the weight of numbers tilts toward the south, but cities on both sides of the border are participants in a shared historical drama.[22]

My discussion covers smaller cities as well as large. There is plenty of attention to Los Angeles, Dallas, Seattle, Denver, and Salt Lake City, but less prominent cities also get speaking parts in the story. Nearly two decades ago I flew to Billings to participate in a conference marking the centennial of statehood for the northern-tier states of Washington, Montana, North Dakota, and South Dakota. After three days to check out the city's hotels and rail-side warehouses, its downtown stores, the restaurants where local business people gathered for breakfast coffee and pancakes, and the minor league baseball park where young players from the Dominican Republic and Venezuela tried to hit and throw their way out of Montana and into the big leagues, I decided that Billings was going to be in any book I wrote about western cities. So Billings appears in the following pages. So do Boise, Butte, Bismarck, Bakersfield, Brownsville, and Burnaby.

This book has generous bounds in time as well as space. More than anything else, cities are vast devices for exchanging information, and changing technologies of transportation and communication have keyed the differences among different urban eras. In particular, western North America over the past five centuries has been part of a sequence of three city types—preindustrial cities, industrial cities, and an emerging type that can tentatively be called postindustrial. Each type is associated with a global shift in the balance between urban and nonurban population. Each development has involved revolutionary changes in settlement patterns and social institutions.

Imagine first a caravan of high-packed wagons and heavily burdened mules plodding the royal road from El Paso del Norte toward Santa Fe in the 1750s, hundreds of dusty miles behind and the treacherous *journada del muerto* yet to come. Then picture a worker on his way to Butte in a smoky coach on the Northern Pacific railroad, a traveling salesman taking the Katy railroad from St. Louis to Dallas, and a family with cut-rate tickets on the Santa Fe Railroad taking their hopes to a citrus farm in booming southern California—all in the 1880s. Finally, remember your last stopover at LAX or Sea-Tac or Dallas/Fort Worth airports, their concourses crowded with business travelers clutching laptops, families chattering on cell phones, and foreign visitors trying to figure out how to transfer to Disneyland.

Along with *metropolis* and *region*, the key word in this urban interpretation of western development is *connections*. No single framework can encompass everything. Every synthesis highlights certain aspects of the historical experience and shrugs off others. Nevertheless, an urban system approach offers a number of advantages for organizing the history of western states and provinces:

It highlights the direct connections between the development of the West and larger historical changes such as mercantile imperialism, industrialization, and the rise of an information economy. It helps to situate the West at the crossroads of the modern world. We can see Arizonans, Albertans, and Alaskans as western *North* Americans, as Pacific North Americans who share history in common with Australasians and East Asians, and as inhabitants of a continental periphery that shares a common history with the American South.

The approach links the eighteenth and twentieth centuries in a single analytical structure and suggests appropriately heavy emphasis on the twentieth. Without ignoring the nineteenth century, it places the decades of initial English-speaking settlement within a larger frame rather than picking out the conquest of a western frontier as a freestanding historical event.

The concern with economic growth and the changing distribution of population emphasizes the essentials of frontier history. However, it also draws attention to cities as arenas for exploring conflict and accommodation among classes, races, and ethnic groups. For the twentieth century, it helps to explain many issues of environmental change as a result of urban demands for previously rural resources.

To close this introduction, I want to illustrate the centrality of cities to ways in which Westerners have defined themselves with two utterly dissimilar documents—a sixty-year-old matchbook cover and a sprawling, challenging novel of much more recent vintage. The matchbook is a souvenir from a road trip that my family took from Tennessee to Idaho in summer 1950, just weeks before I started the first grade. It was distributed by the Casper, Wyoming, Chamber of Commerce. The outer cover shows the Wyoming cowboy in standard profile and proclaims "Casper, Hub of Wyoming. Gateway to the Last Frontier. The Acknowledged Convention and Industrial City of Wyoming." Inside it repeats "Casper, Hub of Wyoming" and adds additional enticements: "Finest Hotels and Tourist Courts . . . Gay Night Clubs" (with no *Brokeback* meanings, I'm sure). On a miniature map all roads lead to Casper from Sheridan, Thermopolis, Riverton, Rawlins, Cheyenne, and Lusk. Here in sparsely populated Wyoming, it is a city that centers the state, drawing together its web of highways, reaching back to the past of the last frontier, and looking forward to the future.

For stark contrast *and* confirmation, turn to Leslie Marmon Silko's *Almanac of the Dead* (1991), a novel that runs a dozen out-of-control life stories

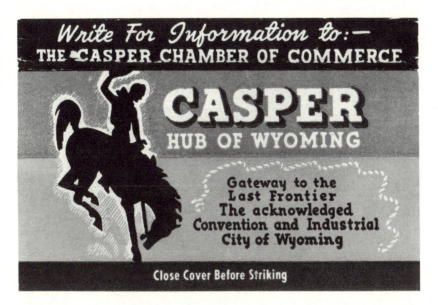

FIGURE 3. All roads lead to Casper. Distributed in 1950 by the Casper Chamber of Commerce, this matchbook combined Wyoming's classic cowboy icon with a series of claims that the small city of 24,000 was the economic and communication center of the state.

in parallel.[23] This half-realistic, half-fantastic book by a Native American writer tries to connect the 1990s to the deep past as it weaves together stories of urban sophisticates and Indians, politicians, coke addicts, laborers, and crooks who deal in real estate, drugs, and smuggled immigrants—all with lives intersecting in Tucson. Open the book to the pages between the table of contents and "Part One: The United States of America" to an equally sprawling map. Tucson is in the middle just as much as Boise or Spokane centered maps in a previous century. Dotted lines and arrow points connect Tucson to El Paso and San Diego and the hinterland of the Four Corners; to Mexico City and New Jersey; to the Caribbean, the Pacific, and Alaska. Tucson—like the other cities of western North America—is central, is socially complex, is internationally connected, is a place where past and present come together to shape the future.

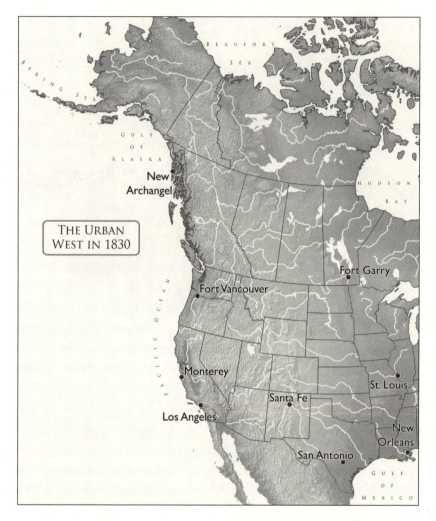

Map labels:

BEAUFORT SEA

BERING SEA

GULF OF ALASKA

HUDSON BAY

New Archangel

THE URBAN WEST IN 1830

Fort Garry

Fort Vancouver

PACIFIC OCEAN

Monterey

St. Louis

Santa Fe

Los Angeles

New Orleans

San Antonio

GULF OF MEXICO

FIGURE 4. The urban West in 1830. After more than two centuries of European interest in western North America, the vast region was ringed by small Russian, Mexican, American, and British settlements and outposts. (Map by Alejandro Bancke.)

CHAPTER ONE

Outposts of Empires

*He came upon Bexar [San Antonio] in the evening of the fourth day and
he sat the tattered mule on a low rise and looked down at the town, the
quiet adobe houses, the line of green oaks and cottonwoods that marked
the course of the river, the plaza filled with wagons with their osnaburg
covers and the whitewashed public buildings and the Moorish church-
dome rising from the trees and the garrison and the tall stone powder-
house in the distance.*

—Cormac McCarthy, *Blood Meridian* (1985)

*In after years, you will think of it as the City of the Little Squares. After
all the other memories are gone—the narrow streets twisting and turning
their tortuous ways through the very heart of the old town, the missions
strung out along the Conception road like faded and broken bits of bric-
a-brac, the brave and militant show of arsenal and fort—then shall the
fragrance of these open plazas long remain. . . . They lend it the Latin air
that renders it different from most other cities in America. They help to
make San Antonio seem far more like Europe than America.*

—Edward Hungerford, *The Personality of American Cities* (1913)

Sitka, Alaska, wasn't much of a town 200 years ago—nor is it all that impressive today with its fewer that 9,000 people—but it was the nerve center for
a Russian trading territory that arced 1,200 miles from the Aleutian Islands to
the Queen Charlotte Islands of present-day British Columbia.

The town had a precarious start. The Russian-American Company placed its original base on Kodiak Island in 1784. As hunting parties ranged farther and farther eastward after sea otter, the company planted an outpost that it named Archangel Michael on the seaward side of what is now Baranov Island. The fort infuriated the native Tlingit people as an intrusion on sacred ground and a usurpation of prime fishing territory. They overran and sacked Archangel Michael in 1802 and remained a potent hostile force after Governor Alexander Baranov refounded the post as New Archangel in 1804 and moved his headquarters there in 1808.

There were strategic reasons for the choice. New Archangel had a superior harbor and better timber. It was far closer than Kodiak to Alta, California, where the Russians bought necessary grain and supplies from the Spanish Mexican rancheros. It interposed the Russian-American Company squarely between the Tlingits and American sea captains who were trading firearms for furs. It helped to fend off the British, who were active along the Columbia and Fraser rivers and looking north along the coast (the islands of what is now the Alaska panhandle, including Baranov Island, were the King George III Archipelago to the British and [Czar] Alexander Archipelago to the Russians).

Sitka grew slowly, starting with fewer than 200 Russians and several hundred Aleut employees in 1810. The Tlingits remained formidable until the late 1830s, when smallpox reduced their numbers and the arrival of some of the Russian navy's first steam-powered ships allowed the Russians finally to outmaneuver Tlingit canoes. Until then, the military barracks, arsenal, and storehouses all crowded for safety inside a fort that perched on a small promontory, but the church, school, and civilian houses stood in constant danger outside the walls. Incessant rain made the looming forest ever darker and more threatening. Wooden buildings rotted within ten years. The only local crops were watery turnips and potatoes. Pork tasted like the rancid fish that fed the local hogs. Some officials argued for a return to Kodiak, an option that remained on the table until Ferdinand Von Wrangell confirmed Sitka as the Russian capital. The population slowly climbed to 1,279 Russians in 1845 and then sagged until the United States acquired the orphaned territory of Russian America in 1867 and made the sixty-year-old Russian capital its base of official operations until 1906.

Far to the southeast, past fjord-lined coast, volcanic peaks, high desert, and granite mountains, Santa Fe was completing its second century at the same time that Governor Baranov was setting up shop in New Archangel. Even with a head start of two centuries, however, it was scarcely more substantial. The town got its start as a privately settled village in 1608. It was formally reconstituted as a royal colony and seat of government in 1610: La Villa Real de la Santa Fe de San Francisco.[1] The villa was part of the far northern frontier of sixteenth-century New Spain, as precariously sited as New Archangel at an extreme of European expansion. Santa Fe's early connection

SITKA
ALASKA

From Aleutski Island in Eastern Harbor. Greek Church bearing N.75°E. true.

FIGURE 5. Sitka, Alaska, in the 1860s. At the time of American acquisition of Alaska, the newly renamed settlement of Sitka clustered around the Russian fort. Similarly to the British settlement at Victoria to the south, its island location provided a measure of security and easy access by water to the surrounding region. (Special Collections, University of Washington Library, Neg. UW 8135.)

to Mexico was a caravan that arrived every third year over the long road from Chihuahua through El Paso. The only salable products were wool and Indian slaves for Mexican silver mines. A great Pueblo Indian revolt in 1680 drove the outnumbered Spanish from Santa Fe and all of the Upper Rio Grande Valley for fourteen years, until Diego de Vargas reconquered the territory and refounded the capital.

Located 1,500 miles from Mexico City and another 6,000 miles from Madrid, Santa Fe was the point through which Spain asserted control over the Rio Grande Valley. Hispanic villages stretched roughly 200 miles through the regions of Rio Abajo (Lower River) south of Santa Fe and Rio Arriba (Upper River) north of the town. Through the eighteenth century, Santa Fe was the starting point for expeditions to explore the Rocky Mountains and Great Plains and military campaigns against Utes, Comanches, and Apaches. It was the place where U.S. Army captain Zebulon Pike spent much of the winter of 1806–7 in custody after straying into Spanish territory on an exploring expedition up the Arkansas River. In the 1820s, it became the terminus for a famous trail from Missouri, along which Americans drove wagons full of textiles and hardware to exchange for buffalo hides, beaver pelts, and horses.

What was Santa Fe like? The first surviving map, which dates from 1766, shows traces of a compact settlement on the north side of the small Santa Fe River. The governor's residence and offices and adjacent barracks were in a low-slung compound on the north side of a rectangular plaza (that's the Palace of the Governors that tourists now visit). A church faced the opposite corner of the plaza, although it would later be blocked when houses encroached on the open space. Beyond the center, it was hard to keep to a grid when the major roads come in on diagonals from Pecos, Galisteo, Santa Cruz de la Canada, and other points, so the rest of the town was scattered buildings of adobe that put farmers close to their fields. The result was not very imposing. Bishop Tamaron of Durango (Mexico), who visited in 1760, wrote that it was "a very open place" with "the houses far apart." Although the town was entering a prosperous period when exports of hides and sheep would support a growing *rico* elite as well as barrel makers, weavers, blacksmiths, and cobblers, Father Francisco Dominguez was equally unimpressed in 1776: "Its appearance, design, arrangement, and plan do not correspond to its status as a villa nor to the very beautiful plain on which it lies, for it is like rough stone set in fine metal. . . . The government palace is like everything else there, and enough said." Seventy years later, when the town had just passed into American control, the lucrative trade with Missouri over the Santa Fe Trail had pushed its population to around 4,500. Nevertheless, first impressions were still negative. Frederick Ruxton thought it resembled "a dilapidated brick kiln or prairie dog town." Travelers who had just crossed the Great Plains must have had rodents on their minds, because A. Wislizenus agreed that it looked from a distance "more a prairie-dog village than a capital."[2]

Both Sitka and Santa Fe—despite their small size and rough construction— played key roles in the European conquest of North America. They epitomize the way that the global empires of Spain, France, Britain, and Russia, and then the new continental nation of the United States, approached and contested western North America through nascent cities. From the 1600s through the early 1800s, each empire planted towns on the continental periphery to serve as trading centers and military bases. Some of these points of entry were crude isolated posts like the Spanish presidio of San Francisco or like Fort Detroit, where tiny French and then British garrisons and their families lived half-starved lives. Others grew into small but diversified towns that were intended to anchor a permanent national claim as strongpoints in imperial rivalry (minuscule as their garrisons of twenty or fifty might be in comparison with the contemporaneous armies of Louis the XIV or the Duke of Marlborough).

In the later sixteenth and seventeenth centuries, before histories of settlement, development, and politics differentiated eastern North America from western, a first generation of trading and garrison towns began to mark the edges of the territory that was to become the United States and Canada. The South Atlantic coast came first, with France (Fort Caroline) and Spain (St. Augustine) battling over northern Florida in the 1560s. The English failed to stick at Roanoke Island but hung on, just barely, at Jamestown after 1607. Quebec dates from 1608; Santa Fe, from 1609–10; New Amsterdam, from 1626; Boston, from the 1630s; Sweden's Fort Christina on the Delaware River, from 1638; and Montreal, from 1642.

Not every tenuous fort or tiny trading post—and there were dozens beyond this list—can be counted as a town. One criterion, surely, was the intention of permanence. A second test is whether and when real estate entered the private market and civilian residents were able to own and pass on property. A third is whether a town was a seat of comprehensive government: Was it the home of a colonial governor? Was it the place where legal disputes could be decisively resolved? A fourth is the development of a diverse local economy that involved something more than directly supporting missionaries or the military: Was it a place that traded with many other places? Did it provide commercial services for smaller, surrounding communities? Had it grown beyond the capacity of its local hinterland to supply it with food and fuel?[3]

These are the sorts of developments that historian Darrett Rutman explores in his classic study *Winthrop's Boston*, which examines how the initial settlement of Shawmut became New England's *city* while other early settlements in Puritan Massachusetts remained fishing villages and farm towns.[4] The catalyst was economic crisis in the 1640s, the second decade of Puritan colonization, when the outbreak of civil war between England's king and Parliament in England commanded the attention and resources of English Puritans. As immigration and investment from England slowed, New Englanders had to find ways to directly support themselves. In the resulting search for markets and trading partners, Boston emerged as the convenient and necessary business center and port. News came to Boston first. Inland communities remained isolated, but Bostonians increasingly rubbed shoulders with shipowners, merchants, and seamen. Non-Puritans built houses and businesses, and the city's merchants began to accumulate modest and then substantial wealth that widened the gap with the rest of the Puritan colony.

More coastal cities followed in the later seventeenth and eighteenth centuries. Charleston, South Carolina, in the 1670s, Philadelphia in 1682, and Savannah in 1733 topped off the list of England's West Atlantic cities. By the middle of the eighteenth century, several were respectable cities. With populations ranging from 7,000–8,000 upward to 20,000, Charleston, Quebec (British after 1763), Boston, New York, and Philadelphia were comparable in size to the provincial centers of Britain—and, on the part of their leading merchants, comparable as well in social ambition. These were places whose economic life revolved around the waterfront. In the decades before the American Revolution, for example, New York's wharves and warehouses crowded the East River at the south end of Manhattan, interspersed with cheap taverns for sailors and dockworkers. A couple blocks back were more warehouses and counting houses, now interspersed with more substantial houses and coffeehouses where merchants could exchange the latest news. The most elegant homes, filled with imported furnishings and china, occupied the lower end of Broadway, close to the fort at the island's tip and cooled by fresh air from New Jersey. The middling classes of artisans and small shopkeepers lived a bit farther from the center, close by public markets and the chapels of dissenting Baptists and Methodists.[5]

The growth and prosperity of the coastal cities depended on a system of country towns and smaller cities that fed the business of the larger coastal ports. Boston continued to dominate regional trade in New England. Village merchants assembled local products that they sold to middlemen in larger towns such as Hartford; Springfield and Salem, Massachusetts; New Haven; and Portsmouth, New Hampshire. These middlemen in turn traded their agricultural products for English manufactured goods imported by the Boston merchants who engaged in overseas trade with Europe, the Caribbean, and Africa. The trade of Long Island Sound and the Hudson Valley as far inland as Albany flowed through New York. Philadelphia dominated Delaware River commerce and reached the Susquehanna Valley with roads to towns like Lancaster, Pennsylvania. Coasting vessels brought goods to Charleston from Savannah and Wilmington, North Carolina. Charleston tapped the Carolina interior at towns like Camden, little more than a country crossroads in appearance but located on the major road to Virginia and Pennsylvania and possessing all the functions of an urban center, with stores, warehouses, flour mill, sawmills, courthouse, jail, and churches.

This growing urban system (although cities and large towns still accounted for no more than 5 percent or so of the population of British and French America) overlapped with the "long eighteenth century" in Europe. Roughly from 1689 to 1815, the dominant elements in European geopolitics were the shifting alliances and wars through which England and other nations tried to contain the rising power of France and to sort out the fortunes of Europe's royal dynasties. In North America, the era saw multilateral contests for Caribbean sugar islands and for the furs, fisheries, and timber of northeastern America. The Anglo–French–Indian wars were part of this larger contest. So were the American revolutionary alliance with France against Britain and the struggle by the new United States to hold its economic independence during the Napoleonic wars.

For a book that focuses on western North America, however, the more pertinent European rivalries are those that extended into the vast, vaguely bounded, mid-continental territories of "Texas" and "Louisiana" and the fur-trading hinterland accessed from Hudson Bay and the northern lakes. Cities like French/Spanish New Orleans, French/Spanish St. Louis, and Spanish/Mexican San Antonio were chess pieces in this imperial game, advanced to strategic spots and trading crossroads. As we've noted, a second rivalry ranged along the Pacific coast from San Diego and Los Angeles to Astoria, Oregon, and Sitka. The end product of the contests—in addition to a long sequence of negotiations, treaties, and territorial exchanges—was a loosely woven net of small but important cities that began to encircle the western half of North America.

Few of these places were physically imposing. They were smaller than the West Atlantic cities by an order of magnitude, with 500 to 2,000 people rather than 5,000 to 20,000. The number of "European" settlers in their backcountry could be counted in the thousands, not the hundreds of thousands. Town dwellers themselves were racially mixed, making it hard for Spanish census takers to sort the *espanoles* from *indios, mestizos,* and *coyotes* (darker-skinned mestizos) and impossible for French officials to enforce absolute sexual distance among white, black, red, and brown-skinned residents.

French traders and missionaries reached the Mississippi Valley from the Great Lakes with the expeditions of Marquette and Joliet, La Salle, and Hennepin in 1673–82. French settlements appeared along the Mississippi River and its tributaries at places such as Kaskaskia and Vincennes. French expeditions to the Gulf of Mexico founded Mobile in 1702 and rebuilt it in 1710, but the most far-reaching of these efforts was to plant New Orleans on a strip of relatively dry land along a bend of the Lower Mississippi. The future Crescent City dates to 1718, when Sieur de Bienville sent a few Canadians to clear the site, but was not formally planned until 1722. It was far from the grand city of 800 fine houses and five parishes described by John Law, whose fervent promotion of his Western Company and its plans for settlement along the Mississippi built into the French financial crisis of the Mississippi Bubble. Nevertheless, New Orleans quickly supplanted Mobile as the center of French activity on the gulf.

Spain responded by pushing along the Gulf Coast from Mexico into Texas, founding a confusing series of often short-lived missions and presidios that reached as far as northwestern Louisiana, with Spanish Nacogdoches only a hundred miles from French Natchitoches. The most important of these Texas settlements was San Antonio, dating from the same year as New Orleans. Fear of French influence and arms trading with the Pawnees and Comanches of the southern plains also gave renewed importance to Santa Fe.[6]

On the Northwest Coast of the continent, Russian explorers Vitus Bering and Alexi Chirikov had reached the Aleutians and Alaska in 1740–42. Spanish interest and concern mounted over the next decades, and Spanish officials decided to move northward along the Pacific coast in 1769–70 to plant three missions plus presidios at San Diego and Monterey. As tourists and California schoolchildren know, more missions as well as presidios at San Francisco (1776) and Santa Barbara (1782) filled in along the coast in the next decades. Recognizing the difficulty of supplying soldiers on far frontiers, an edict from Madrid in 1772 positively encouraged the development of civilian communities around presidios and provided for the distribution of town lots and farmlands to such settlers. In the same interest of supporting the military presence by increasing local food supply, Governor Philip de Neve founded civilian towns at San Jose in 1777 and Los Angeles in 1781.

Britain and the United States added to the imperial vortex in the same closing decades of the eighteenth century. British explorer James Cook probed the coast in 1778. Englishman George Vancouver and American Robert Gray both entered the Columbia River in 1792, a year before Alexander Mackenzie found a route across what are now the Canadian Rockies. While Americans and Russians traded with the coastal Indians for sea otter pelts, the North West Company and then the Hudson's Bay Company consolidated the British dominance of continental fur trading. Americans failed to sustain a trading post of Astoria at the mouth of the Columbia River, opening the way for John McLoughlin to build Fort Vancouver upstream on the Columbia in 1824 as a Pacific center of the Hudson Bay empire (earlier fortified posts had marked the future site of Winnipeg in 1783 and Edmonton in 1801). The unexpected planting of a Russian post on the California coast at Fort Ross in 1811 eventually led the Mexican government to establish Sonoma as the last of the Hispanic pueblos in 1835.[7]

None of these moves and countermoves happened fast. It took years for imperial administrations to digest reports from a distant continent, decide on new efforts, find resources, and set new projects on their way. The results were slow-motion bouts of geo-imperial feints, punches, and counterpunches that dragged out over decades and generations. Nor were strategic decisions in Madrid or Paris or St. Petersburg always implemented by authorities on the scene. For example, the Spanish government decided in 1772 that a line of presidios from the Gulf of California to South Texas should mark the northern frontier of Mexico, but officials continued to put resources into the parts of Texas, the Rio Grande settlements, and California that lay north of the line.

It is remarkable how much importance everyone—that is, everyone whose job was to promote national ambitions—placed on an *urban* frontier. Spanish bureaucrats in Madrid pulled together a set of standards for city planning at the behest of Philip II, who promulgated "the Laws of the Indies" in 1573 to keep distant conquistadors and their successors in line. This list of nearly two score standards and specifications drew on the *Ten Books on Architecture* by Vitruvius, on Leon Battista Alberti's reworking of classic writers on civic design in *De Re Aedificatora*, on garrison towns, and on the growing European art of military fortification as detailed in books like Nicolo Machiavelli's *Arte della Guerra*.[8]

The authorities in England's Chesapeake colonies shared the same city-making impulse: Settlers who concentrated in towns would be easier to control, easier to tax, and easier to civilize through mandated church attendance. The challenge was the abundance of tidal rivers and estuaries that reduced the need for centralized ports. Virginia officials tried in 1662 with an "Act for Building a Towne" and again with New Town Acts in 1680, 1690, and 1706. Norfolk and Hampton were among the few force-fed towns that took. In Maryland, three Proprietary Decrees and seven acts of the assembly between 1668 and 1708 tried for the same goal. Annapolis became a capital and tidewater entrepôt, but other nascent cities such as Baltimore and Georgetown had to wait for farming to spread beyond the fall line.

The Laws of the Indies assumed a particular kind of settlement. Spanish officials knew from their own experience that true cities had centers. City life in preindustrial Europe and the Mediterranean revolved around central squares where cathedrals, guild houses, city halls, and palaces overlooked market days, religious celebrations, itinerant merchants, and gossiping grandees. In cities where everyone moved on foot, the homes of the rich crowded the center, while craftspeople, traders, and workers arrayed themselves in surrounding neighborhoods. The ubiquitous urban form was portable. When Pizarro and his band of freebooters seized Cuzco from the Incas, they easily adapted the old city to new rulers: The central plaza stayed, a cathedral replaced the palace of the Inca, and the massive stone houses of the Indian nobility went to conquistador captains.

The 1573 standards started with the admonition to find a suitable site that not only was healthy but allowed for continued growth. There followed detailed attention to the plaza, which was to lie in the center of inland towns and to face the water for coastal ports. It was to be a rectangle ("this proportion is the best for festivals in which horses are used"), to be the focus of the principal streets, and to be sized according to the expected size of the town—not smaller than 200 by 300 feet or larger than 300 by 800 feet. Bordering the plaza were to be the town hall, customs house, arsenal, and shops. Streets would be laid out on a right-angled grid. As in New England, a new town had rights to surrounding territory of somewhere between sixteen and twenty-eight square miles. New residents were to receive town lots and, beyond a zone of common pasturelands, individual farm plots. New towns were to have at least thirty families with a *cabildo* or elected council. In town after town—around the Caribbean, from Texas to Central America, north to California, and south to Chile—Spanish settlers followed the rules, fixing a central plaza and measuring out right angles with rudimentary surveying tools.

New Orleans, although French rather than Spanish, matched the same urban ideal. A map from 1764 shows a town extending eleven blocks along the Mississippi and reaching four blocks back from the waterfront. Fronting the river was the Place d'Armes (now Jackson Square), bordered by church, convent, jail, guardhouse, governor's house, and powder magazine. Because the site was constricted between a wide, surging river and a swampy interior, New Orleans was compact by necessity, its people building their houses and shops as close to the center as possible.[9]

Most of the other frontier towns, however, were loose and straggling settlements despite their official plans. Santa Fe in the 1766 map stretched for three miles along its river. As Marc Simmons has documented, Albuquerque in the eighteenth century was a series of farms strung along the Rio Grande and the road to Santa Fe. After a church was built and the farms became established, many families built second houses near the modern "Old Town" plaza where they might stay for Sunday but spent more of their time tending their farms.[10] Maps and sketches of Los Angeles at the time of American takeover show a clearly defined center around an irregular plaza with a church and relatively large two-level buildings, but the rest of the settlement sprawled out to the south and east along irrigation canals. Monterey, as depicted in 1842, had the old presidio and Calle Principal at its center, but houses and warehouses spread thinly along the curving bay.[11]

Whatever their layout on the ground, however, colonial capitals and ports exerted powerful centripetal forces. They were political, economic, and cultural centers that drew in activity from immediate hinterlands and tied isolated provinces into global systems of economic and political exchange.

Towns were, first of all, the centers for surrounding farmers and ranchers. Even in Virginia, where the urban system was most rudimentary, landholders assembled at the courthouse crossroads on election days. The more sophisticated Spanish system gave townspeople control over the land within two to three miles of the pueblo or villa, either as commons or as allocated lots and farm plots. Officials expected townspeople to live close to the plaza, even when their farms were two or three miles distant, or to build town houses for Sundays as in Albuquerque. In southern California, the white cupola of

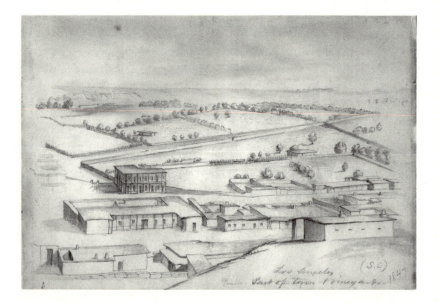

FIGURE 6. Los Angeles in 1847. Los Angeles at the time of the war between Mexico and the United States, here sketched by William Rich Hutton, was a small cluster of buildings amid fields and vineyards that were irrigated from the Los Angeles River. (Courtesy of Henry E. Huntington Library and Art Gallery.)

the church that rose above green trees and gardens marked the center of Los Angeles from fifteen miles off. Land grants in the Mexican era were defined by distance from the front door of the Los Angeles plaza church. Public buildings lined the plaza on one side—granary, jail, chapel—and adobe shops and houses lined the others. Here was where the roads to Santa Fe, Monterey, San Pedro, and Santa Fe converged—the predecessors of I-40, 101, and the Harbor Freeway. As Mary Ryan summarizes, the Mexican plaza was the place where the rancheros worshipped on Sundays, decided public business, and celebrated church festivals at Corpus Christi and Christmas. When Commodore Stockton swept into town in 1846, he reportedly marked American conquest with a band concert in the plaza. "The records of the Pueblo of Los Angeles," writes Mary Ryan, "chart a magnetic field that extended from mountain to sea but pulled a society together at a single point, the Plaza."[12]

The towns of the North American frontiers were also exchange and information centers. In an era when information traveled slowly and unreliably, news of outside markets and political upheavals was precious, and most communication was face-to-face. French adventurers strolled along the New Orleans levee to catch the cooling breezes and shoot the breeze. Atlantic merchants haunted taverns and coffeehouses on both sides of the ocean. The authority of church and civil government simultaneously extended outward from cities and down organizational ladders. When war came—to French Canada in the 1760s, to the Atlantic seaboard in the 1770s, to northern Mexico in the 1840s—to capture a city was to take control of the communications and market economy of an entire region.

As the capital of Alta California, for example, Mexican Monterey had sophistication and prominence far beyond its numbers. First with the trade in sea otter pelts in the 1790s and then with the expansion of the trade of hides and tallow from California ranches, Monterey became a point in circuits of commerce that reached north up the coast, west to Hawaii and China, south to Peru and Chile, and ultimately to the Atlantic economy of England, Spain, and the United States. As John Walton writes:

> Monterey, at the intersection of global markets and productive countryside, fostered a cosmopolitan society. Its population of one thousand persons was international. Spaniards and South Americans merged with various sorts of British and North American immigrants. The leaders were Californios with mixed loyalties to their ancestral Mexico and their own increasingly independent land. . . . California in the 1830s and 1840s was ebullient, multicultural, mobile, progressive, and politically volatile.[13]

And as the capital, Monterey was both the site of local resistance to Mexican authority and the target of American aggression—seized mistakenly in 1842 by Commodore Thomas Ap Catesby Jones, who thought that the United States had gone to war with Mexico, and seized again for good by Commodore John Sloat when war was actually under way.

San Antonio encapsulated these dimensions of centrality. The town originated in 1718 in classic Spanish style as the twinned presidio of San Antonio de Bejar (on the west side of the San Antonio River) and mission of San Antonio de Valero (on the east side). In 1731, fifty-four additional settlers arrived from the Canary Islands as part of a Spanish strategy of global empire building. The authorities made the *Isleños* the sole citizens of Villa of San Fernando de Bexar, located adjacent to the presidio, opening the way for long years of local conflict between Canary Island descendants and civilian *presidiales*.

San Antonio was center to local settlement and regional communication. In the immediate locality—the scale of a day's round-trip by foot—it was the focal point for a string of five missions along a twelve-mile stretch of the San Antonio River. Farms on the west side of the river drew water from two *acequias* (ditches) to feed local civilians and soldiers. Despite dangers from raiding Apaches in the 1740s, who forced farmers to venture out to their fields only in groups, the town continued to grow. At the regional scale, San Antonio was a halfway point between Coahuila and Chihuahua to the south and further Spanish missions on the Red River far to the northeast. Provincial governors lived at San Antonio for convenience even before it became the official capital in 1773. The economy thrived with a long-distance trade with Louisiana in horses and cattle between 1763 and 1800 (when the entire vast realm west of the Mississippi was Spanish territory).

San Antonio entered the 1820s—the first decade of Mexican independence—with a population of 2,000 people. More than half claimed to be Spanish (*espanoles*), 30 percent were mestizo, and the remainder were Indians. There were more women than men, a sure sign of a stable and maturing community, and nearly a third of household heads were women. Trade routes ran northeastward to Goliad and Nacogdoches and southward to Laredo and Saltillo. Local affairs rested in an elected *ayuntamiento* or city council consisting of the *alcalde* (mayor and judge), four *regidores* (councilmen and revenue collectors), and a *sindico procurador* (city attorney). The council raised revenue from city-owned farmland, sales of stray livestock, and taxes on imports and exports of horses and mules. It tried to look after public health, organized disaster recovery after floods, started a school, and supervised public markets.

San Antonio was a pivotal site in the Texas Revolution because it sat astride the main route from Mexico into Texas. The famous 1836 battle between the army of Santa Ana and the American frontiersmen swirled around the walls and grounds of the old Mission Valero (which had been renamed after it was secularized and occupied by one of the local military units, the Alamo de Parras company). Most of the residents huddled in the low adobe houses that surrounded the plaza a cannon shot or two away from the Alamo.

As Texan and then American, San Antonio faced the problems of a frontier city and the competition of new cities like Austin and Houston. Nevertheless it continued to grow to 3,480 in 1850 and 8,000 on the eve of the Civil War. American merchants, soldiers, and adventurers mingled with old Mexican families. German immigrants to the Hill Country to the north looked to San Antonio as the commercial center for new towns like Fredericksburg and New Braunfels, building European-style houses out of "fresh square-cut blocks of creamy-white limestone" to contrast with Texan adobe and the brick hotels and stores of American businessmen. Over the next generation the city would change even more. Railroads would supplant mule trains and wagons. American and German American bankers and businessmen would take full control of the city and regional economy. Neighborhoods would sprawl far beyond the limits of the old villa and mission, increasingly divided by race and economic status. New office blocks and stores would dwarf the old plazas. Population would keep pace with upstarts like Dallas and Fort Worth as the old Spanish villa Americanized, even when tourists like Edward Hungerford in the early twentieth century still saw it as quaint and foreign.

San Antonio in transition is a segue from the first era of western urbanization to the second—from the era of preindustrial empires to that of industrializing nations. For 250 years, Europeans had used cities to stake claims on the vast territories of Texas, California, Louisiana, Canada, and Alaska. These pretensions were tenuous. Rival powers contested them. So did native peoples, who often forced Europeans to form working alliances with the tribes and communities whose resources and territories they coveted. Nevertheless, the small cities along the Pacific coast, the Mississippi River, and the northern frontier of New Spain were important pawns in Europe's global game of power politics.

The long-standing pattern began to change when American settlers pushed in large numbers across the Mississippi River into the Missouri Country and Texas. By the 1840s and accelerating through the rest of the century, the growing nations of the United States and Canada would claim *and* control western North America through the weight of population, through new technologies for condensing distance and manipulating the landscape, and through the organizing capacity of cities that grew to populations in the hundreds of thousands by 1900 and the millions by 1940. It would be the century that fulfilled the prediction of evangelist and social reformer Josiah Strong, who contemplated the future of our country and concluded that "the time will doubtless come when a majority of the great cities of the country will be west of the Mississippi."[14]

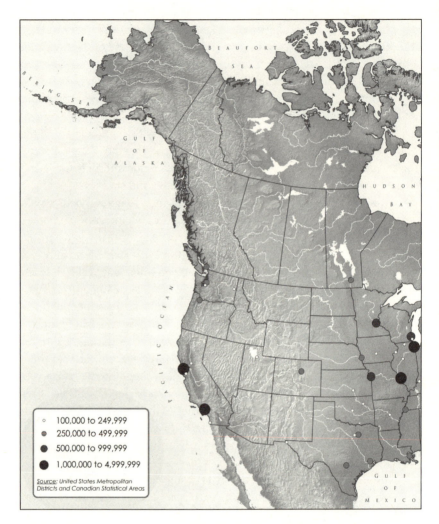

FIGURE 7. The urban West in 1930. The urban pattern of 1930 showed similarities to that of a century earlier, with large cities concentrated on the Pacific and Great Plains margins of western North America. The population categories represent metropolitan district populations as measured by the U.S. and Canadian censuses. (Map by Alejandro Bancke.)

Building a West of Cities,
1840–1940

San Diego, in Southern California, is the largest city in the world.
If your geographies and guide-books and encyclopedias have told you
otherwise, they have lied, or their authors have never seen San Diego.
Why, San Diego is nearly twenty-five miles from end to end. . . . All
of this must be so, because you read it in the green and gold prospectus
of the San Diego Land and Improvement Company (consolidated),
sent free on application.
                                        —Frank Norris, "Boom" (1897)

Things were looking up in the town of Whatcom again. The partners
of a Whatcom land company hoped to persuade the Northern Pacific
Railroad to extend its transcontinental line from Spokane across the wide
Washington Territory, to Bellingham Bay, where Whatcom lay. This
prospect so smote the excitable editor of the new Whatcom newspaper
that he referred to that prominent trade route, "the Liverpool–New York–
Whatcom–Yokohama run"—quite as if this were an everyday expression.
                                        —Annie Dillard, *The Living* (1992)

Every historian of the United States knows the symbolic meaning of the
Eleventh Census of 1890, when federal officials analyzing the returns
declared that it was no longer possible to define a distinct frontier line on a
national map. Less notorious but equally important is the statement in the
same census that "the urban element in the western division . . . has gained

somewhat more rapidly than the total population." Indeed, census takers had recorded an important turning point a decade earlier when their figures showed that the level of urbanization in the Rocky Mountain and Pacific states had passed that in longer-settled parts of the nation. Thirty percent of far western Americans lived in urban areas in 1880 compared to 28 percent for the country as a whole (the census counted both major cities and large towns). By the turn of the twentieth century, 52 percent of Californians were city people, followed by 48 percent of Coloradans, 41 percent of the residents of Washington, 40 percent of Utah, and 35 percent of Montana. Across the border, Canada's 1901 census found that half of British Columbians were also urban rather than rural.

The sober bureaucratic language and statistical tables echoed journalist William Thayer, who reported to eastern readers in 1887 in *The Marvels of the New West*. High on his list were the "populous and wealthy cities that have grown into power and beauty as if by magic." In another hundred years, he predicted, they would surpass eastern cities in enterprise and economic power. The result, he wrote in language that William Gilpin might have appreciated, would be "a national growth and consummation without a parallel in human history." A year later journalist Charles Dudley Warner described the rising ambitions of western cities for the readers of *Harper's New Monthly Magazine*: "New York complains of Chicago's want of modesty, Chicago can see that Kansas City and Omaha are aggressively boastful, and these cities acknowledge the expansive self-appreciation of Denver and Helena."[1]

The process of urbanization—defined as the increasing proportion of city people among a total population—normally involves increases in the size of existing cities and the emergence of new concentrations of people and production. Western North America was no exception, but with the emphasis on new centers. Colonial cities grew, at varying speeds, but the bigger news was the mushroom growth of new places. In 1840, no city west of the ninety-fifth meridian in the future United States and Canada counted more than 5,000 residents.[2] Fifty years later, twenty cities in the western United States had populations of 20,000 or more, from the metropolis of San Francisco at 298,977 to cow town Fort Worth at 23,076. Only five of these places had even existed fifty years earlier—San Francisco, Los Angeles, San Antonio, Galveston, and Houston.

Twentieth-century data show the results of continuing migration to western North America and the consolidation of the region's economy. In 1940, just before massive mobilization for World War II introduced a third era of urban development, 71 percent of Californians were city dwellers. The states of Colorado, Washington, and Utah and the territory of Hawaii had also passed 50 percent. Canadian statistics—although based on different definitions—show urbanization in the Prairie Provinces lagging that in the western United States by roughly a generation. Manitoba became an urban province in the 1940s, and Alberta, in the early 1950s. Saskatchewan, with its seemingly infinite wheat fields and lonely grain elevators marching along the horizon, followed in the 1960s. British Columbia has been more urban than Canada as a whole since the 1950s, and Alberta, since the 1980s. The metropolitan areas of Los Angeles and San Francisco/Oakland had grown to well over a million residents by 1940, and a dozen other cities in the western United States and Canada were now comparable to the San Francisco of 1890: Dallas, Denver, Houston, Omaha, Oklahoma City, Portland, Seattle, San Antonio, San Diego, Seattle, Vancouver, and Winnipeg.

The next eight chapters cover the three generations of intensive western urbanization and regional growth that began in the 1840s and lasted well into the twentieth century, examining the sources of city growth and creation of mature urban communities. Urban history as frontier history deals with the founding of cities, competition with rivals, displacement of native people, expansion of transportation systems, and evolution of raw outposts into permanent communities with diversified economies—in short, with the full incorporation of the West into the system of modern capitalism. These chapters begin at the edges of the West and work toward the deep mountain valleys and high plateaus at its center. They start with the metropolitan centers that have tied the West to the world and move to smaller cities at the "delivery end" of the urban hierarchy. The different sets of cities discussed in each chapter, such as Pacific gateways or irrigation cities, occupy distinct niches in the economic geography of North America, with their roles structured by the interplay of natural resources and changing global markets.

The takeoff for this second era of western urbanization coincided with what Eric Hobsbawm has called the Age of Capital—the years from 1848 to 1873 when a sustained economic boom drew much of the world into a highly integrated economic system.[3] Mass production and marketing of manufactured goods required massive flows of raw materials from India, Southeast Asia, and the Americas. In North America, the expansion of U.S. territory in the 1840s brought economic change in a rush. Newcomers transformed the towns of Mexican California and New Mexico into American cities. Within the space of a generation—from the heyday of the Oregon Trail to the first transcontinental rail line—American settlers built the outlines of a new urban system. For the next fifty years, western communities depended on railroad connections for their growth, and urban history can easily be read as railroad history. Many cities were explicit constructions by railroad companies—Cheyenne, Billings, Vancouver. Others from Denver to Los Angeles to Tacoma begged, blackmailed, and dug deep into their community pockets to get a rail connection of their own.

As the nineteenth century turned to the twentieth, western cities matured as established communities. Second and third generations of businessmen took over civic leadership. Some of them pursued new economic opportunities, while others turned attention to the public services, like water supply, that were necessary for prosperity over the long haul. Members of an expanding middle class of white-collar workers and their families looked to new bungalow belt neighborhoods for a stable setting for family life. At the same time, working men and working women turned to labor unions to protect their interests in increasingly stratified economies.

In the section that follows, chapters 2 and 3 introduce two sets of western gateways. One is the line of cities from Winnipeg to Dallas and San Antonio that grew in the transition zone between the humid East and a drier West and connected an industrializing North American core with western ranching, farming, and mining country. The second group is the Pacific ports from Victoria and Vancouver south to San Diego that made it possible to develop the continental interior from west to east and linked North America to Asia. Chapter 4 then examines the emergence of economic "capitals" that organized and controlled statewide or multistate regions of the interior through nested urban systems—particularly Salt Lake City and Denver, followed a generation later by Spokane, El Paso, Edmonton, and others. Chapter 5 moves further into the western heartland to profile smaller cities that developed at the base of western mountain ranges to serve rich regions of irrigated farming. Chapter 6 travels even deeper into the mountains to find cities of industrial mining such as Butte and Cripple Creek, while also noting the proliferation of factory work in gateway and empire cities.

An inescapable theme is rivalry. No one knew which small settlement was going to grow into another Paris or which California mission would be the seed for another Rome. As journalist Julian Ralph commented,

> A question which agitates the minds of many persons in western Washington is whether it is possible for both Seattle and Tacoma— lying so near one another as they do—to become great cities; and if not, which will eventually become the chief and gigantic seaport. . . . [E]verywhere that I travel I find these rivalries between neighboring cities (Bismarck and Mandan, Rapid City and Deadwood, Helena and Butte, and so on through the list, which rightly begins with St. Paul and Minneapolis).[4]

The roster of competing pairs can be extended to Edmonton and Calgary, Winnipeg and Minneapolis, Vancouver and Victoria, Los Angeles and San Diego, San Francisco and Oakland, Phoenix and Tucson, Dallas and Fort Worth, Kansas City and Omaha, Oklahoma City and Tulsa, Houston and Galveston—and so ad infinitum.

The frantic growth of the nineteenth century tapered off in the 1920s and 1930s in some parts of the West, although certainly not in oil patch cities like Houston, Dallas, Los Angeles, and Tulsa. The rate of western urbanization now tracked that of the United States as a whole after outpacing it for half a century. The same held true in Canada, where the nation as a whole shifted from 49 percent to 54 percent urban from 1921 to 1941, while the four western provinces shifted from 38 percent to 42 percent. These were slower times for Portland and Winnipeg, Denver and Salt Lake City.

This regional pause reflected a new stage in European American industrialization. The earlier decades of explosive growth had coincided with the rise of a steam and steel economy that manifested most obviously in thousands of miles of new railroads. After a global deflation from the mid-1870s to the mid-1890s, the industrial world entered a new phase—a "second industrial revolution" in the opinion of historian David Landes—driven by new high-technology industries such as chemicals and electrical equipment that were best developed out of the industrial and educational base of northeastern North America.[5] Mines and mills found it hard to compete against General Motors, DuPont, or Westinghouse for attention and investment.

This shift followed the consolidation of an industrial core anchored by New York and Chicago. Canals and Great Lakes shipping sketched the outlines in the 1830s and 1840s. Railroads etched it onto the landscape in the 1850s. By the time of the Civil War, trans-Appalachian railroads made it economically feasible for the Northeast and Old Northwest to hold together and prosper even with the closing of the Mississippi River. At the end of the nineteenth century, a thick set of industrial cities reached from Maine to Minnesota to Missouri and back to Maryland. The core retained its national dominance through the first half of the twentieth century. With only 7 percent of the land area of the United States, it held 43 percent of its population in 1950 and accounted for 50 percent of its income and 70 percent of manufacturing output. It was similarly the center of political and cultural influence. The Boston–Chicago axis accounted for a disproportionate share of patents, scientists, major corporate headquarters, candidates for president, and listings in *Who's Who*.[6] In Canada, a narrow corridor from Windsor through Toronto and along the St. Lawrence River to Montreal exercised the same dominance.

While the raw materials of the West stoked the growth of Chicago, New York, and Toronto, western city people increasingly worked to promote progressive urban reform and planning and to cultivate respectable "eastern" culture. The emphasis reflected the demographic maturation of cities. The early communities of unattached young men grew more balanced by sex and by age, with children to educate and middle-aged residents who were happy to marry and settle down. It also reflected the continuing need to attract investment when the era of bonanzas and railroad booms was drawing to a close (except where gushers were making oil millionaires). Cities now needed to sell themselves as safe and sober places to put money or set down roots.

FIGURE 8. Portland, Oregon, impersonating New York in 1929. The City of Portland's annual report for 1929 depicted the city's ambitions, not actual conditions. There *were* new bridges across the Willamette River and the city's new airport *was* along the river close to downtown, but the size of the buildings and the intensity of activity would have been much closer to New York than to Portland's more modest realities. (City of Portland Archives and Records Center.)

Denver is a case in point. By 1900 the local economy had diversified, government services were more fully developed, and socially distinct neighborhoods were firmly established. The census of 1900 reported for the first time that women outnumbered men, and Denverites of both sexes could choose among scores of literary groups, fraternal organizations, charitable societies, churches, and clubs. Visitors arrived looking for the Wild West and found a city not terribly different from Indianapolis. By the 1920s and 1930s, maturity had sometimes turned to stodginess, with journalists calling Denver a "reluctant capital" and "prematurely grey."[7]

Across the Rockies, Salt Lake City's Mormon leaders fought an even harder battle to gain a reputation for respectability. In the 1860s, tourists

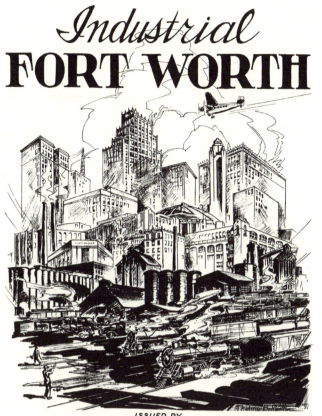

Industrial FORT WORTH

ISSUED BY
FORT WORTH CHAMBER OF COMMERCE

FIGURE 9. Fort Worth impersonating Chicago in the 1930s. In the late 1930s, the Fort Worth Chamber of Commerce promoted "Industrial Fort Worth." Several of the buildings in the picture were new additions to the Fort Worth skyline, but the picture as a whole evoked a future as another Chicago. (Image courtesy of Special Collections, Mary Couts Burnett Library, Texas Christian University.)

came to Utah looking for the salacious and sensational among a polygamous people. Transcontinental railroads opened a new flood of sightseers, prompting church leaders to emphasize middle-class gentility. They cleaned up public spaces, encouraged tree planting and green lawns, and opened Temple Square to visitors. "Come on by the thousand, look at us, see us, and believe your own senses in preference to the distorted tales of scandal-mongers and calumniators," wrote the *Salt Lake Herald*.[8] Officials installed one of the world's largest pipe organs in the tabernacle, and the Mormon Tabernacle Choir in the 1890s became an official ambassador of refinement. By the early twentieth century (after the abolition of plural marriage in 1895), the Mormon era was quaint history.

As with the Utah capital, western cities could market themselves as tourist attractions and places to enjoy a leisured life, downplaying the industries and industrial landscapes that had created them. Chapter 7 explores this evolution of western cities as tourist centers, an increasingly important business that required well-tamed communities that could sell their climate, local color, and access to undamaged nature. Chapter 8 examines another aspect of maturation in the differentiation of compact cities into distinct neighborhoods and downtown districts, describes the resulting cityscapes, and probes efforts to span social divisions in the supposed interest of the city as a whole. Chapter 9 extends the discussion of reform and progress to the ways in which metropolitan centers assured their survival by staking long-distance claims to sources of water and energy and incorporating those resources into the fabric of everyday life, a topic that conveniently links the first part of the twentieth century to its later decades.

CHAPTER TWO

Across the Wide Mississippi

The business interests of this continent have been developed in a series of circles, smaller circles being formed as the necessity has arisen out of larger ones. Fifty years ago the circles environed ports of supply, which were few in number. New York, Boston, Philadelphia, New Orleans, and St. Louis were the only big trading places. St. Louis did all the heavy mid-continent trade; then Chicago sprung up and soon monopolized the northwestern part of it. Westward Kansas City grew and appropriated a section for itself. Within the last ten years Denver has become a point of supply for the larger portion of the central Rocky Mountain region and divided the southwestern business until Albuquerque loomed up. . . . Thus it can be seen how the country becomes subdivided into smaller circles as regards its commerce and how points of supply rapidly rise into importance as a country settles up and develops. The location of these new centers of business are controlled by two factors—through railroad communication and being approximately the geographical center of a newly developing region.

—George H. Tinker,
A Land of Sunshine: Flagstaff and Its Surroundings (1887)

To have an immense production of exchangeable commodities, to force from nature the most she can be made to yield, and send it east and west by the cheapest routes to the dearest markets, making one's city a centre of trade and raising the price of its real estate—this, which might not

have seemed a glorious consummation to Isaiah or Plato, is preached by
western newspapers as a kind of religion.
                    —James Bryce, *The American Commonwealth* (1912)

All roads lead to Winnipeg. . . . It is the gateway through which all the
commerce of the east and west, and the north and south must flow. . . .
It is destined to become one of the greatest distributing and commercial
centers of the continent.
                              —*Chicago Tribune* (1911)

The common image of William Clark is a dauntless explorer. He is the explorer in a canoe, on foot, on horseback, parleying with Indians, probing the sources of rivers, testing treacherous mountain passes, noting the changing landscape. On road signs that mark the parts of his route to the Pacific he stands next to Meriwether Lewis as both peer intently westward. On the emblem of the Lewis and Clark Centennial Exposition, Portland, Oregon, 1905 world's fair, he strides toward the setting sun, arms linked with Lady Liberty, Miss Columbia, or some such allegorical beauty representing the new nation.

In fact, William Clark's life was more closely linked to St. Louis than to the Montana mountains that are now Lewis and Clark National Forest or to western waterways like the Clark Fork of the Columbia River. St. Louis was the starting point for his trek to the Pacific Ocean in 1804–6 and his home as a federal official after his return. In 1807 Clark accepted appointment as superintendent of Indian affairs for the vast Louisiana Territory and settled in St. Louis. President Madison appointed him governor of Missouri Territory in 1813, and President Monroe reappointed him through 1821, the year of Missouri statehood. For those crucial fifteen years he was one of the city's most prominent residents. As Indian superintendent and governor, his task was to keep peace with the Indian nations of the Missouri Valley and manage the trade in furs. He worked to protect tribes against squatters, maintained trade through government agents, and used diplomacy to keep Upper Mississippi tribes neutral in the War of 1812.

William Clark's St. Louis was the epicenter for change from an old urban world to a new. The colonial system in western North America crested in the early nineteenth century. European conflicts pushed France out of its last holdings on the continent soon after 1800. Spanish expansion essentially stopped except for gradual growth and infill in Upper California. Among the European empires, only the thinly scattered Russians and the newly consolidated British fur-trading enterprise of the Hudson's Bay Company were still expanding their far western presence.

St. Louis, the small city that grew from the spot where the Gateway Arch now casts its shadow, dated from 1764, when Pierre Laclède came north from

New Orleans to set up a fur-trading base. The French-speaking settlement was an imperial outpost like many others. It picked up French settlers from the Illinois country as news arrived that the east bank of the Mississippi had become English territory with the end of the Seven Years' War in 1763—even as St. Louis and New Orleans themselves came under Spanish rule in the same treaty. St. Louis counted only 1,000 residents in 1803 when the Louisiana Purchase made it an American town. Nevertheless, it was already a crossing point for the great central valley of North America, perched on high land along the west bank of the Mississippi and easily reached from the Missouri River, the Illinois River (with its route to Lake Michigan), and the Ohio River (with its Wabash, Tennessee, and Cumberland tributaries). It was the jump-off point for French-speaking and English-speaking fur traders and the launch site for military exploring under Zebulon Pike and Stephen Long in addition to Lewis and Clark. It was also a tiny place where every merchant and businessman (who counted) knew everyone else (who counted) and families sealed commercial alliances with marriages.

Over the course of William Clark's tenure in St. Louis, American expansion transformed St. Louis from the imperial outpost of 1803 to a booming commercial city. The fur trade up the Missouri into the upper plains and Rockies expanded, along with a smaller but lucrative overland trade to Santa Fe and New Mexico after 1821. Some merchants were independent and acted on their own behalf, while others were agents of John Jacob Astor of New York. Astor had failed to capture the fur trade of the North Pacific with his failed Columbia River outpost of Astoria, Oregon (1811), but he dominated the business in mid-continent. His American Fur Company allied eastern investors with the powerful Choteau family of St. Louis. Trade goods were purchased on the East Coast or from Europe and consigned to St. Louis, where Astor's agents broke them up into lots for different forts and traders. Each stage offered a markup and profit. Only the actual traders had the risk, hoping they'd be able to bargain for enough furs to cover their costs. The American Fur Company could outlast competitors with the help of Astor's deep pockets. When the beaver pelt trade declined in the 1840s, the company, now under the Choteaus, went into buffalo hides.

Behind fur and hide traders came farmers. After 1815, waves of American settlers pushed the "frontier" west to the great bend of the Missouri River (the vicinity of modern Kansas City, Missouri). The introduction of steamboats on the western rivers revolutionized transportation, moving agricultural produce in volumes that dwarfed the old canoe and flatboat trade. St. Louis was the convenient point to exchange goods moving westward along the Ohio River from Pittsburgh, Cincinnati, and Louisville with the products of the Missouri River Valley. Its wide, sloping riverfront levee was also a convenient place to shift goods between smaller, shallow-draft steamboats that plied the Upper Mississippi and deeper-draft boats on the New Orleans run.

In geopolitical terms, early, polyglot St. Louis was the pivot for efforts to reorient much of western North America toward New York, the eastern seaboard, and the United States more generally. From the Atlantic Ocean, two great embayments reach deep into the continent—Hudson Bay from the far northeast and the Gulf of Mexico from the southeast. The bay gave British fur traders access to the far west of the continent. The gulf gave access for Spanish soldiers, missionaries, and administrators who could follow the long road from Veracruz to Mexico City, then on to Chihuahua, and finally to Santa Fe or Santa Barbara.

Over the middle decades of the nineteenth century, steamboats, railroads, and throngs of English-speaking settlers confirmed the primacy of overland access. St. Louis traders and merchants sketched out the American claim. Texas land speculators and Oregon missionaries added their weight. Diplomacy and aggressive war to conquer California confirmed new national boundaries in the 1840s. Transcontinental railroad surveys in the 1850s looked for ways to turn the political settlements of the Treaty of Guadalupe Hidalgo and the Oregon boundary treaty into practical economic connections, identifying five possible routes from the Mississippi to the Pacific. St. Louis was at the center of the action until railroad builders (and federal land grants) turned ambitions into reality over the next generation.

The growth of St. Louis in the early nineteenth century, both during and after the era of William Clark, was thus the first step in the century-long process through which cities incorporated the central valley of North America, from the Mississippi River and Laurentian Plateau to the Rocky Mountains, into the Atlantic economy. Tiers of "gateway" cities developed in concert with the North American railroad system—not only St. Louis of the future arch and Omaha with its "Gate City" nickname but also metropolitan centers from Winnipeg to Dallas and a supporting cast of smaller cities. Many started as points where pack trains and wagon roads reached water or where small shallow streams reached deeper rivers. They grew as railroads pushed across the Mississippi in the 1850s and across the continent in the last third of the century. They were the spearheads of trans-Mississippi settlement: Their shopkeepers sold the tools and equipment that every homesteading farmer required, their banks supplied credit to help get crops to market, their business communities helped to raise capital to construct roads and railroads, their factory owners turned wheat and meat into salable products, and their merchants identified and organized agricultural markets. The terms of trade between town and country were not necessarily equitable, but the connections made the rural Middle West possible.

The process began with the growth of Mississippi River towns from the 1820s through the 1850s. Some were "naturals" like St. Louis. Minneapolis and St. Paul grew where the Falls of St. Anthony marked the head of navigation on the Mississippi and supplied abundant waterpower. Davenport, Iowa,

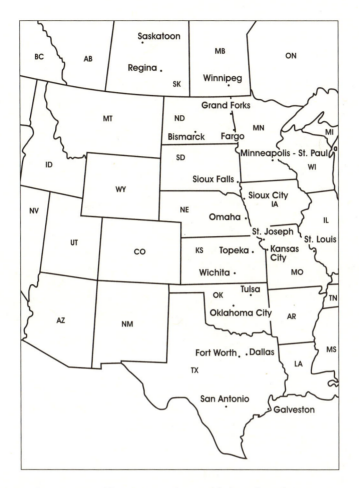

FIGURE 10. Gateway cities. The eastern and western halves of North America interacted through gateway cities that grew in a north–south corridor extending roughly 500 miles west from the Mississippi River. (Map by Jacquelyn Ferry.)

and Rock Island, Illinois, sharing Mississippi River rapids, were aspiring naturals whose boosters remembered the analogy of Louisville, where the Falls of the Ohio River required shipping to pause for a short canal passage.

Elsewhere on the Mississippi were crossing-point towns, none of which had many obvious advantages over the others. The lower river had east-bank bluff towns like Natchez, Vicksburg, and Memphis. Federal legislation to promote railroad construction in Iowa named Burlington, Davenport, Lyons, and Dubuque as riverside termini but left out Keokuk and Muscatine, Iowa, not to mention Winona, Minnesota; Galena, Illinois; La Crosse, Wisconsin; and other contenders in adjacent states. Hannibal, Missouri, for example, dates from 1819. It is famous as the home of Samuel Clemens, but it took the

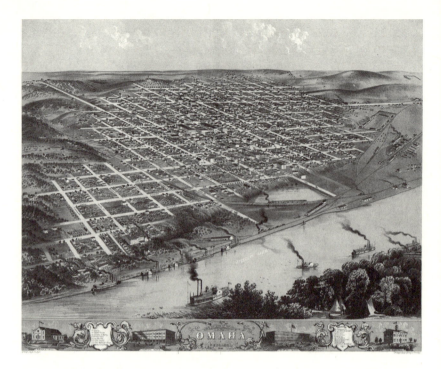

FIGURE 11. Omaha in 1868. In 1868, Omaha was booming as the eastern terminus of the Union Pacific Railroad. This panorama shows the prominence of rail lines and facilities but gives equal attention to the shallow-draft steamboats that plied the Missouri River and exchanged cargoes directly on the riverbank.

completion of a railroad to St. Joseph, Missouri, in 1859 for economic take-off. With the railroad, Hannibal industrialists could float Wisconsin timber downriver, see it into construction material, and ship it west to build fences and farmhouses. The small city grew to 18,000 in 1900, more than a country town and less than an industrial powerhouse.

The process repeated farther and farther west from the 1850s through the 1870s. Fargo, Grand Forks, and Winnipeg grew at crossings of the Red River of the North. Fort Smith sat on a tight loop of the Arkansas River where it entered Indian Territory. In between, where the Missouri River bends from east–west to north–south, Independence, Kansas City, Leavenworth, Atchison, St. Joseph, Nebraska City, and Omaha were contending for business by the onset of the Civil War. Over the next three decades, the era of transcontinental railroad building sorted out the "winning" cities that gained railroad crossings and junctions from the also-ran towns.

For one example, Omaha got its initial jump start by grabbing the Nebraska territorial capital in 1855 from other tiny towns. Congress designated Council Bluffs, Iowa, which had prospered in the 1850s by supplying overland travelers heading to California, to be the eastern terminus of the first transcontinental railroad. Without a bridge, however, supplies and construction materials had to be ferried across the river, making Omaha the effective staging point for railroad work and then the permanent headquarters of the Union Pacific. Its rival Nebraska City, which had prospered with overland wagon freighting in the 1860s, fell behind as Omaha's rail connections attracted outside investment into huge stockyards and processing plants. With Nebraska City safely in the rearview mirror, Omaha entrepreneurs could look to St. Joseph and Kansas City as their next rivals.

On the southern prairies, Dallas and Fort Worth developed similar functions. Sited at a crossing of the Trinity River (noticeable on the North Texas landscape but hardly a barrier as great as the Mississippi or Missouri), Dallas did not appear in the 1850 census but prospered as a Confederate supply center during the Civil War. The Texas Central and Texas and Pacific railroads arrived in 1872–73, soon followed by additional lines. A rich agricultural hinterland produced wheat, cotton, and cattle, supporting local manufacturing of flour and leather goods and making it a sort of mirror of Omaha. Fort Worth, forty miles to the west, aspired to supplant Dallas but remained much more a cattle town—hence its twentieth-century slogan as the city "where the West begins."

Winnipeg predated its U.S. counterparts, originating as a fur-trading fort in 1738 and the nucleus of the Red River Settlement in 1812. Local leaders in the 1870s enticed the Canadian Pacific Railroad (CPR) to bend its route to cross the Red River through the city, offering cash, a bridge, and permanent exemption from local taxes. The town boomed in the early 1880s as the staging point for CPR construction. By the early twentieth century four major railroads converged in the city—the Canadian Pacific, Grand Trunk, Canadian Northern, and Northern Pacific. With 215 kilometers of sidings, the CPR yards were the largest in the British Empire. In 1912, at the height of a great boom that had pushed population from 42,000 to 136,000 in a decade, nearly 5,000 Winnipeggers worked for the railroads as engineers, firemen, conductors, repairmen, and laborers.

Rivers of wheat flowed eastward. It gathered in trickles from farmers' wagons into local railheads, moved in thicker streams on branch lines to the trunk railroads, and cascaded into Winnipeg elevators or rolled through the city on the way to the head of Lake Superior. Immigrants to new prairie farms shared the return trains with carloads of manufactured goods and thousands of commercial travelers who canvassed the needs of small-town storekeepers and kept their shelves stocked from Winnipeg warehouses. Well into the century, Winnipeg wholesalers had a price advantage over Vancouver as far to the west as Revelstoke on the west slope of the Rockies. Its business center was a bustling retail and office district where thousands of shopgirls in their teens and twenties tended sales counters and female "typewriters" produced the voluminous correspondence that banks, insurance agencies, and commercial houses required. The Grain Exchange was the city's largest building: "Here was the nerve centre of a great industry to which hungry men and women of practically every nation in Europe looked to be fed. Here could be felt the nip of early frost in Alberta. . . . Once inside the walls of the building, a man became a citizen of the world, he saw from afar the hands of millions uplifted and heard from beyond the seas the ceaseless cry for bread."[1]

Winnipeg was thoroughly North American in its pace of life. Despite the women who staffed its shops and offices, it was a bachelor city in the early twentieth century, with 10,000 more men than women. It was also a young city, with more than 80 percent of its population under age forty. The streets bustled. Restaurants served up meals in for diners eager—or required—to get back to the job. English visitor Ella Sykes, who came at the height of the boom, marveled over the Land of Youth: "Everything here goes hay presto! Here funerals pass at a smart trot, and I could hardly keep up with the brisk pace at which the choirs led the psalms and hymns in the churches."[2]

Omaha, Dallas, and Winnipeg represent the climax species of midcontinent urbanization—three of the "gateway cities" that grew roughly at the margin between wetland and dryland agriculture. As Chicago and St. Louis grew increasingly "middle" western, Winnipeg, Minneapolis/St. Paul, Omaha, Kansas City, and the Dallas/Fort Worth combo offered the parallel services of the regional metropolis. Because it is efficient to process grain into flour and livestock into meat close to places of production, reducing weight and shipping costs, they became flour-milling and stockyards cities. Because it is efficient to distribute hardware and dry goods from locations close to the stores that actually retail the goods, they became warehousing and wholesaling cities. Entrepreneurs thought in continental terms: What markets were underserved? Where did their cities and regions sit within the large-scale resource exchanges of North America, including flows across the international boundary?[3]

Second-level cities filled in between the metropolitan gateways and grew as secondary trading points a hundred or 200 or 500 miles into the prairies. Regina and Saskatoon, Grand Forks and Fargo, Topeka and Wichita, Wichita Falls and Abilene: The list could be much, much longer. Some started as river crossings in the steamboat era (St. Joseph), others, as stations on new railroads (Saskatoon did not incorporate until 1901). They offered the same commercial services as the larger gateways but to fewer customers and under the shadow of the metropolis. It helped to be a railroad division point where repair and maintenance shops added to the economic base, to be a state or provincial capital, or to benefit from a local mineral resource such as petroleum for Wichita and Tulsa.

Bismarck offers an example of a city that never reached the big time. Lewis and Clark had spent the winter of 1804–5 at the site of Bismarck (well, actually,

FIGURE 12. Winnipeg downtown. Winnipeg's Market Square was part of a thriving commercial core as the city was the gateway to the booming farmlands of the Prairie Provinces at the turn of the twentieth century. (Archives of Manitoba.)

just across the river). It was a Northern Pacific Railroad town site, named to appeal to immigrants from the German Empire. Bismarck prospered from 1873 to 1879, when the Northern Pacific terminated at the Missouri and produce could arrive by riverboat to be transshipped and carried eastward. It also got a boost as a supply center for the Black Hills gold rush in 1874. But when the railroad plunged westward to Billings and beyond, Bismarck business tapered off, even though it secured the Dakota territorial capital in 1883 and state capital in 1889. James Bryce visited in 1883 to hear speakers claim a destiny to be "the metropolitan hearth of the world's civilization" and left perplexed but impressed that the new capitol building was being built a mile out of town "on the top of a hill in the brown and dusty prairie."[4] Bismarck did grow slowly to meet the challenge of closing this gap, but it didn't pass 10,000 people until the 1920s (and had only 60,000 or so by the twenty-first century).

Bismarck was typical of most plains towns as a creature of the railroads. Operating by rule of thumb, railroad executives platted towns at regular intervals along their routes, spacing them close enough to serve all farmers but not so close as to be redundant or so far apart as to offer an opening for a rival line. In railroad offices, writes geographer John Hudson, were "enormous stacks of engineering blueprints . . . showing existing lines in yellow, projected lines in red, competitors projected lines in green."[5] On Colorado plains, for example, the Chicago, Burlington and Quincy created Wray, Yuma, and Akron, and the Missouri Pacific created Brandon, Chivington, Eads, and Galatea. The Texas and Pacific promoted Midland and Odessa. The Burlington and Missouri River Railroad laid out Crete, Dorchester, Exeter, Fairmount, Grafton, and so on alphabetically across Nebraska. The Union Pacific Railroad had a Town Lot Department to market land in places like Cheyenne and Laramie and gave special deals to lumber and fuel dealers who agreed to set up business at new town sites.

Even Bismarck's growth would have looked good to many ambitious townspeople elsewhere on the plains. As the railroad and farming frontiers pushed toward the Rockies, it came clear that only a handful of towns would turn into cosmopolises or even into cities with five-digit or four-digit populations. Grand ambitions met the reality of finite business opportunities. The continued growth of metropolitan centers and smaller regional centers (say, Salina, Kansas, or Brandon, Manitoba, as well as the North Dakota capital) created connections and markets for country crossroads towns and county seats but locked them into even lower levels of the urban hierarchy. The result was the filling out of a hierarchy of cities and towns that ran from Dallas down to West Texas hamlets, from Omaha down to county seats, and from Winnipeg down to stations on the Canadian Pacific and Canadian Northern rail lines.

Buried in the systematic overview, of course, are frustrated ambitions and individual failures. Financial panic in 1857–58, followed quickly by the disruptions of a Civil War that used the Mississippi as a military corridor and battle site, upset the ambitions of many river cities. The worldwide economic depressions of the mid-1870s and mid-1890s frustrated later generations of entrepreneurs. Towns with momentary ambitions, and perhaps with a general store and post office for starters, were far more likely to fade into nothing than to grow into a dot on a modern highway map.[6] Mining ghost towns high in the Colorado Rockies are picturesque and romantic, but Great Plains ghost towns may be nothing more than a patch of wild lilacs overgrowing abandoned foundations. When William Least Heat-Moon drove and walked the landscape of Chase County, Kansas, in the 1980s, as recounted in *PrairyErth* (1991), he encountered abandoned railroad rights-of-way and the remnants of towns sunk into the soil like old graves.[7]

Anyone can see the results who chooses to drive across the Prairie Provinces, or North Dakota, or Kansas, or Texas. The sequence of cities and towns stretches out or attenuates to the westward where settlement was later and thinner. The trip between Fargo and Bismarck is 180 miles, with Jamestown halfway between and Valley City and Steele further subdividing the journey. Bismarck to Billings is 370 miles, with Dickinson and Miles City in between, with Medora and Glendive and Forsyth taking the next level. To the north, the distance from Regina westward to Calgary is more than twice its distance eastward to Winnipeg.

Table 2.1 gives the populations for cities that ranked among the 100 largest in the United States in each of the five census years from 1880 to 1920. Three pairs of cities are grouped: Minneapolis and St. Paul, the two adjacent Kansas Cities, and the two cities that now anchor the Dallas/Fort Worth "metroplex." The table tries to include the potential "gateway" cities in Texas, Oklahoma, Kansas, Nebraska, the Dakotas, and the western edges of Missouri and Iowa, along with the more easterly sited but westward-looking Minneapolis and St. Paul.[8] Several Canadian cities are included for comparison. Only five cities appear in each year: the Twin Cities, Kansas City, Omaha, San Antonio, and—perhaps surprisingly—St. Joseph. Some cities such as Galveston, Lincoln, and Topeka appear in early decades but then drop off because their growth slowed in the twentieth century. Other cities appear

TABLE 2.1. Plains and Prairie City Populations, 1880–1920

City	1880	1890	1900	1910	1920
Minneapolis	47,000	165,000	203,000	301,000	380,000
St. Paul	41,000	133,000	163,000	214,000	234,000
Minneapolis/St. Paul	88,000	298,000	366,000	515,000	614,000
Kansas City, Missouri	56,000	132,000	164,000	248,000	324,000
Kansas City, Kansas		38,000	51,000	82,000	101,000
Kansas City combined		170,000	215,000	330,000	425,000
St. Joseph	32,000	52,000		77,000	78,000
Omaha	30,000	140,000	103,000	124,000	191,000
Galveston	22,000				
San Antonio	20,000	37,000	53,000	97,000	161,000
Dallas		38,000	42,000	92,000	158,000
Fort Worth		23,000		73,000	106,000
Dallas/Fort Worth		61,000		165,000	264,000
Lincoln		55,000	40,000		
Sioux City		38,000			71,000
Topeka		31,000			
Houston			44,000	79,000	138,000
Oklahoma City				64,000	91,000
Tulsa					72,000
Wichita					72,000
Winnipeg			42,000	136,000	179,000
Saskatoon				12,000	26,000
Regina			2,000	30,000	34,000

as replacements: Dallas and Fort Worth from 1890, Houston from 1900, Oklahoma City from 1910, and Tulsa and Wichita from 1920. The picture is clear: By the early twentieth century there were six dominant metropolitan gateways: Winnipeg, Minneapolis/St. Paul, Omaha, Kansas City, Dallas/Fort Worth, and San Antonio.[9]

The new Federal Reserve banking system codified the commercial geography of the United States in 1914. After intense lobbying from city boosters across the country, the Reserve Bank Organizing Committee designated twelve cities for Federal Reserve banks, each to work with local banks in a designated territory. The western winners were San Francisco (never any doubt), Minneapolis (likewise), Kansas City, Missouri (rather than Omaha or Denver), and Dallas (instead of Houston or New Orleans), with Chicago and St. Louis hovering in the rear.[10] The Minneapolis territory extended shallowly eastward into northern Wisconsin and deeply west through Minnesota, the Dakotas, and Montana. Kansas City's district included only a narrow fringe of Missouri but all of Kansas, Nebraska, Wyoming, and Colorado plus northern Oklahoma and New Mexico. Dallas reached from Shreveport to Tucson.[11]

Downtown skylines reflected the relative position of cities in the urban hierarchy. Table 2.2 shows the number of buildings with at least eight floors in a group of Great Plains cities (the data come from 1953 but reflect the situation around 1930, given that virtually no American city added large downtown buildings in the intervening years of economic crisis and world war). The regional metropolis of Omaha, with several corporate headquarters including the Union Pacific Railroad, had the most fully developed downtown. A secondary regional center (Wichita) and two state capitals (Topeka, Lincoln) had similar and smaller downtowns, trailed by the much smaller cities of Fargo and Sioux Falls with only one tall building each.[12]

Another feature of the gateway city landscape was its vast array of mills and warehouses, often the most substantial buildings in town. They grew in size with the scale of merchandising, with the capacity to quickly assemble enough

TABLE 2.2. Tall Buildings in North Plains Cities

City	1950 Population	No. Buildings 8+ Stories	No. Floors in Tallest Building	Total Floors in Buildings 8+ Stories
Omaha	251,000	20	15	200
Wichita	163,000	6	14	60
Lincoln	99,000	4	15	50
Topeka	78,000	4	12	41
Sioux Falls	53,000	1	9	9
Fargo	38,000	1	8	8

FIGURE 13. Omaha downtown. On July 13, 1909, Sixteenth Street from the U.S. National Bank (with columns) to the Post Office (with the tower) was crowded with people waiting for the Barnum and Bailey Circus parade. (Omaha Public Library.)

goods to fill entire railcars. Winnipeg served the needs of the Prairie Provinces from the cavernous floors of six dozen four- to six-story warehouses, some of them covering entire blocks. Omaha had a "Jobbers Canyon" formed by block after block of warehouses. Its showpiece was the huge John Deere Plow Company building, erected on the site of the old Roman Catholic Cathedral.

For some ambitious men, the jelling urban system was a prod to mobility. An ambitious man could always leave the small town for the larger city, as does Carl Linstrum in Willa Cather's *O Pioneers!* People could also try their luck in more than one aspiring town. William Gilpin tried out Kansas City, Missouri, before turning into the prophet of Denver, and William Byers hauled his printing press from Omaha to Denver with the 1859 Pikes Peak gold rushers to publish the *Rocky Mountain News* and settle down. John F. Kinney, not especially notable himself but well chronicled by Timothy Mahoney, tied his fortunes in the 1850s to Keokuk (the "Gate City" to Iowa), in the 1860s to Nebraska City (it was to be the new Chicago), then to Fort Kearney, Nebraska (which he wanted to rename "Empire City"), and finally after 1890 to San Diego ("the Gem of all western cities" and "the great port for Japan").[13]

The alternative was to embrace small city life and the business culture of the midlands, represented in fiction by the figure of real estate dealer George F. Babbitt. The "Zenith" that novelist Sinclair Lewis imagined as

Babbitt's hometown in 1922 might have been on either side of the river, for he had spent weeks in both Indianapolis and Kansas City to soak up atmosphere. Minneapolis held a "Babbitt Week" to celebrate publication, and Cincinnati, Milwaukee, and Duluth claimed to be the model. Although the enthusiasm for Lewis's satirical portrait of middle-class life seems curious from the viewpoint of a later century, it shows the continued self-confidence of cities across mid-continent as they settled into maturity in the 1910s and 1920s.

Local control was beginning to slip in the 1920s, with chain store retailing, the mass culture of movies and radio, and the consolidation of banks and utilities. George Babbitt was proud of his motorcar, likely manufactured in Michigan rather than locally (as a carriage might have been). His "God was modern appliances," again nationally advertised and produced. His own product—houses and building lots—was irrevocably local, but families who bought in one of his subdivisions might well furnish from national catalogs. Pharmacists who affiliated with the Rexall chain likely did better than competitors who remained independent. Grocers began to wonder about competition from A&P and learned that they had to stock nationally advertised products like Campbell's soups.

Let's take a closer look at early-twentieth-century Topeka, when the city was growing steadily from 34,000 in 1900 to 44,000 in 1910 (but not fast enough to stay in the top 100). Residents liked to point out their city parks with entrance gates, bandstands, picnic groves, and small lake and the imposing churches on one or two of the main streets leading from the business district toward the better residential areas. The city was big enough and well enough established to have a *Who's Who*.[14] I sampled the first and last complete biographical paragraphs on each page for the 1905 edition for place of birth (Table 2.3). The results show the power of the east–west migration trail, with very few community leaders from the South. They show the youth of Kansas, with few locally born having made it into middle-class respectability. They also show the limited impact of European immigration on a third-level interior city (contrast New York or Chicago at this time or even Omaha and Kansas City).

A generation later, for comparison, Omaha's leadership was even more provincial. The city that had ambitiously staged a world's fair in 1898 had settled down. From a 1928 *Who's Who* I took the second full biography per page (for roughly 12 percent of all entries).[15] A fifth were Omaha natives, and another third were from elsewhere in Nebraska or Iowa (Table 2.4).

Everyday Omaha was a very different place than its business leadership suggests. As early as 1889, Rudyard Kipling complained that it was "populated entirely by Germans, Poles, Slavs, Hungarians, Croats, Magyars, and all the scum of the Eastern European states."[16] His prejudice aside, Kipling was not too far off the mark. In 1920, after the great era of immigration from Europe to North America, 49 percent of Omaha residents had been born

TABLE 2.3. Birth Places of Topeka Civic Leaders

Place of Birth	Number
Topeka	3
Kansas (other)	16
Missouri	13
Iowa	9
Other Middle West	97
Northeast	88
South	12
Europe	17
Canada	5
Total	244

TABLE 2.4. Birth Places of Omaha Civic Leaders

Place of Birth	Number	Percent of Total
Omaha	40	20
Other Nebraska/Iowa	67	33
Other Middle West	48	24
Northeast	22	11
Missouri/Kansas	4	2
Other United States	7	4
Canada/Europe	16	8

abroad. Germany accounted for 16,748 out of a total population of 191,601; Central and Eastern Europe, for 27,360; and Mediterranean countries, for 6,351. The numbers were enough to give Omaha civic life a Middle Western feel with ethnic voting blocs and machine politicians. In *Jefferson Selleck*, set in a city very, very like Omaha, novelist Carl Jonas describes a central district with Little Poland, Little Croatia, Little Lithuania, Little Czech-town, and "Little almost any country you can think of" and has his title character recollect that "Gateway City from the time of my childhood almost into the 1930s was as bossed a city as Chicago, Kansas City, or Boston is today."[17]

Winnipeg too was increasingly a "European" city, as the Canadian government after 1900 actively encouraged immigration. It had Poles, Russians, Jews (9,000), Germans (8,000), Ukrainians (3,500), Swedes, and Norwegians. A quarter of its residents in 1911 had been born outside the British Empire, and the Prairie Provinces in Winnipeg's hinterland were also an ethnic mosaic. Within the city, the massive barrier of the CPR sliced east and west, dividing the business district from Eastern European immigrants in the North End neighborhoods full of "small foreign-language newspapers, watch-repair shops, a Jewish theatrical company, a Ukrainian dance troupe, small choirs, tap-dancing schools, orchestral groups, chess clubs, and more radical political thinkers per square block than Soviet Russia had known before the Revolution."[18] Nevertheless, the city's middle-class culture continued to sport an overlay of empire loyalty. The elite emulated English social styles, and the city turned out in numbers for the visit of the governor general (a younger brother of the king) and his daughter, Princess Alexandra. The upper crust were already attending parties at the Royal Alexandra Hotel, built by the Canadian Pacific in the same mold as its Empress Hotel in Victoria, British Columbia.[19]

Let's close this chapter by dropping south to Dallas, a city whose popular image often seems larger than life. In Edna Ferber's schmaltz-culture epic *Giant*, Dallas is the city of bankers, lawyers, oil tycoons, and expensive hotels—the control center for Texas ranching and oil production. The movie *State Fair* is set in Iowa, but Hollywood filmed the 1962 version starring Pat Boone at the grounds of the Texas Centennial Expo of 1936, which has continued as the venue for the nation's largest state fair. From 1934 to 1997, downtown had one of the nation's most notable landmarks in the shape of its Flying Red Horse. Two giant thirty-by-fifty-foot signs perched on top of the Magnolia Hotel, their electrified Pegasus standing for the Magnolia Petroleum Company (later Mobil Oil) in winter fog and summer sun. More recently, Dallas claimed a bit of history that doesn't really belong to it with a huge bronze sculpture of dozens of oversized longhorns being driven to market past the Convention Center and City Hall. Fort Worth was the real stockyards town, of course, but the longhorns were funded by Dallas real estate tycoon Trammel Crow, who preferred cattle to bronze oil derricks or bronze shopping bags from Neiman Marcus.

Dallas is also the site for one of the best-known commercial buildings in North America. Located several blocks from the retail and finance center of Dallas, it dates from 1901. Its builder was the Rock Island Plow Company, a farm implement manufacturer from Illinois that wanted a location from which to serve customers across the Southwest. The building remained an agricultural equipment warehouse until the 1930s and then housed a grocery wholesaler and a private company that warehoused and shipped schoolbooks to communities throughout Texas and neighboring states. On November 22, 1963, Lee Harvey Oswald climbed to the sixth floor of what was then called the Texas School Book Depository Building, found a window at the southeast corner that overlooked Dealey Plaza, waited for John Kennedy's motorcade to arrive, and assassinated the president. Its sad encounter with history aside, there is no building whose previous uses better represent the role of gateway cities.

CHAPTER THREE

The First Pacific Century

There are more things in San Francisco's Chinatown than are dreamed on in heaven and earth. In reality there are three parts of Chinatown— the part the guides show you, the part the guides don't show you, and the part that no one ever hears of.
— Frank Norris, "The Third Circle" (1897)

All day the gray low-ceilinged sky had threatened the Puget Sound port of Secoma with the year's first snow, and now, with evening closing in, it had come, muffling the harbor's barnyard chorus of cautiously moving shipping and brushing with ethereal beauty such mundane things as boxcars and freight sheds, docks and barges and anchored vessels.
— Norman Reilly Raine, "Tugboat Annie's Secret" (1949)[1]

Deep in the high desert of eastern Oregon the Owyhee River flows through basalt beds and steep canyons into the Snake River. "Owyhee." It looks like an Indian name, perhaps borrowed from the Paiutes or Shoshones or Nez Perce. Now try an experiment and speak it aloud, and a different possibility surfaces. "Owyhee" is actually a variant spelling for Hawaii, a trace of early contact between Anglo-Americans and the Pacific islands.

First reached by Europeans in 1778, Hawaii by the early nineteenth century was furnishing seamen for European trading ships and workers for the fur trade of northwestern America. Kanakas, the contemporary term for Hawaiian Islanders, appear on the employment rosters of the Hudson's Bay

Company. Hawaiians helped to build and operate Fort Vancouver. They helped to man Fort Langley on the Fraser River, Fort Vancouver on the Columbia, and even Fort Hall deep in present-day Idaho. Early census records of the Oregon Country record Hawaiians along with Scots merchants, French-Indian trappers, and pioneer farmers from Missouri and Illinois. North of the new international border, Hawaiians worked at the coal-mining town of Nanaimo in the 1850s, Victoria had a "Kanaka Row," and the sawmill settlement of Moodyville (the Burrard Inlet predecessor of Vancouver, B.C.) had a "Kanaka Road" to balance its Chinese boarding houses and its "Frenchtown." The Hawaiian government maintained consular offices at Victoria and Port Townsend to promote trade and look after the interests of Hawaiian workers.

In the same era that Hawaiians were serving the European American economy as members of its mobile, maritime workforce, Europeans were remaking Hawaii as an extension of North America. British explorer George Vancouver introduced cattle in 1792 to provide a food supply for naval vessels and trading ships. As the animals proliferated, the Hawaiian monarchy imported vaqueros from California who helped to train a workforce of Mexican Hawaiian *paniolos* (from *espanole*). Protestant missionaries were active from the 1820s, and Honolulu and Lahaina became important supply stations for American whaling ships in the 1830s and 1840s. Merchants from Britain and the United States developed close ties with the Hawaiian royalty and made Honolulu the hub of transpacific trade. When steamships replaced sailing vessels in the later decades, Honolulu was poised for a boom that boosted its population from 15,000 to 45,000 over the 1880s and 1890s.

As David Igler has documented, the commercial colonization of Hawaii was part of the emergence of the eastern Pacific as a distinct realm of trade and economic exchange. Honolulu was in the middle. On one side was Canton, the great mart for luxury goods like sea otter pelts and sandalwood. On the other side were points on the eastern edge of the Americas, arrayed from Callao in Peru through Acapulco and San Blas in New Spain, the small ports of Alta California, trading posts on the Columbia River, Nootka Sound on Vancouver Island, and Russian America. In the 1790s, one or two ships a year called in Alta California, rising to twenty or more per year in the 1830s and 1840s. Nearly half of the ships were American, but many came from Britain, Spain, Mexico, Russia, and more than a dozen other countries. They swapped manufactured goods back and forth for hides, pelts, foodstuffs, and luxuries as they built up lucrative cargoes for China. They enlisted seamen and carried workers from one island or continent to another. They also carried European diseases like tuberculosis, smallpox, and influenza that devastated island and Northwest Coast populations and made areas like Oregon and northern California easy targets for English-speaking settlers in the 1840s and 1850s.

This quick introduction of Hawaii and Hawaiians—not to mention the

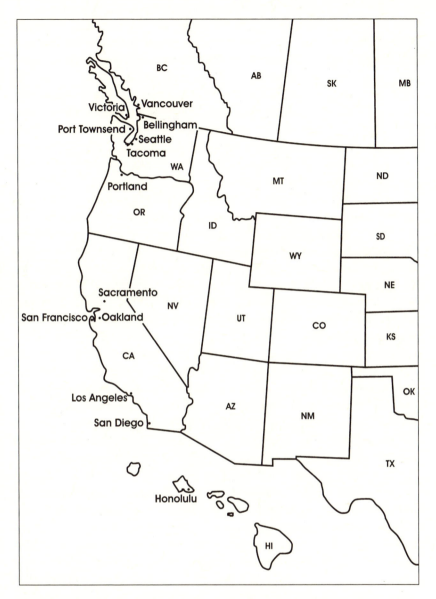

FIGURE 14. Pacific cities. As this map shows, Pacific coast cities fall into two clusters—the California ports from San Francisco and Oakland southward and the northwest ports from Portland to Vancouver. (Map by Jacquelyn Ferry.)

career of Sitka, Alaska, from a previous chapter—is a reminder that nineteenth-century settlers and city makers approached western North America from the water as well as the land. St. Louis, Omaha, and Winnipeg had counterparts in a set of West Coast gateways built on the foundations of early colonial outposts—not only San Francisco and its Bay Area rivals like Vallejo but also San Diego, Portland, and Victoria. These fast-growing cities connected North America to Asia. In the era of water transportation, they also connected the eastern United States and Canada to the Pacific interior.

The Pacific gateways functioned somewhat like the European treaty ports on the coast of China or the European colonial capitals along the west coast of Africa, where Conakry, Freetown, Monrovia, Abidjan, Accra, and Lagos sat astride the routes into different sections of the continent. You could get to Tombouctou from the north or east across expanses of desert and wasteland, but European colonialists found it easier to come inland from the Atlantic coast. In the same way, you could get to Grass Valley in the Sierra Nevada without going through San Francisco or reach Walla Walla without going through Portland, but to do so would be choosing the hard way. Victoria, perched at the tip of an island with access to an expansive range of straits and bays, was a conifer-encircled cousin of Singapore.

San Francisco was central to the entire system during the California gold rush and for a century after. In 1848 and 1849, geography and human action built the city in harness together. San Francisco Bay was the natural place for oceangoing ships to pass their passengers and cargo onto shallow-draft steamers that plied the interior rivers to Maryville, Sacramento, and Stockton, the jumping-off points for the mines. The small settlement of Yerba Buena beat out rivals like Vallejo and Benicia (each of which was briefly the state capital) by changing its name to San Francisco to match the well-known bay and then by the cumulative effect of its growing corps of merchants and business, its new wharves reaching far into Yerba Buena Cove, and its general reputation.

San Francisco merchants and investors built a regional empire on both sides of the high Sierra Nevada range in the heady years of the gold rush and the Comstock silver bonanza that followed. In 1860, San Francisco counted 57,000 people; Sacramento, 14,000; and Maryville and Stockton, between 5,000 and 10,000. The hierarchy of trade mirrored that of the mid-continent, with San Francisco standing in for Chicago and Sacramento, for Omaha. Miners could get the basics in Downieville or Placerville, select from a much wider array of goods and services in Maryville and Sacramento, and buy nearly anything in San Francisco, the city for fine living in Nob Hill mansions and high living in saloons, brothels, and gambling houses. As early as 1851 a British visitor saw it as a place of "precocious depravity," a reputation that the Vigilance Committees of 1851 and 1855 attempted to counter by imposing their own version of law and order through a dozen ad hoc executions. Nevertheless, the Barbary Coast took on much the same reputation as

Five Points and the Bowery in New York. Books like *Lights and Shades in San Francisco* competed with *The Tricks and Traps of New York* in recounting lurid stories of the underworld:

> The "Barbary Coast" proper, is in the northerly part of the city. . . . Like the malaria arising from a stagnant swamp and poisoning the air for miles around, does this stagnant pool of human depravity and crime spread its contaminating vapors over the surrounding blocks. . . . Barbary Coast is the haunt of the low and vile of every kind. The petty thief, the house-burglar, the tramp, the whoremonger, lewd women, cut-throats and murderers, all are found here. . . . And Hell, yawning to receive the putrid mass, is there also.[2]

One of the attractions was high wages and widespread economic opportunity. A booming and fluid economy held pitfalls as well as promise for aspiring merchants. However, it meant good city wages for unskilled workers and openings for women as well as men to operate small businesses. In turn, wealth accumulated from supplying the mines and miners poured into manufacturing, transportation, and real estate. By 1860, San Francisco was the ninth-largest manufacturing center in the United States. The most important specialty was metalworking by firms like the Union Iron Works to provide machinery and pipe for mining and later for irrigation. Blankets and other woolen goods were an important product, soon to be joined by sugar refined from Hawaiian cane. San Francisco and Sacramento furnished the "Big Four" entrepreneurs who organized and built the Central Pacific Railroad eastward from California to connect with the Union Pacific.[3] San Francisco money poured into Nevada mining in the 1860s, with commercial banks to finance mining and refining and a stock exchange to trade Nevada stocks. The 1870s brought further investments in hydraulic mining in California, in newer western mining regions, and in California wheat and California real estate. Data on the sources of California real estate and business loans show its lead in the later nineteenth century (Table 3.1).[4]

As a new community with a rapidly shifting population, San Francisco offered business opportunities to women as well as men. From the earliest years, when men far outnumbered women, many women made their living

TABLE 3.1. Sources of California Investment Loans

City	1879	1899
San Francisco	$11,713,700	$20,932,400
Sacramento	$2,263,700	$2,304,000
Los Angeles	$4,500	$994,500

as small business proprietors specializing in "domestic" businesses like laundries, clothes repair and tailoring shops, restaurants, groceries, lodging and boarding houses, and hotels. In 1880, when the city still had only three women for every four men, 500 women ran hotels and boarding houses, and roughly 1,500 operated businesses of all sorts—about one-tenth of all working women. Historian Edith Sparks suggests that Mrs. Ann Hudson may have been typical, selling "Ladies and Gents New and Used Clothing" from a store at Seventh and Market that "was simply part of the commercial landscape, a customary sight to San Franciscans who encountered women-owned businesses on a daily basis."[5]

San Francisco's commercial influence extended from B.C. to B.C. (British Columbia to Baja California). Goods and information came to San Francisco first, to be distributed by the Pacific Mail Steamship Company; by Wells, Fargo and Company; and later by the growing railroad system. "Capital and commerce center here," wrote Samuel Bowles in 1869: "It is the social focus and the intellectual inspiration, not only of California, but of Nevada, Oregon, and Idaho as well." He might well have added Puget Sound and the British colonies to its north. He commented as well that "all the people west of the Rocky Mountains feel a peculiar personal pride in San Francisco, and, if they would confess it, look forward to no greater indulgence in life, no greater reward in death, than to come hither."[6]

Portland was the first city to seriously challenge San Francisco's sphere of influence, succeeding to a waterborne commercial system sketched out by the Hudson's Bay Company. From 1825 to 1845, John McLoughlin had made Fort Vancouver on the Columbia River the center of a fur-trading empire that fanned out to the four points of the compass. Trappers and traders followed the Columbia upriver to the network of interior trading posts and beaver streams and downstream traveled north along the Cowlitz River corridor or coast to Puget Sound and south up the Willamette River. The Columbia itself was and is the Great River of the West, comparable to the Danube in drainage area and volume of water, with the snowcapped Rockies standing in for the Alps and the volcanic cones of the Cascades for the mountains of Serbia and Transylvania.

Within a group of settlements that included Fort Vancouver, Oregon City at the Falls of the Willamette, and hundreds of new farms hacked out of the Oregon forest and savannas by the 2,000 Oregon Trail settlers of 1843–44, the site of Portland was Oregon's first highway rest area. Native Americans and fur trappers had cleared part of a dry, sloping bank on the west side of the Willamette roughly halfway between Fort Vancouver and Oregon City. It was a good spot to cook a meal, spend a night, or repair equipment. Nevertheless, promoters William Overton and Asa Lovejoy claimed the square mile that would become downtown Portland because they saw the superiority of its site over local rivals. As two British spies compared the new town to neighboring

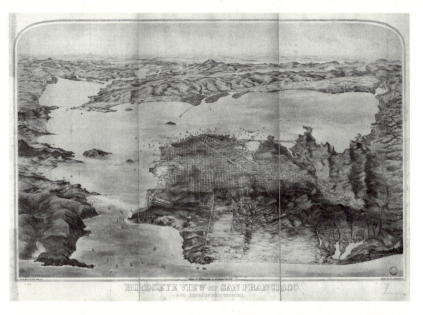

San Francisco panorama in the 1870s. This bird's-eye view of San Francisco Bay was drawn in the late 1860s and republished in the 1870s. Note the rapid development of areas near the bay and the bustling harbor compared to the desolate, windswept dunes that bordered the ocean. (Library of Congress.)

settlements in 1846, "The situation of Portland is superior . . . and the back country of easier access. There are several settlements on the banks of the [Willamette] river below the falls, but the water, covering the low lands during the freshets render them valueless for cultivation, and but few situations can be found adapted for building on."[7]

The California gold rush turned a town site into a city by creating a voracious appetite for Oregon wheat and lumber. Newly platted Portland established itself as the head of oceangoing navigation on the Willamette River after fending off a strong challenge from St. Helens. Thirty miles closer to the open ocean on the main stem of the Columbia, St. Helens built a road over a high steep ridge of the Tualatin Mountains to tap the richest wheat farms. Portland countered with its own plank road on an easier route. Then came the news—in February 1851—that the Pacific Mail Steamship Company of San Francisco was going to terminate its California–Oregon service at St. Helens. The contest hung in the balance for two years until Pacific Mail found it was unable to make full cargoes at St. Helens and began to advertise direct service between San Francisco and Portland, which assembled cargoes with shallow-draft steamboats that plied the Willamette.[8]

After gaining control of trade between western Oregon and California, Portland entrepreneurs looked eastward. From the 1860s to the present, metropolitan growth has been tied to the resources of the Columbia River Valley. Central to the city's prosperity was the Oregon Steam Navigation Company, a Portland-owned corporation that monopolized travel to eastern Oregon, Washington, and Idaho with a fleet of steamboats. Settlers east of the Cascades hated its high freight charges, but Portlanders liked the jobs and money that it funneled to the city. Contemporaries called it Oregon's "millionaire-making machine."[9]

Even after 1883, when the Northern Pacific Railroad linked Portland into the transcontinental rail system, Portland remained a river city. The regional economy has relied ever since on the advantages of location. Columbia River steamers and railroads both used the "water-level" route to the interior that made the young city the bustling entrepôt for the vast Columbia Basin. Lumber and grain schooners crowded the banks of the Willamette to take on cargoes for California markets. East Portland and Albina, on the "wrong" side of the Willamette River, were Portland's Hoboken and Jersey City—industrial suburbs built around docks, mills, factories, and railroad yards for the Union Pacific and Southern Pacific. Boarding houses and small cottages climbed the bluff behind the factories. Up to a thousand railcars rolled in and out of Portland on a busy day in the later nineteenth century. The Pacific Coast Elevator, whose 1,000,000-bushel capacity was unrivaled west of the Twin Cities, could unload grain from eight railcars and load it into two ships at the same time. Planing mills, lumberyards, sash and door factories, and other manufacturing plants filled in along both sides of the river. The surviving symbol of this first industrial era is the Union Pacific rail yard smokestack, built in 1887 on "a foundation that would last for all time."

Industrial growth and the first Willamette River bridges paved the way for the Great Consolidation of 1891—the merger of Portland, East Portland, and Albina into a single supercity seven years before Brooklyn and New York had the same idea. When the census of 1890 showed that Seattle was crowding toward the title of the second-largest city on the West Coast, Portland boosters swung into action. The Chamber of Commerce pushed a referendum on consolidation. East-siders, they argued, would benefit from the removal of bridge tolls. West-side businesses would gain expanded markets. Voters agreed, and Portland kept ahead of Seattle for another twenty years.[10]

Short-term success notwithstanding, Portland's business leaders faced a long-term challenge in the development of the maritime cities of the Salish Sea, a term that embraces Puget Sound in the United States, the Strait of Georgia in Canada, and the Strait of Juan de Fuca that divides the two nations and gives entrance to the North Pacific.[11]

Victoria, perched on the lower tip of Vancouver Island just far enough east for shelter from Pacific gales, was the initial focal point. As Fort Victoria (1843) and then an incorporated city (1862), it was the new center for Hudson's Bay Company operations, the seat of government while Vancouver Island was an

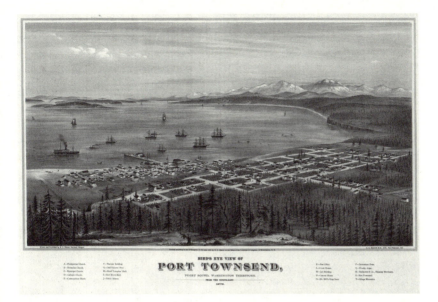

FIGURE 16. Port Townsend, Washington, panorama. Located near the entrance to Puget Sound, Port Townsend, shown in 1878, was an early lumber port whose metropolitan ambitions were dashed as railroads supplanted oceangoing trade and gave the advantage to Tacoma, Seattle, Everett, and Bellingham. North of the border, Vancouver and the Canadian Pacific Railroad similarly limited the economic prospects of Victoria.

autonomous Hudson's Bay Company colony from 1849 to 1866, and then the capital of the combined province of British Columbia. From Victoria ships crossed the Strait of Georgia to the Fraser River, plied the coasts of Vancouver Island to ocean-facing Nootka Sound or the east-shore coal mines around Nanaimo, and sailed south around the islands and bays of Puget Sound. Victoria mercantile houses placed family members in the smaller cities on both sides of the border to act as agents for waterborne commerce. The ambitious American equivalent was Port Townsend, located on a point of land that juts into the entrance to Puget Sound from the Olympic Peninsula.

By the 1880s, Victoria and Port Townsend faced active competition from a long lineup of mainland towns. From south to north in the United States were Olympia, Tacoma, Seattle, Everett, and Bellingham (itself a tense amalgam of four communities around a promising bay). New Westminster and—after 1886—Vancouver continued the series in Canada. Each had its advantages— spacious harbor, potential routes eastward through the mountains, proximity to timber- and agricultural land, and on through the booster litany—but the sine qua non, however, was a transcontinental rail connection.

Vancouver took off when the Canadian Pacific Railroad (CPR) arrived in 1886. Owning impressive tracts of land on the outskirts of the preexisting town, the CPR did its best to profit from real estate development as well as freight and passengers. Victoria held its edge in population into the early 1890s (17,000 to 14,000 in 1891), but Vancouver steamed ahead in the next two decades, with more than triple Victoria's population by 1911. Vancouver became the port of supply for the B.C. interior, developed mills and factories along False Creek, and attracted the head offices of the province's many mining and salmon-canning operations.[12]

All of the U.S. cities secured rail connections in the 1880s (Tacoma first), but Seattle made the most of the opportunity. There is no a priori reason why it outpaced Tacoma and Everett, each with a superior harbor and high hopes, but success built on success. The Klondike gold rush sealed the deal. Publicist Erastus Brainerd and the Seattle Chamber of Commerce jumped to identify Seattle with the Far North in the minds of most Americans. Captured initially in the flush times, Alaska business stayed in the pockets of Seattle merchants, bankers, and boat builders and helped Seattle's population outnumber Portland's by 1910. The city's first steel-frame skyscraper was the aptly named Alaska Building of 1914, decorated with a frieze of terra-cotta walrus heads, and as early as 1921, historian Ezra Meeker wrote that "without Alaska Washington would not now have attained the commanding development that is her pride." Murray Morgan later said it even more directly: "In Seattle, gold spurred growth, and growth battened on growth."[13]

More than a century later, Seattle remained a city of the sea. Unlike Portland, with its water-level route into the interior, Seattle metaphorically backed against mountains and faced the ocean. Huge ferries arrived and departed on crisscrossed routes to half a dozen islands. Cargo vessels made their way in and out of the port located at the reengineered mouth of the Duwamish River on the edge of downtown. Visitor and future resident Jonathan Raban immediately picked up Seattle's stance:

> Seattle looked like a free-hand sketch . . . of a sawmill owner's whirlwind vacation in Rome and Florence. Its antique skyscrapers were rude boxes . . . fantastically candied over with patterned brick and terracotta moldings. . . . All the most important buildings faced west, over the Sound, and Seattle was designed to be seen from the front. You were meant to arrive by ship, from Yokahama or Shanghai, and be overwhelmed by the financial muscle. . . . the world-traveled air of this Manhattan of the Far West. If you had the bad taste to look at Seattle from the back, all you'd see would be plain brick cladding and a zig-zag tangle of fire escapes.[14]

From Burrard Inlet and Puget Sound to San Francisco Bay and San Diego Bay, the west-facing cities of the western coast were the arrival points for hundreds of thousands of east-faring immigrants from Pacific islands and

Asia. From the 1850s into the 1880s they came in great numbers from China to build railroads, work mines, staff factories, and do the dirty work that kept cities going. After the United States and then Canada clamped restrictions on Chinese migration, Japanese workers beginning in the 1890s and Filipino workers after American conquest met much of the demand for labor in both cities and countryside.

The patterns that workers traced around the rim of the Pacific were as complex as the networks of commerce. Chileans, Chinese, and Australians joined the California gold rush along with East Coast Americans. Miners—and then mining engineers—circulated among the western United States, Canada, and Australia. Asian laborers headed to the United States but also to Peru, Mexico, Cuba, and Canada. Immigrants from British India made their way to British Columbia via the United States when the Canadian government erected legal barriers to direct entry. Chinese immigrants used Canada as a route to the United States. By the end of the first century of substantial migration from Asia to the Americas (roughly the 1840s through the 1930s), two-fifths of Japanese in the Americas had settled in Latin America (especially Brazil and Peru), whereas 33 percent of Chinese in the Americas lived in Latin America, 21 percent lived in Canada, and 46 percent lived in the United States.

English-speaking North Americans had as much difficulty then as now in deciding whether to welcome or fend off immigrants. Labor agitation in the late 1870s and early 1880s against low-wage competition from Chinese workers led up to the Chinese Exclusion Act in 1882 in the United States and the imposition of a punitive head tax on Chinese immigrants to Canada in 1885. Continued violence in backwater towns like Rock Springs, Wyoming (1885), and in the growing cities of Seattle and Tacoma (1885–86) helped to push Chinese workers into Chinatowns in Vancouver, Portland (whose Chinese population swelled from 1,700 to 7,800 during the 1880s), and especially San Francisco (whose Chinese population reached at least 30,000).[15] These were overwhelmingly male communities. Handfuls of merchants lived comfortably; thousands of workingmen crowded into cheaply built tenements and shanties. Honolulu's Chinese worked as stevedores, servants, and factory hands. Chinese Portlanders toiled in steamy laundries, cultivated vegetables on the edge of the city, and staffed Columbia River canneries when the salmon were running.

Chinatowns were an "attractive nuisance," easy to romanticize for tourists and easy to raid in vice crackdowns. Although there was little functional difference between the Chinese workers and the transient white males who lived in adjacent skid roads, the lives of Chinese-born workers involved activities that white society defined as vices, particularly gambling and the use of opium. Police officials could stand foursquare for virtue by raiding fan-tan rooms and opium parlors while ignoring the far more numerous gambling joints

FIGURE 17. West Coast Chinatown. San Francisco and Portland had the two largest Chinese populations in North America in the late nineteenth century, the result of their roles as the first major Pacific ports and their relative tolerance of Chinese residents compared with other cities. This photograph from Portland is unusual in showing children because early Chinese immigrants were largely a bachelor society. (Oregon Historical Society, Neg. 3880.)

and saloons with white customers. Tour guides in San Francisco manipulated a narrative of danger and depravity, leading visitors on misleading rambles through Chinatown basements and hiring local residents as fake denizens of opium dens. Tour books called Chinatown a "fantastic realm" where Americans were foreigners in their own country. To novelist Frank Norris it was even more extreme, a "noisome swamp" full of "strange, dreadful life."[16] Chinatowns' very existence gave residents of European heritage the thrill of confronting the "other" while remaining firmly in charge.

It was a short step from fears of Asians as a social threat to fears that Asian communities—undeniably crowded and unsanitary in many cases—posed physical dangers as sources of disease. The fears came to a climax at the very end of the century, when an outbreak of bubonic plague spread from southern China through the Pacific. It reached Honolulu in December 1899, Sydney in January 1900, and San Francisco in March. In both U.S. cities it found its quickest footing in the crowded, rat-plagued blocks of Chinatown. Health officials quarantined both Chinese districts, responding simultaneously to concrete epidemiological concerns and to white fears that it was Chinese residents (not the plague bacillus or its animal vectors) who could contaminate the entire community. In San Francisco the quarantine devastated the Chinese American economy, but the recognized leadership of Chinese merchants was able to deal with the Public Health Service somewhat as equals and negotiate house-to-house inspections to replace the quarantine. In Honolulu, "Chinatown" actually housed 3,000 Chinese, 1,500 Japanese, and 1,000 Hawaiians in densely packed two-story wooden buildings, backyard shacks, and shanties (another 7,000 Chinese lived elsewhere in the city). Chinatown was an overcrowded slum, to be sure, with little fresh water and terrible sanitation. When plague appeared, public health officials resisted panic and racist pressure to raze the whole district in favor of burning only those buildings where plague victims had died. On January 20, 1900, however, a controlled burn blazed out of control, spiraling into a fire that consumed a fifth of Honolulu's buildings, devastated Chinese and Japanese businesses, and forced thousands of residents into tightly controlled refugee camps.[17]

The image and reality of Chinatown changed in the following decades. Immigration for family unification (including the ruse of "paper families" in which immigrants claimed fictitious family relationships with Chinese already in the United States) slowly evened the gender imbalance that made Americans uneasy. In multiracial Honolulu, Chinese merchants and manufacturers had a strong enough voice to block discriminatory laws. In Portland, merchants and professionals began to move out to new neighborhoods, leaving community institutions and businesses behind as "Chinatown." Twentieth-century Chinatowns began to capitalize on their exotic character through tourism managed by Chinese businessmen themselves. After the San Francisco earthquake, Chinese entrepreneurs carefully rebuilt in "oriental style" with upturned eaves, bright red and green paint, balconies, lanterns, and pagodas. The rebuilt neighborhood, said Look Tin Eli, was "much more beautiful, artistically, and much more emphatically Oriental" than the old.[18] Vancouver by the 1930s was staging "tong wars" with actors using rubber knives (like the staged cowboy–Indian fights and staged train robberies that other cities liked to add to their fairs and festivals). Even Charlie Chan, the hero of six novels from 1925 to 1932 and then of four dozen increasingly terrible movies from 1931 to 1949, helped with the transition. As a detective on the Honolulu police force, Chan corralled white criminals in Hawaii and California, displayed the virtues of intelligence and responsibility, and demonstrated the existence of a *relatively* open society in Hawaii.

As Chinatown was slowly demystified and domesticated for American tastes, newer Japanese and Filipino immigrants took their place as social menace. White Americans disliked the entrepreneurial competition from Japanese who excelled in niche markets like truck farming, produce sales, and hotel keeping. In addition, white Westerners were increasingly prone to articulate

sexual fears, for the early twentieth century was an era of "white slavery" pan-
ics and antiprostitution crusades. Filipino men, on their own as migratory
workers or personal service workers, were depicted as sexual aggressors on the
hunt for white women. They were welcome to use the hotels, shops, and pool
halls of Little Manilas in Seattle and Los Angeles for a sense of community,
but they generated hostility when they danced with white women in taxi dance
halls. The possibility of racially integrated classrooms stirred fears of sexual
mixing among schoolchildren. "I am responsible to the mothers and fathers
of Sacramento County who have their little daughters sitting, side by side, in
the school room with mature Japanese," roared one California legislator: "I
have seen Japanese of twenty-five years old sitting in their seats next to the
pure maids of California." The Gentlemen's Agreement of 1908 that curtailed
labor migration from Japan to the United States was triggered by the decision
of the San Francisco School Board to place the city's ninety-seven Japanese
students in a separate "oriental" school. Canada copied the Gentlemen's
Agreement almost immediately to assuage fears in British Columbia, but the
Victoria School Board still segregated that city's common schools in 1922–23
because of the same worries about the sexual consequences of mixing Asians
and white Canadians in the same classrooms.[19]

Americans and Canadians not only legislated against Asians and formed
common anti-Asian organizations like the Asiatic Exclusion League of North
America but also stoked their antipathy with blaring headlines and scare sto-
ries in the *San Francisco Chronicle* and *Los Angeles Times* ("The Yellow Peril:
How Japs Crowd Out the White Race," "Japanese a Menace to American
Women") and apocalyptic novels. Pierton W. Donner in *The Last Days of the
Republic* (1880) fears invasion by Chinese hordes who would overrun the
continent and raise the standard of the emperor over the Capitol. For Homer
Lea in 1909, the newly ascendant Japanese were the threat that required an
expanded military establishment. In *The Valor of Ignorance* he maps out how
Japan might successfully seize Hawaii and the Philippines, land at Gray's
Harbor on the Washington coast to conquer the Northwest, and continue
by taking San Pedro and then San Francisco itself. In 1915, J. U. Giesy in *All
for His Country* depicted a Mexican invasion that would draw off American
forces, opening California to invasion from Japan, with house servants as a
fifth column. By 1921, when Peter Kyne published *Pride of Palomar*, Mexicans
were in good graces again, with Bolsheviks in Siberia now the distraction
from the Japanese threat to California.[20]

North of the border, *The Writing on the Wall* by the pseudonymous Hilda
Glynn-Ward appeared in the *Vancouver Sun* and then between hard covers in
1921. The author inveighs against the tide of Asian immigrants who were supposedly inundating British Columbia and predicts a future in which an Asian
majority—led by the wily and unscrupulous Japanese—had seized control,
disfranchised white residents, and pushed Canada back across the Rockies.

By 1921, she feared, the finer residential neighborhoods of Victoria would be filled with Chinese families, Stanley Park in Vancouver would have been sold to Chinese loggers, and white women would enter the city's Granville Street shops only as menials doing the bidding of Japanese owners.

Some Westerners may have feared China and Japan, but others saw Asia as economic opportunity. California-based history publisher Hubert Howe Bancroft sums up a century of armchair ambition in *The New Pacific* (1900). He ends his boosterish inventory of western resources with the ancient trope of the westward course of empire and the newer American trope of searching for new frontiers. The twentieth century, he proclaims, would be the century of the *new* Pacific, with North Americans shouldering aside tired Europeans and the wealth of the Pacific surpassing that of the Atlantic. The vision is one of classic liberalism, with free trade in goods and ideas lifting the strongest individuals and nations to success:

> The far west facing the far east, with the ocean between, have lain hitherto at the back door of both Europe and America. Now by magic strides the antipodal No-man's-land is coming to the front to claim a proper share in the world's doings. . . . We have no longer a virgin continent to develop; pioneer work in the United States is done, and now we must take a plunge into the sea. Here we find an area, an amphitheatre of water, upon and around which American enterprise and industry . . . will find occupation for the full term of the twentieth century, and for many centuries thereafter. The Pacific, its shores and islands, must now take the place of the great west, its plains and mountains, as an outlet for pent-up industry. Here on this ocean all the world will meet, and on equal footing, Americans and Europeans, Asiatics and Africans, white, yellow, and black, looters and looted, the strongest and cunningest to carry off the spoils.[21]

Bancroft's peroration was tied to a specific moment. In the single decade starting in 1898, the United States annexed Hawaii and parts of Samoa; fought the Spanish American War, acquired Guam, and took control of the reluctant Philippines through four years of colonial war; declared an Open Door policy for trade with China and intervened during that nation's Boxer Rebellion; mediated an end to the Russo-Japanese War; and started work on the Panama Canal. Journalists penned stories such as "The Coming Supremacy of the Pacific" and "The Momentous Struggle for Mastery of the Pacific."[22] Theodore Roosevelt dispatched the Great White Fleet of new battleships on a fourteen-month round-the-world voyage in 1907–9 to demonstrate American military power vis-à-vis Japan, fend off the yellow peril, build a sense of common interest with New Zealand and Australia, and cap a decade of Pacific expansion.

The Panama Canal project, which began with the American-assisted secession of Panama from Colombia and climaxed with the canal opening in 1914, linked Pacific cities with the world of Atlantic commerce. At one end, the creation of Panama and the Canal Zone and digging the canal were an installment in Caribbean ambitions that extended from the Monroe Doctrine through the Spanish–American War, acquisition of Puerto Rico, and repeated twentieth-century interventions in countries such as Nicaragua and the Dominican Republic. At the other end—the Panama City side—the canal was part of Pacific ambitions, with every West Coast city expecting to benefit from the new waterway and from growing Asian trade.

Here came the promoters of San Diego (who were joined in a harmony of booster ambition with Los Angeles, San Francisco, Oakland, Portland, and Seattle): Anticipating the project for visitors to the Louisiana Purchase Exposition in St. Louis, the secretary of the Chamber of Commerce wrote that the canal would make San Diego "an important naval rendezvous, thus adding largely to the gaiety and attractiveness of this beautiful city." A decade later, another booster was convinced that it would soon and inevitably be "the main port of call for vessels going to the Orient, the Hawaiian Islands, and Australia." Maps marched along with the prose. The Chamber of Commerce mapped "San Diego's Advantageous Location," which placed the city as the very pivot of the Pacific coast. T. D. Beasley's *Map of the City of San Diego, California* in 1915 included one inset showing a schematic diagram of the Panama Canal and another showing Middle America with San Diego in the upper left corner and Panama in the lower right, including steamship routes and comparisons of the San Diego–New York distance via Panama (4,000 miles) and Cape Horn (13,000 miles) and boasting the statement: "San Diego: The first port of call on the Pacific Coast north of the Panama Canal and Tehuantepec Route."[23]

Two thousand miles away, the cities of British Columbia were not to be outdone. Visitors had already proclaimed their great future. Vancouver, said a correspondent of *Frank Leslie's Popular Monthly*, was the "sea-port of the twentieth century! The Constantinople of the West!" A few years later, another American visitor was convinced that "Vancouver will be New York's greatest rival. . . . [I]n 60 years it will outstrip Paris and Berlin." But maybe Vancouver was not the perfect location, despite the best efforts of the CPR, and would soon be surpassed by Coquitlam. With the canal in prospect, it too had a prosperous future "nothing short of a world-wide cataclysm can turn aside." Wrote the *Weekly Globe and Canadian Farmer* in April 1913, "Of all the cities on the coast which are looking forward to the opening of the Panama Canal, Port Coquitlam . . . is justified in being the most optimistic."[24]

The first world's fairs on the West Coast looked both westward and eastward. The Lewis and Clark Centennial Exposition and Oriental Fair in Portland (1905) was keyed simultaneously to a history of continental expansion and to

SAN DIEGO'S ADVANTAGEOUS LOCATION

FIGURE 18. San Diego imagined in 1915. San Diego boosters creatively imagined San Diego as the pivot point for trade between Asia and the Panama Canal. This map from John J. Mills's *San Diego, California* (issued by the Board of Supervisors and Chamber of Commerce of San Diego County, California, 1915), was aimed at people attending the city's Panama–California Exposition. (Henry E. Huntington Library and Art Gallery.)

FIGURE 19. Lewis and Clark Exposition of 1905. The ambitious port cities of the Pacific coast called attention to themselves with a series of large-scale expositions and world's fairs, including events in San Francisco in 1894 and 1915, Portland in 1905, Seattle in 1909, and San Diego in 1915. One of the major backers of Portland's Lewis and Clark Centennial Exposition was the local electric power company, which used the occasion to promote its product. (Oregon Historical Society, Neg. 56808.)

Pacific ambitions. The most impressive structure was the Forestry Building of huge unpeeled logs, but most of the foreign exhibits were from Asia. The Alaska–Yukon–Pacific Fair in Seattle in 1909 stated its economic orientation in its name but, ironically for such a sea-centered city, arranged the grounds to frame a view of Mount Rainier. The California–Pacific Exposition in San Diego in 1915 was intended to stake that city's claim to the new trade routes and the U.S. Navy, but its major buildings imitated cities like Seville, and its most interesting attractions were Indian potters and craftspeople from the Southwest.

It was San Francisco, the first and foremost capital of the Pacific West, where the message was most clear. A Chicago company that billed itself as "builders and operators of public utilities" created a model of the Panama Canal for the San Francisco Panama–Pacific International Exposition of 1915 (the direct competitor with San Diego). The model covered five acres with oceans at each end, lighthouses, dams, Panamanian cities, and working locks. Its promoters happily recited its wonders:

It is housed in a special building containing a large oblong amphitheatre that surrounds the model. The model remains in place, and
the seating for 1200 people revolves slowly around the model, powered by electricity, making the circuit in 23 minutes. Each chair on
the moving platform has a telephone receiver and gets a continual
lecture, which is delivered from 60 phonographs that play into
telephone transmitters.[25]

This is the city that Edward Hungerford had just visited and described as
fully cosmopolitan, a city where Portuguese, Italians, and Japanese mingled
with eastern bankers and sourdoughs from Alaska. Its residents claimed
that "Hong Kong or Manila or Yokahama seem nearer to us than Chicago or
St. Louis." The contrast within California was fixed in San Francisco opinion:
"Los Angeles is western," argued a Bay Area businessman: "We are not. We
are 'the Coast,' and be exceeding careful, young man, how you say it."[26]

It was also the city that worried most deeply about keeping its commercial lead as the ports of Los Angeles and Long Beach took off in the 1910s
and 1920s with improved harbors and shipments of southern California
petroleum. In total, U.S. trade across the Pacific increased three times as
fast as transatlantic trade between 1913 and 1929, growing from 6 percent
to 12 percent of U.S. foreign trade. At the beginning of the 1920s, the San
Francisco Chamber of Commerce was confident that "the magnitude of San
Francisco's foreign trade future is assured because San Francisco possessed
the greatest number of natural inducements and offers the largest possibilities of any city in the commercial and industrial world." By 1930, however,
the chamber was hard at work to hold its place with a new international trade
department. By the end of that decade, it was trying to refute a *Saturday
Evening Post* article that called San Francisco a "forgotten port" and stressing
the need to "protect her large and valuable trade with Japan" in the face of
global tensions.[27]

A nervous San Francisco business community and a world lurching
toward war were the context for San Francisco's Golden Gate International
Exposition in 1939–40, which outdid them all as a sort of apotheosis of
American/Pacific expectations. Its 17 million visitors received an art deco
introduction to the Pacific Ocean as an American lake. The style was "Pacific
Basin," an amalgam of Incan, Cambodian, Malayan, and Thai elements laid
on with Hollywood exuberance. Towers of the East cast reflections on the
Lake of All Nations. Pacific House sheltered a relief map of the bottom of the
Pacific Ocean and six murals by Miguel Covarrubias on themes of Pacific culture. Outside, visitors watched Pan American Airways' China Clipper take
off for Asia (service had started in 1937), little expecting that the U.S. Navy
would soon purchase the site to augment the Bay Area's naval facilities for
war with Japan.

CHAPTER FOUR

Inland Empire Cities

The country tributary to Denver. . . . extends far beyond the state of
Colorado and practically embraces the whole of the territory West of the
Missouri River. . . . In this vast region, every new mine worked, every
fresh acre cultivated, every new orchard planted. . . . [a]nd every manu-
facturing enterprise started, react beneficially on and send new life-blood
to the heart—Denver.

—Thomas Tonge, *All about Colorado* (1913)

The later nineteenth century was the last great age of empires: In the same years that William J. Palmer was developing a vision of economic control of the central Rockies, Emperor Napoleon III of France (1852–70) was rebuilding Paris before accepting war with Prussia and surrendering the fortress of Sedan to the army of King Wilhelm, soon to be proclaimed the emperor of a united Germany. Elsewhere in Europe, Kaiser Franz Joseph ruled the Dual Monarchy (after 1867) as emperor of Austria and King of Hungary, reform-minded Alexander II reigned as czar and autocrat of All the Russias, and Sultan Abdulaziz presided over the tricontinental Ottoman Empire. Japan had an emperor, returned to partial power by the Meiji Restoration in 1867. China had an emperor, presiding over the last decades of the 300-year Qing dynasty. India would have an empress after January 1, 1877, although she spent most of her time in Britain. Even in the New World, Maximilian had reigned briefly and incompetently as emperor of Mexico (1864–67), and Dom Pedro II (1841–89) ruled far more successfully over the Empire of Brazil.

In the firmly republican United States, there was no danger of a formal crown imperial, but there could be urban/regional empires of trade and settlement. Empire, Colorado, popped onto the map in 1860 on the road to lofty Berthoud Pass. Empire City, Nevada, flourished for a few decades along the Carson River and then faded into emptiness for a century before developers recycled the site for a golf course. In Cherokee County, Kansas, another Empire City lasted thirty years (1877–1907) before folding into neighboring Galena. Empire City, Oklahoma, still makes it on the map, with an official population of 734 people in 2000.

The real empire cities of the mid–nineteenth century were the regional centers of Salt Lake City and Denver—the sacred and secular capitals of the Rocky Mountains—which emerged in the quarter century after 1850 to serve growing mining and agricultural regions. Both regional empires functioned through a hierarchy of cities and towns, and each was substantially freestanding, its developed territories separated by lightly settled mountains and deserts. The ambitious imperial centers were the starting points for railroad building and sources of capital for processing raw materials. They were also social and cultural centers. Their civic/religious and business leaders fought off the claims of rival cities, took the lead in displacing or incorporating Native Americans, and dominated a network of smaller service and production towns in mining and agricultural districts.

Brigham Young did not name *his* new settlement in 1846 Empire City, but it did start out as "Great Salt Lake City of the Great Basin, North America," and it was nearly instantaneously the first imperial center for the zone of the interior. Cities were central from the start in the teachings of Joseph Smith and the Church of Jesus Christ of Latter Day Saints. Pulling followers together around a complex narrative that ties American Indians to the people of ancient Israel, Smith made the idea of Gathering a central element of the new faith as it developed in the 1820s and 1830s. Awaiting the transformation of the world in the latter days of history, believers were to come together in a single large community "and so fill up the world in these last days, and let every man live in the city for this is the City of Zion."[1] The model may have been influenced by the many small utopian communities that were springing up on the edges of American settlement, but the Mormons realized it far more successfully than any of the other experiments.

The early first attempts to build the gathered community were in the rapidly developing Mississippi Valley. The City of Zion, or Far West, Missouri, came first from 1831 to 1838. The physical city centered on a public square. The political and social city was equally centralized, with a top-down hierarchy of leadership and a church-directed economy in which individuals consecrated their property to the church but retained stewardship. Hostility from non-Mormons drove the community to abandon Missouri to construct a second city in western Illinois. Nauvoo ("The Beautiful") reached 20,000 by 1844. It was developing into a city-state with its own militia chartered by the state of Illinois, and Smith went so far as to suggest that the enclave be made a separate federal territory.

Change came again in 1844, when mob action and the vigilante murder of Joseph Smith in 1844 shifted leadership to Brigham Young and forced the Saints to consider if they had a future in the United States. Not long before his death, Smith had proclaimed that "the whole of America is Zion itself from north to south, and is described by the Prophets, who declare that it is the Zion where the mountains of the Lord should be, and that it should be in the center of the land."[2] Now Young considered moving to Vancouver Island, Texas, California, and other parts of northern Mexico before deciding that the Great Basin was the most isolated location that the Mormons could feasibly reach in large numbers. Familiar with the reports of western exploration by John C. Fremont and Benjamin Bonneville, whose maps hung on the wall at Nauvoo Temple, Young and the Mormon leaders made the decision in January 1846, when the whole vast territory of the basin was still inside the borders of Mexico. By the time the Mormon vanguard reached Salt Lake Basin in 1847, however, the United States–Mexico war was well along, with the massive American annexations of 1848 on the near horizon.

Over the next decade, the Mormons built a city at the base of the Wasatch Mountains and claimed a Great Basin Empire. One step was to organize an unofficial Territory of Deseret with Young as governor and with vast extent through the Colorado River drainage and Great Basin, plus a piece of southern California for an outlet to the sea (territory that would later be shared among nine states). Young planted temporary outposts at Carson City, San Bernardino, and South Pass to anchor the edges of the realm.

There followed a decade of political maneuvering between Mormons and the federal government. The United States would not recognize Deseret but did establish a Territory of Utah to which President Fillmore appointed Young as governor. The territorial boundaries from 1851 to 1859 reached from the Continental Divide to the California border between the thirty-seventh and forty-second parallels, before silver discoveries on the Comstock Lode and gold discoveries in the Rockies caused the government to split off Nevada and Colorado territories. The Utah War of 1857–58—a nonviolent show of force by the U.S. government—resulted in Mormon acknowledgment of national authority but left the church leadership politically dominant—in effect as a semiautonomous protectorate of the sort that European powers were employing to control Asian and African colonies.

Meanwhile the Mormons continued to consolidate their presence in the heart of Utah, settling a core region along two long mountain fronts that run 600 miles north–south through Utah and into southeastern Idaho. American, British, and Scandinavian converts arrived in Salt Lake City to be dispatched in groups to new towns, in an updated version of the way that Puritans occupied

seventeenth-century New England. Most of the settlements were agricultural villages with houses on large lots and fields and stables outside the core. They depended on irrigation water, which the Mormons treated as a public or community resource to be controlled by the local bishop. By 1869, roughly 80,000 Mormons lived in 200 cities and villages. Over the course of his life in Utah, Young oversaw the founding of nearly 350 communities. By the end of the nineteenth century, what geographer Donald Meinig calls the Mormon Culture Region stretched from Rexburg, Idaho, to St. George, Utah. The construction of temples marked the greater importance of the cities of St. George, Manti, and Logan as well as Salt Lake City.

Salt Lake City itself was a secular and spiritual capital that grew quickly from a few hundred people in 1848 to several thousand by 1850. As historians Thomas Alexander and James Allen comment, the city was the gathering place for the colonizers of new towns, the model for their planning and governance, and the religious, political, and economic nucleus of the territory.[3] The streets of the oasis city followed the standard American grid with a large temple square. A bird's-eye view from 1870 shows a prominent stream debouching into the grid only two blocks east of the temple (a stream that still runs through a ravine in the shadow of the state capitol building). Houses and two-story business buildings spread loosely east, south, and west across the level plain, creating a settlement that was urban in function but semirural in its landscape.

Isolation was impossible to maintain. Federal troops threatened the city in 1857–58, the Pony Express galloped through its streets in 1860, the Union Pacific Railroad ran only thirty-seven miles away by 1869, and the Utah Central Railroad tied Salt Lake City directly into the rail network the following year. Prospectors fanned out through the territory, and non-Mormon mining towns grew at places like Park City. Many of the inevitable newcomers were non-Mormon merchants, bankers, miners, and railroad men. The church tried to preserve economic isolation by creating Zions Cooperative Mercantile Institution (ZCMI) to act as the commercial intermediary between "gentile" merchants and Mormon consumers, but the church began to allow Mormons to trade directly with Gentiles in the 1880s. A Chamber of Commerce and Board of Trade with both Mormons and Gentiles appeared in 1887. A double-centered business district had Mormon businesses and hotels clustered around the temple and ZCMI at the northern end, while Gentile bankers, merchants, and hotel keepers set up shop several blocks to the south (and closer to the train station). An apt analogy for Salt Lake City is seventeenth-century Massachusetts, where Boston as the political and economic capital became a partially secularized community while the backcountry towns remained closed agricultural settlements.

The future of Salt Lake City was never in doubt as long as Mormon missionaries continued to meet success in the eastern states and Europe. The Great Basin Empire expanded in its early decades like a balloon inflated by the stream of Mormon migrants who arrived at Salt Lake City and then spread north and south under the direction of the church. Non-Mormons who came with the railroad and mining booms fit neatly into the same framework, utilizing the rail system that centered on northern Utah and establishing their parallel society in Salt Lake City and Ogden. Gentiles, as the Saints called non-Mormons, chafed at the power to dictate local politics. Their Liberal Party finally defeated Mormon candidates for Salt Lake's City Council in 1890. Inept government soon brought a reform mayor with support from both sides, and Utah residents had realigned with the national Republican and Democratic parties in time for Utah statehood in 1896. By 1900, with polygamy officially proscribed and a state capitol building under construction on a hill overlooking downtown, Salt Lake City's 54,000 people made it the largest center between San Francisco and Denver.

Denver followed a path to prominence that was fundamentally different than the career of Salt Lake City. Its business leaders—for Denver was as much a businessman's city as Salt Lake was a religious and cultural center—fought their way past a series of rivals. The battles started with town site promoters who outwitted their literal next-door neighbors and continued at an increasingly expansive scale as Denver's bankers, merchants, and railroad builders pinned more and more towns and cities into subordinate positions within its economic empire. Despite William Gilpin's excited prose, there was nothing inevitable about Denver's growth. Each success looked logical after the fact, but all were hard won at the expense of economic rivals and Native Americans who happened to be in the way.

Gold created Denver, and silver sustained it. Reports of placer gold in the sands of Cherry Creek and the South Platte River triggered fevered reports in the settlements along the Missouri River in summer 1858. Headlines blared: "New Gold Discovery," "Kansas Gold Fever" (Kansas Territory then stretched to the Rocky Mountains), and "Gold! Gold!! Gold!!! Gold!!!! Hard To Get and Heavy To Hold. Come to Kansas." Perhaps a thousand miners set out for the "Pike's Peak" diggings before winter set in. One of them was William Larimer, lately of Larimer City, Nebraska, and Leavenworth, Kansas. On his arrival in November, Larimer found the rival town sites of Auraria and St. Charles staked up on the two sides of Cheery Creek. According to local lore, Larimer fed whiskey to the one resident of St. Charles, convinced him to sign over the site, and renamed it Denver City after the current governor of Kansas Territory. Larimer knew what he was after, writing his family that "we are bound to have a territory if not a state, and the capital will be Denver City with the state house near Will's and my claims."[4]

Denver and Auraria—two separate towns but a single settlement for practical purposes—provided winter quarters for most of the 1858 migrants and a jumping-off point for thousands of new prospectors in 1859, many of whom made their way westward just as merchants were setting up shop in Denver and fueling its first real estate boom. Because most of the gold was deeper in the mountains, prospectors and miners themselves lived in instant towns like Gold Hill, Central City, Blackhawk, and Idaho Springs, which could be approached through foothill towns like Boulder and Golden as well as Denver.

Through the next decade, Denver's instant civic elite fought for success. They contested with Golden for the territorial capital, with rival cliques of politicians known as the "Denver Crowd" and "Golden Crowd" struggling to control the Republican Party. Golden snagged the prize in 1863, but Denver grabbed it back four years later. By that time, railroad wars were heating up as each city tried to be the first to reach the Union Pacific as it built westward from Omaha. The Denver Pacific (DP) had the advantage of hard-driving John Evans (who had already given his name to Evanston, Illinois, before heading west). Evans outhustled Golden and Central City entrepreneurs by striking a deal with the Kansas Pacific, which was building west from Kansas City, simultaneously pushing the DP northward to the Union Pacific in 1870, the same year that Salt Lake City made its rail connection. Denver now had *two* railroads to eastern markets. It was "the proudest year in the whole [very short] history of Denver" according to the first effort to write the city's history.[5]

Denverites had already done the dirty work of driving the nomadic Cheyenne and Arapahoe Indians off the grasslands that stretched back to the farms of eastern Kansas. The Treaty of Fort Laramie in 1851 had given the closely related tribes most of the Great Plains between the Platte and Arkansas rivers. Three hundred Arapahoe lodges dotted the plains around Denver in summer 1859, but the influx of whites prompted the new Treaty of Fort Wise in 1861 that excluded the Indians from the richest hunting grounds near the base of the Rockies. Peace chiefs tried to live within the new agreement, but many of the younger warriors were fed up with the endless stream of migrants and freight wagons and with new ranches encroaching on their territory and staged increasingly bloody raids. Denver leaders knew that prosperity required safe access. The *Rocky Mountain News* called for "a few months of extermination against the red devils." Governor Evans recruited a volunteer cavalry regiment in summer 1864 and gave command to Colonel John Chivington, a former Methodist preacher and Civil War hero, whose sentiments were clear: "I am truly satisfied that to kill them is the only way to have peace and quiet."[6] He took his chance on November 29, 1864, when his regiment attacked a peaceful Indian camp along Sand Creek in southeastern Colorado, slaughtering 150 men, women, and children.

Proponents of ethnic cleansing dominated Denver in 1864 and 1865. Angry crowds intimidated investigators. A meeting to nominate candidates for an anticipated state government called for repetition of Sand Creek "ad infinitum." At a constitutional convention in fall 1865, members of the Colorado 1st Volunteer Regiment proclaimed that "Sand Creek must be vindicated." Sand Creekers assassinated Captain Silas Soule on a Denver street for testifying about the truth of the Sand Creek Massacre before an investigating commission, and other Denverites had screamed at senators holding hearings on the Indian problem, "Exterminate them! Exterminate them!"

At the start of the 1870s, Denver's shadow loomed across the Wyoming border. Cheyenne, which was a creation of the Union Pacific Railroad and the first city at the foot of the Rockies to enjoy an eastern railroad connection, had already been through a boom and bust as railroad workers arrived and then left. Its ambitious businessmen, attracted by the expectation that there could not "fail to be money in a place, that was sure to be always frequented by bull-whackers, miners, and soldiers," now felt obstructed by federal agreements that reserved two-thirds of Wyoming Territory for Sioux game harvesting.[7] Having "preceded civilization" rather than growing up with the territory, Cheyenne's leaders organized the Big Horn Black Hills Mining and Exploring Association in 1869–70 with the stated purpose of finding gold (because a new gold rush would bring customers to the saloon owners, hotel keepers, theater proprietors, and bankers who made up the association).[8] They blithely expected Easterners to flock by the hundreds to join up, even though the unspoken goal—revealed by the organization of the association into military companies—was to shove Indians out of the way by force. President Grant and the U.S. Army, who thought they had secured a few years of quiet on the northern plains, were appalled that tiny Cheyenne, Wyoming, aimed by itself to provoke a new Indian war and blocked the expedition from leaving town—postponing the next Sioux war until the Black Hills gold rush of 1874–75.

The "Big Horn Black Hills" episode may have played out as comic opera rather than tragedy, but Denver continued to purge its hinterland of inconvenient occupants. The Utes of the western slope maintained an uneasy truce with white Coloradans in the 1860s and early 1870s, ceding chunks of land as mining pushed into central Colorado and then the San Juan Mountains in the southwest quadrant of the newly admitted state. Governor Fred Pitkin argued that opening Ute lands would "furnish homes to thousands of the people of the state," while his secretary, W. H. Vickers (an early Colorado historian), called the Utes "thoroughly disagreeable neighbors" who should best be "banished to some more appropriate retreat than the garden of our growing state."[9] A blowup in 1879 that left an Indian agent, eleven other white men, and thirteen soldiers dead turned desire into action. "The Utes Must Go!" thundered Denver newspapers, and go they did, to reservations in Utah and a far corner of Colorado that were too small to interfere with the development of the urban empire.

Denverites were not the West's only bloody-minded city makers. Isolated homesteaders may have been trip wires in white–Indian wars, but city leaders organized campaigns to eliminate Indians by removal or extermination. Time and again, city people used the economic power of urban centers to fund military expeditions and city-centered communication networks to coordinate warfare against Indians. Impatient urban leaders sometimes pushed toward hostilities against the wishes of regular army commanders who were trying to manage Indians rather than kill them.

In the Comstock country of Nevada, the rapid influx of prospectors and settlers in 1859–60 threatened the lands and food supply of Northern Paiutes and Bannocks, who responded to the capture and rape of two Indian girls in spring 1860 with raids and then with the sound defeat near Pyramid Lake of a hastily organized force from the Comstock towns. The defeat galvanized whites from Virginia City to San Francisco, because it threatened the future of Nevada mining. With the help of telegraph lines, the California–Nevada urban network had the capacity to quickly mobilize against Indian threats. It took only a month to assemble a new expeditionary force and defeat the Paiutes in the "Pyramid Lake War." As Eugene Moehring has written, "Urban networks served as reliable defense and communication systems, reinforcing the conquest culture that shaped white attitudes toward Native Americans."[10]

Continued growth of the Reno–Virginia City–Carson City complex fragmented Paiute lands and destroyed food supplies through logging and fouling of rivers, although scarcely fast enough for the Virginia City *Territorial Enterprise*, which continued to call for extermination of the remaining Indians.

Far to the south, Apache raids on mines and ranches constrained Tucson's development. The army tried to diffuse the situation by gathering peaceful Apaches at Camp Grant on the San Pedro River. When raids continued, Tucsonians accused the protected Indians of sheltering young men who staged the attacks. On April 28, 1871, a large group of Anglos, Mexicans, and O'odham Indians from Tucson defied the army and attacked the camp. The Camp Grant Massacre left 144 Apaches dead, mostly women, children, and the elderly. Later in the year, a Tucson jury took only nineteen minutes to clear the participants of murder charges.

Following the work of John Chivington and John Evans in the 1860s, railroad builder William Jackson Palmer shaped Denver's growing empire in the 1870s. Trained in the railroad business with the Pennsylvania Railroad and in the management of large enterprises by commanding Union cavalry forces at Shiloh, Antietam, and Chickamauga, he became treasurer and construction manager for the new Kansas Pacific Railroad in 1865, supervising its completion from Kansas City to Denver. He also assisted in the construction of the Denver Pacific Railroad from Denver to the Union Pacific at Cheyenne. The work confirmed his skills as a railroad executive and introduced him to the undeveloped resources of Colorado and the Southwest.

Palmer incorporated the Denver and Rio Grande railroad in 1870. His plan was to build from Denver south to Santa Fe, with a possible extension to Mexico City. "I thought how fine it would be to have a little railroad a few hundred miles in length," he wrote, "all under one's own control with one's friends, to have no jealousies and contests and differences, but be able to carry out harmoniously one's view about what ought and ought not to be done."[11] Palmer envisioned his railroad as the main street of a self-sufficient economic region, with a main line running along the base of the Rocky Mountains and spurs into the major valleys and over the key passes. He expected the transcontinental lines to detour north and south around the great mass of the Colorado mountains, leaving his railroad to develop and benefit from the mineral wealth of the Rockies. The Denver and Rio Grande reached Pueblo in 1872 and the base of La Veta Pass into New Mexico in 1876.

The next four years saw a bitter and complex battle between Palmer and the new Santa Fe Railroad, which had run a line up the Arkansas River to Pueblo. The two railroads battled for dominance in the Southwest by contesting control of key routes. The Santa Fe won the race over La Veta Pass and the easiest access to New Mexico. The two lines fought to a standoff in the Royal Gorge of the Arkansas River, the logical route from Pueblo to the silver-mining city of Leadville. Palmer gained control of the route in June 1879, implementing a U.S. Supreme Court decision by ousting Santa Fe employees at gunpoint. In 1880 the two companies agreed to divide the territory. The Denver and Rio Grande took the area north of the thirty-sixth parallel and west of its Denver–Trinidad line; the Santa Fe took the territory to the east and south. The agreement turned the Denver and Rio Grande into a Colorado railroad that threw 1,300 miles of rail line over the southern and central portions of the state by 1883. Much of the mileage was narrow gauge, to facilitate construction through narrow canyons and precipitous terrain.

Palmer's vision was social as well as economic. He spoke of the opportunity to create a new commonwealth and condense the progress of centuries. The railroad was not just "a mode of making money, but a large-scale model way of conjoining that with usefulness on a large scale solving a good many vexed social problems."[12] He acted on this conviction through town promotion and industrial development. He laid out South Pueblo as an industrial center and organized the Colorado Coal and Iron Company (later Colorado Fuel and Iron) to manufacture steel rails. To complement the industrial center at Pueblo, he envisioned the "Fountain Colony," later Colorado Springs, as a model community. Two-thirds of the revenues from land sales were to be reserved for community improvements and expenses. As it developed in the 1870s, Colorado Springs became a summer resort and permanent home for members of the upper middle class rather than an ideal city for the working class.

Denver's economy had suffered with the national depression of the mid-1870s but surged again with the expansion of silver mining in the Rockies. The rich strike at Leadville in 1878 brought more investment into Colorado and more profits into Denver. In 1880, 58 percent of the deep mining operations in the state had Colorado owners, most of them from Denver with a scattering of Golden, Pueblo, and Colorado Springs investors active in their immediate vicinities. It was most efficient to bring ore from far-flung mines to large smelters at the base of the Front Range—meaning both Denver with its diversified labor force and Pueblo with its own railroads into the mountains and easy access to coal. Pueblo grew rapidly from 3,127 people in 1880 to 28,157 in 1900 as a smelting and steelmaking town—an industrial island with an immigrant labor force in sparsely settled southern Colorado. Denver remained in charge as the expansion of stock raising and then agriculture on the Colorado plains further diversified its economy. Wealthy mine owners like Leadville's Horace Tabor put their money into Denver real estate, erecting mansions on Capitol Hill behind the gold-domed statehouse and building downtown office blocks to house freight forwarders, insurance offices, real estate salesmen, and bankers who kept the industrial economy spinning. Denver businessmen controlled a high country empire that stretched from the Montana border to the mesas of northern New Mexico, from the dryland wheat farms of eastern Colorado to the canyon lands of Utah. Every civic leader and economic schemer may not have shared the details of William Gilpin's continental vision as summarized in *The Cosmopolitan Railway*, but a journalist in the same years reported that "the people have adopted what they call their 'thousand-mile theory,' which is that Chicago is 1000 miles from New York, and Denver is 1000 miles from Chicago, and San Francisco is 1000 miles from Denver, so that, as any one can see, if great cities are put at that distance apart, as it seems, then these are to be the four great ones of America."[13]

If Denver and Salt Lake City were first-generation capitals of commercial empires, Spokane stood out among second-generation empires, districts that had their takeoff between 1880 and 1910 (see Table 4.1). Its hinterland was smaller than Denver's, but it embraced a full set of resource industries within a 200-mile radius. Mining boomed in 1882 in the Coeur d'Alene region of northern Idaho, followed into the early 1890s by new discoveries of gold, silver, and lead in northern Washington and the Kootenay district of British Columbia. Timber harvesting and wheat farming took up some of the slack when mining began to play out. The Northern Pacific Railroad arrived at the dusty river crossing in 1883, and Great Northern arrived at the now booming city in 1892. By 1900 nine rail lines converged in a thick and sometimes crisscrossing web, helping the city to outgrow Walla Walla and Yakima, Washington, and Sandpoint and Moscow, Idaho. Hydroelectric power promised industrial development from the Spokane River—here a potential rival with Great Falls, Montana, which saw an industrial future in waterpower from snow melting off the eastern slopes of the Rockies.

The settlement called itself Spokane Falls until a devastating fire in 1889 gave an opportunity to rebuild bigger, better, and with more sophistication. Four- and five-story brick buildings for downtown replaced the low wooden

TABLE 4.1. Population of Inland Capitals

Year	Salt Lake City	Denver	Spokane	El Paso	Calgary	Edmonton
1860	8,200					
1870	12,900	4,800				
1880	20,800	35,600				
1890	44,800	106,700	19,900	10,300	3,900	700
1900	53,500	133,900	36,800	15,900	4,400	2,600
1910	92,800	140,500	104,400	32,300	43,700	24,900
1920	118,100	256,500	104,400	77,600	63,300	58,800

Note: The Calgary and Edmonton figures are from the Canadian census taken in 1891, 1901, 1911, and 1921. The seemingly identical numbers for Spokane in 1910 and 1920 are correct, rounding totals that differed by only a few dozen people.

buildings that had shouted "frontier." Mining money financed the new office buildings and hotels and built new residential neighborhoods on hills to the south. With electric streetlights on every corner, Spokane was now "the magic city of the Inland Empire," an interior hinterland that residents energetically began to imagine in maps, pictures, and promotional writing.[14] The Inland Empire was a bit fuzzy at the edges but reached perhaps from Missoula to the crests of Stevens and Stampede passes above Puget Sound, from Boise north to Revelstoke in British Columbia.

Like all boosters, Spokane enthusiasts lived in the future. As Katherine Morrissey has pointed out, their typewriters repeatedly banged out phrases like "bound soon to come," "not many years ahead," and "will be" even when they claimed to be reciting facts. The Chamber of Commerce boosted Spokane's reputation by arguing that no city in the Northwest had a stronger reputation than "the Imperial City of the Inland Empire," using notoriety to feed fame and vice versa. Maps repeatedly showed the railroad web, and the Chamber of Commerce urged western travelers to pay a visit on their way to better-known cities on the coast. The Great Northern Railway agreed that Spokane was "the center of a real empire," although other railroads avoided taking sides in regional rivalry and opted instead for even more sweeping references to "the Golden Northwest."

As the nineteenth century turned into the twentieth, Spokane began to emphasize manufacturing as well as its commercial potential as the Power City of the Inland Empire. Now the Chamber of Commerce map (1904) explicitly surrounded the city's site with the proud label "All Roads Lead to Spokane the Power City." However, Spokane's boom years would soon stall, leaving a city no bigger in 1920 than in 1910. Some raw materials went through Spokane factories, but the city now had too many competitors as the North American rail network built toward its greatest density of routes. Carloads of grain, ore, and logs rolled east and west, to flour mills and furniture factories in Portland, to middlemen in Edmonton, to smelters in Omaha, Denver, Great Falls, and Helena. In the 1930s, moreover, Columbia River dams would undercut the uniqueness of its on-site hydropower.

The population figures in Table 4.1 tell a different story about El Paso, potentially Spokane's counterpart near the southern rather than the northern edge of the United States. As geographer Donald Meinig writes, "The American city was almost entirely a modern creation of the railroads." A dusty crossroads with a few hundred people in the first three decades after transfer from Mexico to the United States, it took off with rail connections in the early 1880s, shooting past the long-established Spanish/Mexican/American cities of Santa Fe and Tucson as the trade center of the Southwest. By 1884, three years after the locomotive chugged into town, El Paso connected with New Orleans, Dallas, St. Louis, Denver, Los Angeles, and Mexico City. Spur lines soon ran into the copper country of southeastern Arizona. Stockmen in town

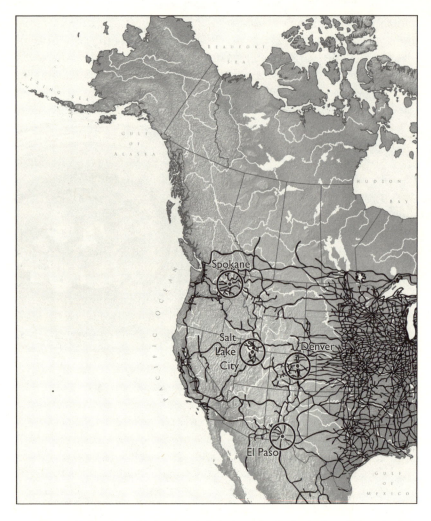

FIGURE 21. Railroads and inland capitals in 1901. At the beginning of the twentieth century, the continental railroad network converged in four nodes in the western interior: Spokane, Salt Lake City, Denver, and El Paso. (Map by Alejandro Bancke, adapted from Jacques Q. Redway and Russell Hinnman, *National Advanced Geography* [1901].)

for auctions and visits to bankers gathered at the Hotel Paseo del Norte. The giant El Paso Smelter belched smoke and enriched eastern investors. With a population two and a half times that of Phoenix, it was "a strong, hardy, pushing city bound to be the Chicago of the Southwest," wrote the *El Paso Times* in 1910.[15]

The problem for El Paso was that half its hinterland lay in Mexico. During his long term in control, Mexican strongman Porfiro Diaz (in power 1876–1911) invited American capitalists and engineers into the northwest provinces of

Chihuahua and Sonora to build railroads and open mines. From El Paso you could easily reach Sonora, the Mexican Pacific port of Guaymas, and Mexico City itself by a comfortable sleeping car service. In 1911, however, insurgents drove Diaz into exile, beginning the ten-year turmoil of the Mexican Revolution. Civil war drove American investors out of Mexico and interrupted El Paso's southern trade. The new relationship was epitomized by the expansion of Fort Bliss, an old army post that served as General John Pershing's base for his 1916 invasion of Mexico in search of the marauding forces of Pancho Villa. El Paso continued to grow in the 1920s, with the military of growing importance for local incomes, but Phoenix now had the advantage. It was, after all, a safely "American" city in contrast to tough-as-nails El Paso, with its large Hispanic population, and the twin city of Juarez, offering liquor and vice for off-duty soldiers, intrepid tourists, and lonesome cowboys.[16]

In the 1920s, both academic sociologists and the U.S. Department of Commerce tried to map out the retail and wholesale trade areas of major cities using data on freight movements, newspaper circulation areas, and similar indicators. Although each map varied from the others, each showed large hinterlands for Salt Lake City and Denver running north–south with the grain of the mountains and lesser hinterlands for Spokane and El Paso (constricted by smaller competitors like Albuquerque and Butte).[17] Nevertheless, between the Pacific coast and the Great Plains, these were the only four cities large enough in 1920 for the Census Bureau to define them as centers of Metropolitan Districts and collect population data on their suburbs. They make a striking appearance on a map of Metropolitan Districts in 1930 prepared by the Urbanism Committee of the National Resources Committee— four black dots standing out against a white background broken only by state boundaries. The import of another map in the same report, *Our Cities: Their Role in the National Economy* (1937), is the same. "Transportation and the Urban Pattern: 1930" shows the way that the rail network converged on these four points, each radiating five or six main lines and a swarm of local feeders. All railroads did indeed lead to Spokane—and El Paso, Denver, and Salt Lake City.[18]

CHAPTER FIVE

Garden Cities

*He knew that there was such a town as Norrison, a metropolis of the
desert plains, named for his father, who had been a Moses of emigration
thither, even to the smiting of the dry hills to furnish water for the
reclamation of the land.*
> —Mary Hallock Foote, *The Chosen Valley* (1893)

> *In that magic carpet country,*
> *Past the blue of Salton Sea,*
> *Lies a charming home-sweet-homeland*
> *Where I long to be.*
> *Panoramic in its beauty,*
> *Nature spreads her very best.*
> *And enchantingly surrounds us,*
> *Here in Brawley, Heaven blest.*
> > —"Brawley, the World's Largest City beneath
> > the Level of the Sea" (1946)

In summer 1950, my parents packed the family into the backseat of our
1941 Studebaker Champion and drove west from Knoxville, Tennessee. My
recall of the trip is incomplete—I was only five—but I remember the water.
We stopped one morning in Gunnison, Colorado, and there it was, running
cool and bright along the sides of the streets. It was tamed water gurgling
clear and peacefully through squared channels, far different from the unruly,

red-muddy slurry that clogged the ditches back home after a rainstorm. A week later, when we arrived to visit my Great-Aunt Helen in Gooding, Idaho, there it was again, flowing water guided carefully along the neighborhood sidewalks. One of the highlights of the trip was to wait for the irrigation water to course through the neighborhood and to help raise the miniature gates that let it soak into Helen's yard.

More than a half century later, as I start to draft this chapter, I've just paid a maintenance assessment from the Dee (Oregon) Irrigation District. We have a small weekend cabin on five acres in Hood River County. Four separate irrigation districts serve the county's orchardists by routing water from springs and streams on the north slope of Mount Hood to nourish 15,000 acres of pear, apple, and cherry trees—and our own summer garden. We're near the end of the line as the irrigation ditch contours down the opposite flank of our side valley, loops around the volcanic outflow that created the rich soils of Dee Flat, and works its way back in our direction. Tomorrow is the county's annual Blossom Festival, when fruit growers invite in city people from Portland, craft shows fill the old schoolhouses, and the Parkdale Grange offers very filling barbecue dinners.

Managed water—and mismanaged water—is one of the central stories of the modern and modernized West. It is a story of utopian dreams and corporate power, of semisuccessful democracy (in my end of Oregon) and bitter conflicts among Indians, ranchers, farmers, and environmentalists (as recently in the Klamath Basin of Oregon and California). Historians can detail the growth of technical capacity and engineering ambition. They can explain the complexities of changing water rights law and the institutions that have allocated scarce water. They can explore and lament the tangled and often unintended consequences of environmental change and the disappointments of irrigation homesteading. They can indict the interlocking progress of capital investment and social inequity.

They can also approach the story of western water as the making of irrigation cities. Scattered through the western interior—embedded within the imperial reach of one large metropolis or another—is a distinct group of smaller cities that have organized oasis agriculture. Town makers sited them at the meeting points of mountain and plain, where steep gorges and canyons spread out into widening valleys and basins and where the rivers that plunged fast and roiled from the high slopes grew slower and more placid. As the landscape gentled, the streams spread out into braided channels, dropped their silt and sediment, and nourished thin green lines of cottonwoods. Up from the riverbeds were alluvial fans, benchlands, and hills covered with tufted grass, sagebrush, and succulents.

These settings were ripe for engineering. If only there were dams somewhere upstream, with head gates and canals to lead the water away from the rivers, pass it through fields, and return it five or fifty miles downstream. The narrow oasis could become a broad garden. Row crops could grow, fruit trees could blossom, and little riverbank settlements could hope to become small prosperous cities, places like Hood River at the mouth of its small valley or Gooding on the Snake River plain. These were the ambitions and frequently the success stories of the irrigation frontier that began with cooperative agricultural colonies in the middle decades of the nineteenth century, grew with private investment toward the end of the century, and expanded with federal funding after the Newlands Reclamation Act of 1902.

We've already visited the first of the irrigation cities at the base of the Wasatch Mountains. Oasis farming was only the starting point for Salt Lake City before it grew into a regional capital, but it was central to the life of smaller Utah communities in the Salt Lake City orbit. Church officials carefully managed the expansion of Mormon settlement, sending exploring parties to find good sites in west-sloping valleys, picking the first settlers for mix of skills, and dispatching them to create new towns like Provo, Fillmore City, and St. George. Settlers customarily received town lots large enough for gardening and farm lots beyond. As the new townsmen constructed necessary irrigation facilities, church officials managed and distributed the water as a common resource.

The counterparts on the northern Colorado Piedmont were secular cooperative colonies. In the *New York Tribune* of December 4, 1869, agricultural editor Nathan Meeker announced a meeting for the purpose of forming a colony for settlement in Colorado. The result was the Union Colony Association with Meeker as president and the *Tribune*'s famous editor Horace Greeley as treasurer. Membership fees were pooled to purchase land, with each member entitled to receive a farming plot and to purchase a town lot. Surplus funds were to be applied to commonly owned "improvements for the common good"—schools, a town hall, and irrigation canals. The first of 3,000 colonists arrived in June 1870 and began to settle in a central town they called Greeley, which was soon a "fixed fact." Water from the Cache la Poudre River soon "came dancing through the flumes like a ministering angel." In 1871, the Chicago–Colorado Colony established Longmont on the model of Greeley. Fort Collins, which borrowed the "colony" name but not the cooperative spirit, came soon after. Taken together, wrote one contemporary, "colonization introduces a new era. It overcomes all the obstacles attending single efforts, and aids materially in the quick development of every industrial pursuit."[1]

Private investment capital followed the communal pioneers, attempting to turn irrigation water into a profit-making commodity in the 1880s and 1890s. As central Idaho mining discoveries slowed, Boise pinned hopes on the "New York Canal." When outside investors in the 1880s gave up in discouragement, Idahoans raised local funds for its completion. Irrigation was an add-on for Denver, where English investors wrapped the Highline Canal

FIGURE 22. Greeley panorama. Greeley in 1882 was twelve years old. It grew rapidly in its first years but, like a number of other cities that grew as service and supply centers for irrigated agriculture, reached a plateau as a small city under the shadow of its larger neighbor, Denver.

around the south and east sides of the city in the 1880s and sold enough of the South Platte River to water 25,000 acres in wet years. It was an essential in southern Arizona. Settlers along the Salt River laid out the town sites of Phoenix, Tempe, and Mesa and dug small ditches as early as the 1870s, gradually expanding the system to 260 miles in twelve canals that irrigated 30,000 acres by the end of the century. William Smythe, the great advocate of irrigation as the basis for democratic utopias, called Phoenix "distinctly modern, and almost wholly the offspring of irrigation."[2]

The Newlands Act increased the scale of investment. Roosevelt Dam on the Salt River was the first federal reclamation project to break ground. The Salt River Project stabilized the water supply and supported agricultural expansion, especially after the federal government purchased all of the valley's private canals and integrated their management, and the farmers in turn bought the services of Phoenix and Tempe. The waterpower city of Great Falls hoped that the nearby Sun River project would give it an extra push as a market for new irrigated crops (an overoptimistic expectation as it turned out). Private investors had failed to turn the Snake River Valley into a garden in the 1880s, but the Arrowrock Dam on the Boise River, the world's largest when completed in 1915, gave the state capital a second wind, part of the transformation of sagebrush plains into a string of small cities from Twin Falls and Burley to Boise, Nampa, and Caldwell.[3]

Grand Junction can stand in for half a dozen other cities that grew into substantial subregional centers—places like Klamath Falls and Medford, Oregon; Yakima, Washington; Garden City, Kansas; or Phoenix before its discovery by snowbirds. Virtually on the heels of federal officials who pushed the Utes out of west-central Colorado came town promoter George Crawford. Drawing on experience that stretched back to the 1850s in Kansas, he selected a site where the Gunnison River joined the Grand (Colorado) River in fall 1881. Private developers dug irrigation canals (many of which would later be completed or expanded by the federal government through the Bureau of Reclamation). Farmers experimented with different crops and fruit trees, learned the local microclimates, and made their first sales to the nearby mining regions.

Grand Junction was the information center of the West Slope. Two lines of the Denver and Rio Grande railroad met there, bringing steady jobs and wider markets to a town that was a halfway point between Denver and Salt Lake City. It was the location of the Western Stockgrowers Association, Mesa County Agricultural and Horticultural Society, and Grand Junction Fruit Growers Association, not to mention the lawyers and land agents who hovered around the Mesa County courthouse. Most Main Street businesses made do with one- or two-story buildings, but the town sprouted its first five-story "skyscrapers" early in the new century. With 3,500 residents by 1900 and close to 10,000 by World War I, Grand Junction dominated possible rivals such as Delta and Montrose.

Grand Junction was a busy place after hours as well as in the workplace. Historian Kathleen Underwood has counted at least eighty churches and voluntary associations organized between 1882 and 1900. Men joined the Masons, Odd Fellows, Elks, and Woodmen of the World. They ran for office, staffed volunteer fire companies, and organized Peach Day festivities. They explored new technologies through the Camera Club and Chautauqua Literary and Scientific Circle. They got exercise with the Grand Junction Wheelmen. Women, whose increasing numbers domesticated the crude town, enjoyed political influence after Colorado adopted women's suffrage in 1893. One cluster, typified by Ella Belle Ackerman, was active in the Women's Relief Corps, the Women of Woodcraft, and the Rebekahs (an auxiliary of the Independent Order of Odd Fellows). Another group, perhaps a bit higher on the economic ladder like newspaper editor's wife Lola Price, tended toward the Women's Library Association, Art League, Children's Home Society, and Grand Mesa Women's Club. There were also the Amazon Guards, a drill team associated with the local militia company that competed statewide, and the Ladies Columbine Band (although each group of women arrayed themselves around a male leader when they sat for group portraits).[4] Undeniably western in its setting below the high, dry wall of the Book Cliffs and Roan Plateau, it was Middle American in the intensity of community life.

FIGURE 23. Grand Junction downtown. Ambitious western cities in the first decades of the twentieth century began to add imposing public buildings, commercial blocks, and elevator hotels to their original low-rise buildings. Grand Junction in this photo taken at Main and Fourth Street was large enough for electric trolley service as well as its first five-story buildings. (Western History Division, Denver Public Library.)

Irrigation cities were different in California—larger, more complex, more contradictory, more "Californian," with that word's implications of the complexities of big money and racial divisions. Wheat was the state's first great agricultural product, but specialized crops that required less land and more water challenged its prominence in the 1880s. Grapes, sugar beets, vegetables, and fruit took hold in the 1880s and continued to expand in acreage into the 1920s, pushing aside wheat in much of the central valley for grapes and beets, taking over the far southern California coast for lemons, using smaller inland valley slopes for oranges, and filling the Santa Clara Valley with cherry and plum trees.

Fresno at first glance looked like Grand Junction on too many doughnuts. It started in 1872 as a dusty railroad crossing in the middle of the "San Joaquin Desert." It grew as the organizing center for intensive, semiurbanized agriculture. It won the county seat in 1873 but only began to grow when irrigation water arrived from the mountains to the east and farmers began developing its environs with twenty-acre farms. The early farm developments were "colonies" in name but business enterprises in fact, as land developers organized group settlement to share the costs of distributing water among small farms. A San Francisco entrepreneur and city money backed the pioneering Central California Colony in the mid-1870s. The were nine colonies around Fresno in 1882, twenty in 1897, and perhaps three dozen in the early twentieth century. These were not so much communitarian experiments as methods to pool capital as water became a commodity—perhaps early versions of the ubiquitous modern home owners' association. Grapes were the big crop, for wine and then for raisins.

The result was a semiurbanized landscape. The city itself boasted a new library and city hall, high school, twenty-eight miles of paved streets (out of 150 miles), forty miles of streetcar lines, fine parks, and the biggest hotel in the central valley. It was "one of the leading provincial cities of the State" with 50,000 people, food-processing and wholesaling companies, and "all the accessories of a high-class modern city." Beyond the formal city limits, as the Chamber of Commerce put it in 1917, "the town and country gradually came into close touch through good roads, schoolhouses, telephones, interurban cars, Rural Post Office deliveries, daily papers, and other conditions which made rural life an attraction, and Fresno County the great exponent of city life under rural conditions." The intensively irrigated and cultivated inner ring combined with more distant farms to make Fresno County "the Banner Agricultural County of the State."[5] The connections were physical, economic, and something more, as the editor of the *Fresno Republican* wrote in 1909: "The welfare of this whole community is so bound up in the prosperity of the raisin business, and the progress of that business is so dependent on organized and more or less public action, that raisin affairs have always been treated, and properly treated, as public affairs."[6]

Fresno elided—or its civic leaders ignored—the issues of race and labor, but the city's growth depended on immigrant workers. Fresno County had 5,300 Japanese residents by 1920, but they were eclipsed by the Armenians who began to arrive in large numbers in the mid-1890s. The intersection of M and Ventura streets was the site of the Holy Trinity Armenian Apostolic Church and the focal point of Little Armenia. On the surrounding farms Armenians grew raisins, figs, and melons. None of this ethnic complexity, however, made it into A. J. Waterhouse's poem "In Fresno Land" for the *Fresno Republican*'s 1897 inventory of the advantages of *Imperial Fresno*:

> In Fresno land, the Summer land,
> Where all the weary mountains stand,
> White-capped and patient, waiting still
> For time and man to do their will,
> Their western slopes reach out to greet
> The grey earth smiling at their feet;
> And life's a dream divinely planned,
> In Fresno land, the Summer land.[7]

Farther south, the rise of the citrus towns helped to define "Southern California" as a distinct region. Charles Nordhoff in *California for Health,*

Pleasure, and Residence (1874) calls everything south of San Francisco the "southern" part of the state. Fifteen years later, boosters had narrowed the focus to the territory south of the Tehachapis as a distinct area, with its own crops, dominant city, and eastward rail connections. The Southern Pacific Railroad reached Los Angeles through the San Fernando Tunnel in 1876, and the city became the focus for a growing network of radiating rail lines—first heavy rail for freight and then the electric interurban passenger service of the Pacific Electric after 1901, soon to reach 1,000 miles of line. The region imported capital by the bucketful, especially in the boom of 1887–88, when speculators platted sixty new towns in Los Angeles County alone. Los Angeles population reached 102,000 in 1900 and 319,000 in 1910.

The network of smaller cities south and east of Los Angeles boomed as well, especially after productive strains of oranges were promulgated in the 1870s. Citrus shipments rose 580 percent from 1894 to 1914, funneled through district exchanges and then the central exchange in Los Angeles. The result was ruralized urban development, a landscape of orchards, processing plants, electric rail lines, and closely packed towns and small cities that sketched the outlines of the metropolis to be filled in over the course of the century. Growth took off during the land boom of the mid-1880s and then continued in spurts through the early decades of the twentieth century. The lowland districts of Orange County around Anaheim and Santa Ana developed intensive agriculture around small farms and small cities. So did the San Fernando Valley, the long corridor at the base of the San Gabriel Mountains from El Monte to San Bernardino and Redlands, and in a different part of the state, the Bay Area fruit belt from San Jose to San Leandro.

The citrus belt was colonial in three senses. Some of the first settlers were idealistic or practical communitarians along the lines of Utah and Colorado. German settlers at Anaheim as early as the 1850s tapped the Santa Ana River with a five-mile canal, placed ownership of water and waterworks in the hands of a mutual stock company, and required that water rights and land title had to be transferred together. Riverside and Ontario, California, followed as the idealistic foundations of the future smog belt. Riverside—the Southern California Colony Association—dated to the 1870s but took off in the 1880s with the land boom and cooperative marketing. Fifteen miles closer to Los Angeles, the brothers George and Ben Chaffey used Canadian money to buy several thousand acres of rancho lands, installed a water system, and sold water rights through a mutual company. Laying out streets in 1882, they built a community center and fountain at the railway crossing before offering lots. Ontario was a "Model colony" because of joint management of water and a compact scale of horticulture, not by utopian aims. It was to be a community of prosperous city people who wanted a rural lifestyle—in short, a Model Arcadia (where alcohol sales were prohibited).

Southern California irrigation cities were colonial as well in their dependence on the circulation of outside capital. The Southern Pacific Railroad, in Douglas Sackman's words, "brought the Mediterranean climate to Southern California" through relentless publicity to attract real estate developers and entice eastern Americans to relocate—bringing their checkbooks.[8] Indeed, the ideal of the "grower" was an emigrant with enough money to buy the land, seedlings, and supplies while someone else did the hard work. George Henderson has identified a literary tradition of "rural realism" in which California novelists in the decades around 1900 tried to acknowledge the full power of metropolitan capital while still holding onto a vision of agrarian virtue.[9]

Third, European or American "colonies" around the world, whether in Kenya, Malaya, or the Ivory Coast, depended on low-wage workers as well as well-heeled investors. In southern California, the new farmers and orchardists who bought into an idea of wholesome, genteel family farming also depended on someone else for the long, careful hours of planting, pruning, irrigating, tending, harvesting, and packing. Ontario, for example, relied on Chinese laborers in the 1890s (who lived in their own camp away from the white utopia). By the early 1900s, Indians and Mexicans did the hard work of picking and packing. The same was true south of Los Angeles, where farmworkers were successively Chinese, Japanese, and Mexican immigrants.

Large tracts of southern California by the early 1900s had become a widely spread and socially bifurcated protometropolis. On one hand were prosperous Anglo-American towns with main streets, expensive churches, clubhouses, new libraries, and white-painted houses or arts and crafts bungalows for middle-class growers and business proprietors. Millionaires Row in Pasadena was Orange Grove Avenue, and more modest cities also offered the supposed best of city and country life together. Riverside was "an urban republic of ten-acre groves" and pleasant neighborhoods where modest working-class homes were scattered among middle-class bungalows, with "all the advantages of an unsurpassed rural district and a model city," according to Southern Pacific Railroad publicists. With its Spanish-revival downtown, imposing Mission Inn, and blossoming trees, the town saw itself as "the kind of city that people from other cities visited on their vacations."[10] If Grand Junction was a piece of the Middle West in the great interior, Riverside—and Pomona and Whittier and many others—were other Middle Western fragments cast even farther toward the Pacific coast.

But a second "suburbscape" for workers threaded around and through the string of proprietors' cities. Upper-class suburbanites needed domestic helpers if they were to live in style. As in the American South, enclaves of Mexicans and African Americans could live in close proximity to their employers because strict racial etiquette instead of physical distance was sufficient to maintain a social hierarchy. An example is the 2,000 African Americans who created their own community in west and northwest Pasadena. As federal housing appraisers commented in the late 1930s, this "old unrestricted area has long been inhabited by the servant class who were employed by wealthy families in the higher grade areas to the west and south."[11]

Also tucked on the outskirts of Los Angeles and its surrounding small cities were labor camps and small company towns. Workers who built and maintained the Pacific Electric Railway were the first settlers of Watts ("Mud Town" because its land was sandy, damp, and cheap) and formed worker enclaves in Long Beach, West Hollywood, and Pasadena. Other camps housed farmworkers who tended vegetables, harvested sugar beets, or maintained the citrus orchards. In Smeltzer, Asian immigrants tended celery fields on the site of the future suburb of Westminster. The Limoneira Ranch built housing for its Mexican workers ($300 per cottage) and its American workers ($2,000 per house), providing a model that the *California Citrograph* urged on other growers.

Over the 1910s, 1920s, and 1930s, many of these camps matured into permanent *colonias* for year-round citrus workers. Segregated Latino neighborhoods developed on the outskirts of towns like Pacoima and El Monte. As of 1920, Riverside's 500 African Americans and 1,000 Mexicans lived only on the east side of town. In some cases, real estate developers marketed explicitly to Mexicans, selling small frame houses or bare lots where worker families could put up tents and build for themselves. The Anaheim Chamber of Commerce encouraged subdividers to market to Mexicans because owners of even the most modest homes would be a permanent labor supply. In the northern half of Orange County alone there were at least a dozen and a half colonias in 1940, clustered around La Habra, Placentia, Yorba Linda, Garden Grove, and Santa Ana. The latter city had only twelve Mexican families in 1900 but 4,000 Mexican residents by 1930, many living in the colonias of Delhi, Logan, and Artesia.

These were poor but vibrant communities. One example is Corona, south of Riverside, where Anglo men worked together through the Lemon Men's Club, while Mexican and Italian immigrants worked their lemon ranches and packinghouses. During the 1920s and 1930s, as Jose Alamillo has shown, Mexican immigrants created their own set of community institutions, ranging from pool halls and saloons where men could relax to churches and Cinco de Mayo festivals where women took the lead. Local baseball teams brought Corona's Mexican workers in contact with their counterparts from other towns and provided a springboard for labor organizing in the 1940s. Civil rights activism followed after 1945, when military veterans and leaders of the Cinco de Mayo festivals battled segregation in the name of the Good Neighbor Policy.

From the perspective of agricultural history, these worker settlements look like part of a rural landscape. Historian Gilbert Gonzalez has called them

FIGURE 24. Irrigation cities. Located in the western interior, most irrigation cities grew to moderate size. The exceptions, such as Phoenix, owed their further growth to activities and industries beyond agriculture. (Map by Jacquelyn Ferry.)

"villages" to emphasize their scattered locations, dependence on agricultural jobs, and lack of urban services, but he also acknowledges that they were linked into "regional communities that gave the people a sense of identity and culture beyond the confines of the individual village." Writing from the perspective of urban history, Becky Nicolaides calls these same communities "farm-fringe streetcar suburbs" and notes that their residents had access to jobs in Los Angeles as well as in nearby orchards. The closer to the big city, the greater the economic connections, which were much more extensive for El Monte at fifteen miles out than for Fountain Valley or Pomona at twice that distance. Matt Garcia similarly agrees with urban critic Rayner Banham that southern California's irrigation cities were a "townscape" in which sub-urbanization *was* urbanization.[12]

Irrigation by itself built small cities: In 1920, 4,000 people lived in Garden City, Kansas, along the Arkansas River and 5,000 people lived in Brawley, California ("the biggest little city neath the surface of the sea"). There were 9,000 in Grand Junction and Modesto, 10,000 in Provo, 14,000 in Brownsville, and 18,000 in Bakersfield. The big irrigation cities were places like Phoenix at 29,000 and Fresno at 43,000. Growth in many of these cities—places such as Grand Junction and Klamath Falls—slowed after the 1920s as local agriculture maxed out available land and water.

The ones that didn't stall had something extra: Boise was the state capital and then the home to the globe-spanning construction firm Morrison-Knudson. Fresno benefited from the scale of production and processing, with a hinterland nearly thrice as populous as Grand Junction's by 1920 and four and a half times Grand Junction's by 1950.[13] In the regions that grew most rapidly, the integrated landscape of cities, orchards, and fields became the armature around which postwar booms would pack new residents in the tens and hundreds of thousands. Phoenix attracted tourists, then defense contracts in World War II, and then relocating industries. It layered subdivisions over the cotton and vegetable fields of the Salt River Valley and connected its separate towns into a single metropolis. Fort Collins and Greeley boomed after 1950 as parts of an urbanized Colorado Piedmont that also included Boulder and Denver. And most spectacularly of all, the citrus towns of Orange, Riverside, and San Bernardino counties were the scaffolding around which postwar migration has wrapped more than six million new residents since 1945.[14]

CHAPTER SIX

Smokestack Frontiers

*I first heard Personville called Poisonville by a red-haired mucker named
Hickory Dewey in the Big Ship in Butte. He also called his short a shoit.
I didn't think anything of what he had done to the city's name. . . . A few
years later I went to Personville and learned better.*

*The city wasn't pretty. Most of its builders had gone in for gaudiness.
Maybe they had been successful at first. Since then the smelters whose
brick stacks stuck up tall against a gloomy mountain to the south had
yellow-smoked everything into uniform dinginess. The result was an
ugly city of forty thousand people. Set in an ugly notch between two ugly
mountains that had been all dirtied up by mining.*

—Dashiell Hammett, *Red Harvest* (1929)

*Now the inbound steamer was laying a streak on the water of Bellingham
Bay below, and dark crowds hung at the rails. From bare hill to bare hill
across Whatcom, the mills sounded their whistles, like birds calling and
answering.*

—Annie Dillard, *The Living* (1992)

The Boston Saloon on D Street in Virginia City, Nevada, didn't look much
different from scores of other barrooms in the bustling mining city. It was
a long narrow one-story building forty feet deep and only fifteen feet wide—
just enough for a bar along one side and tables along the other where customers could drink, smoke, deal cards, gamble with dominoes, and sometimes

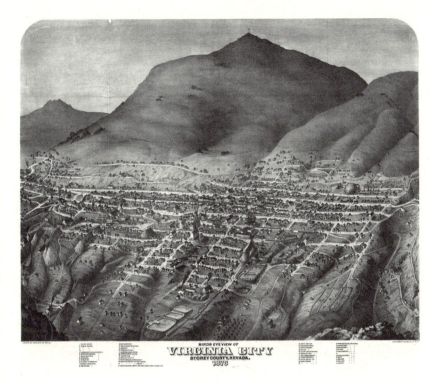

FIGURE 25. Virginia City, Nevada, panorama. Virginia City in 1875 spilled down the side of Mount Davidson with the main streets following the contour of the slope. The main commercial streets are clearly visible running horizontally along the hillside. Managers and business owners lived uphill, while workers, including European immigrants, Chinese, and African Americans, lived downhill among mines and refineries.

listen to harmonica players or an amateur trombonist. Crystal stemware and white china plates showed pretensions to elegance. What set the Boston apart was owner William G. Brown, an African American from Massachusetts. The bar was "the popular resort of many of the colored population" where the city's several hundred African American men and women could relax.[1]

Clinging to the steep dry slope of Mount Davidson, Virginia City was the capital of the Comstock silver kingdom in the boom years that lasted from 1860 until 1875, when a massive fire swept down the hill to consume over 2,000 buildings. The city of 20,000 people spilled down the mountainside with A Street through P Street contouring the bare slope like a series of Inca terraces. Mine managers and successful businessmen lived upslope on A Street. C Street was the main business artery, D was the entertainment and red-light district, and E through K housed a multiracial mix of miners and wageworkers in boardinghouses and small rental cottages.

A worker who pushed out the door of the Boston Saloon to stagger the three blocks downhill to G Street would have passed a brothel, the Virginia Gas Works, and Kee Day's small laundry. If the short stretch of G Street between Union and Sutton streets was home, his neighbors were a typical Virginia City hodgepodge of English, Irish, and German immigrants, African Americans, and native whites. There were boardinghouses and small single-family houses, an African Methodist Episcopal church, and a "German hospital" with twenty-four beds operated by Dr. E. Thiele. The Consolidated Virginia Mine, where many of the residents worked, loomed above the block. The roughly defined Chinatown was just downhill on H and K streets. As people came and went—shifting rooms within the city or moving to other opportunities—neighbors might have included a machinist, a tailor, a miner, a glazier, a barkeeper, and an ambitious businesswoman who opened the "entirely new, thoroughly and elegantly furnished" Virginia Hotel just one week before the big fire swept over the block. Many of the residents were families with children, who left behind marbles, slate pencils, toy wheels, and dolls.

A single house at 18 North G Street, excavated by archaeologist Julie Schablitsky in 1999, testifies to the fluidity and precariousness of working-class life. Mrs. M. A. Andrews operated a dressmaker's shop out of the small building for perhaps eighteen months before her death in 1873, at age thirty-five. In 1875, it housed bartender G. A. Taylor and then the Cooper family of British immigrants—Thomas, Eunice, and three children, who would make their lives in Virginia City. Mrs. Andrews left behind pins and beads for decorating ladies' dresses. Mrs. Cooper lost her French-made porcelain tea set and a cameo in the big fire, and one of her children lost a porcelain doll imported from Germany—all indications that the family aspired to be part of a stable middle class.

Before the socially aspiring Coopers and the straitlaced dressmaker (she was a teetotaling member of the International Order of Good Templars), 18 North G had a seamier past. Under the burned floorboards archaeologists have found a hypodermic syringe and half a dozen needles with traces of morphine, an increasingly popular recreational drug in the years after the Civil War (injecting morphine gave a quicker high than imbibing alcohol or smoking opium). Forensic DNA analysis shows that the needles had multiple users, both male and female, black and white. Was the house a "shooting gallery" where people gathered to share recreational morphine? Or was it a medical office where a physician treated venereal disease (a supposition supported by the nearby find of a male irrigator used to clean the urethra)?

The people of G Street lived in the same city that Samuel Clemens helped to make famous in the stories and vignettes of *Roughing It*, drawn from his experiences in the early 1860s, but their everyday city was gritty rather than colorful.[2] Mining districts may have started with individual prospectors like the forty-niners who swarmed over the central Sierra Nevada, the disgruntled Californians who swarmed to Canada's Fraser River in 1858, or the Pikes Peakers who flocked to Colorado in 1859, but this "Paint Your Wagon" stage was as ephemeral and short-lived as a Broadway musical. To bring gold or silver or copper ore from deep below ground and to process it into usable metal required money, machinery, and disciplined manpower. Successful mining camps quickly turned into industrial cities where skilled workers toiled in regular shifts to blast out tunnels and muck out ore from twisting subterranean lodes and haul it to the surface. Towns that added smelters to put the ore through its first processing could become magnets for an entire mining district, requiring more industrial workers to work the smelters and ship the upgraded ore to big-city refiners. As Josiah Strong realized, "The vast region of the Rocky Mountains will be inhabited chiefly by a mining and manufacturing population, and such populations live in cities."[3] He didn't offer a list, but the roster of specialized industrial cities would have started with Virginia City and added Butte and Anaconda, Montana; Cripple Creek and Leadville, Colorado; and Bisbee and Douglas, Arizona.

One of the hackneyed tropes of western travel writings in the last third of the nineteenth century was to marvel over the change that two or three years could bring to a mining town. Leadville's big silver boom took off in 1877. Three years later it was the largest silver/lead smelting center in the United States, with thirty-seven blast furnaces in fifteen smelters. Writers from *Scribner's*, *The Atlantic*, *Harper's*, *Frank Leslie's Illustrated Weekly*, and other mass-circulation magazines marveled over the "Magic City." It was "roaring," "wild," "fast," "restless, eager, fierce." At night "the miners then drift into town in swarms; a dozen bands are drumming up audiences for the theatres and variety shows, scores of saloons and numerous gambling houses are in full blast, and the entire scene gives the town and place the appearance of one grand holiday."[4] But soon the excitement gave way to steadier growth as it was (briefly) the state's second-largest city. Storekeepers put on coats and ties and appreciated the newly paved streets that eliminated the sludge that used to ooze into their shops. Now journalists took as much pleasure in correcting the image of a wild and woolly town as their predecessors had in creating it. British tourist Phil Robinson thought it was like "some thriving provincial town" whose prosperity had reduced its peculiarity. *Harper's Weekly* reported that modern Leadville was "as steady going as Salem or Plymouth Rock." Ernest Ingersoll summed up the rapid change in 1883: "The rough old camp has crystallized into the city she resolved to become."[5]

What journalists found less exciting were the lunch-pail families on the streets behind the opera house and the everyday neighborhoods beyond the saloon district. Mining cities and mill cities were workingmen's communities where skilled workers joined unions and hoped for a regular payday, where women worked and kept house, where children went to school before jobs beckoned them away in their teens. For all its saloons and its mountain setting, the Virginia City of the Cooper family was a lunch-pail city. So were Butte and Anaconda under the big sky of Montana, Bellingham and Tacoma under the lowering clouds of Puget Sound, and Bisbee and Globe under the blazing sun of Arizona.

If you had paid a visit to Butte with journalist Julian Ralph toward the end of the nineteenth century, you would have found a "wide open" town with an oversized "vicious quarter" of gambling hells, hurdy-gurdy dance halls, and prostitutes and streets as lively at three in the morning as New York's Broadway at noon. You would also have found schoolrooms for 5,000 children, a club for university graduates, and a Women's Christian Temperance Union chapter.[6] Had you left Mr. Ralph's quick tour to talk to the priests in the Roman Catholic churches, the young women packing lunch pails in assembly-line fashion, or the off-duty miners at the offices of the Butte Miners' Union, you would also have found the Gibraltar of organized labor.

A city of copper mines and smelters that reeked sulfurous fumes, Butte was an Irish city and a union city, categories that were difficult to tell apart in Silver Bow County. Marcus Daly, the king of Anaconda Copper, was himself an Irish immigrant and shared culture if not wealth with many members of the Butte Miners' Union, a situation that helped to stabilize labor–management relations in the 1890s and early 1900s, before eastern capitalists bought control of Anaconda and began to squeeze the workers in 1912–13. Like Virginia City, Butte was built on the slope of a steep hill. Like eastern factory cities, Butte had a middle-class side (uphill and upwind) and ethnic neighborhoods closer to the factories and on the lower land of the valley floor: Finntown, Dublin Gulch, Corktown, and Chinatown, plus neighborhoods of Serbs, Croatians, Montenegrins, and Scandinavians. Men worked in the mines and smelters, and women worked as domestic servants, teachers, and clerks. They too had their unions: the Laundry Workers' Union, Teachers' Union, Clerks' Union, and Women's Protective Union for boardinghouse, restaurant, and theater workers.

Pueblo was another smelting center that processed ore from mines as far away as Mexico and Nevada. It was also the site of Colorado Fuel and Iron, the West's first and largest steel mill, with 5,000 employees by World War I. Workers came from Mexico, from Italy via New York, and from Greece and eastern Europe via Chicago. The "Pittsburgh of the West" was closer to an eastern industrial city than to a western commercial city. Its Roman Catholic families attended ethnically segregated churches where Italian or Polish or Czech was spoken as often as English. Workers belonged to ethnic societies like the Croatian Fraternal Union of America, read locally published foreign-language newspapers, and lived in Mexican, Italian, or Slavic neighborhoods that clustered around the mills.

FIGURE 26. Butte after the boom years. Photographed in 1942, the neighborhoods of Butte spill down the long slope below the huge open-pit copper mines. (Library of Congress and Wikimedia Commons.)

In empire cities and irrigation utopias, the rhetoric of economic growth and the vision of smallholder capitalism tried with some success to *conceal* economic inequality and class differences that didn't match up with the booster ideology of growth and opportunity. In mining cities, however, deep economic divisions were impossible to avoid or ignore because their economy depended on a large laboring class. The same was true of lumber mill cities like Everett, Washington, and Coos Bay, Oregon, where factory workers turned the logs of the coastal mountains into shingles, two-by-fours, and window sashes. In the early twentieth century, Astoria, Oregon, New Westminster, British Columbia, and Monterey, California, were cities where southern European and Asian immigrants put fish into cans. The same spot that started out as a promoter's dream or a merchant's home base could develop within a generation into a workingman's city of mills and factories, immigrant neighborhoods, and wage laborers, introducing deep tensions of class and race into the supposedly egalitarian West.

One of the best places to explore this transition from prospector's frontier to smokestack frontier *and* the instability of the resulting communities is Cripple Creek, Colorado. Elizabeth Jameson has painstakingly reconstructed the ways in which the bonds of community were formed in one decade and snapped apart in the next. The city's trajectory is familiar: Gold was discovered on a sparsely developed plateau on the back side of Pikes Peak in 1890, investment poured into mining, rail lines reached the district in 1894–95, and a strike in 1894 led to ten years of relative stability and mutual accommodation between capital and labor. For the next decade—until owners mobilized the power of the state government on their behalf in a fiercely fought strike in 1904—the instant towns of Victor and Cripple Creek were working-class communities. Cripple Creek especially took on cosmopolitan airs, with electric lights by 1892, telephone service by 1893, a solid brick-built business district, thirty churches, nineteen schools with 4,000 students by the early 1900s, and 150 saloons.

Workers and labor unions held the balance of political power after the district was set off as Teller County in 1899, removing the influence of Colorado Springs voters. The county government paid union wage rates and used the labor-friendly *Daily Press* as the official county paper after 1901. Labor leaders worked through established reform parties—Populist, Democrat, Socialist—depending on specific issues, candidates, and chances for victory. The men elected to union offices were usually drawn from the members who were older married home owners. Shopkeepers tended to side with the unionists, who were the overwhelming majority of their customers. *Everyone* participated in labor day festivities, and fraternal organizations and lodges created contacts and fellowship across class lines. Even Sherman Bell, a mine manager who became infamous for antilabor actions in 1904, belonged to Elks, Masons, and Knights of Pythias along with many of his employees.[7] It was a good place to be a member of the skilled working class as long as you were "white," meaning no Asians, Mexicans, and or southern and eastern Europeans were welcome in the mines.

It took the bitterly fought strike of 1903–4, which started in solidarity with smelter workers in Colorado City, to break up the unity of the white working-class city. There was violence on both sides, but it was far more systematic from the Mine Owners Association and the Citizens Alliance formed by business leaders. Former lodge brother Sherman Bell, commanding the Colorado National Guard troops, was now eager "to do up this damned anarchistic federation" (meaning the Western Federation of Miners).[8] In what amounted to a political coup, the owners used the National Guard to suppress local newspapers and to arrest and deport labor-leaning officeholders in favor of their own toadies. "Habeus Corpus, hell," Adjutant General Bell reportedly roared as his men surrounded the courthouse, "We'll give 'em post mortems." The strike split Cripple Creek's middle class. Salaried white-collar workers, most of whom worked for the mining companies, were antiunion. Business and professional men with independent businesses split down the middle, sometimes seeing themselves as part of the "producing classes" and understanding

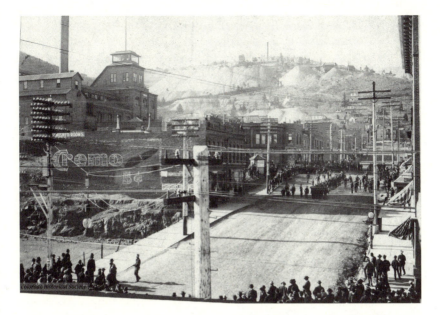

that they had benefited from the high union wage scales, which meant high spending on retail and services.

Things went to hell just as disastrously in Everett, where workers faced a deeply unstable industrial regime. Surviving one boom and bust in the 1880s and 1890s, Everett entered the twentieth century with new aspirations sparked by Frederic Weyerhaeuser's huge new lumber mill in 1902. In 1910, forty-four shingle and lumber mills and dozens of other factories stretched for eight miles along the Everett Bay. Americans, Canadians, and immigrants from northern Europe manned the mills. Many were "shingle weavers," a term that derived from the speed with which workers could stack interwoven bundles of cedar shingles but was applied to anyone in a shingle mill. It was easy to recognize a mill worker from the stubs of sliced-off fingers, for wood processing meant inexorable production lines with high-speed saws. Off the job, many of the industrial workers bought small wooden houses, joined any of twenty-five labor unions, and belonged to any of forty fraternal lodges and another forty churches. It was a family town, a working-class town, and nearly a socialist town (they controlled three of the seven wards). As historian Norman Clark sums up, "The city of smokestacks had become a reality, and it was a distinctly urban reality."[9]

Everett's problem was the endemic overproduction in the wood products industry, as it took very little capital to cut a stand of trees or connect a saw to a steam engine. The city's "sawdust barons," some of whom had been enticed west by railroad king James J. Hill, were fiercely antiunion because wages were one of the few costs that they could control in the face of competition from much smaller enterprises. There was a boom in the early 1900s, a bust from 1913 to 1915, and a new boom in 1916 because Europe now had an insatiable appetite for wooden ammunition boxes and coffins. Union members thought that the new prosperity would allow the promised restoration of wages after cuts in 1913, but the barons demurred. Shingle weavers went out on strike, attracting the attention of the Industrial Workers of the World (IWW) and one of the leaders of the free speech fights. The hint of Wobbly involvement destroyed any hope of bridging the divide between workers and middle class. Sheriff Donald McRae deputized hundred of vigilantes and effectively blockaded the normal routes into the city. On November 4, 1916, the steamer *Verona* from Seattle (roughly thirty miles away) neared the Everett docks carrying scores of Wobblies, met by equal numbers of armed deputies. "You can't land here!" shouted McRae. "The hell we can't!" replied a Wobbly. Someone fired, then many. Five men died on the *Verona* and two on shore before the ship reversed its engines and headed back to Seattle. The Everett Massacre was soon an infamous rallying cry among radical workers, but Everett itself was beginning a fifty-year transition to the place where Boeing would turn out thousands of 747s and other jetliners on vast production lines.

Mines and mill towns were the front lines in labor–management battles at the turn of the twentieth century, but labor conflict increasingly followed manufacturing to metropolitan centers. The mining economy needed rails and pipes, hoists and pumps. The irrigation economy needed farm implements, tools, pumps, leather goods, and a multitude of other tools and equipment. Lumber camps needed steam engines and saws. Everyone needed clothing and cooking utensils, flour for flapjacks, and beer to clear mining grit and sawdust from throats if not from lungs. The result was the expansion of big-city manufacturing, first to serve the resource towns, then to make resource processing more efficient through centralization, and next to supply the growing western population with consumer goods that no longer needed to be hauled across the continent. As early as 1860, the value of San Francisco's manufactured products exceeded the production of California gold. Portland and Seattle workers in the later nineteenth century ground grain into flour, sawed logs into lumber, and turned lumber into ships, furniture, and building components. Denver and El Paso acquired metal smelters and refineries.

Larger cities offered great opportunities for radical organizing, not so much among local industrial workers as among the transient laborers who passed through between jobs in fields and forests. In the depression year 1894, contingents of Coxey's Army—unemployed workers who planned to converge on Washington, D.C., from around the United States—gathered among Tacoma's waterfront dives and Portland's tenderloin before hopping trains bound eastward. Oakland sent 300 men and women. The Los Angeles contingent, 500 strong, hijacked a train and met a friendly welcome in Tucson and El Paso. Organized a decade later in Chicago and drawing heavily from the Western Federation of Miners, the IWW signed up new members from the wintering loggers and harvest hands hanging out in skid row saloons and lounging outside labor exchanges.

Wobblies picked cities with large numbers of single workers for free speech fights in which a long procession of speakers would harangue crowds about the evils of capitalism or the injustice of local officials until they were each arrested in turn, disrupting business and clogging the jails. In Spokane in 1909, a campaign against crooked labor agents escalated into a five-month battle in which Wobblies flooded the city by the hundreds, defied a ban on public speaking, and then crowed the jails at the expense of taxpayers. The drill was similar in Missoula, in Fresno, and in San Diego in 1912. As the latter city was gearing up for the Panama–California Exposition, workers challenged an ordinance prohibiting street-corner speech making in the city center with mass demonstrations and outdoor oratory that was suppressed with vigilante violence and newspaper attacks on the "anarchist horde" of "colonized hoboes" who wanted to undermine prosperity in favor of "an anarchist paradise."[10]

Up the coast, the Los Angeles growth elite had already declared war on organized labor. The city had grown slowly in the mid–nineteenth century as an agricultural center and much faster in the 1880s and 1890s with the southern California real estate and citrus boom. The next step, in the minds of people like *Los Angeles Times* publisher Harrison Gray Otis, was to expand the manufacturing base. To compete with San Francisco required plenty of fresh water (see chapter 9), a deepwater port (developed at San Pedro and then Long Beach), and cheap labor. If San Francisco's unions were powerful, L.A.'s would be weak. In the 1890s Otis and other newspapers wore down the printers' union and spread the open-shop gospel through the city, pushing wages 20 to 40 percent lower than in the Bay Area. A vicious bombing of the *Times* headquarters in 1910 that killed twenty-one people derailed labor's counter organizing efforts and destroyed the chances of a strong socialist candidate for mayor. Union members John and James McNamarra admitted guilt after first claiming innocence. Their trial and execution left the doctrine of "industrial freedom" (hiring without union contracts and vigilance against union organizing) to be proclaimed by the *Times* and enforced by the Merchants and Manufacturers Association.

The Los Angeles story was a prelude to widespread union busting a decade later. All across the country, the militant patriotism of World War I provided an excuse to jail radical leaders and intellectuals and undermine militant unions. In the copper country of southern Arizona, it is debatable whether the corporate-controlled mining and smelter towns of Globe, Bisbee, Douglas, Morenci, and Clifton counted as cities or company towns. There was no doubt, however, that they were the sites of spectacular union building and union busting. The IWW began a concerted organizing campaign in 1916 and claimed thousands of members by the next spring. In June 1917, two months after U.S. entry into the war, the IWW called strikes that quickly shut down Bisbee and Morenci; the Phelps-Dodge Company called the labor action German subversion. With the tacit approval of the state government, Phelps-Dodge recruited and armed 2,000 citizens who descended on Bisbee on July 12, rounded up 1,200 men suspected of being Wobblies, loaded them into cattle cars, and dumped them across the New Mexico border, where the army had to feed and house them. Outside the union halls, local opinion held that Bisbee had been cleansed of Germans, Mexicans, and other subversive aliens, although most of the deportees were native-born Americans.

In the Northwest, the timber industry organized the Loyal Legion of Loggers and Lumbermen to counter the IWW. Portland authorities railroaded physician, pacifist, and civil liberties advocate Marie Equi into San Quentin prison. The U.S. Department of Justice used provisions for the internment of enemy aliens to root out IWW members and sympathizers. U.S. Attorney Clarence Reames thought that "every member of the IWW who is an enemy alien as defined by the proclamation of the President" should be interned until the close of the war. Hungarian-born Paul Seidler agreed that the United States was on the right side in the war but also stuck to his Wobbly beliefs, earning internment. "Socialistic tendencies" got Herman Schreiber into more trouble than did his German sympathies. George Zeiger's mistake was to refer to himself as a citizen of the world.[11]

The effective destruction of the Socialist alternative through wartime repression opened the door for business owners to organize open-shop campaigns to undermine unions (in an open shop, an employer can hire nonunion workers even if some employees have a union contract). Dallas employers went after trade unions with the Open Shop Organization and broke a 1919 strike against Texas Power and Light despite sympathy strikes from building trades unions. In 1920 it was Denver's turn, when streetcar workers took on the Denver Tramway Company and the open-shop campaign of the Denver Employers Association. After a wage cut in the midst of postwar inflation, the Amalgamated Association of Street and Electrical Railroad Employees struck in defiance of an injunction. On August 5, efforts to block streetcars being operated by scabs led to a riot that killed two people and trashed the first floor of the *Denver Post*. The next day, jumpy strikebreakers fired into a crowd, killing five and injuring twenty-five. The police and members of the American Legion used the incident to restore order at the expense of the workers. The open shop was successful even in San Francisco, long a bastion of working-class political power.

The Seattle general strike of 1919 had already confirmed the most inflated fears of business owners. The city's 25,000 shipyard workers expected a wage hike to keep up with postwar inflation and two years of federally enforced wage controls. When federal regulators refused the demands, the alliance of shipyard workers went out on strike on January 21, 1919. Both organized labor and the federal government saw Seattle as a test case, especially after February 6, when roughly 40,000 workers in other unions stayed home in solidarity. The result was as close as the United States has come to a general strike in which the entire body of organized workers walks out at one time. The strike shut down Seattle for four days. The unions organized "eating stations" to replace closed restaurants while war veterans who were also union men kept order on the streets.

The strike in Seattle dissolved as quickly as it had started. The national American Federation of Labor unions withheld support because a general strike was far too radical for their strategy. The strikers were pressured to restart electric service or see the power plants operated by the National Guard. Mayor Ole Hanson, elected the year before with labor backing, decided to act tough and play to the national press. Police crackdowns, the threat of federal troops, raids on union offices and newspapers—all combined to save the city for "Americanism" in the space of four days. Hanson resigned his position and went on a national speaking tour, preaching law and order in hope of securing a national political nomination from the Republican Party (the nomination for vice president in 1920 instead went to Massachusetts Governor Calvin Coolidge, who had received even more publicity for resisting a Boston police strike).

The same wave of unrest pounded Winnipeg, where the General Strike of May 15–June 25, 1919, stands as a pivotal event. Historical novelist Allen Levine has one of his characters draw the connections: "What is happening here is not just about Winnipeg. There's been trouble in Seattle, there's plans for the One Big Union in Calgary. We are on the brink of a Socialist upheaval that is going to make what happened in Russia seem small by comparison."[12] Even more clearly than in Seattle, the Winnipeg General Strike opened all the social fault lines at the same time. It pitted industrial and transportation workers against capitalists, eastern European immigrants against Anglo-Canadians, North End against South End, Winnipeg Trades and Labor Council against the Citizens' Committee of 1000. The federal government helped to break the strike by arresting leaders and sending the North-West Mounted Police charging into a demonstration on North Main Street. Despite sympathy strikes as far away as Victoria, the strike ended with the leaders in prison, a legacy of bitterness, and a story that lived on among the city's Left.

Pacific waterfronts remained a hot spot of labor conflicts into the 1930s.

The IWW had tried to organize dockworkers and sailors, but police and vigilantes crushed a San Pedro strike in 1923. San Francisco shipping companies and stevedoring companies imposed open shop in the same years. After a ten-year lull, the International Longshoremen's Union (ILU) appeared on the West Coast in 1933 with demands for a closed shop, union hiring hall, and coast-wide contract. On May 9, 1934, dockworkers from California to Washington walked out. Stevedoring companies brought in strikebreakers whom they housed on moored ships, a sure recipe for increasing violence. In Portland, U.S. Senator Robert Wagner, in town as an advance man for Franklin Roosevelt's planned visit to kickoff construction of Bonneville Dam, got caught in a cross fire between picketers and police. The threat that FDR might cancel his visit helped to bring the business establishment into negotiations. Tension in San Francisco built to Bloody Thursday, July 5, 1934, when police and ILU battled up and down the waterfront and two workers died. The San Francisco Labor Council called an ineffective general strike on July 14, but its involvement actually put decisions in the hands of moderate labor leaders rather than the ILU. On paper, the companies won, but over the next several years they quietly conceded many of the demands with arbitration agreement and responses to "quickie strikes."

From the Rocky Mountain mines in the 1880s to the Pacific waterfronts in the 1930s, the story so far has been about working *men*, but the twentieth century also brought new militancy among the working women who increasingly staffed factories in the larger cities. New York may have been the heart of the garment industry in the early twentieth century, but thousands of women toiled in clothing factories in California and Texas cities. In 1933, the International Ladies Garment Workers Union sent Rose Pesotta to Los Angeles to organize the thousands of women workers from Mexico, Italy, and Russia. She enrolled members by using Spanish-language radio and focusing on women's issues, leading to a strike by 1,600 female garment workers. The women won a thirty-five-hour week and better wages, although the terms were hard to enforce in a fragmented industry of small producers. A 1935 strike by the thousand women who sewed clothing in Dallas was less successful because of police intimidation.

The Mexican American women, men, and children who worked long hours for pitiful wages in San Antonio's pecan-packing plants were more successful with the leadership of two remarkable women. The industry was notorious for its exploitation of workers, who earned an average wage of $2.25 a week sitting on backless benches in dust-choked rooms cracking pecan shells by hand. When several thousand workers struck to protest wage cuts in 1938, owners enlisted the usual help of the police to break up picket lines and demonstrations with tear gas and clubs. The local leader was Emma Tenayuca, a passionate homegrown radical who had Communist Party ties. Sparks flew as she shared leadership with Luisa Moreno, the sophisticated adviser sent from New York by the national United Cannery, Agricultural, Packing and Allied

FIGURE 28. Industrial cities to 1940. The industrial West included mill cities like Butte and Everett that processed specific raw materials and large cities like Los Angeles and San Antonio that manufactured a wider range of products. (Map by Jacquelyn Ferry.)

Workers Association (UCAPAWA). Moreno came from an upper-class family in Guatemala, had lived in New York, and was fresh from organizing campaigns in Florida. Tenayuca, who came from San Antonio's Mexican westside neighborhood, resented "that Spaniard" (Moreno) and continued to turn the strike into a community movement. Borrowing from the IWW and anticipating future civil rights tactics, one of the strategies was mass protests in which roughly a thousand workers went to jail for the cause. Speaking for the city's conservative business leadership, San Antonio's police chief told a state commission that "if the westside workers were organized by UCAPAWA, 25,000 workers would be lost to the 'Red Banner.'" The strikers won compliance with the new federal minimum wage of $0.25 an hour, vastly better that the $2.00 a week that many had earned in 1934, although mobs and police harassment drove Tenayuca out of the city a year later.[13]

Luisa Moreno's career, which stretched from the 1920s to the 1940s, provides a point of transition across the great divide of World War II. From San Antonio she moved to Los Angeles, where she helped to organize El Congreso de Pueblos de Hablan Espanola, the first national Mexican American political and civil rights organization. She also helped UCAPAWA win a closed shop and improved working conditions for the Mexican American and Jewish immigrant women of the Sanitary Packing Company, one of largest fruit canneries in Los Angeles, and she continued to help workers secure better contracts with canneries throughout southern California in the early 1940s. As World War II blended into the Cold War, however, her grassroots organizing again ran aground on national politics. She retired from active organizing in 1947, a few years before her union succumbed to postwar red-baiting. Three years later she left the United States for her native Guatemala under threat of deportation.[14]

With some accuracy, "industrial West" today suggests "clean" and modern manufacturing—sleek-skinned aircraft on brightly lit assembly lines and semiconductors meticulously fabricated in clean rooms (although don't ask about toxic chemicals dumped into the soil). A century ago, it meant brutally hard work in sweltering mine shafts, clattering mills, and dust-choked packinghouses. Now as well as then, however, much of the work is done by immigrants. Then it was Chinese in Astoria salmon canneries (until replaced by machines known as "iron chinks"), Mexicans in Los Angeles packing plants, Scandinavians in Seattle lumber mills, and eastern Europeans in Denver smelters. In the early twenty-first century it is Chinese and Salvadorean women in garment sweatshops, Mexican workers in other garment factories, and Asian immigrants in chip plants. These are workers who play vital roles in the western metropolitan economy—and around whom regional and national debates about exclusive or inclusive immigration laws still swirl.

CHAPTER SEVEN

Money in the Air

Fair Santa Barbara, to thee
Is given a sacred ministry.
To thee the sick and suffering
Their hopes and fears and sorrows bring.
Would these sad hearts so sorely tried
Might see their longing satisfied.
—All about Santa Barbara, California:
The Sanitarium of the Pacific Coast (1878)

Reno, November 23d. The Marquise de Chelles, of Paris, France, formerly
Mrs. Undine Spragg Marvell of Apex City and New York, got a decree
of divorce at a special session of the Court last night, and was remarried
fifteen minutes later to Mr. Elmer Moffatt, the billionaire Railroad King.
—Edith Wharton, The Custom of the Country (1913)

In June 1915, Miss Bessie Post of Westbury, Long Island, a properly brought-up woman in her twenties, enjoyed a grand western tour that started in southern California and ended in the Canadian Rockies. Halfway through the trip, she checked into Portland's new Multnomah Hotel ("absolutely fire-proof" according to hotel stationery), purchased an umbrella, and lunched on fried fresh salmon. "Well!!" she wrote the folks back home in New York: "I wish you could have seen the size of the order—pieces together 10 inches long and 4 inches wide." The afternoon began with a trolley ride to Council

Crest, where an amusement park topped the 1,000-foot ridge of the West Hills and sightseers could marvel at Mount Hood's massive peak rising to the east. It continued with automobile sightseeing to see Portland's rose gardens in full bloom, which she thought even nicer than Pasadena's, and the Forestry Building left over from the 1905 world's fair. The "Timber Temple" was built from huge unpeeled logs measuring as much as six feet across. "They say wood is cheap out here," she commented in explanation. Although she didn't have time for a steamer excursion along the Columbia River and wasn't much for strenuous hikes, she left Portland a satisfied tourist. Like others who came west in increasing thousands in the late nineteenth and early twentieth centuries, Bessie Post was looking for a relaxing tour, not a strenuous adventure. If Portland houses didn't quite measure up to the mansions of Glen Cove and Oyster Bay on Long Island's North Shore, the city had more than adequate amenities.[1]

Through her whole trip, Miss Post had been enjoying the air—the climate of the Southwest and the Pacific slope. Air, to be sure, is a pretty intangible commodity, but western cities have been selling it for nearly a century and a half through their claims on climate, scenery, and recreational resources. They developed local recreation hinterlands in the later nineteenth century, with some similarities to resort districts around eastern U.S. cities. Southwestern cities prospered as health resorts and winter escapes. Urban boosters cooperated with railroad publicity departments to promote state and national parks and sometimes acquired title to nearby mountaintops for local recreation and tourist attractions. In the 1910s and 1920s they made sure that paved highways pushed outward from the major cities to serve automobile tourists who would come to know Route 40 and Route 66.

All of these activities involved an exploitation of "air." The literal pure, dry air of the Rocky Mountain Piedmont and southern California attracted asthmatics and tuberculosis victims to cities like Colorado Springs and Pasadena. The soft, warm air of southwestern winters was a key resource for leisure and retirement cities such as Santa Barbara, Santa Fe, and the competing cities in Arizona's Valley of the Sun (meaning Phoenix, Tempe, Chandler, and Scottsdale). Noble mountains and exotic deserts to be seen through clear western air brought tourists to and through Denver, Albuquerque, Calgary, and Los Angeles.

Tourism—comfortable visits as distinct from arduous travel—came west in the last quarter of the nineteenth century. In the 1830s and 1840s, to travel westward from the Mississippi River or to voyage into the Pacific was to adventure and explore like Francis Parkman, Richard Henry Dana, or John C. Fremont. By the 1860s it was to report and comment for people who were unlikely ever to observe the new mines and farms and cities for themselves but who could still read books by the likes of Horace Greeley, Samuel Clemens, and Richard Burton. In the 1870s, with pleasure travel affordable

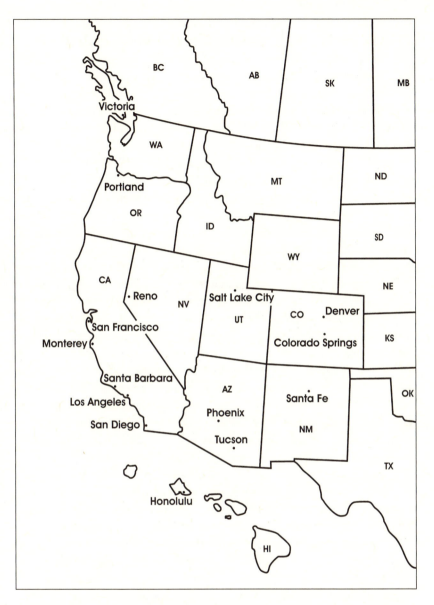

FIGURE 29. Tourist cities to 1940. Cities throughout the West identified themselves as tourism and leisure destinations, offering various combinations of pleasant climate, sea air, and mountain vistas. (Map by Jacquelyn Ferry.)

only to the upper crust, San Francisco newspapers published the list of arrivals by the new transcontinental railroad on their social pages. By the 1880s, in contrast, railroads, urbanization, and the confinement of Indians to increasingly smaller territories had turned travelers into tourists who could expect comfort and convenience along with scenery. The change is apparent from book titles: compare Ovando Hollister's comprehensive *The Mines of Colorado in 1867* to Frank Fossett's *Colorado: Its Gold and Silver Mines, Farms and Stock Ranges, and Health and Pleasure Resorts* in 1880. In 1870, Englishman John White had reported on the rude shanties, bull whackers, and soldiers he met following the route of the half-finished Union Pacific a few years earlier. A quarter century later, a different John M. White offered a travel narrative—*The Newer Northwest: A Description of the Health Resorts and Mining Camps of the Black Hills of South Dakota and Big Horn Mountains in Wyoming*—that directed tourists to Hot Springs, South Dakota, Devils Tower, Wind Cave, and (Heaven help us!) the Custer Battlefield and the site of the recent massacre at Wounded Knee, where a photograph of high mounded graves alongside a fence made a gruesome contrast with pictures of waterfalls and canyons.[2]

Western cities were important stops on the tourist loops that railroads vigorously promoted from the 1880s onward: San Francisco along with Yosemite, Denver along with the 1,000-mile circle through the Rockies, and the Petrified Forest and Grand Canyon on the way to Los Angeles. Smaller cities sometimes looked to leisure spending as the main driver for growth. Big cities competed for tourist dollars to supplement their manufacturing and commerce. Even Hollywood got into the act in Los Angeles when movie superstar Mary Pickford visited a meeting of the Chamber of Commerce in 1926 to argue for parks and beautification, with a touch of "Spanish" flavor retained:

The first impression of Los Angeles would be a beautiful one and the last one something that they can carry away instead of going through packing houses. . . . This is part of the staging of a city. . . . It is a purely business proposition because we are unique I think as a city and we are really a garden spot, and in order to attract people . . . we must be beautiful and charming and all of that and that to me is a business proposition. It is much the same as making a picture.[3]

San Francisco was the first tourist destination of the Pacific West because it was big and because it was the most accessible point by water and rail. It marketed its picturesque hills, Golden Gate Park and Cliff House on its Pacific edge, its blue bay, and a bit farther out, redwood groves and Mount Tam. After the earthquake, it sold its own survival and reconstruction as something that had to be seen to be believed. It also sold its exotic neighborhoods and people, including the Italians of Fisherman's Wharf and the Chinese who crowded so close to downtown. After the fire, Chinese and Anglo entrepreneurs cooperated to rebuild Chinatown in "oriental" style with red-painted balconies and swinging lanterns. Edward Hungerford thought that "architects have brought more of the Chinese spirit into its buildings than the old ever had. It does not lack color . . . but it is now frankly commercial. The paid guides and 'rubberneck wagons' have completed the ruin."[4]

San Diego, a sort of antimatter opposite to San Francisco, had been a key site on the route between Mexico and Alta California, but it was on the fringe of American California. As in many other western cities, its early business-men whistled a happy tune. Writing to refute bad-mouthing by recent visitors, the Chamber of Commerce in 1874 anticipated a direct railroad to New Orleans and predicted that "San Diego will, in the lifetime of her middle-aged inhabitants, monopolize the trade, not only of the rich agricultural and mineral country tributary to her, but also of the great Asiatic nations, and the South Pacific Islands." In the meanwhile, however, it held great potential as a health resort, for one only need voyage south from San Francisco to experience a "most agreeable change from cold and fog to a soft and balmy atmosphere."[5] Countless times over the next decades, San Diegans turned to Italy to describe their climate—ideal for both health and pleasure. Crafting promotional literature to distribute at the St. Louis Louisiana Purchase Exposition of 1904, H. P. Wood of the Chamber of Commerce claimed miraculous powers for the climate: "There is no region in the world as free from any seasonal or accidental disease," wounds heal with unusual speed, and "men of eighty and ninety walk the streets with vigorous step, and why should it be otherwise among such perfect surroundings."[6] Nor would the vigorous tourist of any age be bored, not with the lemon groves of Chula Vista; the exotic scenes of Tijuana; the hotel at Coronado; the charming towns of La Jolla, Encinitas, and Oceanside; and mountain resorts such as Cuyamaca and Descanso—in effect claiming for tourism the surroundings that covered what is roughly the metropolitan region of today.

Tourism entrepreneurs were active up and down the California coast. The Southern Pacific Railroad in 1879 absorbed and improved the Monterey–San Francisco rail connection, bought up thousands of acres of land in and near Monterey, and built the luxury Del Monte Hotel to generate passenger traffic and compete with Santa Cruz (which was tied to the big city by a rival railroad). Farther down the coast, W. W. Hollister had already built the Arlington Hotel in Santa Barbara in 1876, kicking off its career as a resort city that did not have to worry about the reek of drying squid and the smell of sardine canneries from Monterey Bay fisheries. San Diego's Coronado Beach development and Del Coronado Hotel on the ocean side of San Diego Bay were the work of a real estate developer from Evansville, Indiana, and a piano manufacturer from Chicago. Opened in 1887, the hotel included 750 bedchambers, thirty billiard tables, four bowling alleys, and 7,300 feet of verandas, implying five feet of rocking chair space per guest if the rooms were double occupancy.

California notwithstanding, Colorado Springs was the first major western city to develop from the start around the health and leisure industries. For the active tourist, "the Springs" billed itself as "a capital center of innumerable attractive drives and excursions" to the awesome Royal Gorge of the Arkansas River; the "sparkling brooklets, streams and beautiful waterfalls" of Cheyenne Canyon; the sandstone formations of the Garden of the Gods that resembled human figures and animals and the ruins of ancient structures with "bastions, battlements, half-buried marbles, towers, and castles"; and Pikes Peak itself, surmounted by a cog railway in 1891.[7] It was also one of the West's most fashionable resorts, just as William Jackson Palmer had intended. Its many English immigrants earned it the nickname "Little London" and elevated the town's social tone in an Anglophilic age, and wealthy residents and well-to-do visitors could easily live an "Eastern life in a Western environment." In the mid-1890s, one could dine and dance at the Broadmoor Casino; try golf, polo, or pigeon shooting at the Cheyenne Mountain Country Club; shop at stores well stocked with eastern goods; or pass the time in a ceaseless round of parties, dances, social calls, and flirtations.

Thousands of sojourners in Colorado in those same years cared very little about the details of scenery. They came not to uplift their spirits through the sublime and the curious but to cure their bodies by exposure to Colorado's climate. The first settlers had noticed the "Italian" climate (was there any place from Colorado to California that wasn't "Italian," that is, when it didn't look like Switzerland?).[8] In the sheltered valleys and canyons of the foothills, Easterners were advised, picnics could be held in December and trails walked in January. The air was exhilarating, stimulating, bracing, elastic. Colorado's dryness, said several physicians, reduced the capacity of the air to conduct heat and electricity and therefore helped to cure pulmonary diseases. Favorable evaluation of Colorado climate triggered interest in the state's advantages as a health resort. The same journalists who helped to publicize its scenery did the same for its climate. As Samuel Bowles wrote of the whole central Rockies, "Here would seem to be the fountain of health; and among these hills and plains is surely to be many a summer resort for the invalid." The Colorado Territorial Board of Immigration took up the refrain in the 1870s. By the 1880s, outside journalists could agree that, despite some overselling, the now familiar advantages of Colorado had proved the state a "great and beneficial sanatorium" for sufferers from pulmonary diseases.[9] It was a truism among enthusiasts that Colorado provided better conditions for invalids year-round than did even the famous health meccas of Switzerland. Governor Fred Pitkin's claim that "we can almost bring a dead man to life" may be dismissed as boosterism, but many experts of the day agreed that residence in the state quickened and strengthened the functioning of any basically healthy organism.

Tuberculosis was endemic in the later nineteenth century. Spread by impure foods such as contaminated milk as well as crowded living conditions,

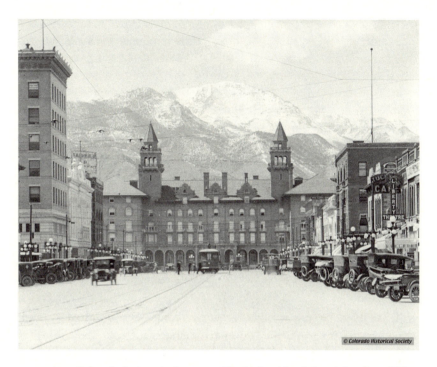

FIGURE 30. Colorado Springs in the 1920s. The Antlers Hotel closed the vista of Pikes Peak Avenue in Colorado Springs with the mountain towering over the city. (Courtesy of the Colorado Historical Society [20005280, CHSX5280], all rights reserved.)

it affected the poor and the affluent alike. Because it is a disease of the lungs, TB or "consumption" in the nineteenth century was often treated by getting victims into fresh clean air. As the spreading rail network made transcontinental travel possible, TB sufferers came west by the thousands to rent a room for a winter, to hire professional treatment in a sanitarium, or to relocate permanently. Las Vegas, New Mexico, a small city conveniently on the Santa Fe Railroad, was a sanitarium center. So was Denver, one of the capitals of the "one-lung army." Pasadena, California, originated as a health colony. Its founder reportedly spent his first nonasthmatic night at the base of the San Gabriel Mountains and decided to build a town. Los Angeles became known as the capital of the "Sanitarium Belt" because of its large number of consumptives. Southern California promoters claimed that the healthy climate added years to life spans and made it difficult to die of old age.[10]

Every November, a wave of asthmatics and consumptives fled the cold, dark winters of the East for New Mexico, California, and Colorado. Thumbing their copies of Mrs. Simeon Dunbar's *Health Resorts of Colorado Springs and Manitou*, hopeful people filled Denver hotels and Colorado Springs boardinghouses recently emptied of summer tourists. Poorer invalids sometimes made do with makeshift accommodations. Visitors reported hundreds of persons living in tent encampments that formed special suburbs of Colorado Springs. In the 1870s and 1880s, the common estimate was that one-third of the state's population was composed of recovered invalids. Although that estimate was passed from writer to writer and quoted by later historians, its validity is impossible to verify. Certainly Colorado Springs had enough resident invalids living on outside incomes to buffer the shock of the 1893 depression. It is also easy to make long lists of distinguished citizens who first visited Colorado as a medical measure, but, again, it is impossible to verify claims that the "one-lung army" of Denver totaled 30,000 in 1890.

Southern Arizona had its own convalescent migration that began after the end of the Apache wars in 1886. The Desert Inn Sanatorium near Phoenix advertised as "especially suited to benefit incipient bronchial and pulmonary cases." Resort hotels in the mountains above Tucson competed for the same clientele, helped with publicity by writer Harold Bell Wright, who extolled the city's benefits in his essay "Why I Did Not Die." Health seekers who arrived in Tucson without money made do with a tumbledown suburb of tents and shacks scattered north of the University of Arizona campus. "As one walked along the dark streets, he heard coughing from every tent," one Tucsonan recalled from his boyhood in Tentville: "It was truly a place of lost souls and lingering death."[11]

The large-scale migration of tuberculars slowed early in the twentieth century. Physicians began to advise institutionalization near the victim's home rather than travel across an ocean or continent. At the same time, the proof that tuberculosis was a contagious disease incited fears in residents throughout the West. By 1901 and 1902, Coloradans were discussing the possibility of quarantining dangerous cases and blaming the flow of health migrants on exaggerations broadcast by "selfish interests engaged in transportation and inn-keeping."[12] Landlords rejected applications for a room or house, and employers slammed their doors in migrants' faces. The best substitutes were the new sanatoriums that offered professional care.

The transformation of tuberculosis treatment from a tourist industry to a specialized medical problem was one of several changes in western tourism in the first decades of the twentieth century. By the 1920s the western travel industry scarcely resembled the genteel business of the past generation. The depression of the 1890s triggered the first alterations. In their scramble for dwindling traffic, western railroads began to offer special convention and excursion rates that they regularized as low summer tourist fares in the first years of the new century. The Denver and Rio Grande railroad in the same years was particularly active in seeking the patronage of middle-class tourists who could now afford a quick trip through the West. An advertising budget of $60,000 per year was used to attract such people as junketeering schoolteachers to its "Around the Circle Tour," on which $28 would purchase a four-day 1,000-mile loop through the best scenery in the Rockies.

Phoenix struggled to turn sunshine itself into a salable commodity, irrespective of its medical benefits. Starting with *New York Tribune* publisher Whitelaw Reid, a trickle of East Coast socialites had begun to take winter vacations in Phoenix in the 1890s. Resorts with tennis courts and golf courses, like the Ingleside Inn in 1910, replaced downtown hotels for long-term visitors. Alexander Chandler laid out an entire city in 1913, named it after himself, and advertised it as the Pasadena of Arizona with a better future than California. City boosters in 1926 mounted a "Let's Do Away With the Desert" campaign to convince residents to plant trees and roses to make the city look more eastern. "Valley of the Sun" came in the 1930s as an advertising slogan to replace "Garden Spot of the Southwest."

Changes at Colorado Springs around the turn of the century illustrate the same live-wire business attitude and go-aheadism. More hotels and cheaper ones were built in the city and up Ute Pass along the Colorado Midland line. "Little London" lost its genteel affectation and showed a new attitude toward tourists, who were now to be welcomed no matter what their manners. As Marshall Sprague has pointed out, the difference between William Jackson Palmer and Spencer Penrose epitomized the change. A member of an established Philadelphia family, Penrose made a small fortune at Cripple Creek and a larger fortune from Utah copper. In 1915, he decided to revitalize Colorado Springs's sagging economy. In tune with the twentieth century, Penrose publicized his holdings in a style that would have made the retiring Palmer wince. The average American soon knew Colorado Springs not as a temperance colony but as the home of "the Highest Zoo in the World" as well as "the Golf, Tennis and Polo Capital of the World." He sank $250,000 into construction of an auto road to the top of Pikes Peak and initiated the Pikes Peak Hill Climb to publicize his new highway.

The new curves and switchbacks winding around Pikes Peak were part of a new era in western tourism in which automobile trips would rapidly replace railroad excursions—but it was a phase in which cities continued to hold many of the cards. Like railroads in the nineteenth century, highways in the twentieth century reached outward from cities. Portland entrepreneurs and engineers built a seventy-mile highway through the Columbia River Gorge in the 1910s, letting adventuresome auto drivers parallel the route of the Union Pacific Railroad past deep chasms and waterfalls. Monterey land developers built Seventeen-Mile Drive along the scenic coast to introduce tourists to a growing complex of resorts and golf courses. Denver acquired a set of parklands in the foothills and Front Range and linked them with new motorable roads as the Denver Mountain Park system. A Parks Committee of Denver in 1912 wrote that "a Mountain Park for Denver will be . . . perhaps the greatest step in the great movement of making our mountains available

FIGURE 31. Columbia River scenic highway, 1915. Dedicated in 1915, the Columbia River Highway eastward from Portland was intended for both commerce and pleasure. Designed after models of mountain highways in the Alps, it opened mountain scenery to motorists. (Oregon Historical Society, Neg. 26000.)

to the people . . . and to take the lead in making Colorado more attractive to tourists than Switzerland."[13]

Initiative shifted to the states in the 1920s. Led by Oregon, state legislatures began to levy gasoline taxes to match newly available federal dollars under the Federal-Aid Highway Act of 1919 and designated key routes as U.S. federal-aid highways such as U.S. 40 from Baltimore to San Francisco,

U.S. 66 from Chicago to Los Angeles, and U.S. 101 along the Pacific coast. Gasoline companies and state highway departments began to issue highway road maps in the mid-1920s, updating them every year to reflect the progress of road improvements. To study these maps in sequence is to watch tentacles of pavement reach outward from the major cities, first connecting with hinterland towns and then groping across the landscape to link with the roads of the next metropolis. In the Southwest, only fragments of pavement reached out from Albuquerque, El Paso, Phoenix, Tucson, Yuma, and Flagstaff in 1930, but the New Mexico Highway Commission assured travelers that the dry climate made bogging down in mud a rare occurrence. By 1932, the Arizona Highway Department map included points of interest and driving distances from Phoenix and showed hard pavement reaching west to Yuma and east to El Paso. Farther north, pavement in the late 1920s crept slowly outward from Casper and Rawlins, Wyoming, and from Bozeman and Butte-Anaconda, Montana. In Colorado and Utah, pavement confirmed the importance of the Mormon corridor from Provo to Salt Lake City to Logan and the Piedmont corridor from Colorado Springs to Denver to Cheyenne, though motorists from more distant towns still had to struggle long miles of bumpy gravel. Not until the mid-1930s did hard-surface highways parallel the most important rail routes.[14]

Twentieth-century cities also knew that the growing numbers of automobile tourists loved national parks. National parks were certainly proud achievements of the growing conservation ethic, but they were also business propositions for big cities. The *Denver Post* and the Denver-based Colorado Mountain Club were the strongest voices in securing congressional approval of Rocky Mountain National Park in 1915. They also pushed, unsuccessfully, for a Mount Evans National Park (which remained instead part of the city's mountain park system). The Seattle Chamber of Commerce and Tacoma Commercial Club made common cause with mountaineers and outdoor enthusiasts, on the one hand, and the Northern Pacific Railroad, on the other, to lobby for preservation of Mount Rainier, first as a forest reserve in 1893 and then as a national park in 1899. The central axis of the Alaska–Yukon–Pacific Exposition grounds—which became the University of Washington campus—framed a view of Mount Rainier and "claimed" it for the city.[15] Tacoma and Seattle businesses continued to push for improved road access through the 1910s and 1920s and provided the capital for the Rainier National Park Company to construct tourist facilities. Seattle's Mountaineers club, organized in 1906, joined San Francisco's Sierra Club and Portland's Mazamas in claiming the magnificent western mountains as recreation grounds for the progressive middle class.

Defining the western mountains and coast as recreation zones required substantial editing of history. Tourism, whether by rail or automobile, increasingly bypassed or ignored the industrial landscape of mining and manufacturing. Nineteenth-century travelers had made sure to include Butte on their Montana itinerary and Leadville on their swing through Colorado. Auto tourists preferred to challenge their Chevrolets with the Going-to-the-Sun Highway over the crest of Glacier National Park or the Fall River Road over the top of Rocky Mountain National Park. Industrial landscapes needed to age and molder a bit before they acquired enough quaintness to be recycled as summer or winter resorts. Cities that were recreational draws and industrial centers at the same time had to hope that working factories, at the least, emitted their smoke and fumes downwind from the tourist facilities.

In Monterey, tourism promoters and land developers battled first over the stench from shoreside squid drying by Chinese fishermen and then, from the 1920s into the 1940s, over the odors from the city's booming sardine canneries. Prevailing west winds wafted the smell of dead fish and fish meal fertilizer over downtown hotels and the extensive Hotel Del Monte properties. Lawsuits and environmental regulations in the 1930s mitigated but didn't solve a problem that continued to grow until the sardine fishery collapsed at the end of the 1940s. One solution was to move the tourist industry around the nob of Point Pinos to Pebble Beach and Carmel-by-the-Sea. Another was to embrace John Steinbeck's portrait of the waterfront in *Cannery Row*. Published in 1945, less than a decade before the canneries and fish meal plants began to shut down, the novel gave Monterey boosters the opportunity to argue that fisheries weren't really smelly and dirty—just part of a colorful past that would gradually be redeveloped into a sort of industrial theme park.

Local color in Honolulu meant leis, luaus, ukuleles, and hula shows adapted—or plundered—from Hawaiian culture. The first tourist hotels and the Hawaii Promotion Committee followed American annexation. Honolulu entrepreneurs tried to convince East Coast travelers to extend their California vacations with a voyage to the tropics, attracting 8,000 visitors in 1919 and 32,000 in fraught and nervous 1941. The vast transformation of Waikiki and the creation of tourist coasts at Lahaina and Kona waited on statehood and jet service in 1959.

Several midsized cities reconfigured history in a somewhat different way by inventing colorful and romantic pasts. Into the early 1900s, Santa Barbara attracted wealthy retirees and winter refugees from the cold corporate capitals of the Northeast with its climate and setting alone. In 1909, however, the Santa Barbara Civic League undertook to restore a historic adobe building and establish a historical museum. Wealthy individuals began their own restoration projects, replacing western frontier architecture with semiauthentic Spanish-styled buildings that enacted the popular image of romantic Old California. The moving force was Pearl Chase, who used the Community Arts Association and a city architectural review board to direct the city's reconstruction as a very tasteful historical theme park. "The Association captured Santa Barbara, politically, bringing the community under the control of a coherent group of

FIGURE 32. Santa Barbara County Courthouse. Santa Barbara self-consciously remade its downtown in "Spanish style" with white-painted walls and red-tile roofs beginning in the 1920s, promoting an attractive image that drew on romantic memories of California's Spanish and Mexican past. (Wikimedia Commons.)

affluent, genteel, preservationist-minded citizens who forced their will, quietly but effectively, on the community," historian Kevin Starr has commented. For these activists, a June 1925 earthquake was an opportunity as much as a challenge, because it leveled State Street and its inappropriate "American" structures. The goals were aesthetic pleasure for locals and attraction for tourists and retirees: "Commercial it may be—but surely the cry of 'Beauty pays' is heard. In Santa Barbara our 'trade' is luring tourists."[16] Indeed, by the 1920s the Los Angeles Chamber of Commerce was worrying that Santa Barbara and San Diego were siphoning off rich retirees and leisure seekers who should have been enjoying the City of Angels.

Santa Fe took Santa Barbara a step further, inventing and then selling itself with a physical and historical image that said as much about American discomfort with the twentieth century as about the city's own past. What started modestly in the 1910s as the development of a particular building style that drew on Spanish and Pueblo traditions for new buildings became a ubiquitous "Santa Fe style" by the 1980s, omnipresent in house and home magazines and even theming a Hotel Santa Fe to provide an authentic American experience for visitors to Euro Disneyland.

In its first sixty years after American takeover, Santa Fe's old *rico* elite and new American settlers struggled to create one more promising commercial town that downplayed its heritage and rebuilt the old plaza as a middle western main street. Spanish, Mexican, and Indian roots were all de-emphasized to counter the American prejudice against "indolent" and "ignorant" Mexico that blocked statehood for New Mexico and Arizona until 1912. After the railroad (the *Santa Fe* railroad) bypassed the city in the mid-1880s for Albuquerque and a direct route to California, however, Santa Fe stagnated as a sleepy territorial capital that tried to market its sunshine and tranquility to TB victims.

Statehood in 1912 changed the equation. Political change removed the need to ignore the past, whose traces in crumbling churches, winding streets, and low-slung adobe houses could be repackaged as quaint and romantic attractions rather than painful anachronisms. The Museum of New Mexico, founded in 1909, took the lead in exploring and publicizing the history of Santa Fe and its surroundings. A Santa Fe City Planning Board, guided by leading figures from the museum, argued in 1912 that architectural image could drive tourist business and reverse the city's decline. The Planning Board and museum outlined the basics of the "New-Old Santa Fe Style" and its differences from California mission styles. Emphasizing flat roofs with protruding beams, low horizontal profiles, adobe colors, and recessed portals, the style was an invented amalgam of Pueblo, Spanish, and generic Mediterranean elements repackaged for tastes influenced by the romantic arts and crafts movement. Restoration of the Palace of the Governors showed how it could be done, and wealthy Easterners began building Santa Fe houses. Writers and artists looking for authenticity moved to Santa Fe and nearby Taos. The Chamber of Commerce soon described Santa Fe as "the City Different," as indeed it was, a tourist-friendly town whose ancient West feel in places like the La Fonda Hotel (1921) was the creation of Anglo newcomers. The four art galleries and shops that sold Indian goods in 1920 grew to twenty-five in 1960 and 295 in 1992. Hotel rooms grew from 205 to 1,150 to 4,116—all the result of a set of aesthetic choices that have provided "a unifying civic identity for the city, a promotional image to attract tourists, and a romantic backdrop for Anglo-American newcomers."[17]

Implicit in Santa Fe's and Santa Barbara's image making, as in San Francisco's cultivation of its colorful, titillating, but ultimately (for tourists) harmless ethnic variety, was a clear racial and cultural message. It was the same message conveyed by the festivals and fairs that contributed to tourist attractions: That which was exotic or looked back to earlier centuries was safely contained. As Catherine Cocks puts it, the "appropriation of non-Anglo histories erased conflict in the past and naturalized class and ethnic differences in the present."[18] Italian fishermen, Chinese souvenir sellers, and Indian craftswomen at the Santa Fe plaza were all carefully positioned *within* cities and their economic systems. Tucson could proclaim itself the "Old Pueblo" in the 1920s and 1930s when its Hispanic residents were safely outnumbered by Anglos. Groups who did not contribute to the "safe but

FIGURE 33. Empress Hotel, Victoria, British Columbia. Built in 1908 for the Canadian Pacific Railroad's steamship line, the Empress Hotel for a century has defined Victoria as a cultured outpost of British society and a suitable spot for affluent tourists on a par with San Diego, Santa Barbara, Honolulu, and Monterey. (Wikimedia Commons.)

colorful" marketing image—Japanese hotel keepers and truck gardeners, Mexican laborers, crippled Scandinavian loggers on skid row—were not part of the lure of San Francisco or the romance of Monterey.[19]

Reno—satirized by the *New York Times* in 1910 as the site of the Hotel Alimonia and the Husbands Exchange Bank—put a triple twist on urban tourism. In the decades before World War II, it offered not only the clear air of the Nevada desert but also a chance for couples to clear the air through quickie divorces. It put the political openness of the West to work on behalf of the economic elite whom western populism was originally meant to combat. And it sold itself to East Coast high society as modern and up to date while simultaneously serving up a cowboy past as a special attraction.

Reno was the second western city to offer a quick route to divorce. Several states in the late 1800s had unusually short residency requirements for voting, provisions that were designed to facilitate attachment to the polity among their very mobile populations, but that also could carry other legal privileges, such as access to local courts for divorces. When South Dakota entered the union in 1889 with a six-month residency requirement, Sioux Falls enjoyed two decades as a divorce mill before the legislature extended the requirement to a year. Meanwhile, East Coast socialites discovered that Nevada had not only a superior climate and scenery to South Dakota but also a six-month residency requirement. Because Reno was Nevada's largest and most sophisticated city, to Reno they came—first Laura Corey to divorce the philandering president of U.S. Steel, then other members of New York society, and then journalists to report on the phenomenon of "going to Reno." Reno divorces were news in the society pages of eastern newspapers by the early teens, when the city of 12,000 might host 300 affluent divorce tourists in a year. In her knife-sharp comedy of manners *The Custom of the Country* (1913), novelist and confirmed *New Yorker* Edith Wharton sent her often-married protagonist Undine Spragg to Sioux Falls for one divorce mid-novel and to Reno for six months and a day in the final pages.

Reno businesses enjoyed the publicity and the cash. Nevada raised the residency to a full year in 1913 but hurriedly returned it to six months in 1915, then to three months in 1927 (doubling the number of divorces from the year before), and then to only six weeks in 1931—the same time that the state legalized gambling as a second way to fight the Great Depression. Now Hollywood was as familiar with Reno as New York society. Mary Pickford got a Reno divorce in 1920 so she could marry Douglas Fairbanks. Over the next couple decades, movie studios cranked out *The Road to Reno*, *The Merry Wives of Reno*, *Six Weeks in Reno*, *Charlie Chan in Reno*(!), and, most successfully, *The Women*, starring Joan Crawford, Norma Shearer, and Paulette Goddard as wives waiting for divorces and trying out new love interests.

As "the Biggest Little City in the World," a slogan that dates to 1929, the city in the 1920s and 1930s marketed four attractions: divorce itself, sophistication, the nostalgic West, and adult amusement. For the men and (usually) women looking for a divorce, the elegant Riverside Hotel offered extended-stay suites and a location across the street from the Washoe County Courthouse (know to jocular journalists as the House of Divide or the Separator). Downtown merchants had up-to-date fashions and offered to reset old jewelry in the very latest styles, while short, bumpy flights to San Francisco after 1929 were scheduled to allow one-day shopping expeditions. At the same time, and often for the same customers, the opposite of New York or Hollywood sophistication was also available in the form of the Nevada Round-Up and dude ranches for women bored with the Riverside Hotel. With the legalization of gambling 1931 and the end of Prohibition in 1933, Reno could also sell "legitimate" naughtiness and scandalous fun. The cowboy gigolo became a stock figure as the western past took on a form less fully sanitized than in red-tiled Santa Barbara. Locals called the Lazy Me Dude Ranch, one of the first to attract long-distance visitors, the "Lay Me Easy."

Reno in the 1930s was a tourist city in transition from one era of leisure to the next. From the 1870s through the 1920s, visitors came by train and took their time for multiweek swings through the parks and scenery or multimonth stays for cool summers or warm winters. The expanding network of paved highways made transcontinental auto trips possible by the later 1930s, with powerful implications for the phenomenon of family vacations. Afford-able air travel followed in the 1960s and 1970s, creating a national convention industry and allowing short junkets from east to west.[20]

Reno also offered a preview of major elements of western tourism. Visitors in search of the *Old* West could visit Virginia City. Tourists interested in actively engaging the outdoors had Lake Tahoe within reach, with its deep blue waters and nascent ski areas. Dude ranches offered a packaged experi-ence that anticipated Disneyland. And as a curious annex of the East Coast elite, the city was on its way from the staged images of divorcées kissing the courthouse pillars in the bright clear sunshine to a run as neon-lit Sin City before Las Vegas—its lights glowing in the clear air of the Nevada desert—added whole new dimensions to the tourist's West.

CHAPTER EIGHT

Cities of Homes

These shacks are tricks. A simple smoke
from wood stoves, hanging half-afraid
to rise, makes poverty in winter real.
                    —Richard Hugo, "Between the Bridges" (1976)

It was just a Spanish house, like all the rest of them in California, with
white walls, red tile roof, and a patio out to one side.
                    —James M. Cain, *Double Indemnity* (1936)

Emily French described herself as a "hard-worked woman" in the remarkable diary that she kept for the year 1890. Divorced, forty-seven years old, responsible for a son and daughter, unskilled but desperate to maintain respectability, she moved from rural Colorado to Denver in April, took a summer job as a cook and housekeeper in the mountains, and returned to the city in the fall. Denver was booming, up 60 percent in population since 1885 and attracting 2,500 newcomers per month—more new hands than even a prosperous economy could absorb. With her experience limited to household duties, her opportunities to earn a meager living were limited to day-to-day and week-to-week work as a housekeeper, seamstress, and nurse for homebound women and children.[1]

Despite her limited circumstances, Emily French wanted a house. She sunk $500, a large part of her meager savings, into a narrow lot in the Fairview district, just west of the South Platte River and south of West Colfax

Street, where a brand new electric streetcar ran downtown. The house was to have four rooms on one and a half floors. She had to borrow money to buy the lumber and hire men to frame it up for her (two successful men from her First Baptist Church cosigned her note) but tried to do much of the finish work herself. Her entries record trips to get single gallons of paint, to buy windows, to find a better door lock. Many dark evenings as winter came on she worked on the interior, nailing up lath to be ready for plastering. We don't know for sure, because her surviving diary ends on a windy New Year's Eve, but it is likely she lost the unfinished house to creditors, because she had another address in the 1891 city directory.

Emily French tried to put down roots in a neighborhood that was up for grabs in 1890. Nearby lived a railroad switchman, carpenter, plasterer, teamster, and rag peddler. Homeless men camped out along the South Platte in tents and shanties. Several small dairies in the half-rural area watered their cows from the filthy South Platte. A bit to the north were small groups of Jewish and Italian immigrants. Desperate to hold onto her self-image as a respectable churchgoing lady in temporarily tight circumstances, Emily scorned these neighbors in the derogatory language of the time as "Dagos" and "Chenes."

We can learn many things from Emily French about the precarious position of single women, about the importance of Protestant piety for self-definition, and about casual attitudes toward animals when they were tools rather than pets. Her story also introduces three important points about the development of western cityscapes. One is the preponderance of freestanding housing among the wide range of housing types. A second is the fluidity of early neighborhood boundaries and their increasing solidity as the nineteenth century turned into the twentieth century. A third is the power of the city center, the destination of converging streetcar lines and the location of social and cultural institutions.

First-generation cities were a confusing hodgepodge. Stores, hotels, storage sheds, fine homes, livery stables, factories, and cheap shanties all crowded together around the landing or the railroad depot. In those first bustling years, workers and merchants needed to be close to the action. Save perhaps in Los Angeles, where English-speaking newcomers took the west side of the Los Angeles River and left the east side to Spanish speakers, nobody knew for sure where the "good side" of town was going to be—although real estate speculators eagerly platted additions of new lots in the expectation of growth.

By the 1890s, however, growing cities like Denver were beginning to display a distinct economic and social geography. Growing downtowns were pushing heavy manufacturing out of the city center to sites with more elbow room and quick access to water and rail transportation. Denver's big smelters belched their smoke downstream along the South Platte. Oakland's waterfront captured an increasing share of Bay Area manufacturing and commerce—

30 percent of shipping by 1910 and still growing. Garment and clothing workers in Los Angeles worked in loft buildings close to downtown, but the large branch plants that made up much of the city's industrial base located three–four miles south of the historic center in the Central Manufacturing District, one of seven industrial districts that the City of Los Angeles designated in one of the nation's first land-use zoning ordinances in 1908.

In place of mills and factories, city centers filled with department stores, new theaters, upscale hotels, banks, and office buildings built in the shapes of U's and W's to maximize natural light. The office buildings brought middle-class men downtown to work, and the department stores brought their wives to shop in increasingly sanitized business districts. Both groups depended on the increasing numbers of women workers. New technologies—telephones, typewriters—meant increasing demand for routine office work. Filling much of the need for desk workers were middle-class women, whose literacy was often guaranteed by the high school diplomas that went disproportionately to women in the later nineteenth century. In 1900 women made up 76 percent of the nation's stenographers and typists and 29 percent of its cashiers, bookkeepers, and accountants. Working in the new downtown department stores and skyscrapers, these white-collar women helped central districts of large cities lose some of their rough edges and grow more respectable as places of shopping and entertainment.

A handful of western cities imitated New York and Chicago by raising soaring buildings like Seattle's forty-story Smith Tower of 1914 and the Los Angeles City Hall, whose hillside location made its 450-foot spire loom even higher over downtown. Most made do with six- to twelve-story downtowns that matched their position in regional urban systems. Fort Worth sprouted a seven-story building in 1907, and Dallas boasted a fifteen-story tower in the same year; and El Paso and Oklahoma City soon had twelve-story mini-towers. One twelve-story building loomed over Fresno's three- to four-story downtown at the time of World War I, when San Diego claimed several new eight- to ten-story buildings. Vancouver's Dominion Trust Building was reputedly the tallest in the British Empire in 1910—a title that it held only briefly before a seventeen-story building rose nearby.

Many architects in the Northwest chose to combat gray winters by coating office and department store exteriors with white and tan terra-cotta tiles whose glazed surfaces reflected the meager sun. When Herbert Croly visited Portland in 1912, he found a mature and cultured (and self-satisfied) city whose solid and dignified "business structures are as good . . . as the average of those erected in the Middle West or in the East."[2] Developers in oil-boom cities that grew rapidly in the 1920s and 1930s—Fort Worth, Tulsa, Oklahoma City, Dallas, Los Angeles—left a legacy of art deco and art moderne building fronts with spare, slick-looking facades and lobbies with exuberant geometric ornamentation. Examples range from the Richfield Building in Los Angeles, whose shiny black facade with gold stripes symbolized the wealth of oil, to the zigzag decoration of Fort Worth's Sinclair Building, to the entire corridor of oil company offices and hotels on South Boston Street in Tulsa.[3]

Big western cities sorted out their people as well as their workplaces. They segregated by race—Chinese and Mexicans increasingly isolated from European Americans. They clustered by ethnicity—Italians here, Norwegians over there, Irish down the hill, Croatians near the factory. They divided by economic status, from skid road to Nob Hill. In between these social extremes, electrically powered cable cars (from the late 1870s) and streetcars (from the 1890s) enabled middle-class families to separate themselves in new neighborhoods three, four, or five miles from crowded city centers.

To find skid row (or *skid road* in the original Seattle terminology), a visitor at the turn of the twentieth century would have headed for the railroad depot and the docks. Western cities were staging points for armies of seasonal workers—harvest hands, railroad construction and maintenance gangs, lumberjacks, and seamen whose work came in the warm months. Men without permanent residence, these workers lived in camps, tents, and bunkhouses for half the year and wintered over in nearby cities. Arriving on a cheap steamer, holding down a seat in an overcrowded railroad coach, or riding the rods to save the fare, they walked into a neighborhood where saloons, cheap hotels, and flophouses occupied two- and three-story walk-ups that more respectable businesses had already discarded in favor of new downtown buildings where elevators served six or eight floors of offices. There was plenty of alcohol on skid row, but these were not yet the exclusive haunts of winos and derelicts that would mark the mid–twentieth century. There was raucous noise from behind the saloon doors but no empty bottles of fortified wine rolling in the gutters. There were also labor agents recruiting for big outfits, employment offices for casual labor, pawnshops, pool halls, cheap theaters, union halls, missions serving a meal for the price of a sermon, and secondhand stores for replacing tools, overalls, and work boots.

Western cities had exceptionally large skid row districts because so much western work was seasonal resource harvesting rather than year-round manufacturing. The first systematic survey by sociologist Donald Bogue utilized 1950 data to discover that five of the ten largest skid rows in the United States were western (San Francisco, Los Angeles, Seattle, Denver, Portland) and another in the top ten was the gateway city of Minneapolis. There is every reason to think that these mid-century numbers reflect the patterns of the previous two generations. In the Northwest, early skid rows swelled after 1898 with the flow and ebb of prospectors heading to the Klondike. All through the West, the depression of 1893 had kicked more men into the marginal workforce, many never to escape (the word *hobo* dates to the 1890s). Most of the districts, like Vancouver's Gastown and Seattle's Pioneer Square, were located for easy access to docks and rail yards for transportation to jobs or cities where the economy might be stronger. Denver's Larimer Street and Portland's Lownsdale and Burnside districts (aka the North End, Whitechapel, or the Tenderloin) also fit the model. Minneapolis and St. Paul recycled outmoded commercial buildings near the Mississippi River. Sacramento's skid row similarly took over the riverfront as the business district moved toward the state capitol. In Los Angeles, Mexican workers made up a large share of the transient workers who hung out in the flats between downtown and Boyle Heights.

Skid rows overlapped vice districts in location and in some of their functions, but they were not identical. The single workers certainly gambled in the card rooms. They patronized the women who sold sex in one-room cribs, brothels, closed boxes at theaters, and the back rooms of saloons, but so did traveling salesmen, local bachelors, and family men out for the night. The immoral trio of alcohol, gambling, and sex was a "social necessity" that maintained a stable society by satisfying men's unstoppable desires without threatening respectable women. Police staged occasional raids, particularly aiming at Chinese businesses, took payoffs, and looked the other way when workingmen's votes helped a local political machine keep office. Portland's first police chief from 1870 to 1883 was also a saloon owner who operated under a separate Board of Police Commissioners that was independent of the mayor. Saloon keeper Edward Chambreau remembered that "the first thing I did when I took charge of this 'Hell Hole' was to fix the policeman on my beat."[4]

On the "other side" of downtown, certainly figuratively and usually literally, new apartment and residential hotel districts housed aspiring white-collar workers—single men, single women, and young families. The white-collar workers who did the grunt work of the paper economy, from processing insurance claims to handling bills of lading, needed to be close to downtown, and their apartment neighborhoods often filled in previously ritzy districts that the bankers and industrialists were now abandoning for greener suburbs. That was the case in Los Angeles, where Bunker Hill filled with boardinghouses and apartments in the 1910s and 1920s; in Dallas, where boardinghouses and apartments pushed into previously upscale East Dallas; and in Denver, where apartments took over Capitol Hill. A flurry of apartment construction in Vancouver's West End drove the city's wealthy to the new Shaughnessy neighborhood in the few years between 1905 and 1913.

Working-class neighborhoods of single-family houses often extended outward from the city center along industrial corridors created by railroad tracks and waterfronts. Land was cheap in these "gritty, humble" neighborhoods, and working-class families often built their own homes, as Emily French tried and failed to do. Family labor could substitute for cash, and materials could be scrounged or purchased a bit at a time while the family lived with and within its building project for months and years from start to finish. Backyard agriculture often supplemented the sweat equity in the

FIGURE 34. Working-class housing in Denver. These small attached houses in the Highlands neighborhood of Denver date from the early decades of the twentieth century and likely housed families whose livelihoods depended on the mills, factories, and rail yards along the South Platte River that bordered the district. (Photograph by the author.)

real estate, with fruit trees and vegetable gardens, rabbits, chickens, goats, and maybe even a cow. Municipal services were limited by neglect from city hall or by choice in independent suburbs. In San Antonio, heavy rains regularly rolled off the limestone hills on the north side of the city to flood the working-class Mexican neighborhoods on the southwest side. Streets went unpaved, and cesspools substituted for sewer connections even as advertisements proclaimed that a Los Angeles community like Home Gardens (or Huntington Park or Compton or South Gate) was a place "where the working man is welcomed and given an even break."[5]

Some of these working-class neighborhoods housed distinct ethnic groups in a manner similar to eastern cities: Scandinavians in Ballard (Seattle), Italians in North Beach (San Francisco), Slavic immigrants in Globeville (Denver). Roughly 10,000 people lived in "Little Mexico," adjacent to downtown Dallas, described in an unpublished Works Progress Administration guide as "a close-packed mass of flimsy, tumbled down frame shanties and 'shotgun' houses threaded by narrow, twisting, unpaved streets."[6] Los Angeles had working-class neighborhoods like South Gate that were all white and others like Belvedere that were heavily Mexican American. As

Mark Wild has convincingly argued, however, the openness and fluidity of fast-growing cities led just as often to "eclectic mixtures of newcomers [who] settled neighborhoods with no dominant ethnic population." Asian immigrants, African Americans, and whites shared Seattle's Central District just south of downtown. The area south of Market Street in San Francisco—to become trendy SoMa in the 1990s—mixed white, black, and Latino. Boyle Heights, on the first high ground east of the Los Angeles River, was Mexican, Japanese, Jewish, and Russian, with these small ethnic groups intermingled so thoroughly that the Federal Writers Project decided that mapping subareas was impossible. The large section of Los Angeles from Central Avenue south to Watts was identifiably African American but shared with Mexicans, Japanese, Italians, and Anglos. They lived in harmony through the 1920s, at least as remembered by people like jazz musician Cecil McNeely, who recalled: "It was complete peace at that time. Spanish, Orientals, and whites. We all went to school together, no problem."[7]

Farther toward the edge of town, socially marginal neighborhoods—half built, self-built, tucked onto undesirable corners and industrial edges—were easy for city officials and tourists to ignore. Until recently rediscovered by historians, they have been the province of novelists and poets. They were places of dogs and chicken coops, run-down houses and sagging shrubbery, heavy drinkers and part-time workers. John Steinbeck's Monterey has "Tortilla Flat," described here for the 1920s:

> Monterey sits on the slope of a hill, with a blue bay below it and with a forest of tall pine trees at its back. The lower parts of the town are inhabited by Americans, Italians, catchers and canners of fish. But on the hill where the forest and the town intermingle, where the streets are innocent of asphalt and the corners free of street lights, the old inhabitants of Monterey. . . . live in old wooden houses set in weedy yards.[8]

Richard Hugo's poems return repeatedly to his childhood in the Duwamish River neighborhoods on Seattle's industrial south side. The narrator in "What Thou Lovest Well, Remains American" describes a remembered cityscape of vacant lots optimistically overplatted in the 1920s, unpaved streets, and roses grown wild between the scattered houses. It was a matter of degree where to mark the distinction between neighborhoods of working-class home owners and neighborhoods for the middle class, but there was an easy rule of thumb: the higher and drier the land, the higher the social status and the more substantial the houses. The rapid development of streetcars let the middle class move out of the crowded center into Bungalow Belts that became a western city trademark. New single-family houses on small lots served a broad "middle" class that ranged from skilled workers to white-collar professionals

FIGURE 35. Middle-class housing in Denver. Bungalows were the ubiquitous housing option for middle-class residents in western cities from Los Angeles to Vancouver to Denver. (Photograph by the author.)

and small proprietors. Their development coincided with increasing social and cultural conservatism as western cities passed into their second or third generation of growth and determined the course of local politics.

The bungalow itself was a specific style of house, imported from colonial India to California, quickly adapted to western landscapes, and spread through the entire region in the first third of the twentieth century. Bungalows usually rose one or one and a half stories, often disguising the second floor with a long, projecting, low-pitched roof.[9] An architect who had recently relocated from California built Boise's first bungalow in 1904; the style caught on quickly as the city boomed in the next few years. Vancouver's bungalow neighborhoods included Kitsilano and Dunbar south of English Bay, often with local variations like half-timbering and curved eaves for an English cottage look. Portlanders built their bungalows from wood, but Denverites used brick and left daylight basements for partial protection from the extremes of the Great Plains climate. White-collar households in Salt Lake City filled the "avenues" to the southeast of Temple Square with bungalows. Albuquerque's equivalent neighborhood rose eastward from downtown toward the University of New Mexico, and Reno's rose southwestward from the city center as described in Walter Van Tilburg Clark's autobiographical novel *City of Trembling Leaves*, where on the south side rises "a high region

FIGURE 36. Middle-class housing in Grand Junction. Grand Junction by the 1910s and 1920s was a far different place than the raw settlement of a generation earlier. Irrigation and hard work had turned raw dirt tracks into shaded streets for the city's middle class of small business owners and professionals. (Courtesy of the Colorado Historical Society [20004422, CHSX4422], all rights reserved.)

of new homes, bungalows, ornamented structures of greater size, a number of which it would be difficult to describe fairly, and white, Spanish houses. This region seems to become steadily more open, windy and sunlit as you move out."[10]

It is easy to view these neighborhoods today because bungalows had modern open floor plans that have stood the test of time—just drive around San Francisco's Sunset District or the environs of Washington Park in Denver, Green Lake in Seattle, Laurelhurst Park in Portland, or the University of Utah in Salt Lake City. You can also visit a well-stocked video store for silent comedies with L.A. neighborhood settings. What you often see on the screen are "Spanish" exteriors to go with the avocado and lemon trees, like the Glendale home of Mildred Pierce in James M. Cain's 1941 novel of the same name. It's

a Spanish bungalow with white walls and red-tile roof. Now Spanish houses are a little outmoded, but at the time [the late 1920s] they were considered high toned. . . . [It had] the standard living room sent out by department stores as suitable for a Spanish bungalow . . . crimson velvet drapes . . . a long oak table holding a lamp with a stained glass shade . . . one table, in a corner, in the Grand Rapids style, and one radio, on this table, in the bakelite style.[11]

Australian scholar Lionel Frost has argued that this sort of low-density neighborhood was characteristic of the "new urban frontier" of the western United States and Canada, southern Australia, and New Zealand. As the centers for rich farming and mining regions, these cities concentrated capital that was available to finance urban services and housing. As cities with high demand for labor and therefore high wages, they also had a population that could afford or at least aspire to single-family houses in new neighborhoods—in contrast to the walk-up slums of New York, London, and Chicago. Melbourne in his analysis is a lot like Los Angeles, Perth a lot like Denver, and Auckland like Vancouver.[12]

In the United States, specific public policy and political decisions followed from the changing city geography. New neighborhoods needed parks and schools. Socially disparate populations needed shareable spaces and symbols of civic unity. The increasing density of downtown workers and shoppers required better transportation. Industrialists wanted more land for factories, while middle-class families wanted to escape noise, dirt, and disreputable people.

Two different versions of middle-class politics emerged from the residential differentiation. One involved populist radicalism that built links between skilled labor and small property owners and proprietors. Members of a reformer/socialist/labor alliance "did not reject the notion of growth as an urban ideal but wanted to extend the benefits of new development into working-class neighborhoods and schools and protect workers from fluctuations in the business cycle."[13] This "radical middle class" was a force to reckon with from the 1880s to the 1910s in cities like Houston, Dallas, and Portland, but its informal alliances were hard put to survive the repression of left-wing voices during World War I, the collapse of the Socialist Party, and antilabor crusades of the 1920s. The alternative approach was solidly middle class. At the neighborhood scale it centered on defense of property and propriety, while at the citywide scale downtown business leaders and newspaper editors looked for issues like transportation improvements and land-use planning that could be understood and sold as benefiting "the city as a whole."[14]

In Portland, for example, the city's well-cultivated image as a conservative and staid city that avoided the social and political extremes of places like Seattle and San Francisco was less a reflection of actual experience than a myth that served the interests of big business and property owners. For the first two decades of the twentieth century, the political operatives who corralled skid row votes and served bankers and utilities faced a deeply rooted populism among small business proprietors, small home owners, and skilled workers, most of whom were residents of the young and fast-developing neighborhoods east of the Willamette River. Like the pieces in a kaleidoscope, different leaders, interest groups, and voters came together in a disparate set of political efforts that were linked by their defense of the right of ordinary citizens to determine their own future.

Portland's radical middle class, as historian Robert Johnston has reconstructed, looks like a curious mix to twenty-first-century eyes. Mayor Harry Lane (1905–9), a penny-pinching moral reformer who went on to serve in the U.S. Senate and resist the American slide into World War I, seems progressive enough on balance. William S. U'Ren, who championed the "Oregon system" of direct democracy through the initiative and referendum processes, still appears in political science texts. Lora Little, however, an east-side housewife who led a fierce grassroots campaign against compulsory smallpox vaccination in the schools, is a harder fit with liberal expectations. Will Daly, a Socialist and small businessman who served on the Portland City Council and nearly won the mayor's office in 1917, demonstrated both the possibility and the frailty of a political alliance among skilled craftsmen, white-collar workers, and home owners.

World War I was the political watershed. It ended Harry Lane's career, and it opened Will Daly to attacks on his previous Socialist membership. George Baker, who defeated Daly in 1917, was a theater impresario and born politician who swayed in the political winds, made the city comfortable for downtown business, and won four terms. Before the war, many residents of the new middle-class neighborhoods had supported the adoption of the commission form of city government in 1913 (to break the power of machine politicians) and had pushed for adoption of the "single tax" on land associated with Henry George (to reduce the power of land-rich corporations and tycoons). In the decade after 1917, many flirted with the Ku Klux Klan and voted for a compulsory *public* education initiative of 1922, which aimed at both the elite and immigrants by banning private schools of all types, whether secular or Roman Catholic.

Politics in Dallas traced a similar trajectory. Populist (1891) and then Socialist (1901) parties had Dallas chapters, which cooperated in shifting coalitions with middle-class reformers and trade unions that were able to challenge or moderate the actions and influence candidate choices of the commercial elite. Socialist and labor candidates could get elected to the School Board and City Council, though not control them. "Dallas radicals emphasized cooperation, education, and the empowerment of producers," and their goals were the "progressive" aims of affordable housing, good public schools, and reliable city services, all issues appealing to skilled trade unionists who were home owners or aspired to ownership.[15] When a Populist and labor activist candidate was in charge of public works, for example, streets got paved in working-class neighborhoods as well as downtown.

The political balance shifted with World War I. The Socialist Party disintegrated in conflicts over pacifism and loyalty during the war, leaving citizens to take their cues from men like George Dealey of the *Dallas Morning News* and other downtown businessmen who simultaneously fought the influence of the revived Ku Klux Klan and advocated citywide planning for efficient growth. The Chamber of Commerce in 1919 created the Dallas Metropolitan Development Association for citywide planning advocacy. Over more than a decade, the civic elite consolidated its control through the Citizens Charter Association, beating back challenges from working-class neighborhoods and from disgruntled politicos labeled the Catfish Club. The outcome was the twenty-year dominance of the Dallas Citizens Council, the embodiment of civic patriotism and business leadership from 1937 to 1957.

The other side of reform politics was moral improvement. On the national scene, the 1920s was a decade when much of the prewar reform seemed to turn sour. Historians have highlighted the fear of southern and eastern European immigrants behind the Red Scare of 1919–20, the rise and fall of the Ku Klux Klan from 1920 to 1925, and negative reforms like Prohibition and immigration restriction. However, middle-class neighborhoods had already become bastions of moral improvement, often by "going dry" through local option. The Dallas suburb of Oak Cliff accepted annexation into Dallas in 1903 only when assured that it could continue to prohibit liquor sales. As saloons crowded into Denver's downtown and clustered around its factories in the booming 1880s, nearly every one of Denver's new suburban neighborhoods went dry. Some prohibited saloons by municipal ordinance, some imposed impossible licensing fees, and some used restrictions in property deeds. With one of the highest ratios of saloons to people in the country (one for every 223 residents according to the 1890 census), Denver's parents worried about bad influences on their children. Montclair established its own school districts so that families could send their teenagers to Montclair High rather than East Denver High, said to be "surrounded by saloons in the center of the city."[16]

Just as middle-class neighborhoods tried to wall off the bustle of downtown and the vice of skid road, outlying or suburban cities could claim superiority to central cities. The Chamber of Commerce of Redlands, in the California Citrus Belt, marketed the city to information seekers with its homes, churches, schools, and absence of saloons. Oakland residents as well as business leaders in the later nineteenth and early twentieth centuries saw the city as a bedroom community and proclaimed theirs a "city of homes" where every dwelling enjoyed "an ever-blooming garden" in contrast to down and dirty San Francisco. Writing in 1911 to the *Oakland Enquirer*, which was fighting a proposal for municipal consolidation with San Francisco, twenty-five-year-old Mona Whalen was enthusiastic about the difference:

> Oakland! Essentially a series of homes, churches, and schools, where good predominates and our boys and girls are shielded from the courser [sic] sights found in a more congested metropolis. Oakland! The City Beautiful. . . . So Oakland, think well before you give over your civic rights to a city that is known as the "toughest town on the Pacific Coast." Think of your open ways and streets, think of your freedom from crime and THINK OF YOUR BOYS AND GIRLS.[17]

The morally mobilized middle class also led new campaigns against the sex business in the years around 1910, when Americans were enthusiastically taking to reforms of all sorts. A national panic about the "white slave" trade and fear that crime syndicates were taking over the sex trade led to the Mann Act of 1910, which attacked the supposed prostitution industry via the interstate commerce clause. New understanding that even "cured" men could transmit venereal diseases to their wives also cued vigorous vice campaigns. Portland's Lola Baldwin, one of the nation's first policewomen, tried to rescue local girls from immorality and worked with federal authorities to arrest and deport Japanese, Chinese, and Russian women. Mayor Harry Lane, whom we've already met, was a physician and social hygiene expert who shared the moral absolutism of his supporters in new middle-class neighborhoods and fired the entire vice squad for corruption. Portland clergy, physicians, social workers, and Women's Union members soon organized a Vice Commission, which operated 1911–12 with $3,000 from the city treasury. Its 1912 report investigated 547 suspect locations (apartments, hotels, rooming and lodging houses). Only 116 made the grade as moral or doubtful, compared to 194 where immorality was countenanced or ignored, 124 where immoral tenants were desired or preferred, and 113 wholly given up to prostitution or assignation.

Vice crusades were one small part of comprehensive efforts to make western cities "work" better through systematic provision of public facilities and systematic planning of land uses—especially to buffer middle-class neighborhoods from the intrusion of unwanted people (residents of low-rent apartments) and activities (factories, saloons, and shops that might cater to riffraff). The first step was often to bring in a nationally known planner to prepare a citywide plan for parks and parkways, which had the advantage of serving the full social spectrum by offering healthy recreation to keep working-class children off the streets in addition to places for Sunday pleasure drives for the refined classes. Seattle and Portland brought in Boston's John C. Olmsted for parks plans, and Oakland brought in Charles Mulford Robinson, the nation's leading advocate of "civic art," in 1906. Denver's Mayor Robert Speer (1904–12,

1916–18) expanded his city's parks and boulevards according to his own vision of Greater Denver and doggedly pursued the goal of a grand civic center surrounded by public buildings—now realized with the classic state capitol and adventuresome buildings by architectural stars Michael Graves (public library), Gio Ponti (art museum), and Daniel Libeskind (art museum expansion).

In some cities, redesigned civic centers were only one element in comprehensive "city beautiful" plans. Examples are the plan that Chicago architect Daniel Burnham and his colleague Edward Bennett prepared for San Francisco (1906), Virgil Bogue's "Plan of Seattle" (1911), Bennett's "Greater Portland Plan" (1912), George Kessler's "City Plan for Dallas" (1912), and Thomas Mawson's plan to turn Vancouver's Georgia Street into the Champs-Élysées and Stanley Park into the Tuileries.[18] The term *city beautiful* has stuck to these plans for three reasons: their ties with the civic improvement and beautification movements, their roots in monumental planning for world's fair sites and Washington, D.C., and their maps and drawings that could make an ordinary U.S. city look like a future Vienna or Paris. In fact, Burnham's plan for San Francisco and Bennett's for Portland were among the first comprehensive metropolitan plans. Their authors hoped to improve the functionality of the center through rationalized division of activities and improvement of transportation, and they tried to order the following elements of the entire metropolis: ports and railroad terminals, industrial districts, major streets including new radial and circumferential highways, civic spaces and sites for public buildings, and parks. In Burnham's influential opinion, the challenge was to plan and design for whole cities.

The problem with comprehensive plans was unrealistic ambition. Burnham's San Francisco plan never had a chance. Delivered days before the great earthquake and fire, it sat on the shelf when property owners rushed to rebuild on preexisting lots and streets. The city's Civic Center is one of the few specific developments that can be traced to Burnham's work. Portlanders received Bennett's plan with great enthusiasm, but the onset of a steep economic recession followed by an equally abrupt economic boom in 1917–18 made it infeasible to consider the huge public investments that it called for. Seattle turned a cold shoulder to a similar plan because its long list of public improvements challenged the city budget.

In the 1920s, cities turned instead to land-use zoning as the best tool to manage growth. Los Angeles had pioneered zoning in 1908 when the city designated several districts for industrial development in order to protect residential areas (although New York's 1916 measure was the first multiuse zoning system). As advised by Californian Charles Cheney and other consultants, cities divided their land into industrial, commercial, apartment, and single-family home zones. In the ideal result, factories could operate in industrial zones without offending neighbors, while home owners could rest secure that unwanted activities would not mar their neighborhood. Real estate investors

ARMSTRONG PARKWAY—HIGHLAND PARK WEST

FIGURE 37. Armstrong Parkway, Dallas. In the mid-1920s, Armstrong Parkway was an elegant feature of the upscale Highland Park development on the north side of Dallas, an example of the ability of western cities to compare favorably with their eastern counterparts.

and home owners both liked the stability that zoning offered. Women's organizations, as Lee Simpson has documented, were also strong supporters of the economic and social benefits of zoning. Oakland's Chamber of Commerce worked closely with Mills College president Aurelia Henry Reinhardt in the 1910s and backed her selection as chair of the Oakland Planning Commission. Speaking to business groups and women's clubs from Ukiah to Los Angeles, Reinhardt sold Oakland just like she sold her college and saw the benefits of public planning for protecting a city of homes.

Part and parcel with parks and planning, which were seen as necessary elements of sober and stable cities, were public celebrations of maturity that ranged from pageants to festivals to world's fairs. Lots of small communities had fairs and festivals to help sell their local products—Watermelon Day in Rocky Ford, Colorado, for example. Larger western cities took up the same habit, in part to zip up business in the down years of the 1890s but also to polish their image as attractive, successful, and well-managed communities. Denver's Festival of Mountain and Plain in 1895 was to attract tourists and blazon forth "the characteristic broad-gauge nature of the people and the wonderful resources and possibilities of the State." Parades of citizens and cyclists took up much of the three-day affair, along with band contests and rock-drilling contests. Phoenix started a Cowboy and Indian Carnival in 1896, featuring Navaho, Pima, and Apache crafts and mock battles: "Cowboys chased Indians while other Indians chased stagecoaches, all in the most colorful style possible."[19]

La Fiesta de Los Angeles, held from 1894 through 1897, had a similar impetus of kick-starting southern California's recovery from the Panic of 1893

FIGURE 38. Omaha park scene. In the early twentieth century, Omaha was a mature city with a wide range of amenities for its comfortable middle class. Parks were one of the features with which cities from Dallas to San Francisco demonstrated their standard of comfortable living. (Omaha Public Library.)

and the collapse of the real estate boom but also served, in William Deverell's telling phrase, to "whitewash" California's Mexican past. The fiesta romanticized old Spanish California while decisively labeling it "history." Each of the grand parades demonstrated the supposed progress of history, starting with Indians, following with Franciscan friars and Mexican rancheros, and ending with up-to-date English-speaking Protestant Angelenos. When the Spanish–American War complicated the task of celebrating American urban progress with references to a Spanish past, the event went on the shelf. But the message had been clear: Chinese and Mexicans were quaint and curious, but the future belonged to the tens of thousands of Middle Americans who had flocked to the city from the Middle West.

Novelist Carl Jonas has described something very similar for "Gateway City," his thinly fictionalized version of Omaha. Sometime near the turn of the century, Gateway City's businessmen had organized Yaw-Et-Ag ("ingeniously constructed from Gateway spelled backward") as a service organization and promotional enterprise. In this supposed city, the Yaw-Et-Ag members were braves and squaws. They were responsible for putting through the bond issue that built a new sewage plant, staged the annual stock and horse show, and constructed "the magnificent coliseum also in Yaw-Et-Ag Park which is generally known as the Teepee." And, not least, they held the annual Powwow as a harvest celebration complete with parades and princesses. As one character proudly says, "The Powwow held each autumn by Yaw-Et-Ag has been called a mammoth promotion stunt for Gateway City, but, while it does bring in business, the description is completely inadequate unless you call Mardi Gras in New Orleans nothing but a promotion stunt also."[20]

Denver suspended its Festival of Mountain and Plain after 1901, turning its attention to other ways to demonstrate its maturity and unity (a touchy subject given the state's ongoing labor wars).[21] With the help of a $100,000 guarantee, Denver businessmen persuaded the Democratic Party to inaugurate its new city auditorium with the 1908 national convention. The *Post* and *News* squeezed every possible drop of favorable comment. Thousands of Denverites wore badges reading "I Live in Denver—Ask Me." Delegates not adequately entertained by politics or alcohol could watch imported Apaches perform war dances or make snowballs from carloads of mountain snow. The purpose of the convention was accomplished when delegates had emptied their pockets and eastern correspondents had written glowing dispatches.

Omaha and Portland had already staged successful world's fairs: Omaha's challenge behind the Trans-Mississippi Exposition (1898) was the spectacular failure of Great Plains agriculture during the recent drought years. Taking the bull by the horns, the Omaha fair had three separate cattle exhibits (Omaha was the third-largest meatpacking center in the world) as well as exhibits touting scientific agriculture and land-grant colleges. Indians from twenty-three tribes participated in ethnographic exhibits and mock battles with whites that were viewed by tens of thousands of visitors including President William McKinley. If Indians were programmed to be losers in Omaha, they were scarcely to be seen except in statuary at Portland's Lewis and Clark Centennial Exposition seven years later. Like Omaha's fair, the Lewis and Clark Exposition ran in the black and impressed eastern visitors. "The enterprise has from the beginning been managed with modesty, good sense, and good taste," Walter Hines Page told the readers of *World's Work*—music to the ears of Portland's civic elite with its New England heritage.[22] Still to come were fairs in Seattle (1909), San Francisco (1915), and San Diego, whose Panama–California Exposition (1915) took place in the new Balboa Park in a set of Mediterranean fantasia buildings that appropriated the California past for business purposes.

To use a modern phrase, all of these community events stayed "on message." These were cities where everyone pulled together (even when labor unions fought world's fair management of construction wages). Everything was up to date, comfortable, and inviting for visitors and investors (and real estate would never be cheaper). These were white people's cities, and the Indians and Mexicans who had preceded Anglo-Americans were now colorful, friendly, or safely vanishing—a trope that obviously ignored the people of the many skid rows and tortilla flats. This said, it is possible to be overly harsh in retrospect. The festivals and fairs celebrated and confirmed the values of bourgeois communities, which is the best single way to describe places like Portland, Omaha, Victoria, Vancouver, Dallas, and Denver in the early twentieth century.

CHAPTER NINE

Water, Power, Progress

Seven hundred feet below streamed what was left of the original river, the greenish waters that emerged, through intake, penstock, turbine and tunnel, from the powerhouse at the base of the dam. Thickets of power cables, each strand as big around as a man's arm, climbed the canyon walls on steel towers, merged in a haze of transformer stations, then splayed out toward the south and west—toward Albuquerque, Babylon, Phoenix, Gomorrah, Los Angeles, Sodom, Las Vegas, Nineveh, Tucson, and the cities of the plain.

—Edward Abbey, *The Monkey Wrench Gang* (1975)

It was money and politics for Dominic. He was aiming to be governor, but he wanted to be mayor first. He wanted to bring in casino gambling and build a Venice on the Rio Grande. . . . Dominic had cooked up a big urban enhancement project. Canals full of Rio Grande water. Casinos. A Disneyland on the river.

—Rudolfo Anaya, *Alburquerque* (1992)

Rudolfo Anaya's novel *Alburquerque* imagines a political contest in a city divided between a disgruntled old guard and a dynamic Hispanic incumbent popular in the neighborhoods. Frank Dominic tries to capture the mayoral election with a bold scheme to "rebrand" Albuquerque as a destination resort. He wants to promise jobs for the Hispanic barrio, cachet for the North Valley yuppies in their adobe-style houses, development opportunities for the real estate industry, and attractions for tourists. The solution: Acquire rural water rights and divert the Rio Grande through downtown in a series of canals and lagoons to create scores of waterside building lots for condos, office buildings, a casino, hotels, and a performing arts center. "The hell with the rest of the state," thinks Dominic. Albuquerque can be Santa Fe and Las Vegas both. The meeting to roll out the scheme is well attended:

> Pete Lupkins, one of the most respected architects in the city. . . . removed the cover from the scale model at the front of the room. The audience leaned forward, and what they saw made them gasp. The pattern of the city was clear, but there were new buildings rising where none now existed. Throughout the city ran the canal system, paths of blue. The Albuquerque of the year 2000. A desert Venice with beltways of green, ponds, and small lakes, all interconnected by waterways that crisscrossed the downtown area.[1]

If it were reality rather than fiction, the "El Dorado" plan for Albuquerque would not stand alone. Tucson in the 1990s considered refilling the dry bed of the Santa Cruz River to revitalize downtown. Other Arizonans have successfully promoted development of the amazingly named Scottsdale Waterfront, where flats, shops, and the Fiesta Bowl Museum will hug the bank of the Arizona Canal as it channels irrigation water along the north side of the Valley of the Sun. In Las Vegas, of course, tourists at the Venetian can enjoy $15 gondola rides "beneath bridges, beside cafes, under balconies and through the vibrant Venetian streetscape."[2]

Fair enough, but Anaya's inspiration was likely the San Antonio River Walk. A Works Progress Administration project at its inception in 1939, the original goal was to combine canalization and flood control with the development of a park that could host festivals ("Venetian night" was one of the first!) and offer cool relief from the South Texas climate. The initial project has been extended several times, and hotels and restaurants started to open basement-level entrances and terraces onto the riverfront sidewalks in the 1960s. Taking cues from New Orleans and Carmel, investors and city leaders transformed River Walk into an early theme park with tacos, tourist barges, mariachi bands, and, since 1988, the built-from-scratch festival marketplace Rivercenter. Three hundred miles away, an artificial canal wends through the commercial center of the carefully planned town the Woodlands (outside Houston) and passes under a bridge copied from San Antonio.

And then there are echoes too of Venice Beach, built on marshy California dunes south of Santa Monica. Abbot Kinney, an eastern industrialist turned southern California conservationist and investor, carved out ocean-side canals and lagoons, put up commercial buildings in Venetian Renaissance style, imported gondolas, opened an amusement pier, and put thousands of building lots on the market on Fourth of July weekend, 1905. Ten thousand Venetians by 1920 lived along the canals and back streets, while tourists and weekenders flocked to the oceanfront amusements. Within a decade, however, the municipal government began to fill canals to accommodate automobiles, and sightseers competed with roustabouts who tended oil wells, "marching in from the east like the broomstick in *The Sorcerer's Apprentice,* surrounding the town, besieging the placid lagoons and glittering canals."[3] By mid-century the town was down at the heels, its pawnshops and bikers awaiting the arrival of avant-garde painters in the 1950s, hippies in the 1960s, sidewalk artists in the 1970s, in-line skaters in the 1980s, and housing gentrifiers along the remaining canals in the 1990s.[4]

Venice Beach in turn is married with the gated golf course developments of Palm Springs in the imagination of novelist Thomas Pynchon. *The Crying of Lot 49* (1966) is Pynchon's headlong rush through 1960s California. The Fangoso Lagoons subdivision was city as theme park long before cultural critics adopted the metaphor.[5] Fangoso "was to be laced by canals with private landings for power boats, a floating social hall in the middle of an artificial lake, at the bottom of which lay restored galleons, imported from the Bahamas . . . real human skeletons from Italy; giant clamshells from Indonesia—all for the entertainment of Scuba enthusiasts."[6]

But hold on, we're still not done with Venice. Leslie Marmon Silko created her own version in her sprawling, semifantastic novel *Almanac of the Dead* (1991). Leah Blue, wife of a Mafia king who has semiretired from New Jersey to Tucson, wheels and deals in real estate. Her big development will be Venice, Arizona, where canals will link a chain of lakeside neighborhoods, and the whole scheme will require an astounding amount of water. Leah plans to rely on wells run deep into an already depleted aquifer with surplus oil rigs from Texas. All she needs is for a pliable federal judge to dismiss an Indian water rights claim in Nevada and she'll have the legal precedent she needs. The judge is happy to offer a favor to his golf buddy Max Blue: "Arne believed in states' rights, absolutely. Indians could file lawsuits until hell and their reservation froze over, and Arne wasn't going to issue any restraining orders against Leah's deep wells either. Max could depend on that."[7]

Silko moves our excursion through aquatic fantasies from the satirical to the sobering. Water in the urban West is about progress as measured in nineteenth-century terms as economic development and growth. It is also power. To control water is to determine the value of real estate and the future of industries—vital choices in a region where every city has been a land speculation. Water is also power in the literal form of electricity, for western cities depend heavily on hydroelectric dams to light their streets and computer screens. In seeking both sorts of power, residents of western cities have reached far into their hinterlands and remade distant landscapes in their own interests. For many Westerners, such efforts were another manifestation of the progressive impulse to political reform, social betterment, and comprehensive planning.

When something is scarce, it's valuable. When it's valuable, it's corruptible, a truth that drives the screenplay for the great film *Chinatown* (1974) and moves our discussion to the most famous episode of North American water politics—the acquisition of Owens River stream flow for Los Angeles.

In brief outline, Los Angeles was located originally to use the Los Angeles River, which drained the San Fernando Valley and made its way to the Pacific through what are now Burbank, Glendale, and Los Angeles. As the Anglo-American city grew on the foundations of Mexican Los Angeles, a private water company replaced the earlier system of communal management in 1868, only to be bought out in turn by the city in 1902 and placed under the management of the Los Angeles Board of Water Commissioners. Mexican law, confirmed by U.S. courts, gave the city rights to the entire flow of the river, and the Water Board quickly moved to more efficient use. It built infiltration galleries to catch underground flow and installed meters that halved per-capita consumption. Realizing (or hoping) that the city would soon outgrow conservation measures, the Water Board turned to the Owens Valley, 200 miles north and east on the far slope of the Sierra Nevada. Against local opposition from farmers and ranchers, the city bought up water rights, secured a right-of-way for an aqueduct with the help of Congress and President Theodore Roosevelt, and passed a bond measure for construction by a ten to one margin.[8]

Completed in 1913, the 225-mile pipeline delivered four times the flow of the Los Angeles River. With southern California still growing, the Water Board in the 1920s quietly bought out Owens Valley irrigation ditches that supplied individual ranchers, triggering acts of armed resistance and sabotage (one might call it ecoterrorism if the actors had not been landowners). In the eventual settlement that dragged through the legislature and courts, Los Angeles bought out most of the valley's rural and town property at 1929 prices during the early years of the depression. The city provided water only within its legal boundaries, leading to the annexation of 250 square miles including the San Fernando Valley. In the result, Owens Valley water initially served Los Angeles agriculture as well as domestic and industrial needs until subdivisions replaced orange groves. At the end of the 1930s, southern California reached out again to the Mono Basin north of Owens Valley and to the Colorado River, now acting through the Metropolitan Water District of Southern California, formed in 1928 by Los Angeles, Pasadena, Long Beach, San Diego, and other municipalities.[9]

Scholars and scriptwriters have long treated the story as a moral parable. City slickers from Los Angeles buy up water rights without explaining their intentions, springing the truth on the valley people after it is too late. Ranchers lament the loss of a way of life, and small towns wither along with agriculture. Efforts to resist the juggernaut, even to the point of dynamiting the big pipe, are futile. The whole scheme is a cynical effort to shift land values by taking water from some acreage and piping it to other acreage, impoverishing virtuous people of the soil to enrich city speculators. Los Angeles destroys an upright community in order to support city neighborhoods that are full of shallow Valley girls at best and gangbangers at worst. Only the intervention of the courts eventually forces Los Angeles to admit its errors and undertake expensive environmental restoration.

There are, of course, some problems with the moral understanding. Los Angeles water officials were sneaky and arrogant, but several leaders of the local resistance were crooks. Los Angeles may have been shrewd in buying water rights, but it purchased something that Owens Valley residents had themselves transformed into a market commodity. Owens Valley people had already manipulated the water through irrigation systems, so Los Angeles did not acquire and pervert something that was purely "natural." Left unanswered is the question of how far water can legitimately be diverted: one mile? ten miles? 200 miles? The story also assumes that some agricultural products (cattle) are more virtuous than others (oranges) and that the production of market commodities is superior to aesthetic uses like flower gardens. There is a strong assumption that it is "unnatural" to live in Los Angeles, but is it any more natural to impose Euro-American agriculture on a semiarid landscape only a mountain range away from Death Valley?[10]

In fact, the more sinful episode in water policy had occurred much earlier. The first L.A. water system consisted of open ditches or *zanjas* that channeled water from the river to small farms. Capture of the zanja system from Mexican Angelenos in the 1860s and 1870s was not a market transaction but an act of culturally biased political power. Mexicans had treated the canals as a communal service maintained for irrigation, domestic water, and waste disposal. In 1873, however, the Anglophone Americans who now ran the city began to replace the open ditches with pipes and conduits that separated potable water, irrigation water, and sewage. There were good reasons of public health and efficiency to move from ditches to pipes. However, nearly all of the sewers built in the next twenty years served white residents but not Mexican American and Chinese neighborhoods. As David Torres-Rouff writes, "The decision . . . created a continuing problem because it produced and reinforced stereotypes of Mexicans and Chinese as dirty and diseased. . . . The initiation of a new public service that was distributed unequally meant that discrimination would be built into the pipes and embedded into the city's foundation."[11]

In the same years that the L.A. Water Board mounted its initial forays into the Owens Valley, a second moral drama played out over another California valley. This was Hetch Hetchy, a deep glaciated rift in the Sierra Nevada that was added to Yosemite National Park in 1890. Engineers thought the narrow entrance was a perfect site for a high dam to store water for San Francisco. The city, especially in the person of Mayor James Phelan, a successful businessman and progressive reformer, thought this a great idea for a metropolis outgrowing its current water sources. Wait! said the eloquent John Muir, the prophet of wilderness. Hetch Hetchy was as beautiful as the Yosemite Valley itself. To drown the scenery would be desecration. In many accounts, the ensuing political contest was wilderness against expediency, beauty against urban greed. San Francisco mobilized its political clout in Washington and won passage of the Raker Act in 1913, gaining the right, with restrictions, to develop the valley for water and power. The city proceeded to build O'Shaughnessy Dam (1923) and turn the green chasm into a wasteland, but the fight gave the environmental movement one of its founding myths. The battle reverberates as a defining moment at which the American conservation movement added aesthetic and spiritual arguments about wilderness to the practical goals of Progressive-era forest and park protection.

When examined in detail, most recently by Robert Righter, the story is again more complex. It is certainly true that San Francisco had closer and less controversial sources for water (some of which Oakland and other East Bay cities decided to use) and that the struggle to use Hetch Hetchy took on its own momentum in excess of its basic value. It is also true that "the politicians of San Francisco, with wealth, power, and sympathy engendered by the 1906 earthquake and fire" had the clout to bend the outcome in their favor.[12] However, Hetch Hetchy preservationists lived in an era dedicated to getting more Americans outdoors as hikers, campers, anglers, and hunters as well as nature lovers. They wanted active and intense recreation with hotels, roads, and winter sports, not pristine wilderness. Moreover, San Francisco needed electricity as well as water—electricity that would be publicly owned rather than monopolized by a rapacious corporation (Muir and Hetch Hetchy protectors could never shake the suspicion that they were pawns of Pacific Gas and Electric).

The San Francisco and Los Angeles stories epitomize the physical appropriation of the empty West by the urban West. Cities have claimed natural landscapes both for old purposes (stands of timber for construction) and for new uses (deserts and salt caves for nuclear waste repositories). Taking claims together, city people utilize outlying lands and resources to stoke and serve the urban metabolism.[13] Like a living organism, metropolitan areas take in energy and feedstocks and cast off waste products. Cities reach into the countryside for wood, gravel, sand, and other building materials, for natural gas, distilled petroleum, and electricity. Water flows through kitchen faucets, fire hydrants, and factory valves because feats of engineering are matched with creative institutional arrangements. Municipalities purchase private water rights, legislatures allocate water supplies, and a variety of public entities direct the purchase or regulation of watersheds. At the other end of the cycle, cities cast particulates and chemicals into the sky, drain lawn fertilizer and street residues into streams, and ship garbage and rubble to leased or purchased landfills that may be hundreds of miles distant.

Most obviously on the landscape, cities need water for household use, for fire protection, for industry, for the adornment of green lawns and parks, and for the power that can be tapped by dams and turbines. Every large North American city has reached into its hinterland for water since Philadelphia built the first steam-powered municipal waterworks on the Schuylkill River in 1822 and New York tapped the Croton watershed of Westchester County in 1842. In the vast expanses of the West, however, reliable supplies have been harder to find, and cities have reached farther and perhaps more vigorously through state regulation and purchase of water rights. The environmental impacts have frequently been inescapable as western cities in the later nineteenth and twentieth centuries gained control over western places as well as products. They stoked urban and industrial development by controlling streams and altering distant landscapes for hydroelectric power. What initially were claims on single watersheds evolved in the twentieth century into vast regional systems like those of San Francisco and Los Angeles.

Metropolitan centers think about water differently than irrigation cities. When water is used for irrigation, the preference is to run it as directly and quickly as possible from natural streams to farms and orchards to prevent evaporative loss and to keep down costs for farmers with little spare capital. The result, as described in chapter 5, was modest cities sitting in single valleys or basins. Regional capitals, in contrast, with growing industries and booming populations, felt no such restraints. Their leaders had the ambition and financial capacity to reach deep into high mountains with increasingly elaborate engineering and eventually to divert water over natural barriers. To this basic challenge of getting enough water from a distance, cities have added other claims on their regional waterscapes. They have claimed "surplus" flow to generate power for urban consumption, they have made the landscape more accommodating by filling waterfronts and hosing down hills, and they have engineered their own environs to cope (not always successfully) with uneven flows and floods.

California's two urban superstars were not the only western cities to outgrow their initial reliance on local streams at the close of the nineteenth century. With growing populations and growing industries, cities typically needed to scale up both geographically and institutionally about a generation into their development. To find an adequate volume of clean water they reached farther and farther upstream and more and more deeply into mountains. To build the necessary dams, aqueducts, and distributing reservoirs required more capital than private companies could raise, leading to public water boards and water commissions that could levy property taxes.

Portland, as a typical example, had started with water from a small creek in the hills west of town and then used water pumped from the Willamette about ten miles upstream from the city. With supply increasingly strained and the river increasingly polluted, the Oregon legislature in 1885 authorized the city to issue bonds to buy out the private company. The early water commissioners, whose names were a who's who of business leaders, selected the Bull Run River, fifty miles away on the snowy and rainy northwest side of Mount Hood. The new water flowed through Portland taps and hydrants on New Year's Day, 1895. The city also convinced Congress to prohibit logging in the Bull Run watershed to preserve water quality, avoiding one of the problems that was to plague Seattle's use of the Cedar River as its main supply.

To the north, the new, fast-growing city of Vancouver bought water from a private company that in 1888 impounded the Capilano River, which falls precipitously into Burrard Inlet from the north. The firm piped the water under First Narrows and through Stanley Park to city users. Five years later, the city bought out the company and in 1910 added a dam on the Seymour River and a pipeline under Second Narrows. At the end of the 1920s, municipal systems consolidated as the Greater Vancouver Water District, but the sources of supply have remained the lakes and rivers on the immediate northern edge of the metropolis.

Cities on the Northwest Coast had it easy, but not a High Plains metropolis like Denver, whose water history started out like Portland's but diverged a third of the way into the twentieth century with increasingly expensive and complex systems. In 1870, the Denver City Water Company sold water straight from a downtown pumping station on the South Platte River. The company reached two miles upriver in 1878, but when booming growth taxed supplies, a rival company formed in 1889 to tap the river at the mouth of South Platte Canyon. Lucky householders briefly enjoyed a rate war in which the competitors sometimes delivered water for free. The depression of 1893, however, forced consolidation as the Denver Union Water Company, which built Cheesman Dam on the South Platte in 1905.

Because the South Platte could never rival Northwest rivers in volume and reliability of flow, the Denver Water Board (which replaced the Union Water Company in 1918 but left the same business tycoons and engineers in charge) ran a pipeline through the test bore for the Moffat Railroad Tunnel that pierced the Front Range of the Rockies. Although the West Slope water doubled the city's supply after 1936, postwar growth and dry years in the early 1950s led to water restrictions that included a notorious "blue line" beyond which no new hookups were allowed. The solution was more water diverted from the west-flowing tributaries of the Colorado River by means of Dillon Reservoir and the twenty-three-mile Roberts Tunnel to the South Platte. The Fryingpan-Arkansas Project, another water transfer under the Continental Divide similarly furnished water for Pueblo and Colorado Springs. By the end of the twentieth century, there were eight separate water diversions from the Colorado River into the valley of the South Platte River and eight more from the Colorado drainage basin into the Arkansas River Valley. There has been a steady shift from farm to city uses. In 1960, only 15 percent of the Colorado–Big Thompson Project water went to urban uses, but the share was up to 50 percent by 2000. The Denver suburb of Aurora, a relative newcomer to water prospecting, was buying and leasing water from Arkansas River Valley farmers, using the water to wash suburban automobiles rather than to plump up Rocky Ford cantaloupes. On the positive side, Aurora now helps farmers adopt more water-efficient practices like drip irrigation to free water for the city without shutting down agriculture.

Something similar happened in Arizona. Fifty years after Los Angeles monopolized water from Inyo County, Phoenix accomplished a similar capture of agricultural water through negotiation with the Salt River Project. They reached agreement in 1952 that the city would pay the reclamation assessments for all land within city limits that was subdivided. In return, the city received the right to water that had previously gone to farmers. Because even the most lush suburban lawns take less water than cotton fields in the desert, the city gained a surplus that grew with every subdivision and every annexation of land served by the Salt River Project. By 2003, 65 percent of Salt River Project water use was urban.

Cities use water as water, and they use the energy of falling water for electricity. Every time I drive from my Dee, Oregon, cabin to McIsaac's store at Parkdale (perhaps for some PVC joints to repair my garden irrigation), I pass under a column of high-voltage transmission lines. They stride over the landscape like the Martian invaders in *The War of the Worlds*. Taking power from Columbia River dams, they march over Bald Butte on the east side of the Hood River Valley, down and through five miles of orchards, up and over the northern shoulder of Mount Hood, down the upper reaches of the Sandy River (Lewis and Clark's Quicksand River, shortened for booster purposes), and on into Portland. Crisscrossing the Northwest landscape, transmission lines are so common as to fade into the background, but they are powerful testimony to the way that western cities have claimed water for generating turbines as well as lawn sprinklers.

To reach back to the Hetch Hetchy story, the alternative to San Francisco's public water and power project was not wild nature everywhere preserved but, rather, private dams for private profit. An example is Great Western Power, a San Francisco–based corporation that tapped eastern capital to dam the Feather River. The company bought up land and water rights and secured a court decision in 1912 to compel sales from reluctant property owners. As Jessica Teisch has noted, the Superior Court of Plumas County found that the generation of artificial power was in the public interest and "thus cemented the supremacy of urban growth over the local economic welfare and the generation of electricity over agricultural activities."[14] In 1914, Big Meadows became Lake Almanor, and Great Western was sending power to Oakland over a 165-mile transmission line strung on steel towers and thence on to San Francisco by cables under the bay (lighting the state capitol in Sacramento along the way). The company was one of six corporate giants that together owned 90 percent of California hydropower and turned the torrents of the Sierra Nevada into urban resources.

The 1930s brought new and bigger dams on some of the West's largest rivers, this time depending on the power of the federal government to assemble the capital and resources. Congress had authorized a dam at Black Canyon on the Colorado in 1928, but the timing of construction made Boulder (now Hoover) Dam a depression-era public works project. The erection of a wedge of concrete in blazing heat that vibrated between canyon walls captured the national imagination. The project gave the Bureau of Reclamation its first large multipurpose dam designed for hydropower as well as irrigation and helped to light Las Vegas neon and Hollywood soundstages.

Grand Coulee Dam on the Columbia River, funded initially by the Public Works Administration in 1933 and finished in 1941, took shape as a project to benefit agriculture. Its biggest boosters were irrigation advocates in the small cities of eastern Washington. The dam's most effective publicist was Woody Guthrie, hired by federal officials in 1941 to sing the praises of Grand Coulee Dam and Bonneville Dam (1938). Guthrie called Grand Coulee "the greatest thing ever done by a man," and he emphasized its rural effects in "Pastures of Plenty" and "Half a Mile from the End of the Line" (that's the electric power line in the decade of the Rural Electrification Act).[15]

However, Grand Coulee and Bonneville had their greatest effects on urban growth, not farming. Congress established the Bonneville Power Administration (BPA) in 1939 to market Columbia River power and finesse competition between Portland and Seattle. The BPA's choice was a grid of power lines connecting Spokane, Portland, and Seattle in a great triangle with essentially equal price service. The decision favored established cities at the expense of new industry near the dams (the possible result if the price of power had risen with distance). When war came in the 1940s, BPA power stoked aluminum production in and near Portland and aircraft manufacturing in Seattle.

The dam-building era in the West lasted into the 1960s, muddling the neat periodization that takes World War II as the dividing event. Vancouver reached 500 miles across the Rockies to draw the largest portion of its electricity from hydroelectric plants on the Peace River in northern British Columbia, tapping its energy early on its journey to the Arctic Ocean. Winnipeg reached a comparable distance to hydro facilities that harnessed the power of the Nelson River before it emptied into Hudson Bay. More than a dozen additional dams rose on the headwaters of the Columbia in the United States and Canada, on its Snake and Willamette River tributaries, and on its main stem. Together they make it possible for the three states of the U.S. Northwest (Washington, Idaho, Oregon) to take two-thirds of their total electricity from falling water. In the Southwest the Bureau of Reclamation finished Glen Canyon Dam on the Colorado River in 1962, inspiring Edward Abbey's fierce and funny novel *The Monkey Wrench Gang* (1975) about efforts to derail the operations of massive energy-production projects.

As the plotline in *The Monkey Wrench Gang* informs its readers, western city folks also powered up their all-electric houses with the help of far-distant

FIGURE 39. Bonneville Dam. The first of many federal hydroelectric and navigation dams on the Columbia River, Bonneville Dam spans the Columbia Gorge forty miles east of Portland. Its construction triggered intense debate over how and where to use its cheap electricity. The upshot was a new federal agency, the Bonneville Power Administration, to distribute the power of Bonneville and Grand Coulee dams evenhandedly among Portland, Seattle, and Spokane. (Oregon Historical Society, Neg. 92822.)

strip mines and coal-burning power plants. A lot of Wyoming has gone up in smoke on behalf of light bulbs and electric stoves. Portland draws power from Wyoming coal burned at Boardman, Oregon, 200 miles east of the city. Wyoming coal in the early twenty-first century stoked the Laramie River Station at Wheatland to light the street lamps of Sioux Falls and drive the computers of students at the University of Nebraska–Lincoln, both 400 miles away. Carried by huge trains that stretched miles across the landscape, it was also the fuel for the steam plants that kept the traffic lights cycling red and green in Dallas, Houston, and Austin.

The dry plains of eastern Wyoming may be forgettable territory to most Americans, but not so the deserts and mesas of Navajo Country where Abbey set his novel. Everyone knows the landscape of Monument Valley from count-less western movies, but not far away—just beyond the dusty town of Kayenta and across Route 160—Peabody Coal opened a huge strip-mining opera-tion on Black Mesa in the early 1970s. Black Mesa coal powered the Navajo Generating Station at Page, Arizona, which in turn shipped electric power 250 miles to Phoenix and 450 miles to Los Angeles. Coal-burning power plants on the Colorado Plateau belched out three-quarters of Phoenix electricity by 1975 to run air conditioners and high-tech factories, keeping Phoenix smoke free but not the Navajo homeland. Carried in a 270-mile-long slurry pipeline, Black Mesa coal also fired the generators at the Mojave Generating Station at Laughlin, Nevada (1971–2005), a mere 200 miles from Los Angeles. As his characters are deciding how best to foul up the works, Abbey includes both a concise summary of the operation and an extended jeremiad:

> All this fantastic effort—giant machines, road networks, strip mines, conveyor belts, pipelines, slurry lines, loading towers, railway and electric train, hundred-million-dollar coal-burning power plant . . . for what? All that for what? Why to light the lamps of Phoenix suburbs not yet built, to run the air conditioners of San Diego and Los Angeles, to illuminate shopping center parking lots at two in the morning . . . to keep alive that phosphorescent putrefying glory (all the glory there is left) called Down Town, Night Time, Wonderville, U.S.A.[16]

The Monkey Wrench Gang is a riff on the fantasy of blowing up Glen Canyon Dam, but what about real opportunities for dam removal? What do city people think about their long-armed and sometimes strong-armed reach for water and power? Los Angeles is now forgoing much of its Owens Valley water to restore Mono Lake and rewater the Owens River Gorge. In the Pacific Northwest, a handful of small, dated power dams are being removed after negotiations with the Federal Energy Regulatory Commission. The desire to restore natural salmon runs has raised the possibility—not yet serious—of breaching four dams on the Snake River between its confluence with the Columbia and Hell's Canyon at costs to urban electric power needs and Portland barge trade. The same question has been raised about removing O'Shaughnessy Dam to restore Hetch Hetchy, even as San Francisco and adjacent communities committed in 2002 to a $3.6 billion upgrade of tunnels and aqueducts. So far, this is not likely, for Hetch Hetchy by the beginning of the twenty-first century was "the city's greatest asset, funding police protection, city park maintenance, and various social services."[17]

Noting the curious and growing propensity for upscale folks to buy water in bottles rather than relying on perfectly safe city supplies, managers of urban water systems have sometimes tried to turn the tables by bottling their own water. Portland bottled Bull Run water in the 1980s, although to little success (perhaps the name trumped the verdant scene on the label). In the new century, with the future of Hetch Hetchy becoming a public issue, San Francisco mayor Willie Brown suggested that the city should make bottled Hetch Hetchy available to consumers around the world so that everyone could appreciate the city's shrewd dam building. The idea ticked off environmentalists and opened the city to more than gentle ribbing. Even if Hetch Hetchy was as tasty as any water in a bottle, commented the *Los Angeles Times*, the plan was still a reminder of San Francisco's long and troublesome reach.

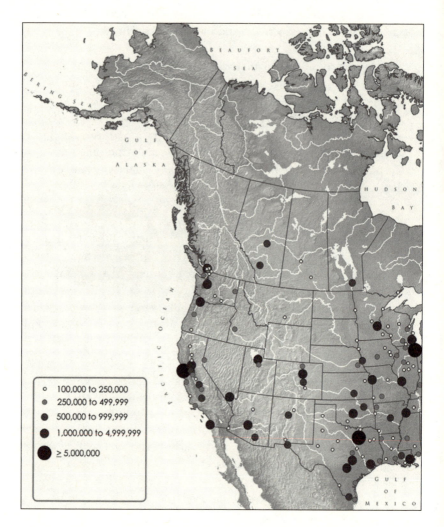

FIGURE 40. The urban West in 2000–2001. At the opening of the twenty-first century, the distribution of large metropolitan areas reflected the rapid growth of the Sunbelt, an increasing Pacific tilt, and the development of the Canadian West. (Map by Alejandro Bancke, adapted from U.S. Census Bureau [2000] and Statistics Canada [2001].)

TRANSITIONS

The Metropolitan West since 1940

*Almost all up-to-date American cities west of the Mississippi are varia-
tions on a basic prototype, and that prototype is Lubbock, Texas. . . . There
is a new kind of city evolving in America, chiefly in the Sunbelt, and on a
small scale Lubbock tells us what these new cities look like.*
                                            —John Brinckerhoff Jackson,
                                            "The Vernacular City" (1985)

*We drove back to the house to crash, each in our separate cars, through the
Campus grounds—22 buildings' worth of nerd-cosseting fun—cloistered
by 100-foot-tall second growth timber, its streets quiet as the womb: the
foundry of our culture's deepest dreams.*
                                            —Douglas Coupland,
                                            Microserfs (1995)

Los Angeles in the 1940s was scarcely fifty years old as a significant
"American" city, yet it was already the site for elegiac nostalgia. Poet Ivor
Winters crafted a long requiem for the passing of time in "On a View of
Pasadena from the Hills." Looking down over the growing city, he muses on
the passing of his father's generation while he sees that "mowed lawn has
crept along the granite bench. . . . Cement roads mark the hills . . . And man-
made stone outgrows the living tree."[1] Setting the scene in the crime novel
The Little Sister, Raymond Chandler also laments the end of simpler times
from a not-so-distant past:

A long time ago. There were trees along Wilshire Boulevard. Beverly Hills was a country town. Westwood was bare hills and lots offering at eleven hundred dollars and no takers. . . . Los Angeles was just a big sunny place with ugly homes and no style, but goodhearted and peaceful. It had the climate they just yap about now. People used to sleep out on porches. Little groups who thought they were intellectual used to call it the Athens of America. It wasn't that, but it wasn't a neon-lighted slum either.[2]

The poet and the mystery writer both wrote as Los Angeles and other western cities were entering an era of extraordinary growth and change. World War II and the postwar boom fundamentally transformed the urban West, setting forces in motion that have made the years since 1940 a distinct era in regional history. These decades have vaulted western North America into a new global position, central rather than peripheral to global circuits of trade and migration. In the process, its cities have filled the valleys with houses, contoured the hillsides with freeways, and lined the highways with the lights of commerce, a process that Winters notes with other lines in the same poem: "Through suburb after suburb, vast ravines/Swell to the summer drone of fine machines."[3]

Between the late nineteenth century and the later twentieth century, North America tilted southward as well as westward. In the decades before World War I, Bostonians and Londoners who came looking for western cities usually covered territory bracketed by Minneapolis, Denver, San Francisco, and Seattle, with stops perhaps in Salt Lake City, Portland, Spokane, Helena, and Bismarck. That's where William Thayer found inspiration for his *Marvels of the New West* in 1887, where Julian Ralph explored the region he details in *Our Great West* in 1893, and where Edward Hungerford found candidates to profile in *The Personality of American Cities* in 1913.[4] It's the same territory that the distinguished English observer James Bryce traversed to research his chapter "The Temper of the West" in *The American Commonwealth*, published in 1888, and which Rudyard Kipling reports on in *From Sea to Sea* (1899), with chapters on San Francisco, Portland, Seattle, Salt Lake City, and Omaha.[5] Served by a thick network of self-promoting railroads, this section of the western United States achieved statehood before the turn of the century, whereas the southwestern territories of Oklahoma, New Mexico, and Arizona had to wait until the early twentieth century.[6]

Anyone making the same sort of high-minded journalistic junket after World War II would have followed a different itinerary. Great Falls, Butte, and Portland were no longer hot news compared to the cities of Route 66—literally Tulsa, Oklahoma City, Amarillo, Albuquerque, San Bernardino, and Los Angeles—to which we could metaphorically add Dallas, Fort Worth, Lubbock, Midland/Odessa, Phoenix, and Las Vegas. This is the newest urban

FIGURE 41. Calgary skyline. Calgary transitioned from a small prairie city to metropolis with international connections in the last quarter of the twentieth century, particularly by hosting the 1988 Winter Olympics and experiencing a wave of investment by energy-development companies that rebuilt its skyline.

America, created by petroleum, global war, air-conditioning, and the Social Security Act of 1935. A few of the cities of the Greater Southwest, such as San Antonio and Los Angeles, should have been in James Bryce's travel plans, but many are twentieth-century phenomena in the manner of Las Vegas.

The urbanization of the Southwest and continuing metropolitan growth through much of the rest of western Canada and the United States has involved headlong participation in the world's third—and ongoing—urban revolution. Patterns of urbanization around the world now reflect the instant mobility of capital in a weakly regulated world financial system. East Asian and South Asian economies are competitors with the established Atlantic core. A networked world economy runs on the services of a handful of world cities and intricate international exchanges among second-level cities. Within western North America, patterns of urban/regional growth have responded to this internationalization, to the global shift toward services (especially those involved with the leisure economy of recreation and retirement), and to the expansion of the U.S. military establishment. Cities like Calgary, San Jose, Honolulu, and Dallas are not only regional centers but also nodes in specialized globe-spanning industries.

Western urbanization has responded to the long fifty-year pulses in the world economy. The mid–nineteenth century was the era of steam and steel, and the early twentieth century, the era of electricity and petrochemicals. The years after 1945 saw the cresting of a third wave and the probable take-off of yet another. From the mid-1940s to the mid-1970s, the drive wheels of economic growth were the scientific–military complex, the maturing of automobile and air transportation, and the postwar housing boom. After a decade of troubled readjustment to high energy costs and the offshoring of much manufacturing, the latest cycle took off in the 1990s with explosive increases in the capacity to exchange and manipulate electronic and biological information.

These sixty-plus years have continued both of the basic processes of urbanization. More and more small cities have grown into metropolitan centers: Canada designated only three western province Census Metropolitan Areas in 1941 but eight in 2001, and the roster of western metro areas recognized by the U.S. Census Bureau rose from forty-one in 1940 to eighty-seven in 2000.[7] At the same time, the largest of the places have claimed a greater and greater portion of the western population and economy. At the start of the twenty-first century, half of the people of western Canada lived in the four largest metropolitan centers, and half of the people in the western United States lived in the region's ten largest metro areas.

Postwar growth has been accompanied by deep restructuring of the metropolitan fabric. Western cities have experienced galloping Manhattanization of downtown cores along with radical decentralization. "Suburbs" like Burnaby, British Columbia, and Mesa, Arizona, rival core cities in size; residential development in Phoenix spills around long mountain barriers into new valleys; and Bay Area workers commute from new subdivisions far into California's central valley. Edmonton was the site for the first supersized superregional shopping mall. Las Vegas, already the pioneer of the suburban strip, now has "neighborhood casinos" where 400-room hotels and surrounding shopping malls colonize formerly residential neighborhoods.

Large-scale tract development may have been happening on Long Island as well as Long Beach after World War II and in Atlanta as well as Aurora, but it was most *visible* in open western landscapes. In 1950, work crews at the Los Angeles suburb of Lakewood started a hundred houses a day as they moved down one side of the street and back up the other, digging foundation trenches, pouring concrete, and working through the dozens of other stages of home building. A set of four aerial photographs of Lakewood's construction process, from bare ground to foundations to framing to closed structures, helped to fix *western* suburbs as the archetype of the new cityscape. They were taken originally as corporate publicity photos. Magazines ranging from *Business Week* to *Time* accepted the images as representing an industrial-strength solution to postwar housing shortages.[8]

It was different a decade later. Architecture critic Peter Blake turned the same pictures into icons of sprawl in *God's Own Junkyard* (1964), as did architect Nathaniel Owings in *The American Aesthetic* (1969).[9] Suburban California was now the prime exhibit of worst practices. "Flying from Los Angeles to San Bernardino," wrote journalist William H. Whyte Jr., "the traveler can see a legion of bulldozers gnawing into the last remaining tract of green between the two cities." A few pages further into his seminal essay, "Urban Sprawl,"

FIGURE 42. Las Vegas Strip. The entertainment corridor universally known as the Las Vegas Strip originated in the 1950s, was vastly expanded in the 1970s, and was reinvented again in the 1990s with huge themed hotel-casinos like Paris Las Vegas, the Luxor, and New York–New York. (Wikimedia Commons.)

he offers San Jose and Santa Clara County as the epitome of voracious farm-eating, land-spoiling suburbanization that shaped a new environment that, quite bluntly, "looked like hell."[10] Malvina Reynolds aimed her popular song "Little Houses" at Daly City on the San Francisco peninsula.

The chapters that follow explore the effects of World War II, rapid regional growth, and the changing global economy of the last half century. Western cities grew with the expansion of the metropolitan–scientific–military complex and the global shift from manufacturing to services, especially those involved in the leisure economy of recreation and retirement. The previously peripheral half of North America has developed into a new center that has begun to change the United States (and certainly has rebalanced Canada).

Three chapters center on changes associated with the Great Boom of 1940–75 (although they carry their story to the end of the century). This was an era in which domestic immigrants, private investment capital, and federal funds (both Canadian and American) poured westward, "tilting" the continental economy toward the Pacific. Chapter 10 focuses directly on the effects of hot war and Cold War, which combined to give western cities a leading role in the development and application of new technologies and emerging industries. Chapters 11 and 12 turn to metropolitan politics, describing the tension and tug-of-war between growth-oriented business coalitions and the competing goals of quality-of-life liberals and ethnic communities.

The final chapters center on the increasingly unbounded urbanization of the most recent decades. Chapter 13 looks at the spread of suburbs and exurbs and the resulting pattern of metropolitan regions and corridors. Chapter 14 returns to the theme of global connections, showing how contemporary western cities function within thick transnational webs of economic and social ties. Chapter 15 looks outward once again at urban claims on rural environments as places of recreation and leisure, claims that have broken down many of the remaining barriers between urban and rural and which parallel the long-standing urban claims on regional water and power.

Wars and Rumors of War

It was five after eight when we pulled into the parking lot at Atlas Ship. . . .
    The gatekeeper said, "Jesus Christ, all you colored boys are late this morning." . . .
    At the entrance to the dock the guard said, "Put out that cigarette, boy. What's the matter you colored boys can't never obey no rules?"
    I tossed it over the wooden craneway, still burning. He muttered something as he went over to step on it.
    The white folks had sure brought their white to work with them that morning.

—Chester Himes,
If He Hollers Let Him Go (1945)

Palo Alto is half bedroom suburb, half futuristic 1970s science fiction movies. . . . The big thing about Palo Alto is that, as a city, it designs tons of incredibly powerful and scarry shit inside its science parks, which are EVERYWHERE.

—Douglas Coupland,
Microserfs (1995)

Laura and Enrico Fermi arrived in the United States in 1939 as refugees from Fascist Italy. In 1938, Enrico had earned a Nobel Prize in physics. By 1942, he was leading the efforts to develop an atomic bomb and presiding over the first controlled nuclear reaction at the University of Chicago. The next year, the Fermis came together with other atomic scientists, engineers, and their families at Los Alamos, a science city built hurriedly on a high plateau in northern New Mexico, where isolation was supposed to ensure secrecy.

Los Alamos sits on a mesa that faces the sunrise over the valley of the Rio Grande, forty miles from the old adobes and new tourist traps of Santa Fe. Built in a hurry in 1943, Los Alamos housed the nuclear physicists and engineers who designed the first nuclear bombs. One hundred sixty miles from the coal deposits of Black Mesa—across plateaus and dry washes still faintly traced with the roads of the Chaco Culture people—Los Alamos has been devoted to the possibilities of a very different kind of energy.

The instant city was a three-way cross between a cheap subdivision, an army camp, and a depression-era federal construction town like Boulder City, Nevada, or Coulee Dam, Washington. To get there you traveled a single washboarded access road that crossed the Rio Grande, clawed its way up the steep face of the Parajito Plateau, passed through a fence and checkpoint, and continued for three more dusty miles before reaching the laboratories and their supporting community.[1] The top scientists lived on "bathtub row," the few houses with full plumbing that were left over from a former boarding school. Most families lived in apartments awash in summer dust and winter mud. Scientists spent their days designing a bomb that would change world politics and returned to dinners cooked on wood-burning stoves. General Leslie Groves, the man in charge of getting atomic bombs produced, commented that the scientists "will like anything you build for them. Put up some barracks. They will think they are pioneers out here in the Far West." He was right. Despite the hardships, Laura Fermi and other residents remembered the sense of community. "I was in Los Alamos only a year and a half," she later wrote, "and still it seems such a big portion of my life . . . it was such intense living." Many articulate residents understood and later represented their experiences in the hectic years of 1943 and 1944 as recapitulations of life on the western frontier, a choice between "adventure or disaster, depending on how you wanted to look at it."[2]

But this very peculiar frontier town had more in common with cosmopolitan San Francisco and Los Angeles than with rural New Mexico. Los Alamos scientists worked in tandem with physicists at the University of Chicago and University of California. Many of them were recent refugees from European fascism and German aggression: Enrico Fermi from Italy, Edward Teller from Hungary, Hans Bethe from Germany, Niels Bohr from Denmark, and Stanislaus Ulam, the only member of his family to survive the Nazi invasion of Poland. Their specific interests and fields were different, but they were a scientific counterpart to the distinguished artists of central Europe who found themselves beached in Los Angeles—Thomas Mann, Arnold Schoenberg, and Bertolt Brecht struggling to stay focused on class conflict in the California sunshine.

Both the Los Angeles colony of European intellectuals and the Los Alamos science city were participants in the reshaping of western North America by World War II. The federal government in 1939 was the leading landlord in the West and its largest general contractor. By 1943 and 1944, it was also the dominant employer. In an era when $1,000 could buy a very good car, Houston, Fort Worth, Wichita, Seattle, Portland, San Francisco, Los Angeles, and San Diego all received more than $1 billion in war-supply contracts. Ten percent of all spending for World War II went to California, twice its share according to population. Californians had derived only 5 percent of their personal income from the federal government in 1930 and only 10 percent in 1940 after a decade of relief and public works programs, but they received 45 percent of their income from the government in 1945 after half a decade of a war economy. The pattern was similar in Colorado and New Mexico, Washington and Hawaii. The effects of World War II still reverberated half a century later. Taken together, the Pacific war and its Asian follow-ups marked the final transition from the old to the new West and made the federal budget the essential drive wheel of western growth.

The armed forces were no strangers in the West in the nineteenth century, but the region's military establishment had faded in the new century. Indeed, boosters in cities throughout the West labored long and hard during the early twentieth century to secure new military bases to prop up local economies. Tacoma's citizens in 1917 voted by a landslide to tax themselves to purchase 70,000 acres for an army cantonment that grew into Fort Lewis, still one of the army's largest bases after eighty years and a decade of base closures. Cities in the San Francisco Bay area vigorously battled among themselves about the best sites for navy bases but presented a common front against the cities of southern California, united with these same cities to defend California appropriations, and stood shoulder to shoulder with cities on both coasts against proposals to shift more defense activities to the national interior. The San Antonio Chamber of Commerce embraced military aviation as the winning card in that city's rivalry with Dallas and Houston. Kelly Field and Brooks Air Base date to 1916–18, and Randolph Air Base dates to the 1920s, all to be vigorously defended by San Antonio's congressmen and businessmen.

The metropolitan–military complex involved mutual dependence. Western cities have wanted military spending, but the armed forces have also needed the strong advocacy of urban leaders to stave off budget cutters in Washington. Particularly during the 1920s and 1930s, the small military establishment cultivated local influentials. From 1931 to 1935, for example, Henry H. Arnold—soon to control tens of thousands of warplanes as commander of the Army Air Forces in the global war against fascism—built the foundations of Edwards Air Force Base by cultivating local leaders. He enlisted the Automobile Club of Southern California and the Los Angeles

Chamber of Commerce, lectured to junior college classes, and staged a private air show for a well-situated Pomona horse breeder.

Prewar mobilization in 1940 brought a new wave of booster opportunities. The Dallas Chamber of Commerce and the Citizens Council (representing the city's preeminent movers and shakers) campaigned in Washington to secure a naval reserve aviation base and a North American Aviation Company plant whose payroll totaled 43,000 by the midpoint of the war. Nearby Fort Worth secured Tarrant Field and a Consolidated Vultee Aircraft (Convair) plant, the latter through newspaper editor Amon Carter's direct lobbying with Franklin Roosevelt. Tucson got Davis-Monthan Air Force Base and facilities for modifying B-24s (which were made at Dallas). Similar combinations of local promotion, political influence, and bureaucratic criteria brought Sheppard Air Base to Wichita Falls, Tinker Air Base to Oklahoma City, and Hill Air Base and Clearfield Naval Depot to the Salt Lake City/ Ogden area.

Production of weapons and military supplies went along with training, staging, and repair facilities. Anticipating shortages of nonferrous metals, the federal government built a huge plant near Las Vegas to produce magnesium with the help of Hoover Dam electricity and a series of aluminum plants at Spokane, Vancouver, Longview, and other sites in Washington and Oregon served by hydropower from the Bonneville Power Administration. It funded steel production at Provo, Utah, and Fontana, California, near San Bernardino. It built the Denver Arms plant, where 20,000 workers made shells, cartridges, and fuses. In Portland and nearby Vancouver, Washington, 120,000 workers built cargo ships and escort carriers. Corpus Christi also built ships, while 35,000 aviators—including future president George H. W. Bush—received training at the new Naval Air Station.

Canada's war effort was more heavily focused on Europe than on the Pacific, but the Vancouver region counted at least 40,000 war industry jobs. Boeing built warplanes in suburban Richmond, while shipbuilding and military shipping clogged Vancouver's waterfronts. Edmonton was the staging area for the rush construction of the Alaska–Canada Highway. Its Blatchford Field was the main refueling stop on the air supply route from the United States to Alaska.

The effects were often startling. After diligently working to secure naval facilities, the cities of the San Francisco Bay area found themselves with more than they had bargained for in 1940 and 1941. The federal government expanded the Mare Island and Hunters Point shipyards, Moffett Field, the Naval Operating Base and new Naval Air Station at Alameda, naval supply depots, and new facilities on Treasure Island, just recently the site of the 1939 exposition. Federal contracts also funded a half dozen huge private shipyards—General Engineering and Drydock in San Francisco, Western Pipe and Steel in South San Francisco, Bethlehem Shipbuilding in Alameda,

FIGURE 43. Portland, Oregon, shipyard. Armies of welders, riveters, and fabricators produced thousands of cargo vessels and warships at huge industrial shipyards in the San Francisco Bay and Portland areas from 1941 to 1945. Their output helped to redress the balance from early naval losses in the Pacific and shifted the balance of the "tonnage war" between German U-boats and Allied convoys in the North Atlantic. (Oregon Historical Society, Neg. 68779.)

Moore Drydock in Oakland, Todd-Kaiser in Richmond, and Marinship in Sausalito. San Francisco itself became a huge dormitory housing war workers, servicemen between assignments, and their dependents. The population of Vallejo and adjoining areas tripled, and workers at Mare Island commuted as far as fifty miles on rationed gasoline. Richmond's job total increased from 15,000 to 130,000. The city imported old elevated railroad cars from New York for a new rail line to Oakland as a way of coping with its transportation problem.

Richmond and Vallejo were not unique, for all of the boom cities of the West suffered a common cycle of problems in which overpriced and insufficient housing forced new workers to locate haphazardly through the metropolitan area and further overburden already overcrowded transit systems. Workers in Seattle's shipyards and Boeing plant scrounged for living space in offices, tents, and chicken coops. A well-publicized visit by the U.S. House Committee on National Defense Migration in summer 1941 found San Diego swamped by 90,000 defense industry workers and 35,000 military personnel. Operating on their own hurried schedules, federal agencies exacerbated the city's problems by locating defense plants and emergency housing on isolated sites, thus forcing extra service costs and creating painful traffic problems. *Life, Business Week, Fortune,* and the *Saturday Evening Post* all described the crowded schools, overpacked hotels, makeshift trailer parks, and raucous nightlife in the "rip-roaringest coast boomtown." San Diego's inadequate and poorly located housing, said one expert, was the "core of every problem and controversy."[3]

Honolulu experienced the war boom in yet another way, as roughly one million soldiers, sailors, and workers passed through Hawaii in the course of the war—four times the territory's population in 1940. Close to the front lines, military officials censored Honolulu newspapers and enforced martial law until late in 1944. The flood of newcomers included both servicemen and war workers. As David Farber and Beth Bailey write, "Hawaii would serve as staging ground for much of the Pacific war. There men trained for the island assault and recovered from battle. Huge numbers of workers were needed to maintain and repair the ships and planes as well as to handle the logistics of troop movement and supply."[4] The armed forces tried to prepare servicemen for the realities of a multicultural society with a *Pocket Guide to Hawaii* and rented the Royal Hawaiian Hotel on Waikiki for submariners on leave, but thousands of men waiting to be shipped out spent their days and nights in the bars and brothels of Hotel Street, where lines stretched around the block by mid-morning. It was a striking change from the upper-class tourism of the 1920s and 1930s, when a round-trip Pan Am flight from San Francisco to Honolulu cost as much as an automobile.

The war also brought entirely new towns. Under the Lanham Act and related programs, the federal government financed one million temporary housing units for wartime use nationwide. Many of the apartments were in the Bay Area at Richmond and the model community of Marin City. Many more—enough for 40,000 residents, were built at the instant "city" of Vanport, Oregon. Rising on the floodplain of the Columbia River, halfway between the Kaiser Corporation shipyards in Portland, Oregon, and

FIGURE 44. War worker housing. Rising in 1942 and 1943 on the Columbia River floodplain between Portland, Oregon, and Vancouver, Washington, "Vanport" housed more than 40,000 shipyard workers and family members in cookie-cutter apartments. From 1945 to 1948, when the flooding Columbia swirled it away, Vanport housed returning veterans and African Americans who found other neighborhoods closed to them. (Oregon Historical Society, Neg. 37471.)

Vancouver, Washington, the first of 9,000 apartments in 600 wooden buildings were ready in December 1942. Painted dull gray to blend into the cold winter rains of the Northwest, the buildings of Vanport included schools, community centers, a day care program, a post office, cafeterias, a fire district, playgrounds, shops, a 150-bed hospital, and a movie theater that ran three double bills per week. Up the Columbia River from Vanport, the science city of Richland, Washington, sprang up on a dry benchland along the Columbia River. Where 300 people had tended peach orchards and asparagus beds in 1940, 15,000 engineers and technicians were supporting the manufacture of plutonium at the Hanford Engineering Works by 1944—plutonium that the scientists at Los Alamos would design into the Nagasaki bomb.

The war meant new people so as to fill the new jobs in the Far West. Americans from Texas, Oklahoma, and the Lower Mississippi Valley followed news of labor shortages and high wages to defense production centers. Seattle's black population jumped from 4,000 to 40,000, and Portland's went

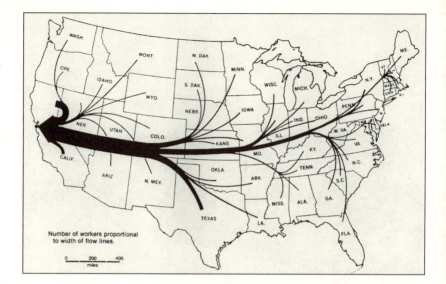

FIGURE 45. Map of World War II migration to San Francisco. War industries in the San Francisco Bay area attracted more than half a million workers from all parts of the United States. Following the migration of Dust Bowl farmworkers in the 1930s, tens of thousands of workers from Texas helped to tie California into the Southwest. (Adapted from the President's Committee for Congested Production Areas, Final Report [1944].)

from 2,000 to 15,000. These newcomers crowded into a few neighborhoods and housing projects carefully set aside in the style of established eastern ghettos. Many found the only affordable housing to be in neighborhoods forcibly vacated by Japanese residents, such as the Western Addition in San Francisco and Little Tokyo east of downtown Los Angeles. Whether in a federal community like Vanport or a housing project like Hunter's Point in San Francisco, new housing preserved the distinction between white and black neighborhoods and set a pattern of suburban segregation for the postwar generation.

Tensions also rose between Mexican Americans and Anglo-Americans in Los Angeles. During the 1930s, tens of thousands of Mexican Americans had permanently settled in western cities such as Denver when their rural jobs as railroad hands and farm laborers disappeared. New migration in the early 1940s swelled the Mexican community in Los Angeles to an estimated 400,000, prompting discrimination and a steady stream of anti-Mexican articles in the major newspapers. On June 3, 1943, off-duty sailors and soldiers led several thousand Anglos to attack Hispanics on downtown streets and invade Mexican American neighborhoods. Blacks and Filipinos were incidental targets. The "Zoot Suit" riots, named for the flamboyant clothes of some young Chicanos, dragged on for a week.

War did open new opportunities for women, who made up roughly one-quarter of West Coast shipyard workers at the peak of employment, two-fifths of Los Angeles aircraft workers, 46 percent of Boeing workers in Seattle, and nearly one-half of Dallas aircraft workers. Aircraft companies, whose labor shortages were compounded by stubborn "whites-only" hiring, developed new power tools and production techniques to accommodate the smaller average size of women workers, increasing efficiency for everyone along the production line. Shipyards turned first to women who were already in the labor force in jobs ranging from shop clerk to farmworker. Many of the "housewives" who responded to recruitment campaigns in 1943 and 1944 were women who needed jobs to support their families. As one of the workers recalled of herself and a friend, "We both had to work, we both had children, so we became welders, and if I might say so, damn good ones."[5] The most common shipyard jobs were clerks and general helpers, but the acute shortage of welders opened more than 5,000 journeyman positions in the Portland operations. A few women even found positions as electricians and crane operators—far more interesting work than waitressing or sewing in a clothing factory.

In aggregate, the organization of a huge military enterprise in 1942–43 shifted the economic and demographic balance in the United States southward and westward. Small cities like Phoenix and Albuquerque became important urban centers within half a decade. Wartime booms accelerated the long-term development of larger cities like Denver and Salt Lake City. From 1940 to 1943, the states with the highest rates of population growth were California, Oregon, Washington, Nevada, Utah, and Arizona (along with Florida, Virginia, and Maryland). The boom touched every major city in Texas, Oklahoma, the Pacific states, and the Southwest as well as selected production centers in the interior West.

Taken after temporary workers had decided whether to stay or head back east, mid-century censuses give an indication of the lasting impact of wartime urban growth (Tables 10.1–10.2). Canada as a whole shifted from 54 to 62 percent urban between 1941 and 1951, but British Columbia, Alberta, and

TABLE 10.1. Western Canada: Changes in Urban Population during the World War II Decade

Area	Percent Urban, 1941	Percent Urban, 1951	Change
British Columbia	54	68	+14
Manitoba	44	57	+13
Alberta	37	48	+11
Canada	54	62	+8
Saskatchewan	33	30	−3

TABLE 10.2. Western United States: Changes in Urban Population during the World War II Decade

Area	Percent Urban, 1940	Percent Urban, 1950	Change
Arizona	35	55	+20
Nevada	39	57	+18
Texas	45	63	+18
New Mexico	33	50	+17
Oklahoma	38	51	+13
Washington	53	63	+10
California	71	81	+10
Colorado	53	63	+10
Utah	56	65	+9
Idaho	34	43	+9
South Dakota	25	33	+8
Nebraska	39	47	+8
Hawaii	62	69	+7
United States	57	64	+7
North Dakota	21	27	+6
Montana	38	44	+6
Oregon	49	54	+5
Alaska	24	26	+2

Manitoba exceeded the percentage shift. The United States in the 1940s went from 57 to 64 percent urban, a shift matched or exceeded by fourteen of seventeen western states plus Hawaii.

Victory in 1945 left the U.S. military extended worldwide. As the "American Century" quickly faded into the realities of the Cold War, the United States prepared for the indefinite projection of power in the Pacific and East Asia and for continental defense through nuclear deterrence. The North Korean invasion of South Korea in June 1950 and the Chinese entry into the Korean conflict in December confirmed the American commitment to a dual strategy of advanced and strategic defense. American military planners during the early 1950s created four strategic "layers" that overlapped the western states and territories—a defensive structure that would be maintained through crises in the Formosa Strait and intervention in Vietnam, Laos, and Cambodia.

The nation's forward presence in the Far East rested on bases in the Philippines, Central Pacific, Korea, and Japan. The need to anchor this first line of defense in Alaska led to a new surge of federal investment greater than that in either the 1910s or the 1940s. Federal agencies and contractors built the Distant Early Warning Line of radar stations across northern Alaska. They expanded military bases like Ladd Air Force Base at Fairbanks and Elmendorf Air Force Base at Anchorage, headquarters for the unified Alaska Command. They upgraded ports, highways, railroads, and airports in the territory's Anchorage–Valdez–Fairbanks core. Alaska's 1950 census counted one uniformed member of the armed services for every 4.3 civilians.

Supply depots, training bases, shipyards, and aircraft-maintenance bases constituted the second layer in the western military system. Admirals presided over navy commands headquartered at Seattle, San Francisco, San Diego, and Honolulu. Each city lay in a cluster of operating bases, shipyards, and air stations. Army and Air Force training facilities were especially prominent in Washington, Colorado, Texas, and Oklahoma. The siting of the new Air Force Academy in Colorado Springs balanced its aging hotels and golf courses.

San Diego also showed the results of the peacetime mobilization. By one estimate, the U.S. Navy alone was responsible for supporting 215,000 people in the San Diego area in 1957. Weapons makers added tens of thousands more. Most residents seemed to believe that what was good for Convair was good for the country. Cruising the harbor, as historian Roger Lotchin has pointed out, one would pass a submarine base, a carrier anchorage, dry docks, shipbuilding firms, ammunition bunkers, and barracks ships: "In the bay, ships ply the waters and retired admirals cruise their sailing vessels; overhead, naval helicopters buzz and jets scream; and downtown, sailors throng the streets."[6] The military was a constant presence in social life and civic activities. Scores of community organizations depended on military surplus goods to support their programs. Initiated in 1953, Air Power Day became a local equivalent of the Pasadena rose festival.

The strategic strike and defense forces that formed the heart of America's Cold War strategy were commanded from cities in the national heartland of the Great Plains. North American air defense was coordinated from a command post sunk deep beneath Cheyenne Mountain at the foot of the Rockies behind Colorado Springs. General Curtis LeMay directed the B-47s and B-52s of the Strategic Air Command from Omaha. By the 1970s, solid-fueled minuteman missiles were targeted for Moscow and Beijing from unobtrusive silos served from northern plains cities like Great Falls and Rapid City.

The fourth "layer" of the defense system was strategic weapons production. Scientists on the federal payroll continued to undertake basic research at the Los Alamos National Laboratory and Lawrence Livermore National Laboratory east of Oakland. The Hanford reservation, supported by the growing Tri-Cities of Richland, Kennewick, and Pasco, Washington, continued to produce plutonium for nuclear weapons. Western Electric operated Sandia National Laboratories at Albuquerque under federal contract after 1949, turning physical theory into workable nuclear weapons. The Rocky

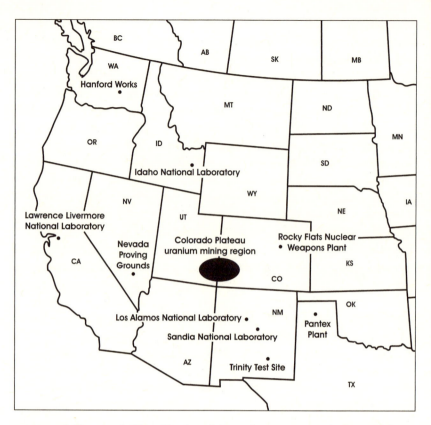

FIGURE 46. The atomic West. The rise of the nuclear weapons industry created new cities like Richland, Washington (Hanford), and spurred the growth of established cities like Albuquerque (Sandia Labs), Denver (Rocky Flats), Amarillo (Pantex), and Las Vegas (Nevada Proving Grounds). (Map by Jacquelyn Ferry.)

Flats facility north of Denver turned the plutonium into triggers for thermonuclear bombs, which another set of workers assembled into warheads at the Pantex plant in Amarillo, Texas.

The federal treasury and the Cold War military not only created an "atomic archipelago" in the West but also supplied the key market for the "fourth-wave" industries that led the economic expansion after World War II. Steam engines and the mass production of textiles had led the first wave of worldwide industrial growth from 1790 to 1815. Steel production and railroads had led the second wave from 1845 to 1890. Chemicals, electrical equipment, and automobiles had led a third wave from 1890 until the Great Depression. After the war, the new leaders were the electronics, communication, and aerospace industries. Whereas the first three waves had worked to concentrate industrial power in the manufacturing belt running from Boston to St. Louis, the Cold War boom had its most profound effects on the American West.

It was chiefly in the West, for example, that the aircraft industry of World War I and World War II evolved into the far more extensive aerospace business. By the 1950s, the cities of Seattle, Los Angeles, San Diego, Dallas, Fort Worth, and Wichita accounted for nearly all of the country's airframe production and assembly. Military contracts supported Lockheed, General Dynamics, McDonnell Douglas, Northrop, and scores of other firms in the Los Angeles region. The location of the Manned Spacecraft Center of the National Aeronautics and Space Administration on 10,000 acres of donated land brought spin-off businesses to Houston. The national space program also drew on the Jet Propulsion Laboratory in Pasadena, as well as Edwards and Vandenberg Air Force bases in California (both economic satellites of Los Angeles).

The promotion of scientific research and applications became another federal industry, especially after the Soviet Union launched *Sputnik* in 1957. The federal subsidy of physical science utilized a combination of federal laboratories, private research and development contractors, and universities. Albuquerque, the self-styled "Atomic City," ranked ninth among all metropolitan areas in its federal research and development contracts in 1977. Colorado's pattern was similar. Martin Marietta Corporation decided in 1956 to build a plant for Titan missiles in the Denver suburb of Littleton. Hewlett-Packard, Honeywell, Sundstrand, and Ball Brothers Research were a few of the other high-technology firms attracted by life near the mountains. It was a short step from defense industries and science-oriented corporations to the research division of the University of Colorado and the federal research agencies located in Boulder—the National Bureau of Standards, the National Center for Atmospheric Research, and the National Oceanic and Atmospheric Administration.

Federal contracts gave the big push for the development and utilization of electronics and information technologies. Stanford Industrial Park in 1951 was the first planned effort to link the science and engineering faculties of major universities to the design and production of cutting-edge engineering applications. Along with the development of companies like Hewlett-Packard, it was the first step in the evolution of Silicon Valley—the nickname for San Jose and nearby South Bay communities—as a center of the electronics industry. Federal contracts, especially for complex challenges like missile guidance systems, have been the Silicon Valley mainstay, driving the innovation cycle from experiment to defense application to civilian spin-off. The invention of the microprocessor in 1971 kicked the electronics industry into high gear. The farmlands of Santa Clara County, California, became a "silicon landscape" of neat one-story factories and research campuses. In 1950, the county had 800 factory workers. In 1980, it had 264,000 manufacturing workers and 3,000 electronics firms.

Historian Margaret O'Mara has pointed out that "suburbs of knowledge" were in part a product of national defense policy during the 1950s.[7] One of the concerns of regional planning in the early atomic age was to disperse vital production facilities to the edges of metropolitan areas to protect them from strategic bombing. Defense procurement policies favored companies with suburban locations. The impact was obviously greatest in young cities with new industries like electronics, peppering the landscape with the clones of the southern California "Yo-Yo-Dyne" factory that novelist Thomas Pynchon satirizes in *The Crying of Lot 49* (1966).

At the same time, suburban tech plants and research extended the historic American taste for the isolated and self-contained university campus. The bucolic campus, often in a small-town setting, was designed to insulate students and faculty from the distractions of the heterogeneous city. The suburban research park in Orange County or the South Bay would likewise be quiet, pretty, and pretty much white in its workforce, at least in the 1950s and 1960s—a nice match with new, quiet, white suburbs. By the 1990s, the workforce was different, but the horizontal suburbscape was much the same. Douglas Coupland's novel *Microserfs*, about Microsoft code writers who trade secure Seattle for a Silicon Valley software start-up in the early years of the 1990s dot-com boom, deftly skews the Silicon Valley environment. His characters drive past "eerie, beautifully maintained lawns that have never felt the crush of a football" and a bit later "through the vine-covered suburbs and carefully mowed, Frisbee-free lawns of Palo Alto's tech parks": "Like most Silicon Valley buildings, EA's headquarters, the Century Two complex, are sleek and clean, and Sony-based aesthetic, where a sleek machine-shaped object contains magic components on the inside that do cool shit. Susan says it's a 'male' aesthetic. 'If men could have their way, every building on earth would resemble a Trinitron.'"[8]

By 1980, western cities were the centers of atomic research and production (still a rising industry after a decade of energy crises and reviving Cold War), aerospace companies, and companies that specialized in instrumentation and military control systems. One industrial cluster in the San Francisco Bay area centered around electronic data processing, another in southern California, around aerospace. Both places had thick networks of suppliers, mobility of workers among competing firms, and relatively open marketplaces of ideas. There were certainly rivalries and trade secrets, but the West Coast style was more open and flexible than rival East Coast centers such as Boston. It was a remarkable manifestation of some of the common, self-satisfied assumptions about the superiority of the "western" style over the eastern.

In the 1980s and 1990s, branch hardware and microchip factories, spin-off companies, and software firms spread the information-processing industry throughout the West. Having seen what the computer industry did for San Jose, every place wanted to be the next Silicon Valley. The information business built on earlier foundations in Dallas (Texas Instruments), Portland (Tektronix), and Phoenix (Motorola). It changed big cities such as Denver and Salt Lake City and radically transformed smaller cities like Boise. Local boosters in the 1980s talked up "silicon prairies," "silicon forests," "silicon deserts," and "silicon mountains." If they were lucky they developed home-grown firms or acquired research arms of large companies, but local leaders were often satisfied with a chip plant or fabricating plant controlled from Mountain View, Cupertino, Seoul, or Tokyo.

In the process of building American scientific capacity, federal initia-tives helped to transform western university systems. Research grants and graduate student aid, especially after the passage of the National Defense Education Act (1958), provided vital funding at a time when regional cam-puses were struggling to cope with the first arrivals from the postwar baby boom. The University of Washington grew from 13,000 to 30,000 students in little more than a decade, in part because of vigorous pursuit of federal grants whose income equaled direct support from the state general fund. The University of California–San Diego was explicitly created to support high-technology research with strong lobbying from the giant defense con-tractor General Dynamics. When federal research and development funding for universities is compared on a per-capita basis, Alaska, Utah, Hawaii, New Mexico, Washington, California, and Colorado all exceeded the national aver-age—with obvious consequences for Salt Lake City, Seattle, Denver/Boulder, and other cities. An analysis of frequently cited scientific papers in twenty-one fields of science and social science, covering 2002–5, reveals that six of the top twelve U.S. universities were in the Pacific states: Stanford, Berkeley, University of Washington, University of California–San Diego, Cal Tech, and University of California–San Francisco.

Direct federal funding and federal markets for science-intensive pro-duction, as well as regional amenities, helped to make western metro areas some of the best educated in the country. Sixteen of the metro areas that had 500,000 or more residents in 1980 reported that 20 percent or more of their adult population (over twenty-five years old) had completed at least four years of college. Ten of these cities were western: Austin at 28 percent; Denver at 26 percent; San Francisco/Oakland/San Jose at 25 percent; and Seattle/Tacoma, Honolulu, Houston, San Diego, Tucson, Salt Lake City, and Dallas/Fort Worth all at between 20 and 24 percent. The West claimed twenty-eight of the fifty metro areas of all sizes with the same high education level—includ-ing not only such likely candidates as Colorado Springs and Santa Barbara but also less obvious cities such as Grand Forks, North Dakota; Boise, Idaho; and Midland, Texas.

These trends came together in the early twenty-first century in a handful of "new economy" cities oriented to the processing and distribution of informa-tion.[9] San Francisco, San Jose, San Diego, Denver, Dallas, and Albuquerque were high on the list. So was Austin, one of those places that seemed to have what it took to attract the "creative class" of artists, software writers, multimedia entrepreneurs, and similar cool people. For one example, an industry magazine in 2006 rated it the number two city in the country for independent filmmakers. With a top-notch university, a pleasant setting (J. Frank Dobie thought "its site one of the most beautiful for a city on the North American continent"), relatively low housing costs, a great music scene, and a critical mass of high-tech companies and research labs, it was the sort of place that attracted mobile college graduates and kept them.[10]

One of the foundations of Austin's success was the digital economy of information technology companies: Texas Instruments and IBM came first, locating facilities in Austin in the 1960s. Westinghouse, McNeil Labs, Cypress Semiconductor, and many other companies came to nearby Round Rock, transforming it from a farm town of 3,000 to a high-end suburb of 78,000 in 2004. Austin in the mid-1980s won a fierce competition for Sematech, a federally sponsored consortium of high-tech corporations that aimed to develop commercial applications for technical innovations. Dell Computer, soon to be a rousing business success story and major employer, opened for business at the same time (later moving from Austin to Round Rock). The 1990s brought Samsung, Advanced Micro Devices, Motorola, and other semiconductor manufactures among nearly 2,000 IT-related companies. IT employment shrank with the dot-com crash of 2001 but still accounted for roughly a quarter of area jobs.

Austin as state capital and university town is also a city of bureaucrats, students, scholars, and similar paper pushers (or in the more high-flown terminology of economist Robert Reich, symbolic analysts). Roughly 125,000 people worked in state and local government in the early twenty-first century. The University of Texas counted 50,000 students, and other colleges added tens of thousands more. Within the city itself, 2000 data show that 41 percent of adults had four-year college degrees, including 16 percent with graduate or professional degrees.[11] Austin in the 1930s and 1940s had been the home to a trinity of Texas intellectuals in the persons of folklorist J. Frank Dobie, historian Walter Prescott Webb, and naturalist Roy Bedichek, memorialized in the sculpture *Philosopher's Rock* in Zilker Park along Town Lake. The 1960s brought the liberal journalism of the *Texas Observer*, and the 1970s and 1980s saw a lively pop music scene develop that blended folk, rock, blues, and country and western. Like Boston, Berkeley, and Boulder, fin de siècle Austin was a comfortable place to be a perpetual student or a creative artist.

The landscape expresses the cultural bifurcation.[12] Downtown is a core of new high-rise offices that many Austinites dismiss as corporate and soulless; the number of buildings ten stories or higher is comparable to that in quite untrendy Cleveland and Cincinnati. Professors, writers, and environmental consultants hang out in the old west-side bungalow neighborhoods with their tree-lined streets (the south side grew up more "country," and the east side, more black and Latino). Outside the older city, high-tech campuses feed every morning at interchanges on the loop highways and I-35 north to Round Rock and Georgetown, sucking in the commuters who fuel their operations. Both towns are in Williamson County, where "Dellionaires" build starter mansions and down off the Balcones Escarpment "gush great rivers of subdivisions, shopping centers, malls, and a bewildering crosshatching of highways."[13]

It is a long reach from Los Alamos in the 1940s to Austin in the twenty-first century, but the links are central to the history of the metropolitan West. The University of Texas in 1940 was a good provincial university. Two generations later it was a megacampus, its growth driven by federal research support and by the prosperity of the American Century—both direct consequences of World War II and the Cold War. World War II proved the importance of scientific research for military superiority (radar as well as atomic weapons). The Cold War created the modern electronics industry and all its spin-offs, from video games to personal computers. At the close of World War II, wartime science czar Vannevar Bush issued a report entitled *Science: The Endless Frontier*, urging continued federal investment in scientific research to promote economic development and sustain national power. Austin's Dellionaires, Seattle's Microsoft millionaires, and Bay Area Web weavers, and the cityscapes they inhabit, are all products of that scientific frontier.

CHAPTER ELEVEN

Progress and Prejudice

When I opened the door I was slapped in the face by the force of Lips'
alto horn. I had been hearing Lips and Willie and Flattop since I was
a boy in Houston. All of them and John and half the people in that
crowded room had migrated from Houston after the war, and some
before that. California was like heaven for the southern Negro. . . . The
stories were true for the most part but the truth wasn't like the dream. Life
was still hard in L.A. and if you worked every day you still found yourself
at the bottom.

—Walter Moseley, *Devil in a Blue Dress* (1990)

On April 10, 1962, when Johnny Podres uncorked the first Major League pitch in newly built Dodger Stadium, the game marked a new era for baseball fans.[1] It also represented the closing chapter in a long struggle between two visions for Los Angeles. The stadium location—Chavez Ravine—had been a 315-acre tract of hilly, wooded land that had managed to escape intense urban development. Its Mexican American population had lived in substandard houses and shacks but maintained a lively sense of pride and identity with their community. Plans from the 1940s for a major public housing project collapsed in 1953 in the face of conservative political opposition. The alternative was to use the site as a Major League Baseball stadium for the newly Los Angelized Dodgers. The city "traded" the ravine, which had already been cleared of its residents, for other property owned by the Dodgers, whose owner Walter O'Malley broke ground for Dodger Stadium in 1959.

Dodger Stadium was one element in a wide-ranging program to promote the economic development of central Los Angeles. In the 1940s, the Los Angeles Housing Authority had planned to replace the run-down apartments of Bunker Hill, located just northwest of downtown, with public housing. However, the land was also a prime target for downtown expansion. Opponents of the Housing Authority used the tensions of the Korean War years to turn the issue into one of "communistic housing projects" and "housing pinks," convincing voters in 1952 to reject public housing by three to one. When Mayor Fletcher Bowron pushed ahead with the Bunker Hill project, to which the city was committed, *Los Angeles Times* publisher Norman Chandler and real estate tycoons looked for a substitute candidate. They ran Congressman Norris Poulson against a mayor whom the *Times* now accused of anarchism. As mayor from 1953 to 1961, Poulson managed to deny Nikita Khrushchev the chance to visit Disneyland. He otherwise let members of the establishment write each year's municipal budget at a special retreat, took his cues from the *Times*, and made sure that Bunker Hill was saved for a music center, bank towers, and costly high-rise apartments.[2]

The contest over housing and redevelopment embodies the clash of two competing interests—or the intersection of two different stories—that found expression among many western cities. We can think of the difference as competing versions of the term *progressive*.

Organizing, striving, and very occasionally succeeding were "liberal progressives" who worked to meet the needs of minorities and the working poor. Their coalitions were a shifting kaleidoscope of Congress of Industrial Organizations labor unions, political leftists, reform-minded liberals, African Americans, and Latinos. Strongest in the immediate postwar years, they shared some of the same ideology as the national Progressive Party that tried to elect Left-leaning Henry Wallace to the presidency in 1948. As in Los Angeles and in national politics, they were also vulnerable to attacks on Communist Party connections.

"Neoprogressives" marched under a different flag. These were businesspeople, real estate owners, and professionals who wanted to embrace and build on wartime growth. Many had businesses and careers that stood to benefit directly from a growing population and an expanding market for cars, appliances, houses, and professional services. Some were also newcomers to the West who were impatient with an older generation of property owners who seemed content with a steady-state economy.

Like their predecessor Progressives earlier in the century, these neoprogressives tried to claim the high ground by arrogating the rhetoric of progress and public interest. They painted their opponents as vice lords and crooked cops, corrupt political bosses, or, at best, small-timers unfitted to guide their city into the modern age. The immediate goal was often to update antiquated municipal administrations and provide a fuller range of city services at a lower cost. Beyond the classic progressive goal of efficiency, the reformers hoped to mobilize public and private resources to build the necessary physical facilities for economic growth. They wanted new docks and airports, an expanded supply of water, new highways, cheaper electric power, and a strong downtown as the core of a growing metropolis.

Pent-up energies fueled a wave of neoprogressive municipal reform between 1945 and 1955. Bright young veterans matched themselves against complacent civic leaders and politicians, sharing the hope of replacing the small-time politics of cronyism with administrations made up of growth-oriented businessmen and bureaucrats. The new politicians lambasted entrenched officeholders, promised to crack down on vice and clean up police departments, and argued for effective planning and efficient city bureaus. During this "revolutionary" decade, civic activists created or reinstated local growth machines, those development-minded alliances of major property owners, utilities, department stores, newspapers, and other local-market businesses that had long been powerful players in city politics. The activists replaced backroom government in Albuquerque and San Antonio; they rationalized the chaotic pluralism that had given Phoenix thirty-one city managers in thirty-five years; and they eased out or bypassed caretaker administrations in Seattle and Denver.

A typical example is San Jose, where ambulance operator and beer distributor Charles Bigley put together a political organization in the late 1920s that controlled a majority on the city council into the 1940s. Like a political machine out of the textbooks, he earned the loyalty of low-income voters with favors and took payoffs from liquor and gambling interests through the police and fire departments. Excited by wartime opportunities, a group of younger, aggressive merchants, lawyers, and industrialists formed the Progress Committee in 1944 to throw the rascals out. Looking forward to the boom that they knew was ahead, they wanted to build "a new metropolis in the place of sleepy San Jose."[3] With the support of the newspapers, they brushed off the opposition of labor unions and large landowners, swept the city council election, and set out to clean house at city hall.

Although the Progress Committee disappeared as a formal organization soon after its 1944 victory, its business agenda dominated city government for the next three decades. City manager A. P. Hamann, hired in 1950 with business rather than government experience, pursued the goal of making San Jose "the Los Angeles of the North." The city recruited new industry. It built new streets, sewers, and an airport. It annexed rural territory in advance of urbanization—growing from eleven square miles in 1940 to 137 square miles in 1970. In the same way that Los Angeles had used its water supply to force annexations in the 1910s and 1920s, San Jose made annexation the price of hookups to its oversized sewer system built originally to serve the local canneries. City officials justified their expansion on the grounds of efficiency—capturing a tax base for public services, coordinating capital improvements, and acquiring necessary land for parks and other facilities.

San Jose boosters also fought to maintain the separate identity of their booming metropolis, resisting inclusion in the San Francisco/Oakland metropolitan area in 1950 and rejecting participation in the Bay Area Rapid Transit system in 1957. The prime beneficiaries and boosters of the Hamann regime were real estate developers and the *San Jose Mercury News*. Under the new ownership of Joseph Ridder after 1952, the *Mercury News* boosted growth and grew prosperous on growing advertising revenues. In Ridder's terminology, that translated into being "a constructive force in the development of San Jose and its territory."[4]

Like San Jose, Salt Lake City ended the 1930s with embarrassingly inept city government. Both the mayor and the police chief landed in jail in 1938 for taking payoffs from three illegal lotteries, three bookies, sixteen brothels, and businesses with names like the Horse Show Card Room. Ab Jenkins, elected mayor in 1939, was a race car driver rather than a politician. His well-meaning efforts to impose some fiscal discipline on the administrative departments of the other city commissioners paralyzed the city with public feuds and turned council meetings into shouting matches. Change came in 1943, when voters turned to radio executive Earl Glade, who would serve as mayor for twelve years. With the support of the *Salt Lake Tribune* and the Chamber of Commerce, the mayor began to plan for postwar changes with the help of the National Resources Planning Board and gradually modernized the city administration.

Business-oriented reform was widely successful through the mountain West. Denver's "interminable Ben" Stapleton was a typical roadblock to change, governing in 1947 as he had twenty-four years earlier. If the city's notoriously bumpy streets and illegible street signs failed to tell newcomers they were unwelcome, Mayor Stapleton could be more direct. "If all those people would only go back where they came from," he responded to complaints, "we wouldn't have a housing shortage."[5] His replacement in 1947 was James Quigg Newton, a Navy veteran who offered new leadership for a city fearful of losing out on the national boom. In his eight years in office, Newton provided efficient, professional municipal management and made Denver safe for ambitious entrepreneurs. Phoenix department store executive Barry Goldwater was among the prominent business and professional men who organized a Charter Government Committee in 1949 to fight blatant corruption in city hall. It swept into office in its first campaign and dominated every city election for the next twenty years. In Albuquerque, the immediate wave of postwar reform had ended the regime of Clyde Tingley, an old-line politico who had made the position of city commission chair into that of partisan boss. Eight years of fragmented politics persuaded middle-class reformers in Albuquerque's "Heights" neighborhoods to organize their own Albuquerque Citizens Committee, which acted as an informal political party to back businesslike candidates.

San Antonio went through precisely the same process. Younger businessmen in 1949 squeezed out an inept political boss (who had once proposed to save money by having the three animals in the city zoo stuffed) and instituted city manager government in 1951. However, swirling factions and noisy political accusations blocked any semblance of efficient government. The city swept through five city managers in three years and ran through dozens of city council members in a series of recall campaigns. In response, fifty of the original advocates of charter reform created the Good Government League (GGL) to raise campaign funds and recruit council candidates. The GGL wanted no sharing of power with the city's partisan leaders, for its stated goal was "retention of the Council–Manager system, creation of good city government geared to community progress with efficient nonpartisan administrations, an end to factionalism, sectionalism, patronage politics, and maneuvering for special selfish interests." The league quickly evolved into another "nonpartisan" party that advocated a well-defined platform, used an anonymous committee to choose council candidates, and backed seventy-seven of the eighty-one city council winners between 1955 and 1971. The "sectionalism" that it claimed to abhor often meant the interests of Mexican American and African American neighborhoods, which were given carefully selected token representation on the city council. Drawing most of its leaders from a few elite neighborhoods, the GGL, as Robert Lineberry has described it, was "a sort of upper class political machine, officing not in Tammany Hall, but in a savings and loan association."[6]

Several of the West's oil cities offered a variation on the pattern of neoprogressive politics in which strong growth coalitions from the 1920s and 1930s persisted into the 1940s and 1950s under the direction of tight cliques of businessmen. Minorities might receive token acknowledgment, but public dissent from the agenda of economic growth was scarcely tolerated. The oil boom of the 1920s had given Oklahoma City a heady taste of growth. As the United States emerged from the Great Depression, the city already had its agenda of urban redevelopment and aggressive annexation well in place. City hall articulated the forthright capitalism of Kerr-McGee Oil, Oklahoma Gas and Electric, the First National Bank, and especially E. K. Gaylord, who owned both daily newspapers and the first television station. While Gaylord's front-page editorials set the tone for the city, the actual plans and programs came from the Chamber of Commerce and its managing director, Stanley Draper. "Mr. Oklahoma City" by resolution of the Oklahoma House of Representatives, he dominated day-to-day policy from 1931 to 1969, just as Gaylord managed the larger climate of opinion. South of the state line, newspaper publisher Amon Carter *was* Forth Worth until his death in 1955. He pushed economic growth, dipped into the federal pork barrel for West Texas, and denigrated Dallas.

Until well into the 1950s, many of the key decisions about the future of Houston were made in Suite 8F of the Lamar Hotel, the private rooms of George Brown, cofounder of the engineering and construction firm of Brown and Root (a predecessor of Halliburton). Over bourbon and a hand of cards, three or four other tycoons would join Brown for storytelling—and decision making. Jesse Jones owned the *Houston Chronicle* and huge chunks of downtown real estate. William Hobby was a former Texas governor and represented his family's *Houston Post*. Gus Worthman was the founder of American General Life Insurance, and James Ellis ran the First National City Bank. Leon Jaworski, a protégé who later became the Watergate prosecutor, recalled that an evening's talk in the late forties or early fifties could "pretty well determine what the course of events would be in Houston, politically, particularly, and economically to some degree." As in Oklahoma City, vigorous annexation was part of the agenda. Mayor Oscar Holcombe in 1949 persuaded voters to double the size of Houston from seventy-six to 155 square miles, protecting future municipal tax revenues while encouraging sprawl.[7]

As in oil cities south of the border, business leadership dominated Edmonton from the early 1930s into the 1960s. Working through the Citizens Committee, the Anglo-Canadian elite who ran local real estate, utility, and manufacturing companies also ran the nonpartisan city government very much along the lines of American neoprogressivism. As the city boomed after 1947 with a wave of oil discoveries, the civic leadership capitalized on the booster spirit of ambitious new residents and cheerleading from the *Edmonton Journal* to pursue "dynamic growth," by which was meant downtown redevelopment, highways, and sports teams.[8]

Vancouver mirrored Edmonton. Contentious class-based politics in the depression years of the early 1930s led business interests and the middle class to vote to abolish ward representation on the city council in order to thwart the Cooperative Commonwealth Federation. With backing from the Canadian Pacific Railway, BC Electric, downtown department stores, and similar economic interests, corporate managers and professionals worked through the Non-partisan Association to control at-large council elections from 1937 until 1968. The "Vancouver Club agenda" was, once again, government assistance to downtown reinvestment and freeway construction to keep people funneling into the urban center.

As basic services were put on track and physical infrastructure began to catch up with the growth of the 1940s, civic attention focused more and more narrowly on revitalizing central business districts. Downtown urban renewal became a central policy issue of the 1960s, just as the professionalization of government had been a leading issue of the 1950s. Western cities were slow to sign up for federal renewal dollars, in part because of the conservative political values of the 1950s. Portland backed off its first urban renewal proposal in 1952 because of neighborhood resistance, and politicians did not try again for six years. Seattle held back from passing enabling legislation until 1957 because of the taint of socialism attached to any federal spending program, at least in the mind of Mayor Gordon Clinton. Salt Lake City voted six to one against accepting renewal dollars in 1965 after a campaign that described urban renewal as a violation of the divinely given right of property ownership. Phoenix leaders made an about-face between 1958 and 1961, first proposing urban renewal and then backing off when far-Right grassroots conservatives conflated urban renewal and housing code inspections as government tyranny (in the process painting Barry Goldwater as a Communist dupe). Omaha voters rejected urban renewal proposals on three different occasions. Dallas, Fort Worth, and Houston also saw no need to reinforce their booming private economies with suspect federal dollars.

Nevertheless, downtown renewal was the climax of two decades of business government in the majority of western cities from Tulsa to Fresno. Advocates sold the program as a tool for enhancing the overall competitiveness of their city. Downtown Tulsa Unlimited (1955), a coalition of business leaders, helped to pass bond issues in 1959 and 1965 for a $55 million civic center. It also supported an adjacent renewal project that cleared land for a hospital, a community college, and apartment and office buildings. The Central Seattle Association looked for ways to confirm its edge over Portland, and Portlanders wanted urban renewal to fight back against Seattle. Boosters of renewal in downtown Denver hoped that the thirty-seven-block Skyline Renewal Project (1967) would let the city throw off the influence of the Federal Reserve Bank cities Kansas City, Missouri, and Dallas. At the same time, San Franciscans hoped to preserve preeminence as a national metropolis through the Golden Gateway Center, which replaced the wholesale produce market near the ferry terminal with office towers shaped like Nabisco vanilla wafers. Industrialists C. B. Zellerbach and Charles Blyth got the project off the ground in 1955 by forming a business committee to advance planning funds to the city. In the 1960s the Golden Gateway development triggered a private construction boom that Manhattanized the San Francisco skyline. The neo-Egyptian obelisk of the Transamerica Pyramid was the most conspicuous among the dozens of buildings that added 10 million square feet of office space for bankers, corporate moguls, and other leaders of a national metropolis.

The redevelopment agenda conceived of western cities as the homes and headquarters of the white middle class. To the growth establishment and neoprogressives, poor people were an impediment, especially when they lived on the edges of downtown. The fate of Bunker Hill was widely shared. Tucson paved over its skid road. Denver's downtown renewal left only two isolated blocks of the old workingmen's district near the railroad station, blocks that survived only when recycled as Larimer Square, with shops and restaurants for the middle class. Portland left skid road alone but took out South Portland, where elderly Jewish residents remembered the delicatessens and

elderly Italian Americans remembered movie theaters that used to sell $0.05 tickets to double features in Italian. Seattle dropped the spacecraft of the Century 21 world's fair of 1962 onto the Warren neighborhood, a somewhat seedy area where old and single people with little money lived in run-down hotels. The redevelopment put the squeeze on the cheap housing and social services in Belltown, between downtown and the new Seattle Center, marking it for the triumph of condominium developments, expense-account restaurants, and yuppie bars in the 1990s.

San Francisco similarly targeted eighty-seven acres of cheap hotels, parking lots, and warehouses south of Market Street for a convention center and office towers. City bureaucrats saw expanded tax revenues, the Convention

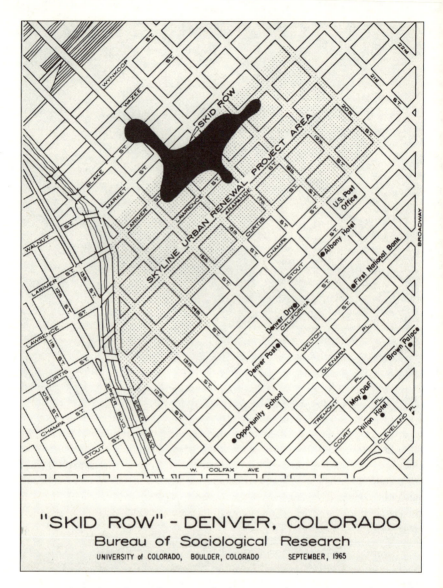

"SKID ROW" - DENVER, COLORADO
Bureau of Sociological Research
UNIVERSITY of COLORADO, BOULDER, COLORADO   SEPTEMBER, 1965

FIGURE 48. Larimer Street, Denver, and urban renewal. In 1965, researchers at the University of Colorado prepared this map of blighted areas in downtown Denver. Much of the area under the inkblot was cleared as part of the Skyline Urban Renewal Project, although a portion of Larimer Street itself was saved by historic preservation activists and recycled as an entertainment district. (Bureau of Sociological Research, University of Colorado, 1965.)

FIGURE 49. Coors Field and the new downtown Denver. Like Seattle, San Francisco, and San Diego, Denver recycled its nineteenth-century warehouse district on its downtown fringe for spectator sports. Coors Field opened in 1995 just to the east of the skid road district marked on the 1965 map. (Wikimedia Commons.)

and Visitors Bureau saw flush times for the hospitality industry, and the Building and Construction Trades Council saw more jobs. Community activists saw the eviction of 3,000 poor people. Public protests and litigation starting in 1968 blocked federal funds for several years and secured 1,200 low-rent apartments for the elderly, but a generation later the SoMa district would be the site of the Moscone Convention Center, the San Francisco Museum of Modern Art, and scads of trendy dot-com workers in the 1990s.

Also in Los Angeles, the urban poor after 1945 were frequently people of color, for the Great Depression and then World War II had brought tens of thousands of American Indians and hundreds of thousands of African Americans and Mexican Americans into Rocky Mountain and Pacific cities. Denver's permanent Mexican American population doubled in the 1930s with displaced farmworkers and again in the 1940s, when the black population also doubled. Portland's African American population increased tenfold because of wartime job opportunities. The number of African Americans in Seattle jumped eightfold and doubled even in out-of-the-way Tucson.

Crowded into a handful of central neighborhoods, the new minority communities were often directly in the way of progress, as at Chavez Ravine. Many of Portland's new African Americans scarcely had time to unpack before officials in the 1950s evicted them from neighborhoods in the northeast section of the city to build a Memorial Coliseum and run Interstate 5 north to the Columbia River. San Francisco redevelopment disrupted the Asian American community west of Van Ness Street, and Vancouver would gladly have put the squeeze on Chinatown to facilitate redevelopment east of downtown.

On the northern plains, it was often aboriginal peoples who lived in the roadbed of progress. Novelist Louise Erdrich has described Fargo's North Pacific Avenue as "the central thoroughfare of the dingy feel-good roll of Indian bars, Western-wear stores, pawn shops, and Christian Revival Missions that Fargo was trying to eradicate."⁹ Two hundred miles to the north, Winnipeg used a freeway to bisect Main Street. The highway divided a section with brighter redevelopment prospects from a North Main district of single-room occupancy hotels, missions, and, in the words of one bluntly prejudiced politician, "poor and drunk Metis." Twenty years later, a sympathetic Winnipeg journalist described "a grungy gauntlet of skid-row hotels, pawnshops, soup kitchens. . . . Winnipeggers, the kind who locked their car doors as they drove past, saw only Aboriginal faces on North Main Street. To them it was the biggest urban 'reserve' in Canada."¹⁰

There was as much continuity as change in the evolving Chinatowns, deeply embedded skid rows, and even the new black neighborhoods. What African American newcomers found in the Pacific West, as Walter Moseley's fictional detective Easy Rawlins knew, was in some ways a westward transposition of the racial practices of the trans-Mississippi South. Most of the black migrants were from Texas, Louisiana, Oklahoma, and Arkansas (nearly half of new black Angelenos from 1930 to 1970, for example, were Texans and Louisianans). They found cities where white southern migrants were helping to shape public attitudes. In Portland, wartime migrants from the Mississippi Valley states helped to defeat a local public housing ordinance and blocked efforts to build public housing for African Americans displaced from wartime projects by a Columbia River flood. Oklahoma native Lincoln Ragsdale, a Phoenix civil rights leader from the 1950s to the 1970s, found a city where white migrants from the southern states had created a racial system much like what he had left behind.

At worst, this "southwestern" heritage reached back to memories of the Tulsa race riot of 1921. In little more than a decade, that city's black community had built a thriving neighborhood north of downtown, with two newspapers, thirteen churches, and a hospital. Because blacks were barred from shopping downtown, Deep Greenwood had prosperous businesses in two- and three-story brick buildings. But Tulsa was also a raw "frontier" town with inconsistent law enforcement and many white newcomers from the Mississippi Valley South. When a white teenager accused a black youth of assaulting her in a downtown elevator, the city exploded. A white mob gathered outside the downtown jail ("To Lynch Negro Tonight" was the *Tulsa Tribune* headline), while blacks armed themselves for self-defense. After shots were fired downtown, the white mob armed itself and invaded the black district in the early morning hours. Blacks fought back until daybreak brought a larger mob that burned or trashed roughly 1,000 homes and businesses. There is no good count, but the death total was probably fifty to seventy-five, with significant numbers of fatalities on both sides. Thousands of black Tulsans spent the next year in tents as they scraped together the funds to rebuild.

Behind the sexual fears and white aggression that were found elsewhere in World War I–era racial riots (in Washington, D.C., Chicago, East St. Louis, Springfield, Illinois, and many other locales), something was different in Tulsa. The city was brand new, booming with the oil business and growing from 1,300 residents in 1900 to nearly 90,000 by the early 1920s. In this new, fast-paced city, blacks had been able to claim their own territory from the start. Rather than taking jobs away from white workers, they helped to meet a high demand for labor. Rather than intruding into established white neighborhoods, as in Chicago, they developed their community from the ground up as a parallel downtown on the other side of the railroad station. White Tulsans torched Deep Greenwood in part out of racial animosity but also to seize well-located, developable land from black Tulsans who had taken advantage of economic opportunity in a boom city. As the mayor said succinctly, "Let the Negro settlement be places farther to the north and east . . . a large portion of this district is well suited for industrial purposes rather than residences."[11] And, indeed, part of the burned-out district was soon reused for a railroad terminal.

Los Angeles too had been a place of opportunity for blacks as well as whites in the early twentieth century. Mindful of race relations in the South and in northern cities like Philadelphia, W. E. B. Du Bois wrote that "Los Angeles was wonderful. . . . Nowhere in the United States is the Negro so well and beautifully housed. . . . Here is an aggressive, hopeful group—with some wealth, large industrial opportunity and a buoyant spirit."[12] In 1910, 40 percent of African American households owned their own homes, five times the rate in Chicago and fifteen times that in New York. Housing opportunities remained good in the next decades, even with all-white covenants enforced in many neighborhoods. As the black community grew through the early twentieth century, increasing numbers made it more prosperous and stable but simultaneously provoked whites to impose more restrictions. Black leaders positioned themselves as pragmatic activists, to use Douglas Flamming's term, adopting whatever tactics "seemed likely to help blacks live better lives in their half-free environment."[13]

For Mexican Americans, Los Angeles was both a home base and a relief valve for fluctuating demand for farmworkers. The Mexican population of Los Angeles swelled to roughly 400,000 during the war. Newspapers responded with inflammatory articles and played up the Sleepy Lagoon case in which several young Mexican Americans were convicted of murder (later to be exonerated). On June 6, 1943, off-duty servicemen attacked young Mexican Americans whom they branded as criminals and draft dodgers because of their flamboyant hipster clothing of long, wide-shouldered jackets and narrow-cuffed trousers. The disorder dragged on for a week of sporadic attacks on black people and Filipinos as well as Latinos. The "Zoot Suit" riots were a climax of interethnic tension, but they followed a two-year campaign by the Los Angeles Police Department against an alleged crime wave by young Mexicans, which itself followed police Red Squad harassment of Mexican American labor organizations in the 1930s. Bad relations continued through "Bloody Christmas" in 1952, when Los Angeles police violently beat groups of Mexican American prisoners who were already safely behind bars—an event that leads off the 1998 movie *L.A. Confidential.*

In the face of hostile majorities and closed institutions, members of ethnic communities in the postwar decade sometimes found common ground in mixed neighborhoods, schools, progressive labor unions, and wartime experiences. In Seattle, Chinese, Filipinos, and Japanese returning from internment camps shared south-side neighborhoods like Rainier Valley and Beacon Hill with recent African American migrants. The same groups shared parts of Fillmore in San Francisco, where community centers and high schools made it possible to reach across racial lines. The area from Makiki to Kalihi in Honolulu was a setting where pan-Asian alliances could develop among multiple groups with East Asian roots. In turn, shared schools and neighborhood proximity helped to nurture political cooperation among Asian Americans, African Americans, and Mexican Americans, often with the help of Jewish radicals in community organizations and Left-leaning labor organizations.

Los Angeles was the site of a significant breakthrough. Multiracial Unity Councils and the Human Relations Committee set a postwar pattern of interethnic cooperation. Distinctly ethnic organizations—the NAACP, the Japanese American Citizens League, the Chinese American Citizens' Association, and the American Jewish Congress—began to pursue joint projects. The Boyle Heights neighborhood east of downtown was a shifting mix of first- and second-generation Jewish immigrants, Japanese Americans returning from internment camps, and growing numbers of Mexican Americans. A sympathetic journalist called it a "U.N. in microcosm," whereas unfriendly federal housing officials thought it "hopelessly heterogeneous" and therefore unsuitable for mortgage guarantees. Jewish activists helped to organize the predominantly Mexican Community Service Organization, which provided the community base for voter-registration efforts and political campaigns that won Edward Roybal a city council seat in 1949.[14]

Elsewhere in the Southwest, blacks and Latinos worked in parallel but not in concert to expand the range of civil rights. After World War II, Latino organizations such as the League of United Latin American Citizens (formed in Corpus Christi in 1929) and the newly organized G.I. Forum battled job discrimination and ethnic segregation. In 1946, the federal courts had prohibited segregation of Mexican American children in California schools in *Westminster v. Mendez*.[15] Eight years later, the Supreme Court forbade Texas from excluding Mexican Americans from juries. Both decisions paved the way for the recognition of African American civil rights but did not directly protect them. With greater numbers, a distinctly Catholic religious tradition, and a racial identity that did not fit neatly into the black–white dichotomy, Mexican Americans in Phoenix tended to pursue their own political and economic goals. In San Antonio, black and Mexican leaders struck their own accommodations with the Good Government League (GGL) elite. Henry B. Gonzalez, for example, followed a political career similar to Ed Roybal's, being elected to local office in 1951 and Congress in 1961, but did so without directly challenging the GGL.

By the mid-1960s in Denver, Chicano activists increasingly emphasized self-help and self-determination. Rodolfo Gonzales established the Crusade for Justice in 1966, dedicated to organizing Chicanos and concentrating their political power. His "Plan for the Barrio" in 1968 emphasized Hispanic cultural traditions, community control of schools, and economic development. By the early 1970s, Crusade was running a school and publishing a newspaper. The Second National Chicano Youth Conference in 1970 adopted the similar "Spiritual Plan of Atzlan," named after the northern homeland of Mexican Indians. Gonzales organized La Raza Unida to contest elections. Although its candidate for governor in 1970 got only two percent of the vote, it forced major parties to court Latino voters.

In the larger picture, structural changes in metropolitan economies and geography undercut efforts at progressive coalition building across ethnic and racial lines. Well-paying industrial jobs that had attracted African Americans to western cities in the 1940s began to leak to suburbs in the 1950s, placing barriers of distance and housing discrimination between black workers and job opportunities. Los Angeles blacks had made significant gains in shipbuilding, port jobs, and heavy manufacturing concentrated in prewar factory districts, but the fast-growing aerospace industry added new economic frustrations with rapid dispersal and continued racism in hiring.[16] In Washington, Boeing added suburban assembly plants in Everett and Renton to its older, centrally located facilities at Boeing Field.

Oakland shows how the two forces of suburbanization and redevelopment worked together to disadvantage African Americans. Following World War II, the immediate postwar years opened the door to a progressive political movement that was labor based and racially inclusive to fight issues such as rent control and public housing. A general strike in 1946 failed to achieve immediate goals but helped five pro-labor city candidates win city council seats the next year. Working on a very different agenda, however, Oakland's civic elite picked a strategy of industrial decentralization and residential segregation that undercut the nascent biracial coalition. Factories located or relocated in the new suburbs of San Leandro and Milpitas, whose housing markets were open to white workers but effectively closed to blacks. Meanwhile, the Oakland Planning Commission introduced a massive redevelopment plan in 1959 with the forecast that Oakland could become the metropolitan center for northern California. To accomplish this ambition, the city cleared much of West Oakland for port expansion, highways, and rapid transit, displacing 6,000 African Americans. Oakland fell short of matching San Francisco while its East Bay suburbs flourished and its marginalized African Americans simmered in frustration.

The same sorts of structured disadvantage lay behind the disorder that exploded in the summer of 1965 in Watts, a black neighborhood on the south side of Los Angeles. Watts was an extension of the South Central neighborhood that had developed a vibrant community culture in the prosperous years during and just after World War II. Visitors like Jack Kerouac found the black metropolis as mesmerizing as Harlem, describing the scene in *On the Road*: "Terry came out and led me by the hand to Central Avenue, which is the colored main drag of L.A. And what a wild place it is. . . . The wild humming night of Central Avenue—the night of Hamp's 'Central Avenue Breakdown'—howled and boomed along outside."[17] Despite residential segregation and increasing physical deterioration in south-side neighborhoods, the National Urban League as late as 1964 ranked Los Angeles as the most desirable American city for African Americans.

Nonetheless, big trouble erupted on the evening of August 11, when a white highway patrolman arrested a young black for drunken driving. The mother of the arrested youth protested loudly. A crowd assembled, and a scuffle ensued with the arresting officers. The arrival of the Los Angeles police incited the crowd, which turned into an angry mob that stoned passing cars and threatened the police. Rioting, looting, and arson spread through the entire Watts community the following day, with the police powerless to intervene. The California National Guard arrived on the evening of August 13, two days after the trouble started, and effectively laid siege to Watts. By August 15, the National Guard occupied a quiet and pacified neighborhood. Novelist Walter Moseley re-created the aftermath:

On Avalon and Central and Hooper the burned buildings outnumbered the ones still intact. There was at least one torched car
hunkered down at the curb on almost every block. Debris was strewn
along the sidewalks and streets. Smoke still rose here and there
from the wreckage. . . . and the police made their presence felt. They
were still riding four to a car, some wearing riot helmets or holding

shotguns upright in their laps. They were still jumpy from days and nights when the Negro population rose up and fought back.[18]

The Watts riot resulted in thirty-four deaths, 1,000 injuries, and 4,000 arrests, with damage to at least 600 buildings. It also frightened white Americans by turning the tables of racial violence. In Chicago and Tulsa forty-five years earlier, blacks had been the victims and whites had been the instigators who used collective violence to keep the newcomers in their place. In Watts, however, blacks were the aggressors, while white "civilians" who were unlucky enough to be in the wrong place at the wrong time found themselves victims. The real targets, however, were two symbols of white authority—the police and ghetto businesses with reputations for exploiting black consumers. As the National Advisory Commission on Civil Disorders concluded in 1968, most property damage was a deliberate response against white-owned businesses that the black community considered unfair or exploitative. Underlying factors included continued housing discrimination and the bitter frustration of disappearing blue-collar jobs. In short, the riots in Watts and other cities were protests—attempts by frustrated members of the black community to call attention to the problems and disabilities of ghetto life.

Resistance in Oakland took the form of political organizing by the Black Panther Party rather than mobilization in the streets. The Panthers drew on the generation of Bay Area blacks who grew up as children of war workers during the 1940s. Bobby Seale was born in 1936 in North Texas but grew up in Berkeley's Codornices Village housing project—one of the segregated legacies of the World War II boom. Huey Newton was born in 1942 in Louisiana but grew up in Oakland. They met as college students and developed an ideology of community empowerment on the basis of Frantz Fanon's anticolonial Marxism, Seale's work in the North Oakland Anti-poverty Center, and personal experiences on the streets of Oakland. In a city where less radical efforts at community control and economic development had few results, Newton and Seale created the Black Panthers in 1966, began to carry firearms, and recruited a visible and articulate ex-convict named Eldridge Cleaver. The Panthers confronted what they saw as biased police. The Panthers shadowed police patrols to prevent mistreatment of African Americans and carried weapons into the California State Legislature in May 1967 to protest gun control. The Panthers also promoted community-based self-help efforts, such as a free breakfast program for schoolchildren and medical clinics, and ran political candidates. In contrast to the rioters in Watts, the Panthers had a political program, if not the ability to carry it through.

The movement was shaken when Newton was convicted of manslaughter for killing a police officer and Cleaver fled to Algeria. Panther chapters imploded when they attracted thugs and shakedown artists as well as visionaries. Nevertheless, the Panthers survived as a political party, registering black voters and running Bobby Seale as a strong candidate for mayor of Oakland in 1973 and Elaine Brown for city council in 1973 and 1975 before supporting African American Lionel Wilson in his successful mayoral campaign in 1977. Former Panther Bobby Rush entered Congress representing Oakland in 1992—in a decade when African American and Latino officeholders in western and southwestern cities would be counted in the hundreds and thousands.[19] Indeed, the story of the second generation of postwar politics after 1970 was to be the revitalization of liberal progressivism around the old aims of minority representation and civil rights and new goals of neighborhood protection and environmentalism—diverse and sometimes conflicting objectives for diverse constituencies that skilled leaders could still shape into winning coalitions.

CHAPTER TWELVE

The Politics of Diversity

John stepped off the elevator, ignored offers to go for beers, and walked through downtown Seattle streets. There were so many white men to choose from. Everybody was a white man in downtown Seattle.
—Sherman Alexie, *Indian Killer* (1996)

Later that evening, everyone would remark at one time or another how roomy 2932 West Sixth Avenue had become all of a sudden. . . . Within a week, Eleven (or perhaps Speed) would remark that the single-family bourgeois dwelling had a lot to recommend it, that the commune was a thing of the past, and that he was thinking of moving into a suite of his own in Kitsalano, provided that it was not full of drug addicts.
—John Gray, *Dazzled* (1984)

O n August 19, 1969, Riverfront for People held a picnic on a highway median strip in downtown Portland, Oregon. On a midsummer day when the mountains and coast beckoned many Portlanders, 250 adults and 100 children spread their blankets and opened their coolers and baskets on a barren strip between four lanes of busy traffic on Front Avenue and an even busier four lanes on Harbor Drive, a 1940s freeway that divided downtown from the Willamette River. Meeting at nearly the precise spot where pioneers had erected Portland's first buildings, the throng comprised young and enthusiastic activists who thought that Portland deserved a park along its downtown waterfront.

The motive was the scheduled demolition of a great white elephant—a two-block building constructed in the 1930s as a public market. The structure sat between Front Avenue and Harbor Drive. For highway engineers, removal opened up the possibility of *more* lanes for *more* traffic along the river. For the hastily organized Riverfront for People, it opened the chance to replace concrete with grass, speeding vehicles with people strolling the downtown riverfront. The City Club of Portland, a good-government study group, weighed in with a report that called for "varied public use . . . and attractive pedestrian access to the esplanade and the river itself."[1] In October the activists convinced the powerful state Highway Commission that a park was at least a possibility. There were two more years of study and debate before the city ripped up Harbor Drive. But it was the activists who introduced the idea, fought off halfway measures (burying Harbor Drive in a tube and topping it with sod was one idea), helped put open-minded leaders on the city council, and deserve the credit for what has grown into Tom McCall Waterfront Park.

Nearly half a continent away, Mexican Americans in modest neighborhoods of San Antonio's west side were growing increasingly dissatisfied with token representation in city government. Fire stations on the west side had the city's older equipment and less experienced crews. Parks were more likely than elsewhere to be poorly maintained fields without play equipment. Low-lying west-side neighborhoods lacked both storm sewers and sanitary sewers, flooding when heavy rains poured off the higher north-side neighborhoods where most civic leaders lived.

The catalyst for action was a flash flood on August 7, 1974. The organization that was available to channel the frustration was Communities Organized for Public Service (COPS), a coalition of neighborhood groups that had grown slowly over the past year with the assistance of the Catholic archdiocese. COPS defined a list of very specific grievances, dug out supporting data, and confronted decision makers. COPS members staged "deposit-ins" when they gummed up the operation of local banks by repeatedly making small deposits and withdrawals. COPS packed city council meetings and forced the city manager to attend a public assembly on the west side, where he faced 500 residents more than ready to talk about storm sewers. The direct result was a bond issue to implement a drainage plan that had mildewed on the shelf since 1945. An indirect result was the erosion of Good Government League influence and the election of independent Latinos to the city council.

The majority of COPS members came from the Mexican American middle-class, churchgoing, achievement-oriented families with steady but limited incomes from government jobs and small businesses. The organization was particularly successful in utilizing the talents of Mexican American women, whose previous public involvement was limited to church groups and PTA meetings. The organization wanted specific service improvements, but it also wanted a seat at the table, and it wanted the specific needs of moderate-income neighborhoods to be given adequate weight in consideration of citywide priorities.[2]

Riverfront for People and COPS introduce an important turn in western city politics from neoprogressivism to a politics of diversity. Citywide planning and growth agendas did not disappear, but new political activists chipped away at postwar growth coalitions from the mid-1960s through the 1970s. The neoprogressives often failed to reproduce themselves by recruiting new leaders to replace an aging generation. More important, they were challenged by constituencies with new ideas about minority rights, community conservation, and environmental protection. African Americans, Latinos, middle-class Anglos, and women all learned to use spatial concentration and neighborhood networks as political resources. The challengers to the growth coalition, with its claim to speak for the all-encompassing public interest, therefore created city council districts, neighborhood organizations, and community groups that could use their geographic bases to articulate a variety of public interests. Across these and many other cities, a common element was an emphasis on the importance of older neighborhoods—as residential communities to be conserved and as political units to be represented through district-based elections.

Many of the "antigrowth" activists were members of the postindustrial middle class. Scientists, professors, government workers, and executives of large corporations depend on the national demand for their talents rather than local markets for goods and services. They are "cosmopolitan in outlook and pecuniary in interest," as sociologist Harvey Molotch has pointed out. They view their cities more as residential environments than as economic machines. Salaried employees who were caught in the inflation of the 1970s, they were also intensely interested in the availability of affordable and convenient housing. We can call these activists quality-of-life liberals. In a manner that ironically recalls the prewar elites of places like Denver, they worried that breakneck development was fouling the air, eating up open space, sacrificing neighborhoods to automobiles, and deferring the costs of remediation to future decades.

Generational change also drove the introduction of new issues. The extraordinary wartime migration of people in their twenties and thirties intensified the impact of the national postwar baby boom in western cities. As the first of the western boomers reached voting age in the mid-1960s, they found appeal in new ideas about cities and communities that had just been articulated in books such as Jane Jacobs's *The Death and Life of Great American Cities* (1961), Rachel Carson's *Silent Spring* (1962), and Michael Harrington's *The Other America* (1962).[3] The new activists came of age and progressed through high school, college, and their early careers during the great era of confidence and prosperity from 1945 to 1974. In the United States and Canada, that prosperity and optimism were especially characteristic of western provinces, states, and cities.

Denverites staged an early and surprising quality of life revolt over the 1976 Winter Olympics. The Chamber of Commerce, Governor John Love, Mayor Bill McNichols, and nearly every other mover and shaker agreed that the Olympics was a symbol of progress, capable of "breaking Denver from the shell of provincialism . . . and catapulting it before the world as a truly international city."[4] Ballooning cost estimates and fears of environmental damage to the Rockies raised popular doubts. Opponents gathered 77,000 signatures to place on the November 1972 ballot a state constitutional amendment and a Denver city charter amendment to prohibit further use of public funds for the Olympics. Citizens of Colorado's Future (CCF) reiterated that the primary beneficiaries of the Olympics would be the tourism and construction industries, while ordinary citizens would bear the cost through higher taxes. Counterattacks on CCF as political amateurs were more accurate than insulting, and the measures carried easily. The community mobilization launched Patricia Schroeder's national political career and enabled Richard Lamm, a leader of the anti-Olympics effort, to win the statehouse in 1974.

Seattle's quality-of-life liberals organized around amenities with powerful symbolic values as well as practical attractions. Downtown redevelopment plans threatened the quaint and ungainly Pike Place Market until University of Washington professor Victor Steinbrueck helped Seattleites articulate their affection for funkier parts of the cityscape. Pioneer Square—a skid road that became a pioneering historic district—reminded residents of the city's literal golden age during the Klondike gold rush. Environmentally oriented residents rediscovered nature in the city and campaigned to turn the surplus lands of Fort Lawton into Discovery Park, twining nature walks around decommissioned antiaircraft missile sites.

Seattleites were important participants in a network of West Coast activists who worked on proactive environmental policies around energy use, recycling, transportation, and food systems. The *Whole Earth Catalog* and *Seriatim: The Journal of Ecotopia* emerged from the post-hippie ambiance of the Bay Area, which housed the Farallones Institute (publisher of *The Integral Urban House: Self-Reliance Living in the City*) and the Portola Institute (the umbrella for the *Whole Earth Catalog*). A grassroots revolt in Eugene, led by "middle-class, well-educated, reformist, politically liberal" activists, fended off a proposed nuclear power plant in 1970, reversing a technocratic decision by the Eugene Water and Electric Board under the banner of citizen involvement.[5] Portlanders created *Rain* magazine to share options for living lightly on the land. Seattleites advanced counterculture environmentalism through neighborhood recycling in the Fremont district and the promotion of sustainable food systems through organizations like Tilth. Berkeley resident

Ernest Callenbach caught the enthusiastic spirit of radical innovation, if not the reality, in his best-selling utopian novel *Ecotopia* (1975).[6]

Political change in Austin also tapped environmental concerns and built directly on student activism at the University of Texas. As late as an open housing referendum in 1968 and the city council elections in 1969, Austin came down solidly on the side of property rights and economic development. Two years later, however, antiwar activists and environmentalists led a referendum that rejected city participation in a nuclear power project. The Coalition for a Progressive Austin organized in 1975 to back liberal candidates, and it maintained an uneasy alliance with home owners, whose vocal neighborhood associations fought intensive development. The Progressive Austinites was essentially a slow-growth group in opposition to the business agenda of the Greater Austin Association. It won a majority on what was quickly termed the People's Council, but it was soon clear that it was very difficult to please middle-class slow-growthers, radical university populists, and minorities who were happy with economic development if they could get a fair cut. The coalition's ability to govern dissipated, but the episode did add neighborhood and environmental issues to the city's political agenda.

Among other changing cities like Denver and Seattle, Portland stood out for implementing a *comprehensive* set of public policies and constructing long-lived political coalitions around several planning goals. Portland had many of the same problems as other cities. Downtown parking was inadequate, the bus company was bankrupt, and a new superregional mall threatened downtown retailing. At the same time, older neighborhoods were at risk from schemes for large-scale land clearance and redevelopment, concentrated poverty, and racial inequities. Many cities understood the situation as a zero-sum competition in which downtown businesses and home owners battled over a fixed pool of resources. Portland is one of the few cities where the "growth machine" business leadership of the 1950s made a graceful transition to participation in a more inclusive political system. The resulting political marriage was a mobilization of the open-minded middle.

The chief architect and beneficiary of the political transition was Neil Goldschmidt, a poverty attorney elected to City Council in 1970 and mayor in 1972, at age thirty-two, representing a city with an increasing proportion of residents in their twenties and thirties.[7] Goldschmidt and his staff were strongly influenced by the 1970 census, which showed the effects of a declining proportion of middle-class families on neighborhood diversity and city tax base. Goldschmidt's "population strategy" emphasized public transportation, neighborhood revitalization, and downtown planning. Better transit would improve air quality, enhance older neighborhoods, and bring workers and shoppers downtown. In turn, a vital business center would protect property values in surrounding districts and increase their attractiveness for residential reinvestment. Middle-class families who remained or moved into inner neighborhoods would patronize downtown businesses, and prosperity would support high levels of public services. Neighborhood planning would focus on housing rehabilitation and on visible amenities to keep older residential areas competitive with the suburbs.

Preservation of a user-friendly downtown was the cornerstone. Business worries about suburban competition and parking problems coincided at the end of the 1960s with public disgust over a blighted riverfront. The public concern sparked by Riverfront for People in 1969 not only paved (unpaved?) the way for the removal of Harbor Drive but also fired imaginations about radical responses to other downtown problems. The Downtown Plan of 1972 offered integrated solutions to a long list of problems that Portlanders had approached piecemeal for two generations. It was technically sound because its proposals were based on improvements in access and transportation. It was politically viable because it prescribed trade-offs among different interests as part of a coherent strategy. Specifics included new parks and plazas, high-density retail and office corridors crossing in the center of downtown, better transit and new parking garages to serve the corridors, districts for special housing incentives, and pedestrian-oriented design.

The complement to downtown revival was a "neighborhood revolution" that began when more than a score of neighborhoods began to argue vigorously for their own versions of local revitalization in the later 1960s. Indeed, the critical mass of neighborhood protest required attention not as single problems or single neighborhoods but as a neighborhood movement. In 1974, the City Council established the Office of Neighborhood Associations to assist local organizations through central and district offices. Neighborhood groups were part of a deep transformation of community life, with the rise of scores of grassroots and issue-based organizations that turned Portlanders into inveterate civic participants whose levels of involvement bucked national patterns by trending steadily upward.[8]

Omaha's formal planning process showed the same shifting goals as did planning for downtown Portland and Seattle. The Omaha Plan of 1956 had scarcely recognized the downtown as a problem and emphasized investment in the city's infrastructure. Ten years later, the Central Omaha Plan recognized special downtown needs but placed its faith in interstate highways and urban renewal. The next seven years, however, brought a generational shift in civic leadership and a willingness to focus on the multiple experiences that downtown had to offer. A new central business district plan in 1973 divided the city center into eight "neighborhoods." As in Portland, planners hoped to bring younger Omahans back downtown with a variety of functions and attractions, including a Central Park Mall (1980).

Canadians reacted just as strongly against urban renewal and freeway plans that threatened historic neighborhoods and comfortable middle-class communities. As a Canadian specialist in urban politics has written, the late 1960s brought movements to counter the neoprogressive agenda with "preference for smallness over bigness [and] opposition to the notion that public works were necessarily good works."[9] To counter slating committees that called themselves citizens' committees and nonpartisan associations, the grassroots opposition devised their own clever acronyms: TEAM for the Electors Action Movement, COPE for the Committee of Progressive Electors, and URGE for the Urban Reform Group of Edmonton.

The latter group grew out of middle-class opposition to a massive highway plan, unveiled in 1964, that would have run five freeways into the center of Edmonton. Leaders of the resistance included faculty and staff at the fast-growing University of Alberta, many of whom were newcomers with new ideas. These quality-of-life liberals forced transportation planners back to the drawing board to produce a new plan in 1973 that reduced reliance on freeways and included a light-rail system. URGE grew out of this effort, advocating for citizen participation and decentralization of decisions. First contesting council elections in 1974, it was increasingly successful in the 1980s and represented Edmonton's relatively progressive tilt within conservative Alberta politics.

A freeway plan—this time in 1967—was also a catalyst for change in Vancouver. With its threat to Americanize Vancouver by shooting freeways into the core of the city, the plan set off a great freeway debate that forced its withdrawal. A year after the plan appeared, a newly organized Strathcona Property Owners and Tenants Association successfully fended off urban renewal proposed for the large Chinatown east of downtown. Historic preservation advocates undermined a Canadian Pacific Railway scheme to redevelop Gastown, the original Vancouver town site and more recently its skid road. On the west side of the city, condominium and apartment construction invaded run-down hippie neighborhoods like Kitsalano, generating new activism around neighborhood conservation. By the early 1970s, new interests and constituencies were making themselves heard. Racial minorities, the new middle class with its quality of life concerns, university-trained activists, and environmentalists "all resisted any land-use change that was propelled by rapid growth and orchestrated by inaccessible politicians and their technical staff."[10]

With the city in political ferment, the middle-class reformers of TEAM won a strong victory in 1972 and held onto power until 1978. Its left-center quality-of-life liberals found their hand strengthened when B.C. electors voted in the progressive New Democratic Party (NDP), with its base in labor unions, to replace the business-oriented Social Credit government. TEAM introduced local area planning to help older neighborhoods define their future. It also redeveloped the south side of False Creek, the outmoded industrial backyard of the city, with moderate-density housing and open space in a model project in the context of the 1970s.

The 1980s brought a series of shifts and countershifts in Vancouver politics. TEAM faltered as the somewhat vanilla middle-of-the-road option, opening the way for COPE to come on strong in 1980. Two years later, Vancouverites voted 57 percent in favor of a return to ward representation. While COPE and its NDP allies held a slim majority in the city, however, the Social Credit Party regained control of British Columbia in 1983 with a Thatcherite agenda of reduced social spending, economic development, and encouragement of outside capital. The province turned its attention to the north side of False Creek for a new stadium and for Expo '86, the provincially sponsored world's fair. After the fair closed, the province moved to redevelop the site with a forest of tall, slim residential towers built with East Asian capital. While the city and province argued over density, affordable housing, and the family-friendliness of the redeveloped districts, outside investment continued to remake central Vancouver in the image of Singapore.[11]

The rise of neighborhood liberals in cities like Austin and Portland was closely associated with the increasing importance of women as direct participants and leaders in local politics. An obvious indicator has been the long list of women elected mayor of major western cities. Portland voters chose attorney Dorothy Lee to head a reform administration as early as 1948. Patience Latting followed in Oklahoma City in 1971. In the next twenty years, the list expanded to include Dallas, Fort Worth, Austin, Houston, Galveston, San Antonio, Corpus Christi, El Paso, Phoenix, Santa Barbara, San Jose, San Francisco, Modesto, Stockton, and Spokane. In 1987, women served as mayor in twenty-six western cities of at least 50,000 residents, just under half of the national total.

Relative ease of access to leadership positions, especially after 1970, reflected the same institutional openness that assisted neoprogressive reform after World War II. We can derive several hypotheses about political empowerment and capacity building from the special character of western cities and their impact on middle-class women. First, the cities of the postwar West were communities filled with newcomers who lacked ties and obligations to extended families, churches, and other community institutions. Women who had satisfied their responsibilities to their nuclear families were therefore relatively free to devote time and energy to political activity. Second, the spreading suburbs of western cities were "frontiers" that required concerted action to solve immediate functional and service needs, such as adequate schools and decent parks. Because pursuit of the residential amenity package has often been viewed as "woman's work" (in contrast to the "man's work" of economic development), burgeoning suburbs offered numerous opportunities for women to engage in volunteer civic work, to sharpen their skills as political activists, and finally to run for local office. Their work on behalf of neighborhood amenities, of course, could easily overlap with the issues of quality-of-life liberalism. Third, western cities had fewer established political institutions such as political machines and strong parties. In the same way that it had helped the neoprogressives, a system of personal, nonparty politics was open to the influence of energetic women.

San Jose and Santa Clara County showed the specific impact of these processes in what some called the feminist capital of the nation.[12] Voters in 1980 made women a three-to-two majority on the Santa Clara County Board of Supervisors and a seven-to-four majority on the San Jose City Council. That majority included Mayor Janet Gray Hayes, elected in 1974 with the slogan "Let's make San Jose better before we make it bigger." By 1982, fourteen of the fifteen cities in Santa Clara County had women on their councils, and four had a woman as mayor. Mainstream as well as radical candidates hoped for endorsements from the major women's political organizations.

The roots of political achievement lay in grassroots organizing in the 1970s that blended issues of neighborhood quality and environment, equal services for Chicanas, and feminist issues such as comparable worth and shelters for battered women. Janet Flammang has argued that women and their organizations such as the League of Women Voters, the National Women's Political Caucus, the National Organization for Women, and the Chicana Alliance filled a political vacuum in the nonpartisan arenas of Sacramento and Santa Clara County. They defined issues, educated the electorate, recruited candidates, raised campaign funds, and rang doorbells for candidates. In affluent Silicon Valley, the lead in the 1970s came from slow-growth environmentalists and neighborhood activists whose husbands had secure professional careers. These middle-class women joined an informal coalition of minority and labor groups to convince the citizens of San Jose to switch to district council elections. By lowering the cost of campaigning and increasing the relative importance of door-to-door canvassing, district elections helped women as well as minority candidates.

Women's participation in local politics also drew on their success in filling high-level professional and managerial jobs. The relative openness of western cities to the economic advancement of women can be measured by women's share of executive, administrative, and managerial positions—jobs such as accountants, labor relations specialists, transportation planners, insurance underwriters, and purchasing managers. Among large metropolitan areas nationwide in 1980, the proportion ranged from 23 percent in Scranton, Pennsylvania, to 38 percent in Washington, D.C. The West accounted for eight of the top ten metropolitan areas and had only one metropolitan area under 30 percent. Opportunities were especially good in San Diego, San Francisco, San Jose, Sacramento, and Honolulu. Statewide census data show that the West is also hospitable to women entrepreneurs, as measured by the ratio of woman-owned businesses to population. Eight of the top ten states in 1987 were western, and every western state was in the top twenty-five.

The growth of political power among Hispanics and African Americans in the 1970s amplified the impact of middle-class activism. During the decades of growth policies, the business establishment in cities from San Antonio to Dallas to Phoenix tried to satisfy minority demands for influence on public decisions by consulting informally with carefully chosen community leaders and running single black or Hispanic candidates on citywide tickets. The bargain was minority votes in return for possible improvements in legal treatment, city jobs, or public housing.

The catalyst for change was the Voting Rights Act of 1965, with its amendment and extension in 1975. The widespread adoption of at-large elections and small city councils in southwestern and western cities in the early twentieth century had reduced the political influence of Hispanic and black voters and favored well-known majority candidates (that is, progressive white business leaders). Even after World War II, Waco moved to at-large council elections after a black candidate nearly won a council seat in 1950. As late as 1980, 12 percent of all Texans but only 0.8 percent of elected officials were African American. Hispanics were underrepresented across the Southwest.[13] In the West Texas city of Abilene, where a slating group called Citizens for Better Government picked candidates who ran at large, only seventy-six Mexican Americans and thirty-one African Americans bothered to vote—out of a minority population of 19,000.

After 1975, however, section 5 of the Voting Rights Act allowed the U.S. Justice Department to review proposed changes in election systems in specified states for their effects on minority voting.[14] A sympathetic Justice Department helped with enforcement during the Carter administration, and Congress in 1982 renewed the legislation and restored provisions weakened in the courts. Minorities can also argue in federal courts that election systems violate equal protections and voting rights guaranteed under the Fourteenth and Fifteenth amendments. In particular, minorities used the federal courts to obtain ward systems where at-large voting effectively eliminated the impact of their votes. By so doing, they could convert neighborhood segregation and concentration from a liability to a political resource.

In the typical case of Houston, the Justice Department invoked the preclearance process, which allows a federal veto of changes in local election systems. Houston had abolished its five council districts in 1955 in favor of at-large elections. In 1979 the department ruled that major annexations in 1977 and 1978 had diluted minority voting strength and could go forward only if the city modified its at-large council elections. The acceptable plan included five at-large seats and nine from districts. The new council elected in November 1979 had three blacks, two white women, and a Latino.

The annexation of 55,000 suburbanites to San Antonio in 1972 had similar consequences. The change to district voting in 1977 came in a city where the Good Government League (GGL) had grown old without recruiting new leaders among suburban north-side developers and businessmen with little patience with the health of the central business district. While the "Texas A&M clique" of north-siders battled with GGL leftovers and independent minority candidates, the Mexican American Legal Defense and Education Fund challenged the annexations. In 1976 the Justice Department disallowed voting in the annexed area, disfranchising thousands of middle-class San Antonians and threatening the city's bond rating. Under federal pressure, the city council submitted a plan for ten council districts. The Anglo-American north side, homeland of old neoprogressives and new suburban frontiersmen, voted twenty to one in opposition, but a twenty-to-one margin in favor from Mexican American neighborhoods was just enough to carry the plan. The first election under the new charter brought a council balanced among five Mexican Americans, one African American, and five Anglo-Americans. Elsewhere in Texas, Corpus Christi, Forth Worth, El Paso, and Dallas were among the larger cities to abandon at-large systems. Statewide, twenty-one city councils shifted to districts during the 1970s, roughly tripling the number of African American and Latino council members in California.

A number of other western cities adopted district elections because of grassroots campaigns rather than federal mandate. The impetus in Sacramento (1971), Stockton (1971), Albuquerque (1974), San Francisco (1977), San Jose (1980), Oakland (1981), and Phoenix (1982) came from local variations on labor, liberal, and minority alliances. Each group saw itself gaining an enhanced voice through small-area representation. Denverites carefully expanded their city council in 1971 to create two "black" seats and two "Chicano" seats. Stockton's liberal–minority coalition narrowly pushed through district elections against that city's entrenched conservatives. Sacramento's white Democrats made explicit commitments to well-organized minority groups in a successful 1969 campaign against a dominant conservative coalition. The insurgents then instituted district elections to secure their political position. In both cities the change brought blacks and Hispanics a larger share of city jobs and greater representation on appointed boards and commissions. In the early 1980s, the council included men like Ralph White in Stockton and Joe Serna in Sacramento, both of whom had been militant minority community organizers fifteen years earlier. At the same time, the degree of change should not be overstated, for the *Sacramento Bee* in 1979 listed only two minorities among that city's fifty "most powerful" people.

The changing political landscape also seems to have opened new economic opportunities for minorities. A U.S. census survey of minority-owned businesses in 1982 found that western cities supported large numbers of black and Hispanic businesses relative to the size of their black and Hispanic populations. Los Angeles, San Francisco/Oakland, and Houston were the top three metropolitan areas for black businesses, followed closely by San Diego and Dallas/Fort Worth. Although the top spot for Hispanic businesses was Miami, southwestern cities—starting with McAllen, Texas, and Santa Barbara—occupied the third through twenty-fourth slots.

In the 1980s and 1990s this era of ethnic and neighborhood revolt gradually yielded in turn to a revised version of growth politics. The results in some communities were rainbow growth coalitions that pursed economic expansion along with a list of community goals including empowerment of ethnic minorities. In fact, western cities converged on the center from two directions. On the one hand, cities like Dallas and Houston moved gradually toward the political middle, as business leaders decided to co-opt rising minority populations and project a progressive image in the era of international trade and information industries while minorities wanted a bigger slice of a *bigger* pie. At the same time, the neighborhood and ethnic rebels of the 1970s discovered that they needed business allies in Ronald Reagan's 1980s. With declining federal funds for social services, housing, and pollution control, they needed to generate local economic growth to provide both jobs and tax dollars. At the same time that quality-of-life liberals were aging into quality-of-life consumers and the yuppie was replacing the granola eater as the standard image of urban thirty year olds, the recession years of the early 1980s occasioned some particularly sharp rethinking of public priorities.

If any western city was open for business in the 1980s, it was Diane Feinstein's San Francisco. The "hyperpluralist" city experienced a brief triumph of the neighborhood revolution in the late 1970s. George Moscone won a narrow victory in the mayoralty race in 1976 with votes from white-collar liberals, Latinos, blacks, and gays. The same coalition supported the adoption of district elections, which allowed direct representation of ethnic minorities and gays on the board of supervisors. However, the changes were supported by only a precarious electoral majority. The murder of Moscone and council member Harvey Milk in 1978 brought to the surface the city's deep social divisions among its liberals, minorities, and residents of working-class neighborhoods.

As the city's new mayor, Feinstein led the return to citywide elections for the board of supervisors in 1980. By restoring an electoral system that dampened the impact of neighborhood agendas, commented Frances FitzGerald, "she could proceed to steer the city back to a more conservative, pro-business course. Though she was a liberal Democrat, she would not be out of step in the eighties." A nationally applauded downtown plan adopted in 1984 was a serious effort to preserve the special aesthetic of downtown San Francisco, but it also made full provision for the continuing growth of office facilities. As Feinstein told journalist Neal Pierce, "The plan recognizes that growth has to take place. Without growth you get dropping retail sales, vacancies, and blight."[15]

Vancouver mayor Gordon Campbell was something of a Feinstein equivalent. A liberal in the 1970s, he moved to the right in the 1980s. In his first term as mayor (1988–90) he facilitated the intensive redevelopment of the

Expo '86 site. In the 1990s, the center-right Non-partisan Association (NPA) and COPE split the city council seats, and Campbell won reelection with the help of the old Anglo-Canadian business interests and the new, entrepreneurial Chinese middle class (the single new NPA council member was a Hong Kong–born banker). Campbell himself was a "developer and businessman, young, personable, well-educated, well-traveled . . . epitomized the free market internationalization of the world city."[16]

Cities in the desert Southwest also moved toward the political center. Albuquerque voters in 1977 elected Mayor David Rusk on a platform of neighborhood preservation, public transit, downtown revitalization, and planned growth. "I can't get hysterical," he commented, "about big factories not going up all over the countryside."[17] Four years later, however, Rusk's identification with environmentalist rhetoric fueled his defeat by the more business-oriented Harry Kinney. Terry Goddard entered Phoenix politics as a neighborhood rebel but turned into an alliance builder soon after his arrival in the mayor's office in 1983. By the time of his reelection in 1985, however, Goddard had proved to be a friend of downtown revitalization and had made peace with much of the development industry, preparing for an unsuccessful run for governor in 1991.

Houston was a decade behind many of the other western cities. The more broadly based Houston Chamber of Commerce had succeeded the 8F crowd as the guardians of development interests. Moderately liberal Roy Hofheinz, mayor from 1974 to 1978, accepted federal community development funds and nudged the city closer to the American mainstream. A further slide toward the center came in 1981 with the election of Kathy Whitmire with wide liberal and ethnic support. Whitmire was far from a "no-growther," but she looked moderate when compared to opponents like former mayor and Chamber of Commerce president Louis Welch. Whitmire's appeal spanned gays, yuppies, and blacks. In office, she earned overwhelming black support in return for improving public services and signaling a new direction in law enforcement by hiring African American Lee Brown as police chief. In working to modernize and expand Houston's minimal public sector and incorporate the black middle class, Whitmire was essentially offering an updated version of the neoprogressive agenda that had worked so well for Atlanta in the 1950s and 1960s. In concert with the restructured city council, she helped to give Houston its first decade of genuine pluralist politics in the postwar era. However, she was forced to de-emphasize social issues in favor of economic development as the Texas recession deepened and after voters rejected an equal employment opportunity measure for homosexuals in 1985. By 1989, Whitmire was firmly in the business camp, speaking on behalf of the privatization of public services, low taxes, and a good business climate. That she has been interpreted variously as a coalition builder, an agent of change, and a business-oriented conservative shows the synthesizing nature of 1980s politics.[18]

The attractions of the political center were most visible in Denver and San Antonio, where Federico Peña and Henry Cisneros promoted what might be called neo-neoprogressive agendas. In each case, a young Hispanic politician brought new ideas into city government. Cisneros defeated a representative of San Antonio's downtown establishment in 1981, and Peña ousted crusty, fourteen-year incumbent Bill McNichols with the help of 3,000 volunteers. If the campaigns had come a decade earlier, they might well have split their communities. In the 1980s, however, Peña and Cisneros ran as technocrats and neighborhood advocates simultaneously. Their administrations accepted the primacy of economic development policies but also took minority concerns far more seriously than had their predecessors. They were explicit that economic development should justify itself by producing jobs and other benefits for the poor.

Peña took office in a city with a leadership vacuum not too different from that of 1947. Like Ben Stapleton a generation earlier, McNichols had grown indifferent to any but routine services. The energy industry building boom was largely guided by the private Denver Partnership rather than the city, allowing the greatest beneficiaries of downtown development to plan its course. Peña's campaign tapped neighborhood activism that had been dormant under McNichols but also enlisted major business backers. His slogan "Imagine a Great City" was broad enough to encompass a rainbow of groups and interests. Over two terms, his accomplishments included a $242 million bond issue for public works infrastructure, a comprehensive plan that paid attention both to neighborhoods and to the downtown, and, most spectacularly, a new multibillion-dollar airport to compete head-on with the Dallas/Fort Worth airport. The range of the 1980s coalition is defined by two of Peña's statements. "What you heard today from the voters was the sound of Denver taking off," he commented after the voters approved the airport in May 1989. At the same time, he has claimed that his greatest achievement was breaking down barriers against citizen access to city government: "Now environmentalists are not fighting the planning board; they are serving on it. That's going to have a lasting effect."[19]

Henry Cisneros gave San Antonio its new political center six years after the collapse of the Good Government League. A pragmatic liberal with experience in Washington, he had carefully followed economic development issues as an urban studies professor and as a city council member since 1975. Overwhelming reelection margins in 1983, 1985, and 1987 gave him the chance to develop "Target '90," a strategic plan on which several hundred civic leaders signed off. Cisneros was described as a "state of the art civic entrepreneur," trying to link government and business and to project a new national and international reputation for his city. Underpinning his agenda was a desire to expand job opportunities for Hispanics and to build up the Hispanic middle class from which Cisneros himself had come. By

1988, burnout from more than twenty years on the fast track and a crisis in his personal life forced Cisneros to opt out of a fifth term as mayor. In eight years, however, he had managed to unite a deeply polarized community around his vision of San Antonio as a leading city of the twenty-first century.

At the beginning of the 1990s, Los Angeles displayed the possibilities and contradictions of the politically diverse western city. Tom Bradley's election as mayor in 1973 depended on a coalition of blacks, white liberals, and environmentalists who supported community development and affirmative action programs that were a breath of fresh air after previous administrations. Massive downtown redevelopment was sold to the same alliance as a form of job creation in 1975; but the new programs gave downtown business and real estate interests a growing voice at city hall. By the 1980s, claims critic Mike Davis, the largesse of land developers had eroded any real distinctions between a Bradley administration and the entrenched Republicanism of the burgeoning suburbs.

Into this managerial middle-of-the-road regime, the "Rodney King riot" of April 1992 was a stark reminder of the limits of neo-neoprogressive politics— as well as the nation's inattention to the problems of race and poverty and the continued antagonism between police and minorities. Rodney King was a black motorist who had been clubbed and kicked by police officers while being arrested after a car chase on March 3, 1991. A nearby resident captured the beating on videotape from his apartment. Within two days, the tape was playing and replaying on national television. The grainy pictures shocked the nation and confirmed the worst black fears about biased police behavior. Early the next year, the four officers stood trial before a suburban jury for unjustified use of force. The televised trial and the unexpected verdict of not guilty on April 29 stirred deep anger that escalated into four days of rioting.

The disorder revealed multiple tensions among ethnic groups and was far more complex than the Watts outbreak of 1965. African Americans from South Central Los Angeles participated, but so did Central American and Mexican immigrants in adjacent districts, who accounted for about one-third of the 12,000 arrests. The disorder spread south to Long Beach and north to the edge of upscale neighborhoods in Westwood and Beverly Hills. Rioters assaulted the downtown police headquarters, city hall, and the *Los Angeles Times* building. As in 1965, some targets were white passersby and symbols of white authority. But members of competing minority groups were also victims, as angry black people targeted hundreds of Korean-owned and Vietnamese-owned shops as symbols of economic discrimination. Four days of disorder left fifty-eight people dead, mostly African Americans and Latinos.

Also unlike Watts, the 1992 disorder did not portend a series of long hot summers with repeated outbreaks of interracial violence, and its deadly narrative can be balanced with analysis of recent changes in neighborhood segregation. The news is a mix of encouraging and discouraging.[20] On the negative, the sheer increase in numbers of Mexican immigrants and other Latinos in western cities from 1980 to 2000 worked against neighborhood integration, as newcomers tended to double up with friends and relatives and to fill up areas where Spanish was in common use. Several important western metropolitan areas saw increases in Hispanic–white segregation over those two decades—Houston, Dallas, Las Vegas, Salt Lake City, and virtually the entire urbanized coast of California. In contrast, residential segregation of Hispanics held steady or declined slightly in Bakersfield, Phoenix, Tucson, San Antonio, Denver, Austin, Corpus Christi, El Paso, and Albuquerque. Because Hispanic residents are such a high proportion of total population, isolation remained highest along the Texas border in Brownsville, McAllen, Laredo, and El Paso and other South Texas cities like Corpus Christi and San Antonio.

Data for African American segregation are more encouraging, at least for the fifty metro areas with the largest African American populations in 2000. This number includes only seven metro areas in the West. All of them showed a decrease of the segregation index ranging from 19 points for Dallas and 18 points for Fort Worth to 8 points for Houston. The most segregated—Los Angeles and Houston—were only eighteenth and nineteenth overall among the fifty; Oakland was thirtieth, San Diego was forty-second, and Riverside was forty-seventh. The record in terms of isolation is also encouraging. The highest isolation level in 2000 was found in Houston, at thirty-fourth place overall, with a value of 47 compared to 70+ in Cleveland, Birmingham, Memphis, or Detroit. The other six western cities were way down the ladder between fortieth and fiftieth place, and all seven cities showed very substantial declines in black isolation.

All politics is dialectic. We can end this chapter with the most recent oscillation in Los Angeles politics. After a business-oriented neoprogressive administration under Mayor Richard Riordan and a liberal caretaker government under Mayor James Hahn, Antonio Villaraigosa won city hall with a resounding 59 to 41 percent margin in May 2005. A former labor organizer and speaker of the California State Assembly, he was perhaps the most Left-tilting mayor since the 1940s. Villaraigosa took 84 percent of Latino votes, 55 percent of Jewish votes, and 48 percent of black votes. Most surprisingly, he was also the choice of 48 percent of white voters in the San Fernando Valley, an area that had thought seriously about seceding from the city only a few years earlier.

According to one close observer of Los Angeles politics, the election was a "victory for LA's progressive movement, which since the 1992 riots has forged an increasingly powerful grassroots organizing and political coalition of unions, community organizations, religious institutions, and ethnic civic groups."[21] Early actions included adoption of a "living wage" law, an antisweatshop policy, and a municipal housing trust fund. What remains to be seen is whether this progressive trend will permanently mitigate some of the multiracial tensions of 1992.

CHAPTER THIRTEEN

Reshaping the Metropolis

*At Colorado Avenue she turned. It was the first through boulevard she
had been on, and the traffic signals were off, with yellow blinkers showing.
So she gave the car the gun, excitedly watching the needle swing past 30,
40, and 50. . . . The car was pumping something into her veins, something of pride, of arrogance, of regained self-respect.*

—James Cain, *Mildred Pierce* (1945)

*Now they lived in Mill Valley. . . . A tract house on the Sutton Manor
flatlands; it was big enough, comfortable, and just barely affordable.
Besides, the first time they'd seen it, a racing green '63 TR-4 was parked
in the driveway, a strong indication that the house's owners were okay
people. If they could live in a tract house, so could Kate and Harvey. . . .
And it was still Mill Valley, though just barely; Kate still hated to tell
people, when she gave directions, to stay on East Blithedale all the way
out, as if they were heading for 101, turn left at the Chevron station, go
past the Red Cart, and turn right at the carwash.*

—Cyra McFadden,
The Serial: A Year in the Life of Marin County (1977)

*Los Angeles is rather like a big earthworm that might be chopped into
twenty pieces and not killed. . . . You get the impression that a medium-
sized urban centre has schizogenetically reproduced itself twenty times.*

—Jean-Paul Sartre, *Literary and Philosophical Essays* (1955)

S eventy years after Emily French struggled to finish her small house near
the South Platte River, another Denver family moved into a new, almost finished house—but this time in the absolutely new neighborhood of Hoffman
Heights in the booming suburb of Aurora. Their experience—dad, mom,
Susan, Tom, Bobby, and Bud—mirrored that of millions of other families, but
we can revisit it through the memories and meditations of Robert Michael
Pyle. His memoir *The Thunder Tree* relives his childhood and youth in the
1950s and early 1960s. Summer days along the High Line Canal, explorations
of abandoned farmhouses, and trips to the public library (which kept getting a
bigger building and following population eastward) all fed his fascination with
wild nature in its losing contest with the suburban frontier.

Aurora was booming in 1953, when the Pyles moved into their new four-
bedroom home, yellow brick on a concrete slab. The kids woke to the "acrid
odor of roofer's tar . . . field marks of a new suburb still under construction."[1] Their parents struggled to turn the bare dirt yard into lawn and garden with the help of the kids, who dug dandelions for a nickel a bucket.
Chinese elms were the tree of choice, brittle but fast growing. The Cold War
funded Aurora's Fitzsimons Army Hospital, Lowry Field with its training
jets and Titan missile silos, and Rocky Mountain Arsenal to produce and
store chemical weapons. Aurora's 3,000 residents in 1940 grew to 30,000 in
1953 when Bobby Pyle and his family moved out from the city, to 50,000 in
1960 when he entered high school, and to 276,000 by the end of the century.
In alliance with Colorado Springs, the city built its own transmountain water
system to pump snowmelt across the Front Range independent of what suburban developers saw as the tyrannical Denver Water Board.[2] Community
leaders annexed undeveloped tracts of prairie, marketed the city as an office
and industrial location, and envisioned Aurora as a new Minneapolis with
Denver relegated to the role of St. Paul without *Prairie Home Companion*.

Bobby Pyle fifty years later is a biologist and nature writer of international
reputation. Then he roamed the edges of Aurora with the eye of a nascent
naturalist. He observed the transformation of the short-grass prairie, first by
invasive species like cheatgrass, then by the Kentucky bluegrass of domestic lawns and city parks, then by the asphalt of church and shopping center
parking lots. His family drove east into the prairie to see pronghorn antelope,
a trip that grew longer with each year. His naturalist's eye also spotted the
changing species of housing: the old round barn, the rural house across from
the new mall, the abandoned farmhouse from a vanished farm, the two new
ranch-style houses built adjacent, "scouts for the suburb that was preparing
to pounce."[3]

Robert Pyle's family were enlistees in the suburbanizing generation
that remade the nation after 1945. The immediate postwar decades brought
a perfect storm of housing demand: Couples who had deferred marriage
now walked down the aisle. Those who had deferred children rushed to

form families. The proportion of adults who were unmarried dropped to its twentieth-century low in 1960, as young people married quickly and had an average of three children spaced closely together. Meanwhile wartime savings were available for down payments on mass-produced tract houses as families longed to move out of cramped apartments or quit doubling up with relatives. Builders pushed the number of new houses to a peak of nearly two million in 1950, industrializing production with standardized components and specialized crews. "On-site fabrication" was mass production without an assembly line. In Robert Pyle's suburban Denver, "growth advanced southeasterly from Denver's hinterland toward the Cherry Creek Reservoir, northeast along Sand Creek, due east on Colfax. All obstacles fell, all proportion fell away. With the advent of the town house and condominium, a powerful new tool came on line. Colonies of cloned domiciles stormed the remaining countryside."[4]

By the time Robert Pyle had left for graduate school, photographer Robert Adams was turning his eye to the same landscape. A highly admired landscape photographer, Adams often chooses to show the small works of humanity against the vast spaces of the world. His first book in 1970 was *White Churches of the Plains*, a stunning series showing small-frame churches standing forty or eighty years old on the windswept land of eastern Colorado. For his second book, in contrast, he photographed suburban Denver. *The New West: Landscapes along the Colorado Front Range* (1974) hearkens back to the Lakewood photos but takes the new suburbscapes on their own terms as the epitome of the emerging West. The genre—the western suburb through the camera—continues to flourish with books like Laurie Brown, Martha Ronk, and Charles Little's *Recent Terrains: Terraforming the American West* (2000) and Ann Wolfe's *Suburban Escape: The Art of California Sprawl* (2006).[5]

The surge of western population that began with World War II has yet to crest, let alone recede. In 1940 the West was a region of large and small cities speckling the plains, straddling small rivers where they escape the mountains, and dotting the coast. By 2000 it was home to vast metropolitan regions that reached out to each other across deserts and prairies. The message of the census has been consistent. To find nineteen of the nation's twenty-five fastest-growing metropolitan areas in the 1940s, Americans had to look west across the Missouri and Sabine rivers. The same western states counted as sixteen of the twenty-five fastest-growing metropolitan areas during the 1950s, slipped to twelve for the 1960s when Americans were discovering the Sunbelt Southeast, and then recovered to sixteen for the 1970s, sixteen for the 1980s, and fourteen for the 1990s.[6] Between 1940 and 2000, Phoenix moved from seventy-seventh place to fourteenth among American metropolitan areas; San Diego, from forty-seventh to seventeenth; Sacramento, from eighty-second to twenty-fifth; and Austin, from 123rd to thirty-eighth.

The first suburban generation built cities with and for automobiles. Auto dependence was not exclusive to western communities, but Denver was tops

FIGURE 50. War boom housing in Los Angeles. This Associated Press photo from the early 1950s carried the following caption: "They met housing needs then. These small unpretentious homes in a Los Angeles suburb were built just after the war when thousands of home-hungry people needed places to live." (Hearst Collection, Department of Special Collections, University of Southern California Library.)

among major cities in the ratio of automobiles to population in both 1960 and 1970 (the result is the same counting all registered vehicles and passenger cars only). Los Angeles, Houston, and even San Francisco were also high on the list. Phoenix, perhaps surprisingly, was a bit further down but still ahead of Detroit, Chicago, and Washington, D.C.

The increasingly elaborate youth culture of the postwar era depended heavily on the rise of multicar families, and observers looked to western cities to understand their implications. Drawing on his own teen years in Los Angeles, Harvard professor James Q. Wilson tried to describe the cultural importance of automobile ownership for a skeptical East Coast intelligentsia.[7] He drew on the same background that shaped Angeleno Charles Bukowski's memories in his poem "Waiting," which recalls Los Angeles of the 1930s as a land of freedom "if you had a car and the gas."[8]

Arriving without preconceived ideas in the 1960s, British architecture critic Rayner Banham saw the same landscape as "autopia" (and "surfurbia") in *Los Angeles: The Architecture of Four Ecologies* (1971). Automobiles in the

FIGURE 51. Westchester, California. Along with nearby Lakewood, the community of Westchester, photographed in 1949, epitomized the national image of Los Angeles as a place of endless horizontal sprawl in look-alike subdivisions. (Courtesy of the California Historical Society/Ticor Title Insurance Los Angeles, Department of Special Collections, University of Southern California Library.)

form of "kustomized kars" are the featured exhibit in pop trend spotter Tom Wolfe's 1965 essay "The Kandy-Kolored Tangerine-Flake Streamline Baby." They play the competing roles of anesthetic and redemption in Joan Didion's novel *Play It as It Lays* (1970).[9] They are vital to the action in *Rebel without a Cause* (1955), with its suburban Los Angeles setting, and they *are* the action in *American Graffiti* (1973), which uses San Rafael and director George Lucas's hometown of Modesto to reproduce the feel of the early 1960s.

Life in a new, auto-oriented suburb like Lakewood, California, was not quite the same as the notorious photographs suggest. Its 17,500 houses *were* built on bean and sugar beet fields, and they were small (950 to 1,100 square feet), but they were up to date (Lakewood was "garbage free" because each house had an in-sink disposal), and they did not all look alike. Dozens of parks and playgrounds helped to divide the development into distinct communities. Residents of each neighborhood staked a claim to "their" park, and kids only ventured into other parks at the invitation of a friend. Most of the residents would have agreed that it was "Tomorrow's City Today," with its very large shopping center and big new high school that was the "jewel of the town."

Lakewood in the 1950s and 1960s was an optimistic and very homogeneous community. Its dads were veterans of World War II and Korea who worked at the Douglas Aircraft plant or the Long Beach Naval Station. Moms stayed home with the kids, by and large. Boys growing up in Lakewood had a clear trajectory to success: high school sports, the military, and a job in the defense industry. It was also very, very white, completing a monoculture in terms of age, family patterns, economic class, and race. As one thoughtful native has commented, it was "the American Dream made affordable for a generation of industrial workers. . . . They were oriented to aerospace. . . . They worked at all the places that exemplified the bright future that California was supposed to be."[10] The flip side of the successful 1950s and 1960s, however, would be an inability to adapt to racial integration and the disappearance of industrial jobs in the 1980s and 1990s. With no layers of history, writes another of Lakewood's "original kids," the community "has the feeling of a club—the feeling that because everyone started out together, residents are entitled to lifetime 'charter membership.'"[11]

Milpitas, California, was another 1950s suburb built for and by the automobile. Located in the East Bay northeast of San Jose, Milpitas grew to serve the new Ford assembly plant. Most of the new worker-residents moved out from Oakland. They brought their union membership and working-class politics with them. They got a quieter community with a new and nicer house, just as in Lakewood. They left behind marginal neighborhoods that suffered from losing households with steady incomes. They also left behind African American neighbors and coworkers who found it much more difficult than whites to make the suburban trek from tenement to tract house.

The western cities that rushed to build freeways in the early decades of the U.S. Interstate Highway program, initiated in 1956, began to choose different transportation options in the second automobile generation that followed the oil shocks of the mid-1970s. In the camp of highway engineering were cities like Denver, which began a controversial boundary-busting freeway loop in the 1980s, and Phoenix, which scrambled to catch up with freeway mileage after a slow start and was still building its valley loop into the new century. In Texas, however, the Houston and Dallas/Fort Worth regions both planned in the early twenty-first century to add 3,000 miles of freeway and tollway lanes, and Austin projected another 1,000 lane miles.

The alternative to highway investment was to build new commuter rail systems to preserve the centrality of historic downtowns and to concentrate new development in corridors and nodes. The Bay Area Rapid Transit system went into operation in the 1970s and grew over the next three decades, helping to bring intense development to outlying centers like Walnut Creek. Portland rejected a planned radial freeway in the mid-1970s and has proceeded to develop an extensive light-rail system. Seattle finished a second north–south freeway in the 1980s and then paused for a seemingly interminable debate about the right public transit investments (bus tunnel? more monorail? light-rail?). San Diego also took light-rail seriously as a system of interconnecting lines. Sacramento, Los Angeles, Denver, Dallas, Salt Lake City, and Phoenix undertook more limited rail systems after 1990, although some of them continue to expand (as in Denver and Phoenix). One consequence is that four cities of the western U.S. ranked in the nation's top ten for percentage of journey-to-work trips made by public transit, with San Francisco/Oakland comparable to Washington, D.C., Honolulu comparable to Philadelphia, and Seattle and Portland comparable to Pittsburgh.[12]

North of the border, Edmonton opened light-rail in the 1970s, followed in the 1980s by Calgary and then by Vancouver's SkyTrain (which runs both above and below the surface). Without the temptation of huge chunks of highway money from their national government, Canadian cities were much more reluctant to build extensive freeway systems. Instead, places like Edmonton and Vancouver have opted to tie their growing regions together with rail transit, improved bus service, and upgrades to existing highway systems—a choice that is obvious to any American tourist who expects to cruise blithely into the city center.

The second generation of suburban development also fostered super-suburb municipalities that began as suburbs or satellites of a larger city but now have populations of 100,000 or more. In 1990, thirty-five of the forty-six supersuburbs in the United States were located in the West. By 2000, the western share was sixty-six of eighty-nine. At the even higher threshold of 200,000, the West in 2000 claimed twelve of fourteen, including giants like Long Beach at 462,000, Mesa (Arizona) at 396,000, Santa Ana (California) at 338,000, and Arlington (Texas) at 333,000. Specialists in urban government place the threshold population to support efficient full-service municipal government at between 50,000 and 100,000. A community of this size can employ a diversified professional staff, maintain sophisticated support services, and realize economies of scale in service delivery. To the U.S. examples we can add Burnaby, Surrey, Coquitlam, and Richmond in the Vancouver region.[13]

Two of the large suburbs are among the most successful of the comprehensively planned "New Towns" that developers promoted around the United States in the 1960s and 1970s. The availability of large tracts of empty land in single or limited ownership near western cities made New Towns relatively easy to create as real estate deals. The Woodlands, on harvested timberland fifteen miles north of Houston International Airport, was the brainchild of George Mitchell, a futurist and energy mogul in the early 1970s. Set among lakes and pine woods, the city sold a combination of small-town nostalgia and high-tech communications infrastructure. Although hit by ups and downs in the Texas real estate market, the Woodlands by 2000 had 56,000 residents. On a different coast, the roots of Irvine, California, date to the 1860s and 1870s when James Irvine acquired title to several ranches in what became Orange County. The Irvine Company moved from agriculture to land development in the 1950s, leasing lots in expensive coastal subdivisions around Newport Bay. Between 1959 and 1964, architect William Pereira and Irvine Company employees developed plans for a 40,000-acre tract between Newport Bay and the site of a new University of California campus. They envisioned a set of semi-independent residential communities linked to two industrial sites, the university, and a Newport Center "downtown." Large builders erected the new housing on leased land, leaving the company in long-term control. Covering only part of the Irvine Company lands, the incorporated city of Irvine counted over 110,000 residents by 1990, 143,000 by 2000, and 194,000 by 2006.[14]

By the 1970s and 1980s, supersuburbs (or "outer cities") were able to push their own development agendas in direct competition with central cities. Their goal was to have the best of both worlds: industrial and commercial real estate development to generate property taxes and sales taxes, coupled with upscale residential development that would bring sober, taxpaying citizens who would want good schools, parks, and libraries but include few welfare cases and crime-prone families. This municipal agenda also suited new suburban industries whose managers thought little about the needs of central cities. Aerospace, defense, and electronics companies cared far more about suburban highways and world markets than about fading downtowns and neighborhoods. The Industrial League of Orange County, which represented major defense and technology corporations, consistently overrode efforts to slow the pace of growth or mitigate its effects on older communities.

San Jose has also battled through tensions between the center and periphery. During the 1950s aggressive annexation by the city of San Jose disrupted efforts to plan for controlled growth in Santa Clara County. By the 1970s, in contrast, the growth of Silicon Valley challenged the primacy of the central city and its downtown business interests. Represented by the Santa Clara Manufacturing Group, the newly rich diluted the remaining influence of downtown, which was no longer a major concern for corporations that built low-rise offices and factories in nearby cities like Mountain View, Sunnyvale, Santa Clara, and Palo Alto, not to mention the occupants of more than 40 million square feet of office space within San Jose's Golden Triangle at the intersection of Routes 101 and 280. Beginning in the 1980s, however, a new generation of city leaders (including mayors Tom McEnery and Susan Hammer) pushed a downtown revival, with new hotels, office buildings, a park, a convention center, two museums, a light-rail line, municipal buildings, and a public library (innovatively shared with San Jose State University). The center of the new San Jose is Plaza de César Chávez, bordered by a science museum designed by a Mexican architect, reviving a new multiethnic downtown on the ashes of the dying white downtown.

Metropolitan Phoenix similarly developed multiple power centers. Phoenix, Tempe, and Scottsdale waged an annexation war through the 1960s as each tried to snag developable land, battles that were revisited more recently among Phoenix, Buckeye, and Peoria. The valley's multiple growth nodes created new, localized sets of business and investment interests different from those of the postwar civic leadership. New centers with their own groups of economic and civic leaders included Scottsdale, Glendale, Mesa, Tempe, Chandler, and the growing Camelback/Biltmore and northwest districts. Mesa boosters, for example, pursued residential, commercial, and industrial growth. The city bought up water rights, promoted its business district, and sought new businesses. Glendale in 1984 offered a $20,000 bonus for the first person to bring a 100,000-square-foot factory to town. Business and civic groups such as the East Valley Partnership, the West Valley Partnership, and Phoenix Together gave lip service to regional cooperation but "competed for everything from sports facilities to educational institutions in order to offer unique advantages to residents and businesses. For the most part, metropolitan pluralism prevailed in the Valley of the Sun."[15]

Center cities and supersuburbs remain in constant tension, something immediately apparent to anyone who follows major league sports. In the Bay Area, San Jose acquired the Sharks of the National Hockey League as part of its downtown redevelopment and efforts to become a "big league city." The San Francisco Giants moved to a new downtown stadium for the twenty-first century, but the Forty-Niners of the National Football League announced plans in 2006 to build their new stadium in Santa Clara in the heart of Silicon Valley. The Oakland Athletics planned to move twenty miles south from the Oakland Coliseum to Fremont. In the Dallas/Fort Worth area, Irving and Arlington used liberal Texas annexation laws to expand aggressively in the decades after World War II, taking in vast tracts of undeveloped prairie land that lay in the path of metropolitan growth. Arlington, for one example, grew from a few square miles in 1945 to nearly 100 square miles, giving it plenty of land for a university campus and a Major League Baseball park, while Irving got the NFL stadium. Chula Vista, California, grew to fifty square miles and close to 200,000 people by 2007, enabling it to make a bid to lure the San Diego Chargers from their old Mission Valley Stadium. And enough said about the curiously named Los Angeles Angels of Anaheim.

Supersuburbs have their occasional downtowns and concentrations of development around superregional malls and freeway interchanges, like Las Colinas northwest of Dallas or the South Coast Plaza complex in Orange County, places that fit journalist Joel Garreau's category of Edge City. However, such mid-rise islands and oases account for only a fraction of metro area employment and retailing. Instead, other experts depict a fractal landscape organized at a much finer grain. The edgeless city is the ordinary landscape that we don't really notice—small office parks, scattered factories and warehouses, and highway-side strips where insurance agents, CPAs, and yoga studios sit next to take-and-bake pizza places and car stereo stores. It is the place where "office park dads" (a phrase coined by political consultants in 2002) are busy at work while their spouses juggle the duties of "soccer moms." These findings support Anne Vernez Moudon's argument that most clustering of activity in suburban zones is at a much smaller scale than in Edge Cities. Her research on Seattle has found what are, in effect, suburban neighborhoods of 3,000–4,000 residents in which a commercial strip or small shopping center (perhaps with multiplex cinema) forms a core. Surrounding it are inward-turned sets of low-rise apartments that have urban densities but nothing of urban appearance and single-family houses. The Seattle region, for example, has two or three Edge Cities such as Bellevue and the Kent Valley but roughly 100 suburban clusters.[16]

These suburban clusters are new melting pots where Asian and Latino immigrants settle and acculturate to North American life. Some minority suburbanization is overspill from established ethnic neighborhoods like East Los Angeles. Much more, however, is the result of conscious initial choices by new Americans and Canadians. Many immigrants prefer new houses that don't require Home Depot handyman skills. At the same time, the combination of new construction with home owner association restrictions promises to insulate property values against any feared effects of racial integration. Minorities in 2000 accounted for more than half of suburban residents in McAllen, El Paso, Honolulu, Albuquerque, Fresno, and Los Angeles and more than 40 percent in San Francisco/Oakland/San Jose, Stockton, San Antonio, and San Diego. There were big gains in the minority share of suburbia in Las Vegas, Houston, Dallas, and Bakersfield as well.

There were still Ozzie and Harriet families (two parents and children in the same household) in western metropolitan areas, but they were most likely to be living in the suburbs and to be named Núñez or Nguyen rather than Nelson. They might have picked a new planned community in Chula Vista, outside of San Diego. The population of Eastlake Greens, for example, consisted of 3,822 whites, 2,380 Hispanics, 2,383 Asians, and 465 African Americans. The nearly identical new houses, the strict design controls, and the curving streets and cul-de-sac layout offer the newly successful immigrant family economic security in a location without embedded ethnic tensions. The same pattern is true of El Paso, Denver, San Jose, Sacramento, and the suburbs south and southeast of Vancouver.

The change can be traced in southern California's Orange County–John Wayne Airport country that was an early home base of Cold War conservatism. Orange County suburbs burgeoned in the 1950s and 1960s with defense industry jobs and white families. This was receptive ground for the John

Birch Society and its Communist conspiracy theories, for grassroots organizing for conservative causes, and for Barry Goldwater's run for the presidency. The people whom Lisa McGirr has termed "suburban warriors" were easy targets for satire by novelists like Thomas Pynchon in *The Crying of Lot 49*, but they acted from a combination of self-interest and political conviction.[17] As the Cold War faded, however, voters continued to fight off higher taxes but showed increasing interest in environmental and social issues. Local residents, moreover, were increasingly Asian Americans and Latinos who embraced "family values" but not the cultural biases that the phrase encoded. By the 1990s there were two "Orange Counties," multiethnic in the northern half closer to Los Angeles and still white in the southern half. The 1998 congressional election marked the shift, when Chicana liberal Loretta Sanchez defeated conservative cold warrior Robert Dornan in a district including Anaheim, Santa Ana, and Fullerton.

Absorbing all these forces of change—suburbanization of housing, transportation investment, immigration—western cities at the opening of the twenty-first century had a distinctive imprint on the map. They were simultaneously centralized (although in a different way than Chicago or Detroit) and multicentered, the locales alike for high-rise corridors, suburban cores, and randomly scattered mini-malls.

At the center of the midsized western metropolis is not so much a traditional, tightly bounded downtown as an expansive but still dominant central district. Extending outward from the central core of banks, government offices, and convention facilities in the last quarter of the twentieth century, it embraced new condo clusters for empty nesters, secondary shopping nodes, "old town" historic districts, and sports venues. Covering perhaps 3 or 4 percent of the entire developed area, it included most of the major public facilities and institutions. The "uptown" end might be anchored by a secondary office concentration (a sort of "edge city" embedded in mid-metropolis), by a major shopping node, or by a university campus such as the University of New Mexico, University of Texas, University of Arizona, Boise State University, or University of Washington.

In the space of eight square miles, about 2 percent of its whole region, a visitor to Salt Lake City will find virtually every reason she has come to visit. Temple Square and the key Mormon landmarks anchor the core. The secular state overlooks the city from a capitol building perched on a steep hill to the north. Convention facilities and sports arenas are just west of the commercial district and its enormously wide streets. City hall, the public library, and other parts of the local government are on the other side of the center, a mile or so south of the capitol. A light-rail line runs three miles east to the University of Utah.

Densities of western cities are surprisingly high. It remains surprising to many people that Los Angeles is more densely populated than Detroit,

Cleveland, or Pittsburgh. There were forty-nine metro areas in the United States with one million or more people in 2000. Ten of the twelve most densely populated were western—Las Vegas, Los Angeles, San Diego, San Francisco, Phoenix, Sacramento, Seattle, Portland, San Antonio, and Salt Lake City.[18] The statistics do not mean that western cities look like Manhattan or the Chicago lakefront, with mile after mile of high-rising apartments. They do mean that few western cities actually match up with the overworked term *sprawl*, with its implications of scattershot housing tracts and isolated subdivisions tossed randomly across the landscape. Instead, they have been growing low-rise but compact, nudging out incrementally into their hinterlands rather than leap-frogging over the dales and hills.

Drive south from Sky Harbor Airport, grind up the high, massive ridge of South Mountain, and look down on Phoenix. You see a big metropolis for sure, with Phoenix, Tempe, a bit of Mesa, and a fringe of Scottsdale all in view. You also see a large uninterrupted urban fabric, with little vacant land except for the undevelopable slopes of Camelback Mountain and Squaw Peak. Phoenix is a typical southwestern/far western metro area that has been holding its density while gaining population. Adding population and urbanized land at roughly the same rates since the 1980s, it looks from on high like a soft blanket of development draped over the Salt River Valley. Denver has been described as folding over the Colorado plains and foothills like a "lumpy pancake." Los Angeles, agrees architecture critic Brendan Gill, has "hugged the ground on which it was built." Alison Lurie describes the same low-rise intensity in her uncharitably titled novel *The Nowhere City*: "She gestured at Mar Vista laid out below the freeway: a random grid of service stations, two-story apartment buildings, drive-ins, palms, and factories, and block after block of stucco cottages."[19]

Contrast Atlanta or Indianapolis or Orlando. Here there are few environmental constraints of topography or water, allowing development to sprawl endlessly into surrounding counties at very low densities. In Tom Wolfe's novel *A Man in Full*, 1990s Atlanta is erupting with real estate development like a sea of lava. Far on the suburban fringe, Forsyth County is changing from a "Redman Chewing Tobacco rural outback into Subdivision Heaven." The typical eastern or southeastern city intertwines into the surrounding region, but as Wolf describes a flyover of Atlanta: "The trees stretched in every direction. They were Atlanta's greatest natural resource, those trees were. People loved to live beneath them . . . for the past thirty years all sorts of people . . . had been moving beneath those trees, into all those delightful, leafy, rolling rural communities that surrounded the city proper."[20]

Indeed, the entire "dry Sunbelt" of California, Arizona, Nevada, Colorado, Utah, and New Mexico added new urbanized land and population in roughly equal rates from 1982 to 1997 according to the National Resource Inventory, whereas the "wet Sunbelt" (Alabama, Florida, Georgia, Tennessee, the

Carolinas) added developed land at twice the pace of population growth. Between 1982 and 1997, again, the South averaged 1.4 new residents for every newly urbanized acre, while the West averaged 3.6 residents. In the 1990s, Charlotte converted forty-nine acres of rural land to housing for every 100 new residents, and Nashville converted forty-two acres. In contrast, Las Vegas converted fifteen, Phoenix converted sixteen, and Salt Lake City converted nine acres.

So, in fact, western cities lie relatively lightly on the land. "Urbanized area" is the U.S. Census category that measures the extent of such lands. Unlike the better-known metropolitan area (an economic concept), the urbanized area is the land that is actually settled at urban densities—the aggregate urban footprint, if you will. In Washington, for example, urbanized areas in 2000 ranged in size from twenty-seven square miles for Wenatchee to 954 square miles for Seattle. In Oklahoma they ranged from thirty square miles for Norman to 322 square miles for Oklahoma City. Urbanized areas claimed only 0.02 percent of Alaska (no surprise there), 0.2 percent of the northern plains states, 0.8 percent of the total expanse of the central Rocky Mountain states, 1.1 percent of the Northwest states, and just 1.7 percent of compact Hawaii.[21] Only Texas at 2.0 percent and California at 4.1 percent were more extensively built over. Canada does not publish data in a form precisely comparable to the U.S. urbanized area, but use of the more expansive Census Metropolitan Area (CMA) boundaries gives a comparable result: 0.4 percent of British Columbia within CMAs and 1.4 percent of the three Prairie Provinces.

There is another message to take away from South Mountain. Phoenix and its sister cities form a "conurbanized" corridor. The term *conurbation* comes from Scottish planner Patrick Geddes, who coined it early in the twentieth century to describe the way in which sets of originally independent cities were growing into each other to form a larger agglomeration, as with the Randstadt cities of Holland, the Ruhr cities of Germany, or the industrial cities of the English Midlands.[22] In the twenty-first-century West, it is rival real estate promotions and historically competitive commercial centers rather than factory towns that have grown together into single metro-organisms. There are some conurbations that include historically "twinned" cities like Dallas/Fort Worth, Houston/Galveston, and Seattle/Tacoma and others in which the one city such as Denver or Portland has always overshadowed the secondary center(s).

The typical western conurbation stretches long and narrow, twice or three times farther along one axis than the other. Environment may not be destiny, but the topography of shorelines and mountains has again taken the upper hand. The Phoenix conurbation runs seventy-five miles from Buckeye to Apache Junction, constrained into a central corridor (and secondary parallel corridors) by the topography of east–west mountain ranges and contouring irrigation canals. Pugetopolis, centered nicely on Sea-Tac Airport, runs

FIGURE 52. Lions' Gate Bridge, Vancouver. Opened in 1938, the Lions' Gate Bridge (officially the First Narrows Bridge) connected Vancouver to the north shore of Burrard Inlet. Arching over the entrance to Canada's western port with a 5,890-foot suspension span, it is a northern equivalent of the Golden Gate Bridge that opened just a year earlier, and it played a major role in the development of Vancouver's northern suburbs. (Courtesy of North Vancouver Museum.)

eighty miles from Olympia to Everett, squeezed between the water of Puget Sound and the rain-soaked foothills of the Cascades. Utah's conurbation—ninety miles from the south edge of Provo to the northern edge of Ogden—is confined by a different sort of saltwater to the west and the high, dry Wasatch Range to the east. It's seventy miles from Oceanside to Tijuana, with San Diego in the middle; eighty miles from Salem, Oregon, to Battleground, Washington, with Portland in between; a hundred miles from Castle Rock to Fort Collins, with Denver in between; and sixty miles from West Vancouver to Chilliwack along the axis of Burrard Inlet and the Fraser River. Medium-sized cities like Albuquerque and El Paso also stretch along a single axis—in these cases constricted along the course of the Rio Grande by mountain ranges and military bases. Seen from Tantalus Drive high behind the city center, Honolulu is a narrow, twenty-mile arc of urban development that wraps around the southwest side and base of the Koolau Range from Pearl City to new communities around Koko Head.

The scale and visibility of western conurbations combined, in several cases, with their relative economic and social homogeneity to support interest

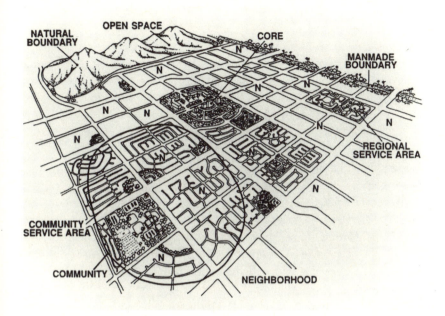

FIGURE 53. Phoenix urban village plan. In the 1990s, many western cities developed regional plans that proposed to combat sprawl by focusing growth on regional and neighborhood centers. The City of Phoenix Planning Department, for example, proposed in 1993 that the city be planned as a set of neighborhood clusters of "urban villages" that could provide a wide range of jobs and services within a relatively localized area.

in metropolitan growth management. Often spurred by the specter of suburban gridlock and other threats to the quality of daily life, the growth management impulse has drawn on neighborhood activists, quality-of-life liberals, environmentalists, and open-space advocates.

One strategy by urban planners and public officials has been to bring order out of the randomness of market by promoting development around outlying centers or nodes. Phoenix talked about promoting "urban villages." Portland's "Region 2040 Plan" (1994) designated a hierarchy of "regional centers" and "town centers." The Puget Sound Regional Council in 1996 defined nine established downtowns in the Seattle/Tacoma area and twelve suburban locations as "urban centers" that are to absorb most new employment and receive most transportation improvements. Salt Lake City residents in the 1990s undertook an elaborate Envision Utah program that built consensus around the need to strengthen regional community centers and development corridors. The legislature in 1999 established a Quality Growth Commission to help channel state infrastructure funding to communities that planned their development according to the growth management goals.

Americans could look north for examples of innovative responses to metropolitan growth such as the Winnipeg Unicity. In 1960, the provincial government created the Metropolitan Corporation of Greater Winnipeg with an elected council to serve as a second tier of government dealing with regional issues while the old city and suburbs handled local concerns. Twelve years later, the leftist New Democratic Party used its control of the province to create a single unified Unicity with a fifty-one-member city council (now shrunk by two-thirds). The price for a uniform tax rate and uniform services was a government in which suburban areas outweighed the old core. According to urban politics specialist Christopher Leo, the term *Unicity* was seldom used by the twenty-first century—just Winnipeg.[23]

Advocates of regional planning often journeyed to Vancouver for inspiration. The Greater Vancouver Regional District (GVRD), created in 1967, has responsibility for regional parks, transit, water, environmental services, and planning. Its Livable Region plan in 1976 proposed to focus future growth on central Vancouver plus four outlying nodes in Burnaby, Surrey, Coquitlam, and New Westminster. Although the plan made great sense in the physically constrained setting of Vancouver, the provincial government of the 1980s gutted the authority of the GVRD. With further swings in local politics, the GVRD in 1990 updated and reissued the Livable Region plan with claims of "moderate success" (although central Vancouver was still far ahead of outlying centers in its share of commercial and office space).[24]

Another option was to manage the entire footprint of a city by directing growth onto certain lands and away from others. Here too, Canadian cities took the lead. Having acquired large tracts of tax-forfeiture land during the bad years after 1920, Saskatoon in 1945 found itself owning 8,500 building lots. It acquired additional farmland in the 1950s and 1960s with the goals of promoting compact development and moderating land costs. In 1953 it adopted a policy of maintaining a fifteen- to twenty-year supply in public ownership, selling to developers at a profit and simultaneously ensuring that growth would be orderly and contiguous. Edmonton used both purchased and tax-foreclosed land to influence the location and character of development, establishing a partial greenbelt and encouraging large, mixed-use neighborhoods with town centers such as Mill Woods in the 1970s. British Columbia's parliament in 1973 passed Bill 42, which created an Agricultural Land Reserve. The province has put the most productive farmland, much of it in the Fraser Valley, off-limits to urbanization. The effect has been to limit the eastward sprawl of Vancouver and to keep smaller, fast-growing Abbotsford a true city in the country, where population and farm revenues both doubled from the mid-1980s to 2006.

Hawaii set the pace in the United States with a 1961 law to protect pineapple and sugarcane plantations by dividing the areas into urban, rural, agricultural, and conservation areas (somewhat like the British Columbia program).

California created a commission to regulate filling and development around all of San Francisco Bay in 1965. Oregon adopted a statewide land planning system in 1973 to fend off what Governor Tom McCall called "the unfettered despoiling of the land" through "sagebrush subdivisions, coastal condomania, and the ravenous rampage of suburbia in the Willamette Valley."[25] A key tool was the establishment of Urban Growth Boundaries that protect productive farm- and forestland and keep metropolitan areas compact.[26] The Washington Growth Management Act in 1990 adopted a similar although less stringent policy of Urban Growth Areas.

Las Vegas—the newest supercity—developed compactly even while growing a spectacular 83 percent in the 1990s. The opening aerials in television's *CSI: Crime Scene Investigation* show the surprising conservativeness of its urban footprint. An intensely developed core area includes not only the Strip but also hospitals, a university, banks, and business towers. Low-rise neighborhoods spread from Boulder City and Henderson to North Las Vegas, but they are constrained by military land, by a basin and range landscape that channels development into a corridor, and by the costs of supplying water in a desert. This is a metropolis with good union jobs in the hotel and restaurant industry and a service economy that is diversifying from gambling and tourism.

For permanent residents, Las Vegas offers a new variation on the venerable idea of development around neighborhood units with what historian Hal Rothman has called "post-urban pods." Writing for the local newspaper, he has commented that "each Station or Coast casino defines a new node, a six-square-mile area in which people live and play." Far from the Strip, these "community casinos" include restaurants and hotels and attract adjacent mixed-use development with shopping and housing. As he wrote a few months before his death, "Right by my house is a casino . . . that has next to it a faux village with condos, restaurants, and high-end stores. That development has morphed across the street, giving me a Whole Foods within range of my wheelchair."[27]

Las Vegas, like most of the metropolitan West, is also part of an even larger pattern. Somewhat in the way that astronomers see stars grouped into galaxies, galaxies into clusters, and clusters clumping unevenly at astonishing scale, geographers see cities grouped into conurbations and conurbations grouping into larger ribbons of urbanization. In 2005, the Lincoln Institute of Land Policy revisited Jean Gottmann's idea of the "megalopolis" as reshaped by a half century of Interstate Highways. It defined ten Megalopolitan Areas for the United States and adjacent border areas. Each has a distinct historical and regional identity, is organized around high-volume transportation corridors, and is projected to have at least 10 million people by 2040. In the east the list includes the Boston-to-Washington and Chicago-to-Toronto clusters that were apparent as early as the 1960s. In the West, from larger to smaller population, are the Santa Barbara–Los Angeles–Tijuana "Southland" (which extends a spur to Las Vegas); north-central California reaching from the San Francisco Bay deep into the Central Valley; the Texas Triangle, with its corners at Houston, Dallas, and San Antonio; Cascadia (Portland–Seattle–Vancouver); and Phoenix–Tucson. Some might add the Rocky Mountain Piedmont from Pueblo to Cheyenne or, with a very big stretch and lots of open country, Calgary–Edmonton.[28] To return to the astronomical metaphor, these are the West's night-view megacities, the bands and constellations of brightness that show so sharply on nighttime satellite images and contrast so starkly with the dimly lit mountains, plateaus, prairies, and forests between.

CHAPTER FOURTEEN

Transnational Urbanism .

In an ironic way, the invasion from the South had been good for business
to this point because it had driven the entire white middle class out of
Los Angeles proper and into the areas she specialized in: Calabasas,
Topanga, Arroyo Blanco. She still sold houses in Woodland Hills—that's
where the offices were, after all, and it was still considered a very desirable
upper-middle-class neighborhood—but all the smart buyers had already
retreated beyond the city limits.
> —T. Coraghessan Boyle, *The Tortilla Curtain* (1995)

The beginning of December 1999 was not the time to head to downtown
Seattle for some holiday shopping at Nordstrom's or an expensive dinner
at the Dahlia Lounge. Bricks were flying through store windows. Police were
chasing ski-masked rioters through the streets. Members of the global economic elite were trapped in high hotels, thinking (perhaps) that they could
have stayed home in Caracas or Kiev if they'd wanted disorder in the streets.

The cause of the disorder was the World Trade Organization (WTO), the
international consortium of governments that administered the complex
rules that regulate international trade and travel. Mayor Paul Schell and other
Seattle officials, committed to promoting Seattle as a "world-class" city, had
lobbied long and hard to bring the 1999 meeting of the WTO to the shores
of Puget Sound. With the expected presence of finance and foreign affairs
ministers and even some heads of government, it was supposed to give
Seattle world attention. Instead, it gave the city a headache. Fifty thousand

anti-WTO protesters converged on the meeting, held from November 30 to December 4, 1999. Most demonstrators were peaceful, but several hundred started a rampage through downtown that triggered overreaction by unprepared police.

The battle of Seattle was part of an international movement. Similar disturbances had marked an earlier WTO meeting in Geneva, Switzerland. Large demonstrations soon followed against the International Monetary Fund in Washington, D.C., in 2000 and against a WTO meeting in Genoa, Italy, in 2001. Protesters were convinced that the WTO is a tool of huge transnational corporations that tramples on local labor and environmental protections in the name of "free trade" that benefits only wealthy nations and their businesses. WTO defenders pointed to the long-term effects of open trade in raising net production in the world economy and thereby making more wealth available for developing nations. Opponents asserted, in turn, that such wealth never reaches the workers and farmers in those nations. American opponents demanded that U.S. firms, such as sportswear companies, that make their products overseas make sure that those overseas workers have decent living conditions and wages.

The context for WTO policy is a global network of economically advanced cities that drive and steer the engines of world trade, and the Seattle/Tacoma metropolis was a full-fledged member. The lumber mills and smelters that had once lined their waterfronts were gone by the end of the 1990s, leaving space instead for cruise ship docks and bike paths. There were far fewer factory workers than a half century earlier and many more residents who earned their living by trying to sell airplanes to international carriers, handling containers full of Chinese-manufactured shoes and toys, writing software and searching for killer applications, teaching science to students from abroad, peddling books over the Internet, and taking cappuccinos global. Each Seattle worker who did punch in at a factory time clock produced an average of $129,000 in exports—the highest figure among all U.S. metro areas. For Seattle there was also a special irony about December 1999: The scale of the protests caught authorities by surprise because much of the organizing had taken place online through Web sites, list serves, and chat rooms that many of the protesters accessed through Microsoft Windows–operated PCs.

Before the WTO embarrassment, Seattle's business and political leaders had already been staking their claim to international importance. Seattle and Tacoma competed for the lion's share of transpacific container trade with business leaders standing (metaphorically) with their backs to Mount Rainier and their eyes to the ocean. As the North American Free Trade Area was following the Canada–United States Free Trade Agreement, a local think tank published a key report on "international Seattle."[1] The state of Washington and province of British Columbia had already tried efforts to market the region for biotech and environmental engineering investments, and Seattle Mayor

Norm Rice pushed cooperative area-wide trade promotion efforts in the early 1990s. Paul Schell, as dean of architecture at the University of Washington and then as Rice's successor in the mayor's office, promoted the idea that Seattle and Vancouver should think of themselves as a single transborder region called "Cascadia" whose combined forces would make it a global economic powerhouse.

Seattle was not alone: All across the West, boosters and entrepreneurs recognized that the scale of economic activity and decisions was shifting from regional to continental and transoceanic. The explosive growth of major western cities after 1940 had made them national power centers by the 1970s. Their continued growth in the globalizing economy of the late twentieth and twenty-first centuries has made several western cities *international* power centers.

International connections were certainly on the agenda of every western mayor and business organization. San Francisco after World War II enjoyed its established role as an international contact point with every expectation that it would continue to benefit as a "focal point for increased trade with hitherto underdeveloped countries in the Pacific Rim and South America," and its leaders like to point out that world statesmen created the United Nations in its War Memorial Opera House.[2] In the 1940s and 1950s, coastal cities counted the number of steamship lines that made regular calls. By the last quarter of the century they were battling for direct flights to Tokyo, Taipei, Frankfurt, and Paris. Official propagandists in the 1980s called Houston "an international city with a dazzling future," a city where a "global consciousness" was attracting "world attention." Anchorage benefited as the best stopover on the great circle air routes, making it a logical site for refueling and transshipping cargo, whether from Singapore to Mexico City, Beijing to Los Angeles, or Honolulu to Frankfurt. A consortium of cities and business groups published a profile of the Dallas/Fort Worth "metroplex" that included a map showing the entire world pivoting on its international airport. Los Angeles no longer had a port but a "Worldport."

This sort of globalizing rhetoric might be ill-matched to reality in some cities (is Tacoma likely ever to become the Dublin of America?), but it had a solid grounding in the western- and southernmost of U.S. metro areas. Just as nineteenth-century Dallas and Kansas City were intracontinental door-keepers, twentieth-century Honolulu was an intercontinental stepping-stone between Asia and America. The islands of Hawaii were an outpost for New England missionaries and whaling ships in the early nineteenth century and then an agricultural paradise where California capital put Chinese, Japanese, Filipino, Portuguese, and Puerto Rican immigrants to work in pineapple and sugarcane fields. In World War II, Honolulu was the staging point for the U.S. war effort in the western Pacific, a role that it repeated during the war in Vietnam, when the 5,000 military personnel who flew to the city each week for rest and recuperation accounted for one-fifth of its tourist business. Many of its other tourists in the 1970s and 1980s were newly wealthy Japanese who thronged to the beaches and hotels of Waikiki.

Realizing that both defense spending and tourism were deeply tied to international relations, local leaders during the Cold War consciously worked to build a specific geopolitical role keyed to Honolulu's location. The East–West Center at the University of Hawaii was created as an intellectual meeting place. Hawaii's multiracial population was a domestic obstacle for statehood (triggering fears among southerners of racial amalgamation), but it also allowed advocates to proclaim that statehood could make Hawaii and Honolulu a symbolic and practical "bridge to Asia." State officials developed a Pacific Rim strategy in the 1960s, and Hawaii built its own pavilion at the Osaka world's fair in 1970. Politicians and civic leaders envisioned Honolulu as an information exchange center with a future as a Geneva of the Pacific.

Economic activity flowed both ways. Hawaiian corporations in the 1950s and 1960s diversified out of local agriculture into overseas ventures. Castle and Cooke moved into banana production in the Philippines and manufacturing in South Korea, Thailand, and Singapore. The Dillingham Corporation undertook construction projects all around the Pacific: power plants in Korea, harbor facilities in Singapore, transportation projects in New Zealand and Australia, pipelines in Thailand. In the same decades, Japanese investors put billions of yen into Hawaiian resorts and residential real estate. At the beginning of the 1990s, Japanese owned half of the hotel rooms on Waikiki. Real estate investments of $6 billion by the end of the 1980s put Honolulu third behind New York and Los Angeles in attracting Japanese capital, with money continuing to flow into second homes as well as hotels and office buildings until a peak in the mid-1990s. Boosters rebranded downtown Honolulu as the "Plaza of the Pacific." Like Miami for Latin America, Honolulu was a comfortable location for Asian firms to open a U.S. office and a convenient location for U.S. companies with interests west of the Pacific.

Vancouver was simultaneously booming as Canada's single doorway to Asia. After World War II, Vancouver and Victoria were well matched as stodgy and very "British" cities (not unlike Christchurch and Wellington in New Zealand). Vancouver had a great natural setting, two classy hotels, dull neighborhoods, and the National Exposition farm show. With less ethnic variety than Winnipeg, it was Wichita with water. However, Canadian immigration policy changed in 1967, dropping a "preferred nation" list for a system that awards points to individuals based on age, education, wealth, and special skills, meaning fewer Europeans and more Asians in the mix. The two most popular destinations were Toronto and Vancouver. At the 2001 census, Asian Canadians totaled 24 percent of metropolitan Toronto and a huge 32 percent of Vancouver (compared to 11 percent for Los Angeles and 18 percent for the San Francisco Bay region). Vancouver's population included 343,000 Chinese and 164,000 South Asians, followed in decreasing population size by Filipinos, Southeast Asians, Koreans, and Japanese.[3]

Expo '86, the world's fair that was instigated and promoted by the British Columbia provincial government, was a catalyst and showcase for internationalization. Attracting 22 million visitors, especially from the western U.S. and Pacific nations, it was part of an expansion of the market for Vancouver's high-end business and professional services, which added Pacific Rim clients to western Canadian customers. Along with traditional business and professional consulting firms, a new business specialization developed in the 1980s teaching English to Asians. Vancouver continues to evolve from an essentially provincial service center to a Pacific Rim city tied to the future of Asian and Pacific markets.

The changes have been obvious on the Vancouver landscape. Kingsway, the major arterial avenue that runs eastward from the city center, traverses a long sequence of ethnic communities, much like Danforth and Dundas streets in Toronto. The province sold the Expo '86 site to a Hong Kong developer; the transaction was a harbinger of internationalization of the city's real estate market and the growth of an entire forest of slim residential highrises. After 1978, when the Canadian government allowed immigration for anyone investing $250,000 in a Canadian business, "investor immigrants" from Hong Kong, Taiwan, Malaysia, Macao, the Philippines, and the Middle East supplemented the more usual working-class immigration. Chinese money poured into leafy neighborhoods of the west side, frequently cutting mature trees and replacing modest-sized cottages with new mansions of 5,000–6,000 square feet, artificial landscaping, imposing walls, and towering front entrances. The fierce public reaction to "monster houses" was essentially a clash between two deeply held cultural values: the English tradition of green, picturesque, and understated landscapes and the Chinese preference for carefully managed architecture under the principles of feng shui.

Asian immigration after 1965 transformed U.S. Pacific cities as well as Vancouver. Immigration reform legislation in 1965 lifted national quotas for permanent entry to the United States, opening the door for Asian immigration to increase from 6 percent of the national total in 1965 to nearly half by the 1990s. The migrations brought ethnic variety to every Pacific coast city. Honolulu in 1980 had more than 50,000 Chinese, Japanese, and Filipinos. San Francisco had more than 50,000 Chinese, Vietnamese, and Filipinos. Los Angeles had more than 50,000 of all four groups. These are the sort of connections the novelist Robert Stone references in *Dog Soldiers* (1974), a book that careens through the settings of the emergent Pacific Rim economy circa 1970 as its characters converge from all directions on the Bay Area.[4] In its transpacific world, Samoan immigrants muster out of the Coast Guard to work for the petty gangsters, San Francisco flight attendants smuggle pot from Bangkok, East Indian women spin topless in seedy bars, Japanese military brides work for Filipino dentists, and the outlaw hero draws inspiration from Native American warriors and East Asian warrior religion.

Drawn from the 2000 census in the United States and the 2001 census in Canada, Tables 14.1 and 14.2 show the continued concentration of Asian-origin residents in the western states and provinces. The U.S. data compile individual self-identifications for the "race" category on the census questionnaire. The Canadian data are for "Visible Minorities." For comparison, the western states in aggregate account for 33 percent of the U.S. population, and the western provinces account for 30 percent of the Canadian population.

To take a single national group, the number of ethnic Chinese in the United States in 2000 was a tenfold increase over the number in 1960. New Chinese neighborhoods developed in Houston, Oakland, and San Diego, while immigrants from Taiwan, Hong Kong, and all parts of the PRC joined the old families from Guangdong in the historic San Francisco Chinatown. Social and

TABLE 14.1. Asians in the United States and the Western States

Group	Total in United States	Total in 19 Western States	Western Total as Percent of U.S. Total
Chinese	2,433,000	1,313,000	54
Filipinos	1,850,000	1,319,000	71
Asian Indians	1,679,000	541,000	32
Vietnamese	1,123,000	730,000	65
Koreans	1,077,000	533,000	49
Japanese	797,000	607,000	76

TABLE 14.2. Asians in Canada and the Western Provinces

Group	Total in Canada	Total in Four Western Provinces	Western Total as Percent of Canada Total
Chinese	1,029,000	483,000	47
South Asians	917,000	296,000	32
Filipinos	309,000	131,000	42
Southeast Asians	199,000	67,000	34
Koreans	101,000	43,000	43
Japanese	73,000	45,000	62

economic divisions appeared among upwardly mobile and assimilating students and professionals, Chinatown businessmen, and an insular workforce in sweatshops and service jobs. Tensions arose between the old elite, which operated through family associations, district associations, and the Chinese Consolidated Benevolent Society, and newcomers with a wide range of political experiences and ideas. John Keeble tried to capture the differences in his novel *Yellowfish* (1980), which starts in San Francisco's Chinatown, visits the environs of Spokane, crosses the border to Vancouver, and returns to San Francisco by way of a Chinese-owned casino in Reno. Set in 1977, the story involves the smuggling of a probable Chinese political agent and three illegal Chinese immigrants (the "yellowfish") from Canada to California. The plot pivots on a struggle for power between factions and generations in Chinatown. The immigrants themselves endure the dangers of the backcountry to obtain the expected security of cities that are fully part of the transpacific economy.[5]

Like Chinese immigrants, ethnic Koreans have brought a strong entrepreneurial orientation. Portland's 15,000 Koreans in 1990 owned 700 businesses, supported eighteen churches, and chose among twenty public associations. The Olympic Boulevard area in Los Angeles in the 1970s had approximately one-third of the area's Korean households but relatively few long-term residents. Instead, it was a place of initial adjustment, much like European immigrant neighborhoods of earlier generations. "Koreatown serves as a launching pad for many Korean newcomers," according to demographer Eui-Young Wu: "Very few of them stay very long. The zip code analysis of the Korean directories also shows that growth rates of the Korean population are much faster in the outlying and suburban areas than in Koreatown. The Koreatown of Los Angeles will probably develop into primarily Korean shopping and service area."[6]

The comment about Korean immigrants holds true as well for other national groups from Asia, who are fully as suburbanized as the general U.S. population. If we separate out the twenty-five large cities (those with 100,000 or more residents) that had the highest proportions of Asians and Pacific Islanders in 2000, we find that eight were western central cities and fifteen were western suburbs—Bellevue, Washington, Fremont and Fullerton, California, and many more. Daly City, on the peninsula south of San Francisco, was a prime exhibit of suburban sprawl in the 1950s and 1960s. By the twenty-first century it was a majority-Asian community where upwardly mobile Filipino and Chinese families were recycling the fifty-year-old houses for a new generation. Milpitas in the last quarter of the twentieth century changed from a white factory town to a high-tech town that was more than 50 percent Asian American. In southern California, Cambodians clustered in Lakewood; Samoans, in Carson and Wilmington; Thais, in Hollywood; Japanese, in Culver City; and Vietnamese, in Westminster.

Monterey Park, a city of 60,000 eight miles east of Los Angeles, gained national attention in the 1980s as the "first suburban Chinatown." In the 1970s it began to attract Chinese Americans enjoying second-generation and third-generation mobility out of crowded ethnic neighborhoods. Soon after, enterprising real estate entrepreneurs marketed the city to potential immigrants from Hong Kong and Taiwan as an "Asian Beverly Hills." *Time* magazine in 1983 featured a photograph of the city council with two Hispanics, a Filipino, a Chinese, and an Anglo, and two years later *USA Today* named it an "All-American City." However, the influx of new immigrants with money generated complex tensions. Third-generation Chinese Americans who had struggled for success sometimes resented rich newcomers who shared their ethnicity but not their history. Whites resented the replacement of familiar stores with Asian shops and supermarkets filled with unfamiliar products ("I feel like I'm a stranger in my own town," one said) and pushed an "English-only" agenda.[7] By 1992, however, whites made up less than one-eighth of the town's population and presumably few members of the 35,000-person crowd who watched its first Chinese New Year parade.

For the United States, of course, immigration from Latin America was an even bigger story than immigration from Asia, adding southern gateways to Pacific gateways. Border cities from Brownsville to San Antonio and their Mexican twins dominate a borderlands region of daily interaction between the two countries. The region in the 1980s extended roughly seventy-five miles south of the border, the distance at which the Mexican government established its checkpoints for visas and tourist cards. On the north it included the four U.S. metropolitan areas that had Hispanic majorities by 1980, among them Laredo at 92 percent—an international city in fact rather than booster literature. Like W. H. Timmons's characterization of El Paso and Juarez, the cross-border communities are "Siamese twins joined together at the cash register."[8] Green-card workers cross from Mexico to the United States as service workers. American popular culture and investment flow south. Bargain hunters and tourists pass in both directions. San Diego State University researchers estimated in 1978 than Mexican citizens spent $400 million in San Diego County in 1978. A major shopping center in Chula Vista reportedly made 60 percent of its sales to Mexicans, and developer Ernest Hahn conditioned the construction of downtown's Horton Plaza shopping mall on the completion of the Tijuana Trolley, the light-rail line to the Mexican border. Going the other direction, most of the signs for roadside attractions for dozens of miles south from Tijuana are in English rather than Spanish.

The binational cities of the Southwest share labor pools as well as consumers. The Mexican government in the mid-1960s began to encourage a "platform economy" by allowing companies on the Mexican side of the border to import components and inputs duty-free as long as 80 percent of the items were reexported and 90 percent of the workers were Mexicans.

FIGURE 54. El Paso. El Paso/Juarez is the second largest of the U.S.–Mexico border cities. Originating as a trading point central to the Gulf Coast, the Pacific, the Rocky Mountains, and Mexico, it grew in the twentieth century with the two M's of military bases and maquila manufacturing.

The intent is to encourage American corporations to locate assembly plants south of the border. Such *maquila* industries can employ lower-wage workers and avoid strict antipollution laws (leading to serious threats to public health on both sides of the border). A series of further incentives followed, such as allowing total foreign ownership of factories. *Maquiladora* plants proliferated, especially after devaluation of the peso in 1982 and the adoption of the North American Free Trade Area in 1993. The 600 maquiladora plants of 1982 grew to 3,000 plants employing 1.2 million workers by 2005. The seven major border city pairs in 2005 had more than 5,100,000 Americans and 5,250,000 Mexicans.[9] In rank order they are San Diego/Tijuana; El Paso/Juarez; McAllen/Reynosa; El Centro/Mexicali; Brownsville/Matamoros; Laredo/Nuevo Laredo; and Nogales, Arizona/Nogales, Sonora.

Among the U.S. cities, the cross-border economy has had the most substantial effects in El Paso.[10] The city emerged as a clothing-manufacturing center because in the 1950s and 1960s its access to Mexican workers allowed companies the Third World advantages of inexpensive labor and weak labor regulations without leaving home. The first industrial park specially for maquiladoras was built a few miles away in Juarez in 1969, and the industrial connection expanded explosively in the 1980s and 1990s. Thousands of American workers in new El Paso factories made auto parts and other components, and thousands of others provided indirect support in transportation and finance. Across the border, 100,000 Mexicans, most of them women, were staffing maquila plant assembly lines.

San Antonio is not a border city, but it continues to be an institutional center and staging ground for Mexican and Central American immigrants. The expansion of civilian jobs at army and air force bases in the 1940s and 1950s helped to create a substantial Hispanic middle class that would assert political power and transform the city's political balance between Anglo and Latino in the 1980s. At the same time, peripheral growth on the Hispanic west side involved the scattering of mobile homes and low-cost housing on poorly drained land. The interpenetration of low-income housing with the crop and grazing lands of southern Texas provided a symbol of the city's historic role as refuge and reservoir for Spanish-speaking farmworkers.

Los Angeles is San Antonio written in capital letters. East Los Angeles is a huge city within a city that stretches twenty miles eastward from downtown Los Angeles and houses more than two million Latinos. By the 1979–80 school year, half the first graders in Los Angeles County were Hispanic. On the negative side of the balance, growing Latino populations have created contests over political power in heavily African American municipalities like Compton as well as racial tension in previously all-white communities like Lakewood. The Watts riots of 1965 were narrowly black against white, but the "Rodney King riots" in 1992 involved Latinos as much as African Americans and targeted businesses owned by Korean and Vietnamese immigrants.[11] On the positive side, Mexican and Central American neighborhoods in southern California cities show the dynamism that Mike Davis has termed "magical urbanism," as residents remake drab, aging rows of bungalows into colorful blocks where front yards become front rooms and transform neighborhood streets from traffic channels to centers of community life.

Latinos have also staked dynamic claims on the center of Los Angeles. On March 25, 2006, hundreds of thousands of peaceful demonstrators packed the plaza and streets around City Hall to protest punitive immigration legislation. Photographed from the *Los Angeles Times* building, the participants in the Gran Marcha made central Los Angeles public space in the same way that waves of political activists have utilized Pennsylvania Avenue and the National Mall as sites of civic action. Someone who wandered around downtown Los Angeles a few days earlier or later would have realized that the action was along Broadway and Spring Street—where the old retail district of the 1920s and 1930s was now booming with Hispanic shops in the old storefronts and Mexican movies in the old film palaces—not a few blocks west from where the dreary caverns of the Arco Plaza and Bonaventure Hotel housed the servants of late capitalism.[12]

Downtown at afternoon rush hour is also a reminder that metropolitan Los Angeles remains divided by ethnicity and class. While darker-skinned Angelenos wait at street corners for buses to take them south to and east, affluent professionals who might have modeled for the *L.A. Law* TV show swing out of subsurface garages and chase the setting sun on their way to Bel Air and

Pacific Palisades. T. C. Boyle's 1995 novel *The Tortilla Curtain* describes a typical destination neighborhood in the hills on the western side of Los Angeles County, where the occasional presence of a "disreputable" automobile inspires politically progressive whites to erect gates to keep out the Mexican hordes. At the other end of the metropolis, a sharp demarcation runs across the middle of Orange County. To the north are increasingly Latino cities like Santa Ana. To the south are affluent cities like Irvine (70 percent white and 30 percent Asian). As ethnographer Kristin Hill Maher discovered, residents of Irvine have mobilized a thick set of social norms to accommodate their desire for low-cost Latino workers to repair their houses, tend their yards, and watch their children while simultaneously seeing Mexican and Central American immigrants as threats to be kept at bay.[13]

Aggregate census data allow us to zoom out from specific metropolitan areas for a comprehensive measure of immigration. The proportion of foreign-born residents in a metropolitan area is an indicator that gets at the cumulative effects of immigration. For the United States, thirty-six of the fifty metro areas with the highest proportion of foreign-born residents in 2000 were located in the West. Those with more than 20 percent foreign born—the top end of the list—included Los Angeles, San Diego, and San Jose plus smaller cities in the southwestern borderlands and agricultural areas like Brownsville, McAllen, Laredo, and El Paso in Texas; Yuma in Arizona; and El Centro, Fresno, Merced, and Madera in California.[14]

To the north, Statistics Canada in 2001 found that 38 percent of Vancouverites had been born in other countries; 21 percent in nearby Abbotsford; and 21 percent in Calgary. For seven of the eight Census Metropolitan Areas of western Canada, more foreign-born residents arrived in the 1991–2001 decade than in any previous decade. The exception is Victoria, where a much larger portion of immigrants are British and Europeans who arrived in the 1960s and 1970s.

Data also provide a more recent snapshot. For 2000–2005, thirteen metro areas in the West had net international migration of 50,000 or more (compared with only ten in the East). The list includes Dallas, Houston, Denver, Las Vegas, Seattle, and Portland in addition to California cities. Other substantial gains were recorded for cities not popularly viewed as immigrant destinations, with more than 10,000 for Tulsa and Salem, 8,000 for Wichita, 6,000 for Richland, 5,000 for Ogden, and 2,000 for Fargo.

Many of the immigrants to cities like San Francisco, Las Vegas, and Dallas have been participants in a globalizing economy in which North American cities are increasingly nodes in global industries such as electronics, energy, entertainment, and tourism that make international peer cities more important than continental neighbors. San Jose and the surrounding Silicon Valley communities are the home ports for high-tech mother ships like Hewlett-Packard, Intel, Google, Cisco, and Sun. Here are fleets of head offices, research facilities, and factories that thrive on the circulation of ideas and skilled workers. Their roots are in the Cold War defense budget, but their workers are now drawn from a global labor pool. In 1970, almost all high-tech workers in Silicon Valley were U.S. born. Thirty years later 42 percent were foreign born, including 36 percent of the Ph.D. scientists and engineers. AnnaLee Saxenian has calculated that Chinese and Indians ran 30 percent of Silicon Valley tech companies in the early twenty-first century. She argues that there is now a "brain circulation" between the western United States and Asia, rather than a one-way "brain drain."[15] Current technology even allows some high-skilled and highly paid immigrants to maintain dual households and "commute" between California and Taiwan, Hong Kong, or Korea.

Pivoting on Silicon Valley is a constellation of other cities on both sides of the U.S. border, each with its own specializations. Austin is a center for research and development. Seattle is the capital of a software empire. San Francisco has been a hotbed for multimedia applications. Phoenix has a Silicon Desert complex, Dallas has a Silicon Prairie, and Portland has a Silicon Forest with an orientation to measuring and imaging devices.[16] Across borders and oceans, Guadalajara and Suzhou offer high-skilled process engineering and low-cost factory operations to turn U.S.-designed innovations into a flow of salable products. Bangalore's industrial parks—cloned from Redmond, Washington, and Sunnyvale models—house branches of American and European information technology companies that have decentralized, plus homegrown software design, coding, and testing specialists—not to mention thousands of tech support staff in computer and software call centers.

Petroleum production and processing make up another high-tech industry with a very different style. The Energy West has extended from Houston and Dallas eastward into Louisiana, west through Texas and New Mexico, north through coal and oil fields at the base of the American and Canadian Rockies, and even farther north to the North Slope of Alaska. Houston and Dallas are centers of the Energy West but so are Midland, Odessa, Tulsa, Denver, Calgary, and Edmonton. After World War II, Texas expertise and capital exploited oil and gas fields on the northern plains. North Dakotans learned to be suspicious of cars bearing Texas license plates as they crisscrossed rural counties in summer 1951 to lock up oil leases, but bankers and newspaper publishers in Minot and Dickinson were glad to see Texans as emissaries of industrial progress. As far as historian Eugene Hollon could tell a decade later, Billings was indistinguishable from Odessa or Amarillo.[17] Texas investors were meanwhile stirring up Denver, buying up downtown real estate and putting up high-rises like the Petroleum Club and Continental Oil buildings. When oil exploration shifted to the North Slope of Alaska in the 1970s, so many oil workers flooded into Fairbanks that local residents began to defend themselves with Texas jokes.

The American oil industry crossed the international border into Canada after the opening of Alberta's Leduc oil field in 1947. American companies

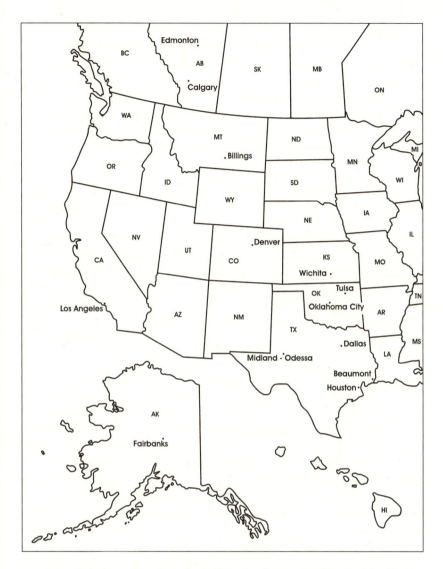

FIGURE 55. Petroleum cities. From the Gulf Coast to the margin of the Canadian Rockies and Alaska, the twentieth-century and twenty-first-century petroleum industry has spurred the growth of a dozen major cities and numerous smaller production centers like Dickinson, North Dakota, and Rock Springs, Wyoming. (Map by Jacquelyn Ferry.)

controlled 70 percent of Canadian oil production at the end of the 1950s and took a leading role in the 1970s in exploring the tar sands of northern Alberta. Tulsa oil companies hired experts to analyze the difference between Oklahoman and Canadian culture. While Edmonton grew as an operations center and base for Canadian oil firms in a prolonged boom from 1947 to 1982, Calgary became a second Denver, with scores of administrative offices for American-owned oil operations. By 1994, eighty-two Fortune 500 companies had offices in Alberta—sixty-seven in Calgary and only twelve in Edmonton. Ironically, by 1981 Canadian investors were responsible for half the new office construction in downtown Denver as they looked for a repeat of the Calgary boom in which U.S. dollars had primed the pump for Canadian fortunes.

Houston itself not only exports petroleum products and petrochemicals but also sells relevant production equipment and expertise—oil field equipment, drilling supplies, petroleum geologists, and petroleum market specialists. During the frantic years of the energy crisis in the 1970s, at least a hundred Houston companies operated in the oil fields of the South China Sea and another hundred in the countries around the North Sea. Houston's numerous foreign banks directly serve its international petrochemical business. The oil industry helped to multiply the value of trade through the Port of Houston by a factor of ten during the 1970s. The city's leading trading partners were the oil companies of Caribbean and Middle Eastern nations. Exceeding even agricultural products and petrochemicals, its leading export group was construction, mining, and oil field equipment—helping to give it fifth place in export sales per capita among U.S. cities. Until the company decided to uproot to the Persian Gulf, the oil production and construction giant Halliburton—itself an amalgamation of several Houston petroleum industry corporations—placed a public face on the city's global economy.

International tourism is another global industry that expanded enormously in the age of the Boeing-747 and similar transoceanic jumbo jets. In 1988, Texas, Arizona, California, Washington, and Hawaii each hosted more than a million foreign visitors. Data on top cities for overseas visitors in 1999–2000 show New York at the top with 22 percent of market share and Los Angeles second with 14 percent of market share (roughly 3,500,000 visitors per year). San Francisco was fifth with 11 percent, closely followed by Las Vegas and Honolulu with 9 percent each; all three of these cities received more than 2,000,000 foreign travelers. Also in the top twenty were San Diego, San Jose, Anaheim, Dallas, Houston, and Seattle with 2–3 percent each. In total, the West accounted for eleven of the twenty top destinations.[18] In the swirl of international travel, Las Vegas competed with Hong Kong and Macao, San Francisco competed with Paris, and Honolulu competed with Bangkok, not to mention other island vacation air-travel destinations like Denpasar (Bali), Palma, and Las Palmas.

As all these industrial examples show, the traditional "horizontal" connections between western cities and their resource-producing hinterlands have been overlaid with "vertical" connections that tie small cities into national and international networks that skip over intervening landscapes. Boise still ships locally grown potatoes (to Asia as well as the United States), but it is also home to electronics and international engineering firms. As early as 1975, according to data compiled by geographer Allen Pred, its twelve largest corporations controlled only 5,600 jobs in the Boise area but 57,400 elsewhere in the United States and Canada and 14,000 in other countries. New York is still the financial capital of the world, but Citicorp moved its international credit card division to Sioux Falls at the start of the 1980s, taking advantage of well-educated workers with good work habits and low wage levels and creating 2,500 new jobs in "depository institutions." As a business and professional center for the Upper Columbia River Valley, Spokane boomed in the 1970s and suffered in the 1980s with the rise and decline of farm, timber, and metals prices. In the mid-1980s, however, it attracted spillover jobs from congested, expensive Seattle. The businesses included a credit card–processing office for Seafirst National Bank and back-office work for Seattle-based Safeco Insurance. In addition, a handful of small software and high-tech companies moved from costly coastal cities. The Guardian Life Insurance Company made the far longer move of back-office functions from New York to Spokane in 1986. Such new businesses substantially widen these cities' range of direct contact outside their regional hinterlands. Long-distance phone lines have joined the Union Pacific, Burlington Northern, and Chicago and Northwest tracks as key economic infrastructure.

At the same time that some finance and management jobs moved down the urban hierarchy, a handful of cities have emerged as dominant centers in the control and management of global capitalism. These "global cities" house interrelated sets of banks, corporate headquarters, advertising and public relations firms, management consultants, international attorneys, and national media—all involved in receiving, creating, and directing huge flows of financial and economic information. They also attract trade associations, think tanks, and nonprofit organizations that work on a global scale. The deregulation of international finance and the explosive spread of instant electronic communication in the 1980s and 1990s confirmed the importance of a handful of global decision centers.

The top of the global hierarchy has long been occupied by London and New York, with Tokyo joining them with Japan's postwar economic recovery. Just below the supercities have been a handful of regional trading and finance cities that edged above their regional rivals. San Francisco in the first postwar decades was one of three major international banking cities in the United States and was the best place west of the Mississippi to find lawyers versed in trade law and international negotiations. As late as 1961 it ranked third in the number of consular offices (after New York and Washington, D.C.) and was home base for the country's second- and third-largest shipping lines. It accounted for 3.2 percent of total sales by the largest American manufacturing corporations but for 5.4 percent of their foreign sales, for a "multinational index" of 1.69. The care and feeding of these global ties remained a central concern, from a postwar effort to develop a World Trade Center to

FIGURE 56. Port of Vancouver. Vancouver is Canada's gateway to Asia, with port facilities on both Burrard Inlet (shown here) and the Fraser River. (Wikimedia Commons.)

Mayor Diane Feinstein's efforts to sell an "Invest in San Francisco" program to Asian businesses from Manila to Seoul.

By the 1980s, however, Los Angeles was elbowing ahead as "a control and managerial center for international capital . . . a global capitalist city of major proportions."[19] The change was apparent in foreign investment in downtown real estate, in the growing roster of European and Asian banks, in the global entertainment industry, and in communications, with the *Los Angeles Times* emerging as one of the nation's three global newspapers, with six bureaus in Europe, five in Asia, five in the Middle East and Africa, and five in Latin America as of 1990. As late as 1967 Los Angeles and Long Beach together loaded and received essentially the same value of goods ($2 billion) as did San Francisco, Oakland, and other Bay Area ports ($1.8 billion). By 1986, L.A. trade at $63.8 billion was 3.5 times that of the Bay Area. Other West Coast ports found it increasingly difficult to compete for import trade because the rich southern California market draws overseas shippers and shipping lines. Los Angeles/Long Beach in the same year handled 23 percent of all U.S. imports and more than half of imports through the West Coast. The Port of Long Beach, which called itself "the trade center for the world," and the immediately adjacent facilities of the Port of Los Angeles now constituted the largest port complex in the United States.

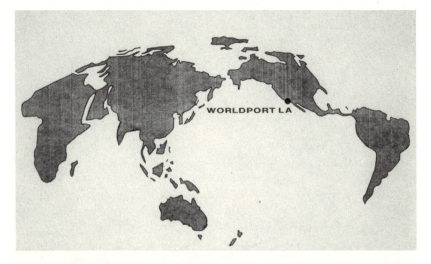

FIGURE 57. Worldport L.A. As the international commerce of the United States shifted increasingly to Asia and the Pacific in the 1980s, the Port of Los Angeles placed itself squarely in the center of global trade. The Port of Los Angeles and the adjacent Port of Long Beach, "trade center for the world," constitute the largest foreign trade complex in North America.

There are many ways to rank the importance of cities in the world economy. We might compare the number of foreign bank offices, value of exports, international conventions and events, offices of international nonprofit organizations, immigrants, foreign tourists, or even direct flights overseas. To pick three indicators, San Francisco, Los Angeles, Houston, and Dallas in the early 1980s were ranked 2, 3, 5, and 6 among all U.S. metropolitan areas in commercial banking assets; 2, 4, 5, and 7 in airline passengers; and 2, 4, 6, and 7 in major corporate headquarters.[20]

Looking at more recent data, Geographer P. J. Taylor and his colleagues have tried to measure the global connections of major cities by analyzing the office locations of the hundred largest international firms providing high-end business services in accounting, advertising, banking insurance, law, and management consulting. They placed Los Angeles ninth in the world. The western cities of Los Angeles, San Francisco, Dallas, Houston, Seattle, and Denver made up half of the nation's top twelve, a share far out of proportion to the region's share of population.[21]

In the world economy of the twenty-first century as much as the earlier industrial economy, skyscrapers nevertheless remain a token of a city's importance. It took forty years for the Sears Tower in Chicago to top the Empire State Building, but the rivalry was thoroughly globalized by the twenty-first century as Kuala Lumpur and then Taipei claimed the world's tallest building. For sheer number of tall buildings of ten stories or more, Los

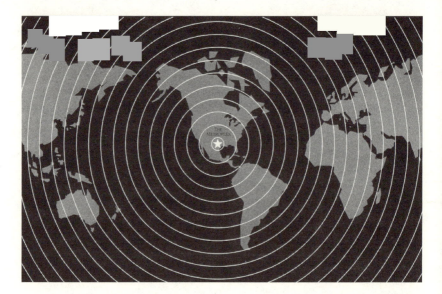

FIGURE 58. Dallas, Fort Worth, and the world. By the 1980s, Dallas/Fort Worth had joined the many western cities that were trying to illustrate their centrality to world commerce. This promotional graphic was published in "The Metroplex Dallas/Fort Worth" profile by a consortium that included the Fort Worth Chamber of Commerce, the City of Garland, the Dallas Partnership, the North Texas Commission, and the Dallas/Fort Worth International Airport.

FIGURE 59. Dallas skyline. By the early twenty-first century, the skyscrapers of downtown Dallas towered over the Texas prairie like an artificial mountain. (Wikimedia Commons.)

Angeles in 2006 ranked sixth in the world; Vancouver, fourteenth; Calgary, nineteenth; Edmonton, twenty-third (just behind Singapore); and Las Vegas, thirty-first (just after São Paolo).[22]

Tall buildings also figure in the cinematic imagery of the international city of Houston. Like an accomplished repertory actor, Houston played a variety of roles in the movies of the 1980s. It is America's boomtown in *Urban Cowboy*, crammed with blue-collar workers trying to become instant Texans. It is Space City, U.S.A., in *Terms of Endearment*, a city where it seems natural to have a lecherous astronaut as next-door neighbor. The city's most telling appearance, however, comes in the low-budget film *Local Hero*, an ironic comedy that transports a quintessential yuppie from the high-rise offices of an international energy company to a sleepy village on the coast of Scotland. A master of the transoceanic telex, the wheeler-dealer is supposed to incorporate the village into a Houston oil empire. Although he fails (of course), the closing cut from cold, rocky beaches to a Texas condo tower is a reminder that the distance between Houston and the world is no greater than the distance to Baytown or Texas City.

CHAPTER FIFTEEN

The Long Arm
of the Metropolitan West

*He answered an ad promising travel and went to work for a crew that
drifted around the country wrecking old houses and hauling the doors,
chandeliers, windows, and hardware back to Los Angeles for use in houses
that duplicated other periods. They even demolished a few mansions in
Montana. . . . [T]he billiard table of a Butte mining baron ended up as a
striking salad bar in Van Nuys and numerous farm wagons and buck-
boards met a similar fate in steak joints, shrimp joints, kingcrab joints.*
    —Thomas McGuane, *Nothing but Blue Skies* (1992)

Larry McMurtry grew up in the 1940s and 1950s on a ranch near Archer
City, Texas. Located miles northwest of Fort Worth, Archer City is a town
of 2,000 that peaked in the 1920s and then struggled to hold its own through
the second half of the twentieth century.[1] Starting with *The Last Picture Show*
(1966), McMurtry turned the experience of Archer City into a series of novels
about the ways in which "Thalia, Texas," has met the larger world.

Thalia stands in not only for Archer City but for similar towns across
the Canadian and American plains. The first books highlighted the decline
of Thalia businesses in the late 1950s and 1960s as the surrounding cattle ranches and cotton farms failed to keep up with changing markets. The
local movie theater went broke—its doors swinging forlornly in the prairie
wind in the 1971 movie version—but increasingly mobile Thalians found
their family entertainment, models of sophistication, and thrills in Wichita
Falls (population 68,000 in 1950 and 104,000 in 2000). Twenty-five years

later, the middle-class Thalians of *Texasville* (1987) readily drove 140 miles to Dallas for a half-hour business appointment or professional consultation. Their daughters sped across two states to dance and cruise the bars. "Shoot," says twenty-year-old T. R. in *Some Can Whistle* (1982), "me and Dew went up to Oklahoma City two nights ago looking. We didn't find a thing so we came back and looked in Fort Worth, but the pickings were so slim we got home just after breakfast. These towns are tame up this way. Too many cowboys."[2]

Thalia embodies two distinct story lines. One is the continued bleeding of population and business from small town to large town—and from large town to metropolis. By any reckoning, the combination of nineteenth-century town boomers, overoptimistic farmers, and hypercompetitive railroads that saturated the Great Plains with thousands of miles of track created far more small towns than necessary. Shakeout was predictable as early as the 1920s. The second story is the many ways that more and more of the rural West has been incorporated directly into metropolitan systems and global economies. The western heartlands—Snake River Valley, Montana plains, San Juan Mountains of Colorado, Utah Canyonlands—were scarcely touched by Europeans in the eighteenth century. In the nineteenth century the new system of commercial cities tied the backcountry into the national economy. In the twentieth century, these same cities staked new claims on their surrounding communities as urban recreation, commuting, and amenity zones in the later twentieth century, while cities have continued to entice country people. Even the rural North Dakotans in Louise Erdrich's novel *Love Medicine* (1984) feel the attractions of Fargo's bright lights. There may be parts of the West that have emptied out, but few places are now isolated from metropolitan influences.

As historian David Wrobel has most recently pointed out, nineteenth-century city boosters used a language of common interest between city and hinterland. They constructed and envisioned the prosperity of entire regions (like the interior empires of Denver and Spokane) and presented "the towns and the agricultural communities surrounding them . . . as symbiotic parts of a whole."[3] They looked at rural–urban differences and saw complementarity. In the hinterland were resource producers and consumers, in the city were markets and services that added value to rural products—and perhaps returned *some* of that value to farmers, ranchers, and miners. City and town were a "regional package."

City and country were still a regional package in the late twentieth and twenty-first centuries—and one in which the metropolis still writes the script. What has changed is the range of demands and balance of power. Agriculture, mining, and forestry became more and more efficient over the twentieth century as resource owners substituted machinery for man power. Falling numbers of rural workers meant declining rural markets for city goods and services. The rationalization of rural production also turned economically redundant coastal and mountain communities into attractive and initially affordable locales for recreation and vacation investment. Thomas Andrews has pointed out that mining towns didn't become quaint and colorful until clattering mills, smoke-belching refineries, and grimy industrial workers were well in the background or in the past—with the transformation of Aspen, Colorado, from half-abandoned mining camp to cultural mecca and tourist trap after 1945 being the prototype of change.[4] The result is a rural western landscape that still serves the needs of city people but now for its surfaces of scenery, hiking trails, ski slopes, and crashing waves rather than the rich soils and minerals beneath those surfaces.

One of the most obvious effects of the metropolitan shadow has been the decline of Main Street in just the way chronicled by McMurtry. The spread of automobiles and interstate highways pushed retailing and service business up the hierarchy of towns and cities. Authorized by Congress in 1956, the interstate system finished half of its 42,000 miles by 1965 and three-quarters by 1970. Construction crews graded and paved the last large gaps in Texas, California, Colorado, Utah, and Montana in the 1970s. Some of the highways have linked entire sets of cities into new constellations like the I-35 corridor from San Antonio to Kansas City by way of Dallas, Oklahoma City, and Wichita. Others plunge through hours of virtually empty mountains and rangelands, like I-15 running 200 miles from Idaho Falls to Butte with Dillon, Montana, at 4,000 people, the largest town in between.

Especially in the far-flung West, the interstate system has had a special importance in reducing what geographers call the friction of distance. When an hour's travel can take you past the county seat to a small regional city with new stores and supermarkets at the freeway interchange and a second hour can take you to an emergent metropolis with big-box retailers *and* an 800,000-square-foot mall, Main Street merchants and professionals have a hard time competing. As geographer James Shortridge puts it for Kansas, the typical county seat town in the early twenty-first century, "although still able to attract customers to its grocery stores, churches, and gasoline stations, is increasingly unable to do so for even slightly more expensive or specialized items such as household appliances or accounting services."[5] A systematic comparison of changes in trade centers on the northern plains from 1960 to 1989 documents what was obvious to travelers: "Small towns persist— more than 3,000 in the seven states—but they provide a diminished set of functions compared to 1960. Similarly, metropolitan areas continue to thrive and grow, affecting not only their immediate areas but also growing circles of adjacent communities."[6] On average, the number of businesses in metropolitan areas and regional centers—places like the Twin Cities, Omaha, Lincoln, and Bismarck—nearly doubled. In contrast, small towns and hamlets struggled to hold onto clothing stores, banks, auto dealers, and other businesses that once lined Main Street—a challenge that has only grown as Wal-Mart has saturated small-city America.

At the same time, not every main street meets the same fate. Some small cities have declined, but others have found special roles that allow population to stabilize or even grow. They can be exurban refuge, resource town, "brainville," or recreation community.

Some are close enough to major cities to become part of the exurban fringe, more disconnected than suburbia but dependent on daily or weekly commuting. Statistics Canada developed the Metropolitan Influence Zone or MIZ for its 2001 census to identify the degree to which municipalities outside Census Metropolitan Areas and Census Agglomerations are connected to those larger population concentrations. "Strongly" and "moderately" influenced zones accounted for 7 percent of the British Columbia population, 11 percent of Alberta, 13 percent of Saskatchewan, and 15 percent of Manitoba.[7] An earlier study of commuting to U.S. metropolitan cities in the 1960s and 1970s showed that much of the wide-open West had been incorporated into automobile commuting zones. The zones for Oklahoma City, Salt Lake City, Stockton, and Midland/Odessa all doubled in size during the decade. By the 1970s, western cities were drawing at least a few daily workers from fifty or seventy-five miles away. Houston's zone embraced Bryan and Beaumont, and Corpus Christi reached to Victoria. Tulsa and Oklahoma City shared portions of a single labor market, as did Fresno–Bakersfield and Austin–San Antonio. By the 1990s, even Archer City had begun to pick up residents who commuted to Wichita Falls.

Interspersed among the upscale exurbs are pockets of economically marginal rural sprawl of the sort that claims the southern fringe of Albuquerque at the same time that tastefully planned New Urbanist neighborhoods claim the north side. San Diego has low-rent sprawl southward toward Tijuana and a "libertarian fringe" of small towns and ranchettes nestled into the dry mountains that back the land side of the metropolis. Many of the residents would rather be Butch Cassidy than a La Jolla scientist, pursuing a lifestyle that emphasizes landscape and lack of social obligations. On the outskirts of Portland, which climb both east and west into mountain foothills, there are a mix of aging leave-me-alone hippies and stranded loggers who sourly watch suburban estate development replace the timber industry. The town of Estacada in the Cascade foothills is now a commuter suburb of Portland, but its annual highlight used to be its Timber Jamboree, complete with court of plaid-shirted young women wielding axes and saws.[8]

Others may be centers for new raw materials industries like Wyoming coal mining and Alberta oil production, although the resource economy is easy come, easy go. Gillette, Wyoming, boomed in the 1970s with coal production; Rock Springs and Kemmerer, in the 1980s with petroleum; and Pinedale, in the new century with natural gas. Small ranching towns turned into townscapes of trailer parks, motel-style apartments, and bars and into social landscapes of uprooted families, bored roustabouts, drinking, and drugs. For the wives of the pipeliners, equipment operators, and roughnecks, Chilton Williamson has observed, "Kemmerer was a sour mirage in the American High Plains to which they had been dragged from comfortable surroundings in lovely lush suburban towns near Oklahoma City, Albuquerque, or Bakersfield."[9]

Only in small cities with a more diversified economic base have the resource booms been absorbed without totally upending the community. Fairbanks was the staging point for Alaskan oil development that brought in as many as 30,000 workers for pipeline construction in 1974–76, but it also had military bases, a university, tourism, and a vast (if sparsely settled) hinterland. Grand Junction boomed in the early 1980s when oil companies explored the feasibility of extracting oil from huge beds of western Colorado shale. Towns on the front lines such as Rifle were swamped by the boom, but Grand Junction was stabilized by its position as a mini-metropolis. The boom and bust of the oil shale business inflated and then deflated housing prices and trapped some overconfident real estate developers. It also left a new airport and dozens of new churches as newcomers searched for family stability and a sense of community. The telephone book in 1985 listed twenty-eight mainline Protestant and Catholic churches, twenty-four Baptist churches (reflecting the Oklahoma and Texas roots of many oil workers), and more than fifty Pentecostal, Bible, and Evangelical congregations.

More sedately than energy towns, hinterland cities have also benefited from the great expansion of higher education from the 1950s through the 1970s that built campuses from scratch and turned dozens of tiny teachers colleges into regional state universities in places like Hays, Kansas; Denton, Texas; Ellensburg, Washington; Chico, California; and Prince George, British Columbia. The same education boom transformed sometimes lonely cow colleges into research universities with cosmopolitan faculties who can support sophisticated community services and often attract "new economy" industries. When Bernard Malamud put in a stint teaching English at Oregon State University in the 1950s, he found the inspiration for the deeply provincial society that he caricatures in *A New Life* (1961). The people of "Cascadia College" hunt, fish, loaf, and prefer the practicalities of grammar to the nebulous realms of literature. A half century after Malamud went back to New York, Corvallis was still small but scarcely provincial, supporting thousands of Hewlett-Packard workers, engineering consultants, and globally networked university researchers.[10]

The most common bypass around small-city decline has been the expansion of the leisure economy in the "nice" and "beautiful" parts of the West, most obviously in the "weekendlands" that lie in symbiotic proximity to large metropolitan areas. A few western weekend zones for the upper crust developed along railroad lines in the first half of the twentieth century, and Richard White has examined the "urban shadow" that Seattle vacationers and real estate developers began to cast on Whidbey Island in Puget Sound even before World War II.[11] It was the postwar automobile age, however, that democratized outdoor recreation and turned lakeshores, oceanfronts, deserts, and mountain valleys into RV zones and second-home districts—the "coastal condomania" and "sagebrush subdivisions" that Oregon governor Tom McCall lambasted in the early 1970s. These are areas within a half-day's drive of major cities where the urban middle class can conveniently maintain second houses, condos, and time-shares for regular use—areas such as the shores and islands of Puget Sound, south-central Texas, and the central Colorado Rockies in Grand, Summit, Eagle, and Park counties. The recreation zone of the San Francisco Bay conurbation rises up the slopes of the Sierra Nevada range like a snow-machine tsunami. Weekendland as a mass phenomenon was a product of affluence in the 1960s and again in the 1980s and 1990s, abetted in the new century by low interest rates and a phalanx of aging baby boomers. For one recent example from 2004, more that 30 percent of the residential mortgages along the northern Oregon coast and 29 percent in Deschutes County east of the Cascades were for second homes.[12]

Roslyn, Washington, eighty miles east of Seattle on the back slope of Snoqualmie Pass, is a symbolically laden example of the weekend transformation. Originating as a company town for coal miners in the 1880s, it shifted to logging in the 1950s and 1960s when the California market for building products was booming and then served as "Cicely, Alaska," for the offbeat television hit *Northern Exposure* from 1990 to 1995. From the quirky opening credits with a moose stalking along main street, the theme of the show was the power of the small frontier town to transform a random passel of city people into a community whether they wanted the change (like Detroit debutante Maggie O'Connell and Seattle storekeeper Ruth-Anne Miller) or not (like retired astronaut Maurice Minnifield or New York physician Joel Fleischman). A decade after the show ended and the tour buses have disappeared, however, the real Roslyn is being reinvented again for city people. The Suncadia resort, on land sold off by Plum Creek Timber, which acquired what were originally Northern Pacific Railroad timberlands, projects thousands of million-dollar vacation homes on the hills around town, aiming at Microsoft millionaires and other Puget Sounders who want woodsy luxury. Said the town's mayor in 2006: "It was a boomtown when coal mining was going on. Then logging came in. Now, in place of logging, we have development."[13] The rural West may have transformed city slickers in the fiction of TV, but the city people will surely transform the town to their own purposes in the reality of real estate.

Beyond the range of day-trippers and weekenders are communities that specialize in serving long-distance mass-market tourism. This is a role that dates back to the nineteenth century. It embraces historic destination resorts that have grown into substantial second-tier cities like Colorado Springs,

Reno, and Monterey along with new destinations like Aspen, Vail, and the rest of the downhill archipelago. The category also includes gateway towns like Flagstaff for the Grand Canyon, Rapid City for the Black Hills, and Hilo for the Big Island. Gateways offer scheduled airline service. They may have attractions of their own, but their tourist businesses also benefit from people who spend time and money on their way to and from the backcountry. They're found on the west slope of the Rockies, on the east slope of the Sierra–Cascade complex, on Pacific shores, and along the Rio Grande and Colorado River corridors.[14]

In a third, overlapping category are lifestyle enclaves for retirees and time-flexible workers, the latter made possible by the ubiquity of air travel since the 1970s and the explosion of electronic communication. These are "fly-in communities" in contrast to the notorious "fly-over country" of the North American midlands. Generally smaller than the gateway cities, they may be places deep in the western interior (St. George, Utah; Telluride, Colorado; Moab, Utah) or on its far edges (Homer, Alaska; Makalao, Hawaii; Tofino, British Columbia). They're something other than weekendlands because few people live close enough to drive there on a Friday night and back on Sunday afternoon. These enclaves of metropolitanism may embrace several towns and spread for twenty or thirty miles in mini-conurbations, like the Kalispell/Whitefish/Columbia Falls complex west of Glacier National Park or the Bend/Prineville/Sisters district east of the Oregon Cascades. Some have been officially captured by the new U.S. Census designation of "micropolitan" area: for example, Ukiah, California and Oak Harbor and Port Angeles, Washington.[15]

Natural amenities are the most powerful attractors for hinterland growth.[16] Retirees, telecommuters, weekenders, and national and international tourists all share locales like Estes Park, Lake Tahoe, the Columbia River Gorge, and the Sunshine Coast and Gulf Islands of British Columbia. Large towns like Lander, Wyoming, and small cities like Bozeman, Montana, are the service centers for a new rural economy whose produce is scenery, sometimes enjoyed pristine and sometimes with the help of golf courses and ranchette subdivisions. We should add in here the "nice small city" whose sociocultural amenities are greater than its environmental and scenic attractions. Examples might be Kerrville, Texas, in the hill country between San Antonio and Austin or university cities such as Lawrence, Kansas, and the twinset of Pullman, Washington, and Moscow, Idaho.

Some of these places remain viable year-round communities where the newcomers put down roots, whereas others fill with superexpensive trophy houses and "ghost houses" used only a few weeks each year. In all the cases, the new economy is driven by capital acquired elsewhere and often spent with little attention to local customs and social networks: Those folks from Dallas and Los Angeles have a tendency to do what they want and don't ask.

FIGURE 60. Missoula. At the time of this 1952 photo, Missoula was a farm and forestry center with a small university, with Higgins Avenue stretching between its two railroad stations. A half century later, it was a center of environmental education and activism as a part of a "New West." (Montana Historical Society.)

The result may be the "devil's bargain" described by historian Hal Rothman. Local businesses that may have initiated the tourist industry are swamped by corporate capital, newcomers price workers out of their houses, and decisions about the community's future are made in city office towers rather than the old downtown coffee shop.[17] At its worst, the consequence is the "Aspenization" of recreational hot spots—the headlong transformation of local economic and social systems that leaves the entire supporting population of firefighters, schoolteachers, and service workers on the outside.

The U.S. Department of Agriculture has tried to systematically measure the different economic factors that now affect the rural United States by sorting counties into a variety of categories. The old economy is represented by "mining-dependent counties" and "farming-dependent counties." Mining counties appear in four relatively small clusters: western Texas; the north-central Rockies from Price, Utah, to southern Montana; central Nevada; and the North Slope of Alaska. The overwhelming majority of farming-dependent counties cover the Great Plains from Texas and New Mexico to Montana and North Dakota (the same economy certainly crossing into the

Prairie Provinces). In contrast are "retirement destination counties" where the number of residents aged sixty or older grew 15 percent or more by in-migration during the 1990s and "nonmetro recreation counties." Together such counties cover much of central Texas, the Rocky Mountain states, the Pacific Northwest, Alaska, and Hawaii.[18]

One common response to the pressures of metropolitan reach in the retirement and recreation zones has been regional land-use regulations to preserve scenery for city people, for without strong land-use controls—unlikely in many parts of the rural West—new development is scattershot (much of Colorado's Front Range looks like it bears the scars from a bad case of smallpox). None of these efforts is fully successful, for it is a fine challenge to preserve the attractions of scenery and rural landscapes *and* make them accessible to city people without turning orchardists, viticulturists, ranchers, and ocean fishing crews into museum exhibits.

California, where pressures of population on landscape have been most pronounced, has been the locale of multiple experiments to meet urban demands for recreation while protecting older resource industries and the natural environment (themselves incompatible goals). California citizens in 1972 approved an initiative to protect 1,100 miles of coastline. As amended in the California Coastal Act of 1976, the state works with coastal counties and cities to separate rural and urban uses and balance public access, environmental protection, and resource industries. The Golden Gate National Recreation Area and the Point Reyes National Seashore applied direct federal control to large tracts of the coast on both sides of the Golden Gate. On the eastern edge of the state, California and Nevada since 1969 have used a controversial bistate commission to protect the natural systems of the Lake Tahoe Basin in the face of extreme development pressures that have made the area a sort of San Francisco/Sacramento exurb. The California Desert Protection Act in 1994 transferred three million acres of the Mojave Desert from the Bureau of Land Management to the National Park Service, which has to balance existing mining and ranching with environmental protection and recreational pressures from Los Angeles. Whether the specific environment is craggy coast, snow-topped mountains, or sere desert, the underlying issue is the same: how to manage the landscapes for urban users with care for natural systems and at least minimal concern for old resource industries.

Federal legislation to create a Columbia River Gorge National Scenic Area in 1986 similarly reflected the power of Portlanders to shape a regional agenda around the goal of scenic protection. Indeed, the legislation climaxed a steady expansion of Portland's use of the gorge as a recreation zone through the twentieth century. Portlanders had begun to savor the scenery of the Columbia Gorge in the later nineteenth century with steamboat tours and camping expeditions. "Here wonder, curiosity, and admiration combine to arouse sentiments of awe and delight," wrote historian Frances Fuller Victor in 1891.[19] Steamboats gave way to automobile tourism with the completion of the Columbia River Highway from Portland to The Dalles in the 1910s. Sections remain in use as scenic byway or hike/bike trail within sight of the streaming traffic on Interstate 84. The Scenic Area Act, however, built in tension by adding the second goal of economic development to the first goal of resource preservation. Senator Mark Hatfield reflected this understanding of the scenic area when he told a gorge audience that the legislation "was never intended to dry up those communities in the gorge or to be a blow to the future of those communities."[20] In specific, the legislative goals are to "(1) protect and provide for the enhancement of the scenic, cultural, recreational and natural resources of the Columbia River Gorge, and (2) protect and support the economy of the Gorge by encouraging growth to occur in existing urban areas and by allowing future economic development in a manner that is consistent with paragraph 1."[21]

In effect, the act requires the Forest Service and a bistate Columbia River Gorge Commission, the specified management agencies, to preserve and create jobs for country people while managing scenery for city people. The tool is a land-use management plan on the Oregon model, not a particularly popular choice among property-rights fundamentalists on the Washington side. A homemade billboard outside Lyle, Washington, depicted the congressional proponents of the scenic area as horses' asses. The act divides the gorge into Special Management Areas (largely federal land where little development is expected, with the Forest Service as the lead agency), General Management Areas (largely private land where carefully controlled development is expected and a bistate commission is the lead agency), and thirteen urban areas that are exempt from the act and remain under local planning control.

The scenic area is a multiple balancing act. As an effort to plan for environmentally sensitive economic development, it faces the challenge of reconciling sometimes competing activities within the same limited space. Protection of natural areas competes with resource production; both may conflict with new industries such as tourism. Closely related is the need to mediate between differing and sometimes clashing community cultures and worldviews that belong to an "Old West" of loggers and ranchers and a "New West" of bureaucrats and Internet entrepreneurs. The intent of the Scenic Area Act and related programs is to plan and manage the changes that usually come piecemeal and sometimes overwhelmingly to resource regions. Substantive goals try to balance the forces of change against the claims of existing social and economic systems. Implementation requires ranchers, loggers, and other "Old Westerners" who pride themselves on bluntness to learn the customs of committee work and bureaucracies. It likewise expects the sophisticated city-based interest groups that generated the legislation to accept rural communities as partners and agents of change.

These regional regulations are product and producer of the cultural contradictions mentioned at the beginning of this chapter. The invasions of summer people and winter people are part of the economic development process by which smaller cities have long sought outside investment—whether from railroad builders, irrigation speculators, or industrialists whom they hope will open a factory in the new industrial park built with U.S. Economic Development Administration dollars. These other deals to attract capital can be viewed as devil's bargains just as much as tourism. A nineteenth-century town that mortgaged itself for a railroad spur was mortgaging its self-control; a twentieth-century town that gave whopping tax breaks to attract a factory sacrificed its schoolchildren for new jobs. Nevertheless, the leisure economy looks and feels different, particularly to men who would prefer to be chain sawing trees or chasing cattle. Country people and small-town people, especially in the deep West, often need the money transferred in from the information economy, but they don't have to like it.

In Thomas McGuane's novels about Deadrock, Montana (a town somewhat like Livingstone on i-90 between Billings and Bozeman), the cattle range country in the heart of the West is linked inextricably to the larger world. The land in *Keep the Change* (1989) may be special in itself, but it is also a commodity, a launching pad for a career, and an opportunity for an exotic vacation from worldly Florida. To try to bail his uncle out of a business deal gone bad, the protagonist has to drive to Billings to meet the attorney for the Continental Divide Insurance Company, a no-nonsense pro who explains that any outcome has to have enough ascribable overhead to help cover the rent on the company's twelve floors in downtown Denver. In the West of *Something to Be Desired* (1985), anything can happen in a "land of Japanese horseshoes, Taiwanese cowboy shirts, and Korean bits."[22]

This tension is the center of Peter Decker's thoughtful discussion of the transformation of Ouray County, Colorado, on the northern slope of the magnificent San Juan Mountains. Change came big and fast in the 1980s as the booming national economy and stock market put money into the hands of professionals, corporate managers, and entrepreneurs. As elsewhere in the mountain and coastal West, an affluent leisure class that could vacation, buy second home properties, and even relocate on a semipermanent basis discovered the ranching and mining towns of Ouray (newcomers included Ralph Lauren as well as dozens of "little millionaires" from Texas and California). The last Ouray County mine (the Camp Bird) closed in the 1980s, at the same time that ranch land was getting far too expensive for ranches to expand through purchases.[23] By the 1990s, more than half of Ouray Co. income was from dividends, interest, rents, and transfer payments, and retirees outnumbered ranchers and ranch workers. Water rights bought from ranchers were keeping the Log Hill golf course development green. The town of Ridgway had a new retail environment with mountain bike shops, hairstylists, bakery, astrologer, chiropractor, and kitchen cabinet maker as well as post office and café. To the social environment of 4-H, Rebekahs, and the Volunteer Fire Department the newcomers added yoga, music, investment, and photography clubs.

Under the shadow of urban money, a new leisure ethic conflicted with an old work ethic. As Decker writes, "A rancher looks at a meadow and sees hard work. . . . The summer resident looks at the same meadow and sees . . . a rural painting of infinite beauty."[24] Newcomers question all the old, established ways of doing things and make land-use planning, school curriculum, and similar community issues into contested territory. Each group is convinced of its superiority: Rural residents scorn people who don't *work*, and the successful pushers of words or numbers assume that their college degrees and corporate standing make them obviously superior. At worst, the big outside money fences off new estates, blocks hunting and fishing, and ignores the local community. At best, newcomers introduce new ideas and force old-timers actually to articulate and defend their preferences rather than imposing them through political power and inertia.

We're left with a question: What kind of place is a metropolitanized West that is incorporated socially and culturally into the spheres of major cities? The North American interior is still the Empty Quarter from the air or the automobile window (try driving Wyoming 28 or Alaska 4 or Saskatchewan 21 in addition to I-15), with a handful of urban oases like El Paso, Las Vegas, Salt Lake City, and Calgary; small prairie and plateau cities; scattered farms and ranches; and plenty of lonely grassland and high wilderness. In our popular understanding, the West used to be a place of isolated individuals and small groups in scarcely formed communities—mountain men, prospectors, Oregon Trail families, and homesteaders living in very little houses on a very big prairie—and much of the landscape appears to support this view.

Tensions between rural imagery and urban reality are deeply embedded in regional culture. Essayists chronicle the work of geologists and naturalists as the modern equivalent of miners and mountain men. Regional novelists choose their contemporary protagonists from ranchers, farmers, loggers, rodeo riders, and river rafters. Their topics are Native Americans, nature, and life in the land of sun and storm. The public most easily recognizes as "western" those writers who deal with small towns and open landscapes. Wallace Stegner and Ivan Doig are western writers, but Maxine Hong Kingston and Sherman Alexie are ethnic writers. Ross McDonald, Walter Moseley, and Octavia Butler are all genre writers. Thomas Pynchon, Joan Dideon, and Douglas Coupland are mainstream. Larry McMurtry is western when his topic is a nineteenth-century cattle drive but not when writing about contemporary Houston or Las Vegas. Literary historians remember Walter Van Tilburg Clark's stories about nineteenth-century Westerners more often than his novel about twentieth-century Reno.

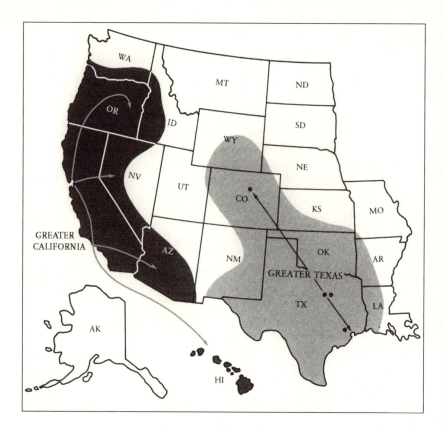

FIGURE 61. Greater Texas and Greater California. The metropolitan areas of Texas and California dominate much of western North America as markets, corporate centers, and sources of investment, workers, and consumers of recreation. (Map by the author, from Gerald Nash and Richard Etulain, eds., *The Twentieth Century West* [Albuquerque: University of New Mexico Press, 1989]).

The same contrast shows in the reception of two painters who came to the Southwest as outsiders and remained to be captivated by the clarity of southwestern light. Englishman David Hockney's reaction to Los Angeles in the 1960s was a series of stunning depictions of lawn sprinklers, high-rise buildings, and swimming pools. The surfaces glare and stare back at the viewer in the "Technicolor daylight" of California. The clear light of New Mexico similarly drew Georgia O'Keefe to paint and repaint the sun-bleached skulls of cattle. The international art world has applauded Hockney's urban and suburban images. The middlebrow public in the United States has adopted O'Keefe's traditionally regional subjects as national icons. Canadian Emily Carr, who painted the trees and totems of Pacific Canada with sweeping brushstrokes in the early 1900s, has become a similar touchstone for many

Canadians. As with literature, North Americans prefer to neglect the urban West to admire what they know to be comfortably western.

Embedded here is also a continuing preference for a white people's West. White Canadians and white Americans have patrolled the racial boundaries in the West since the 1850s, copying each other's restrictive legislation and engaging in copycat violence like the anti-Asian riots that passed from San Francisco to Bellingham to Vancouver, B.C., in 1907. By the twenty-first century, Native Americans and First Nations people are also OK (note the huge increase in the number of people claiming Native American ancestry between the 1990 and 2000 censuses in the United States), but there is less certainty about the Samoans, Salvadoreans, Sikhs, and other newer racial, ethnic, and religious minorities whom twentieth- and twenty-first-century urbanization have brought to the region. The heroes of *western rural* films in the 1940s and 1950s were most commonly white men who were confident in their racial identity, even when they extended friendship across racial and ethnic lines (e.g., Gregory Peck in *The Big Country* or James Dean in *Giant*). The protagonists of *western urban* films in more recent decades were far less certain that whiteness was the winning card (Michael Douglas in *Falling Down*, Harrison Ford in *Blade Runner*).

It is a commonly noted irony that cities like Phoenix and Los Angeles—now solidly multiethnic and multilingual—sold themselves as refuges from the polyglot East. Phoenix emphasized its whiteness in competition with Tucson, whose Mexican heritage and population remained locally important into the twentieth century. *Los Angeles Times* publisher Harry Chandler famously called his city "the white spot of America." The Chamber of Commerce and city officials in Los Angeles talked about living in the most American of cities and the home of red-blooded Americans. In 1924, for example, the Chamber of Commerce magazine editorialized that "for centuries the Anglo-Saxon race has been marching Westward. . . . [T]he apex of this movement is Los Angeles."[25]

The issue of race is a reminder of long-standing parallels between western North America and the U.S. South. Both were colonies of the northeastern industrial heartland, attached permanently to the core through the Civil War, the civil wars between white and red Americans, and the Anglo-Canadian conquest of mixed-race and French-speaking métis territory on the prairies. In the last third of the nineteenth century, the work of economic reconstruction in the South after 1865 had similarities to the development of the West, in both cases involving efforts to build a system of railroads and focal cities to integrate mineral and agricultural resources with the industrial core. In turn, Northeast cities like Montreal, Toronto, Boston, and New York controlled investment capital and set limits for local southern and western civic elites during the economic cycle of 1890–1940. New South rhetoric was the equivalent of western urban boosterism. Southern mill towns along the two sides of the Appalachians were the equivalents of western lumber and smelter cities. We can set Gastonia, North Carolina, alongside Everett, Washington, as mill towns and Kingsport, Tennessee, alongside Longview, Washington, as planned factory towns. The same was true at a larger scale for Denver with its Guggenheim smelters and Birmingham with its U.S. Steel mills. The deflationary collapse of southern and western resource industries in the 1920s and 1930s accelerated out-migration from wheat farms and cotton belt to regional cities. The reactive politics of the KKK found comfortable homes in Atlanta and Denver, Memphis and Portland. The South nurtured regional writers and agrarian theoreticians; the West, its own regionalists and plundered province Jeremiahs.

Since 1935, in contrast, much of the economic and military power of the nation has been mobilized to promote and develop the peripheral regions. Federal spending on public works, rural modernization, shipbuilding, aircraft, atomic energy, and military bases inexorably altered the balance between rural and urban opportunities. The resulting migrations mingled the cultures of the Mississippi Valley and Southwest and made Bakersfield a second Little Rock or Nashville. Commentators in the 1970s and 1980s recognized the transformation of the old periphery into a new core marked by increasingly independent cities by popularizing the term *Sunbelt* for the fast-growth region reaching from the Carolinas to California. Multiracial migration and the application of the Voting Rights Act to both Hispanic and African American minorities in 1975 created common preconditions for metropolitan politics. It is easy to pair up western and southern cities: Washington, D.C., and Los Angeles as information cities; Miami and Las Vegas as resort cities; Norfolk, Virginia, and San Diego as military cities; Knoxville and Albuquerque as atomic energy cities; Atlanta and Seattle as regional/international trade centers—and, of course, Anaheim and Orlando as vacation destinations.

Ironically, cities have been the anchor points for the regional intellectual traditions that have celebrated both the rural South and the wide-open West. The retrograde writers of the Fugitive movement celebrated the preindustrial South from the comfort of Nashville before scattering outside the region. Washington, D.C., New Orleans, and Chapel Hill/Durham attracted intellectuals and scholars with a serious interest in southern history and society in the decades before World War II, and Atlanta took on some of the same role in the second half of the twentieth century.

Western cities have played similar roles. Greater San Francisco has been an artistic marketplace and nurturer of talent since the nineteenth-century heyday of *Overland Monthly* and the meteoric careers of Jack London and Frank Norris. After World War II, the city hosted a remarkable set of poets and novelists to learn from each other, argue, and address national audiences. The mix included academically based writers from Berkeley, alumni of the wartime conscientious objector camp at Waldport, Oregon, East Coasters drawn by the California tilt, and a handful of Bay Area natives. Continuity came from Kenneth Rexroth, Lawrence Ferlinghetti, William Everson, and Josephine Miles. Creative and personal sparks came from Muriel Rukeyser, Gary Snyder, Allen Ginsburg, Jack Kerouac, and Ken Kesey. Meanwhile the creative writing programs that flourished in the 1960s and 1970s at San Francisco State University and Stanford University with instructors like Wallace Stegner, Ivor Winters, and Walter Van Tilburg Clark launched dozens of successful regional writers.[26]

Western cities have also played key roles in defining and preserving regional cultures that include the arts within much broader cultural systems. Salt Lake City and Provo house the interconnecting institutions that support and disseminate Mormon culture—universities, scholarly research, religious gatherings and outreach, and genealogical archives. The University of Texas has helped to make Austin the center for exploring, explicating, celebrating, and complaining about the Texas character. Walter Prescott Webb and J. Frank Dobie dominated the scene in the 1940s and 1950s, giving partial place in the 1960s to the feisty liberal perspectives of the *Texas Observer*. The efflorescence of literary activity in Montana and the production of the massive and valuable state anthology *The Last Best Place* benefited from the concentration of talent in Missoula. At the same time, cities led the increasing complexity of Montana society, where the new state constitution in 1971 was "an environmentally conscious monument to a modern, urban, self-confident state." The narrow margin for ratification came from eight of the state's ten largest cities.[27]

To summarize the changing relations of city and country, let's visit The Dalles, Oregon, eighty miles east of Portland on the Columbia River. Now a city of 12,000, it was sited at the foot of a nine-mile stretch of surging rapids and cascades where a great dike of basalt narrowed the river into "swelling, boiling & whorling" chaos, in the words of William Clark. The falls were a challenge to migrating salmon and an opportunity for uncounted generations of native fishermen. As a rich fishery and interruption to navigation, Celilo Falls and the Long Narrows were a natural trading center where the villagers of the lush coast exchanged fish, shells, cedar bark, and baskets for hides, buffalo robes, and obsidian gathered by the people of the dry interior. It was the "great emporium and mart of the Columbia."[28]

As an American settlement, The Dalles grew steadily with the expansion of steamboat navigation on the Columbia River and with agricultural expansion, but boosters after World War II pinned their hopes on electricity. The Dalles Dam, completed in 1957, flooded the rapids and destroyed the Indian fishery, but it also promised industrial development in what the Chamber of Commerce called "the best dam town in the USA."[29] Heavy industry *did* come in the form of aluminum smelting, an electricity-guzzling business that supported hundreds of good jobs in classic economic development. Fast-forward a half century, however, and overseas competition had undermined the Columbia River aluminum industry, leaving The Dalles with only 200 jobs at one smelting and casting company. In place of the old economy, there is money to be made serving the international set of windsurfers who first discovered the mid-Columbia breezes in the 1980s. The Dalles also scored a Google data center in 2006. Local amenities helped Google executives with the decision. So did the availability of cheap electricity to run all those servers—the same hydropower that once attracted manufacturing. As a "branch plant" town that answers to folks in Mountain View, California, The Dalles will now be "shipping" intangible data from search hits to instant consumers all around the globe.

Urban Frontiers

Los Angeles is beneath us, a huge, silent fairyland. The lights glitter as far as the eye can see. Between the red, green, and white clusters, big glowworms slither noiselessly. Now I am not taken by the mirage: I know that these are merely street lamps along the avenues, neon signs, and headlights. But mirage or no mirage, the lights keep glittering; they, too, are a truth.
—Simone de Beauvoir, *America Day by Day* (1954)

Here is where I go back to the first small crack in the shell of time, to when I was happiest. Myself and the others, empty pagan teenagers lusting atop a black mountain overlooking a shimmering city below, a city so new that it dreamed only of what the embryo knows, a shimmering light of civil peace and hope for the future.
—Douglas Coupland, *Girlfriend in a Coma* (1998)

The view across the Los Angeles Basin from a house high on the hills entranced European intellectual Simone de Beauvoir, at first enthralling her with the spectacle and then intriguing her with the city that lived beneath the light. Novelist Douglas Coupland placed his protagonist on the ski slopes of Grouse Mountain with Vancouver lying below, opening a fictional meditation on the balance between individual desire and social responsibility. Their rhetorical turns invert the founding metaphor of European

American city making—John Winthrop's assertion that the Puritan presence in Massachusetts would be "as a city on a hill" that modeled the just society for the world—but they carry the same hope that the new cities of western North American can, somehow, be better cities.

It would be foolish to build an extensive interpretation on a few turns of phrase, but a basic question remains in several permutations: Have western cities been different from those of eastern North America? If they were different, have they been better—meaning places of greater equality or opportunity? Have they been more self-conscious, with leaders and citizens who have realistically understood their strengths and weaknesses? If they were different in the nineteenth or twentieth centuries, what about in the twenty-first?

A common cultural preference for the elemental West—for unspoiled nature and, paradoxically, for the men and women who have altered it most drastically in their efforts to make a living—draws on firmly embedded understandings of the regenerative power of wild places, whether American West or Canadian North. That's an appealing view that draws on deep values and popular history, but—as this book has tried to show—it is also incomplete and misleading. Neither the social nor the chronological dichotomy of popular history holds. There are contrasts between then and now, as well as contrasts within the West, but it is not the simple opposition of old and lonely frontier versus new, crowded, and corrupting city. Recall that Europeans planted the seeds of cities as early as the 1600s with their arrival in western North America. Remember as well that the U.S. West has been the most urbanized part of that nation for more than a century and that Canada's western half now equals its eastern as a region of city dwellers.

Underpinning all of this book is the assumption that cities, as communities of people, have a simple right to exist, that the residents of concentrated settlements have justification in fairly utilizing natural landscapes or rural land as their workshops and dwelling places. As human societies have invented and reinvented cities multiple times over the last 6,000 years, this belief that urbanization is a legitimate use for land has usually been unstated and uncontested. We realize how axiomatic this claim is only when the contrary message jerks us to attention, whether in the writings of bucolic utopians who regard urbanization as an original sin or in the actions of the monomaniacal Khmer Rouge.

Cities are economic machines that make civilization possible. They increase the efficiency of production by facilitating the exchange and processing of goods and ideas. In so doing, they reduce the costs of necessities as well as luxuries. Cities more than pay for themselves by making it easier for human beings to gain protection from the cold, shelter from the storm, and respite from hunger. This is the trade-off that justifies urban claims on their landscapes and on relationships with their environs. Only on the margins do we explicitly weigh the relative virtues of a few more subdivisions against a few more berry fields or orange groves. Knowing that time will soon enough have its way, few of us are rushing to cast down the walls, rip up the pavements, and invite the fireweed and thistles to repossess Boise or sagebrush to reoccupy El Paso. Were we to abjure cities, and with them the benefits of civilized society, we would all be huddling and howling with Lear on the windswept heath.

There is no real alternative to an urban West. The urbanization of western North America creates opportunities for immigrants and continually redistributes the population of the fifty states and the thirteen provinces and territories among economically troubled and booming cities. Cities reach far into the countryside for food, clean water, energy, and building materials. They restructure the lives of rural residents in "weekendlands." For better or worse, they reshape valleys and hillsides and impinge on the lives of deer and condors, mountain lions and sea lions. They are an inescapable fact of twenty-first-century Canada and the United States.

We *can* say that the cities of western North America have come into their own. In the seventeenth, eighteenth, and nineteenth centuries they represented European imperialism and Atlantic capitalism. They were subordinate points in systems that reported across continental distances to New York, Boston, Montreal, and Mexico City; across the Atlantic to London, Paris, and Madrid; across the Pacific to Canton and Manila; and even across Siberia to St. Petersburg. In the twentieth century and into the twenty-first, they have increasingly generated their own investment capital, exerted their own political clout, and made their own connections with the global economy. They have also been the centers for economic and cultural innovations that articulated the twentieth century and are shaping the twenty-first, from Disneyization to Starbucks, e-commerce to iPods.

One distinguishing characteristic of western cities is the presence of their natural settings and landscape as an active physical and cultural force. These are places that you can *see*. Philadelphia or Atlanta, tucked within thick vegetation, jumbled hills, and small sheltered valleys can only be experienced as a series of neighborhoods and a succession of scenes unfolding at eye level. Los Angeles (or at least a substantial part) we can see all at once. "Once in the fall of '64," writes Christopher Rand,

> I got a fine view of the whole West Side [of Los Angeles]. . . . I was walking southward in the Santa Monica Mountains, and suddenly I rounded a peak and saw the ocean. . . . Small waves were breaking on the beach, which ran off below me, in a graceful curve, to the dune-shaped, hazy height of Palos Verdes, twenty miles away. Inland from the beach, from all twenty miles of it, lay the sprawling city, stretching on to the interior and finally meeting the distant faint brown hills that rimmed the L.A. Basin.[1]

FIGURE 62. Vancouver skyline. The high-rise apartments of Vancouver's West End rise above English Bay as the high peaks of the north shore tower over the heart of the metropolitan region. (Wikimedia Commons.)

Versions of this view of Los Angeles from its mountains have become a cliché in everything from *Fortune* magazine photo spreads to advertisements for new Buicks, but it is a cliché because it forms and confirms our image of how we view and understand the urban complex of southern California.

Other southwestern cities are equally open to inspection. When architect and city planner Daniel Burnham prepared his grand plan for San Francisco in the early twentieth century, he worked from a studio on Twin Peaks overlooking a panorama of the whole city (at least on days without fog)—the city that Jean-Paul Sartre described as "a city of air, salt, and sea, built in the shape of an amphitheatre."[2] Phoenix we've already viewed from South Mountain. Santa Barbara and Oakland are built against coastal hills; Honolulu, against the central peaks of Oahu; Tucson, below the Santa Catalina Mountains; and Vancouver, along a steep-sided fjord. Salt Lake City lies just as Richard Burton saw it 130 years ago, occupying "the rolling brow of a slight decline at the western base of the Wasatch . . . stretched before us as upon a map."[3] River cities like Denver, Boise, Billings, and Grand Junction sweep up broad, shallow slopes from the stream at their center. When we find the proper vantage points on the ridges and escarpments that mark the margins of their valleys, we can take them in as single metropolitan units. Butte, Helena, and Reno lie on long open slopes. Built along the Truckee River as it pours out of the Sierra Nevada, Reno is defined by "the vigor of the sun and the height of the mountains." From the hills that line the north side of the city, wrote a novelist about the 1920s and 1930s, "you look down across the whole billowing sea of the treetops of Reno [and] . . . see the tops of downtown places, the Medico-Dental Building, the roof sign of the Riverside Hotel." To the east the city spilled into the widening valley, where "the light spreads widely." Like the other cities of the West, Reno is a city built to be seen.[4]

In these visible cities, metroscape and landscape connect through *air*. Water has been a utility and a luxury, but air made San Diego and Honolulu and Denver and Los Angeles special places to live—crisp air for TB sufferers, warm air for vacationers, clear air for chamber of commerce brochures. The favored image of Denver is a skyline silhouetted against the rampart of the Front Range. No one, it seems, can talk about the pleasures of Austin without invoking the soft landscape and the soft, soothing air. Looking 1,200 miles westward, Alison Lurie took light as the symbol of the intrusive newness of Los Angeles. The California sun shines with "impartial brilliance" on the transplanted New Englanders in *The Nowhere City*, filters through the drawn drapes of their new house, floods them at the beach. The central character stands on his front walk and looks up at the "intense blue overhead, crossed by trails of jet vapor, dimming to a white haze at the horizon."[5]

Mild climate has had special attractions for the elderly. Retirees populated Sun City, Arizona, and Leisure Worlds in southern California in the 1960s and, since then, dozens of other communities for older adults. Texas, Arizona, and California in the 1960s and 1970s received more than their proportionate shares of state-to-state migrants in their sixties or older. Military retirees have been an identifiable subgroup in military base cities such as Denver, San Diego, San Antonio, Honolulu, and Seattle/Tacoma, which offer access to clubs, medical facilities, and old friends. To the north, mild climate and the rain shadow of Vancouver Island have made Victoria a city that cultivates an image of gentility to attract both vacationers and retirees ("the newly wed and the nearly dead"). It had the highest percentage of people aged eighty or older among Canadian metropolitan areas at the start of the new century. Meanwhile, several metropolitan areas in the Sunbelt saw increases in the number of Social Security beneficiaries from 2000 to 2004 at more than half again the national rate of 5 percent. The list includes Houston, Dallas/Fort Worth, Austin, Albuquerque, Phoenix, Las Vegas, and Riverside.

The tension between landscape and cityscape has also been manifest in the tension between imitation and innovation. Western cities in their first 300 years copied the social systems and culture of Europe—and then of eastern North America. Imperial officials drew the first plans and sent inspectors to distant frontiers to make sure that early settlers were still properly French, Spanish, or Russian. The first and second generations of Anglo-American Westerners were convinced that respectable social institutions were one of the best inducements to investors and immigrants. Western Anglo-Canadians, struggling with the double burden of demonstrating their soundness to London as well as to Toronto and Montreal, were eager to demonstrate their Victorian propriety. Journalist and political theorist Herbert Croly's comment in 1912 that Portland had "buildings of exceptional interest and merit" and an air of "dignity and solidity" would have pleased any civic elite from Dallas to Winnipeg, Pasadena to Victoria. So would the opinion of editor Walter Hines Page that Portland handled its affairs with "modesty, good sense, and good taste."[6]

But western cities were also places where old ideas and ways of life could be rethought and reassembled. Thomas Pynchon vividly describes nighttime Los Angeles from the freeway as a scene of pure energy: "speeding like bullets, grinning like chimps, above the herds of the TV watchers, lovers under the overpasses, movies at the mall letting out, bright gas-station oases in pure fluorescent spill . . . the adobe air, the smell of distant fireworks, the spilled, the broken world."[7] A spilled and broken world is one that is begging to be picked up and reassembled according to new plans and specifications. As sociologist Nathan Glazer noted in 1959, the cities of the postwar West were consciously chosen environments that matched many of the preferences of their residents. In the judgment of Los Angeles architect Richard Neutra, new metropolitan residents of southern California were open to new forms of culture because they had deliberately left behind the traditional communities of the East. This is the spirit of change that novelist Don DeLillo captures in the musings of a protagonist who has uprooted from New York to Phoenix:

I ran along the drainage canal wearing a wireless headphone. I listened to Sufi chanting while I ran. I ran along the palm alleys and through the winding streets of orange trees and handsome stucco homes—streets of westward dreams, the kind of place my father could have taken us half a century earlier, lightward and westward, where people came to escape the hard-luck past with its gray streets and crowded flats and cabbage smells in the hallway.[8]

The design and decoration of western cities express a vernacular exuberance that offers sharp contrast to the classic American model of the tidy New England village. From Tulsa to Fort Worth to Los Angeles, the downtown streets of twentieth-century oil-boom cities are lined with stores and office towers faced with the forward-looking styles of art deco, zigzag moderne, and 1930s streamline. Sunbursts, chevrons, brightly colored zigzags, and sleekly turned corners tied the growing cities to the imagined future. Examples ranged from L.A.'s gemlike Oviatt Building and Richfield Oil Building to Fort Worth's Aviation Building, Sinclair Building, and Texas and Pacific Terminal. The heir of prewar streamlined architecture is southern California's "coffee

shop moderne." The mobile society of Los Angeles devised atomic-age restaurant shops that were open twenty-four hours a day under sweeping cantilevered roofs. "Coffee shop moderne" meant open spaces and bold geometric shapes, frozen sparklers and sunbursts, and glittering surfaces of plastic, glass, and chrome that imitated gull-winged Chevrolets and finned DeSotos. Bowling alleys, supermarkets, and motels tested out the same styles, and Las Vegas made them famous.[9] Frank Gehry's Disney music pavilion and Experience Music Project, Rem Koolhaus's Seattle Public Library, and Daniel Libeskind's Denver Art Museum addition are recent high-art versions of the same ebullient and experimental aesthetic.

Western cities also display the energy of a fantastic and unfettered people's architecture. Some are individual projects like Sabato (Simon) Rodia's famous towers in Watts, a vernacular monument to California exuberance constructed over decades from scrounged materials. Street murals pepper the blank walls of Berkeley, San Francisco, Santa Monica, Compton, and East Los Angeles. The Old Woman of the Freeway began to look out over the Hollywood Freeway in 1974. Visitors to the beachfront community of Venice are reminded of the moral of the Fall of Icarus. A hundred miles down the coast, Chicano Park lies beneath the ramps of the San Diego–Coronado Bridge, which disrupted the Mexican American community of Barrio Logan in the early 1960s. The community fought back first for the park and then for public art on the concrete bridge supports, where Mexican American artists painted immense murals— a thirty-foot Virgin of Guadalupe, towering serpents, and heroes of Mexican self-determination from Emiliano Zapata to Rejes Tijerina and César Chávez, not to mention artist Frida Kahlo and the Aztec emperor Cuauhtémoc.

Otherwise conservative organizations have constructed entire fantastic townscapes. Anaheim's Disneyland, said its builder, was the place for California "to demonstrate its faith in the future."[10] Houston's Astrodome was the brainchild of politician and entrepreneur Roy Hofheinz. Opened in 1965 as the world's first domed stadium, the Astrodome reflected Houston's flamboyance and its disregard for traditional forms, in which baseball parks nestled within active urban neighborhoods. It became an instant tourist attraction because of its Texas size and its entirely new and high-tech approach to the classic architectural challenge of enclosing large spaces. In another branch of architecture, most instant universities in the United States—from the University of Chicago in the 1890s to Duke University in the 1930s—have sought the hallowed respectability of Gothic quadrangles. The University of California at Irvine, in contrast, offers its students a set of buildings that illustrate the full range of uninhibited postmodern architecture. Similarly, the multicolored buildings of Oral Roberts University in Tulsa look like a television spaceport set down in the American West. They declare their allegiance to a popular technological future rather than a European past.

FIGURE 64. Watts Towers. Immigrant Sabato (Simon) Rodia single-handedly constructed two ninety-nine-foot towers and a dozen other buildings between 1921 and 1954 in the community of Watts in Los Angeles County. The towers are twisted steel covered with concrete that is decorated with glass, tiles, and found objects. The site is now protected as a State Historic Park and National Historic Landmark. (Wikimedia Commons.)

Openness—or hyperopenness—to economic opportunity has paralleled innovation in design. Houston, Dallas, and the other cities across the Southwest symbolize the American frontier as business enterprise. Texans, says native son Larry McMurtry, like their "cities as raw as possible, so as to allow free play to what's left of the frontier spirit." "Wheelerdealerism," he continues, "is an extension of the frontier ethos, refined and transplanted to an urban context." Settled from the Middle West as well as the South and tied economically to St. Louis and Chicago as well as New Orleans, Dallas has often presented itself as the archetypal American city. Transplanting Midwestern boosterism to an expansive "metroplex," the business-based Dallas Partnership says that the spirit of Dallas is "dynamic, optimistic, and action-oriented." The Goals for Dallas program of 1966 was "boosterism at its most grandiose," according to historian Martin Melosi. This updated entrepreneurial frontier meets the world as a business town pure and simple—"a dream location for business."[11]

Phoenix has been an even newer version of the same dynamic individualism. Reporter Neal Pierce has commented that Phoenix has appropriated much of the Texas image of endless opportunity: "They all view the civilization here as an opening book, full of promise and opportunity." This "Headquarters West of the American free-enterprise ethic," Pierce writes, has been as firmly committed as Houston and Dallas to the ideology of private initiative. At the same time, the "quintessential Sun Belt boomtown" has lacked strong institutions for community decision making and an ethos of public responsibility. As Peter Wiley and Robert Gottlieb put it, Phoenix has been an example of "free enterprise in the saddle, the market as king southwestern capitalism's quest for immortality."[12]

In much popular imagery, late-twentieth-century Los Angeles supplanted late-nineteenth-century Paris as the world capital of consumption. The city's boom coincided with the postwar wave of consumer demand. In the popular media, Beverly Hills and Rodeo Drive came to rival New York and Fifth Avenue as homes of unlimited charge accounts. In the 1950s or even the 1960s, the young person from the provinces might long for breakfast at Tiffany's. In the 1980s, success was much more likely to mean making it in L.A. The image of the Valley girl satirized southern California as the land of consumerism, whereas teenaged prime-time soaps like *Beverly Hills, 90210* (1990–2000) and *The O.C.* (2003–7) took it almost seriously. Academic evaluations from both sides of the political spectrum also stressed the liberating effects of Californian abundance. Conservative political scientists were impressed by the ability of residents to pick and choose among different packages of public services in the region's scores of small cities. Liberal Los Angeles county supervisor John Anson Ford was saying much the same thing when he asserted that "it must not be a second congested London or New York, but a population center with many new characteristics adjusted to the outdoor life of the region and to the era of greater leisure, greater mobility, and a wider distribution of the skills and culture of modern society."[13]

If Los Angeles represented freedom to enjoy yourself, postwar San Francisco represented the freedom to be yourself. Prewar San Francisco and Oakland were among the most "eastern" of western cities, with strong labor movements, large European immigrant communities, substantial industrial sectors, and a heritage of machine politics.[14] Within a decade after 1945, however, San Francisco and its satellite cities were laying the groundwork for a "culture of civility" that tolerated efforts to define a wide range of self-conscious "communities" in older neighborhoods around the bay. Poet Gary Snyder, best known for deeply engaged writing about the natural world, has commented that "San Francisco taught me what a city could be, and saved me from having to go to Europe."[15]

The coalescence of the beat writers in San Francisco's North Beach neighborhood in the 1950s reached back to Bay Area radicals and bohemians from the early twentieth century (Jack London, Ambrose Bierce) but was also grounded in the survival of the political Left. At the center was City Lights bookstore, the most famous of a cluster of cafés, bars, bookstores, and other gathering places. Disaffected writers, poets, artists, and musicians drifted in and out of San Francisco and Berkeley. Common themes were a rejection of materialist culture, a longing for community, and a celebration of both straight and gay sexuality. The district attracted national attention in the years after Allen Ginsberg first recited "Howl" at the Six Gallery in 1955, triggering an obscenity challenge that reached the Supreme Court.

The explosion of political protest and social experiment in Berkeley and San Francisco in the 1960s built on the earlier political and cultural critiques. The metropolis was fertile ground, with its unrooted populations and clashing ideas. Berkeley's radical reputation and open atmosphere began to attract leftists from around the country: "Max Scheer, the founder of the Berkeley *Barb*, came from Baltimore; Jerry Rubin, a deeply alienated young newspaper reporter, from Cincinnati; and Mario Savio, the Catholic leftist, from New York."[16] Results included the Free Speech Movement at the University of California in 1964, one of the earliest challenges to the authority of well-meaning educational bureaucracies, and one of the most vigorous movements against the Vietnam War. While Berkeley stood as a model for university/hippie districts from Boulder to Seattle, San Francisco hosted thousands of permanent hippies and tens of thousands of short-term visitors in 1967's "Summer of Love."

The rise and fall of free expression in Haight-Ashbury had the additional effect of paving the way for the public emergence of San Francisco's gay community in the 1970s. The city had had a strong homosexual community since World War II, when most gays who had served in the armed forces in the Pacific theater were processed out through San Francisco. Openly gay poets such as Allen Ginsberg were prominent among the beats, and many North Beach bars were gay and lesbian as well as bohemian. Gathering places began to arise in other parts of the city at about the same time that *Life* magazine proclaimed San Francisco the country's "gay capital" in 1964. The same period saw the Castro district go through the stages of a gay bohemian influx in the late 1960s and early 1970s, a gay middle-class transition in the mid-1970s, and a "bourgeois consolidation" in the 1980s. The assassination of Mayor George Moscone and City Council member Harvey Milk in 1979 and the crisis of AIDS dampened the growth of the gay community, but San Francisco as an exemplar of personal freedom helped to open other cities to the free expansion of gay communities.

San Francisco was about styles of life, but San Francisco and western cities generally were also about new forms of political participation and careers open to talent. As early as the 1850s, middle-class San Francisco women played a role in civic life as commentators on public order and the vigilance committees. At the turn of the century, Julia Morgan was launching a stellar career in the traditionally masculine profession of architecture after breaking into the all-male realm of Paris art education, Phoebe Apperson Hearst was using philanthropy to open new opportunities for women, and Mills College president Aurelia Henry Reinhardt was a fully participating member of Oakland's civic elite.

A string of examples does not prove an unmeasurable assertion that western cities were always empowering environments for women, but they are good settings to think about the broadening of civic life to include someone other than the white males who ran eighteenth- and nineteenth-century cities. Perhaps more open social and political institutions, ranging from the scarcity of eastern-style political machines to the fact that thirteen states of the western U.S. granted women the vote in advance of the Nineteenth Amendment, created a wider array of opportunities for women to participate in public life from politics to labor agitation.

Certainly that was the case for two contemporaries of Morgan and Reinhardt whose careers briefly crossed in Denver. Emma Langdon earned her way into labor history between midnight and dawn on the cold night of September 30, 1903, as she worked to print the next issue of the *Victor Record*. As members of the National Guard hammered on the office door demanding entrance in the name of the governor of Colorado, she composed the morning issue on the cumbersome Linotype machine. When householders in the strike-torn mining town stepped into the crisp morning, they saw a headline that read: "Somewhat Disfigured, But Still In The Ring!" At 11:05 the previous evening, a squad of armed soldiers had arrested Langdon's husband and other members of the newspaper staff as "prisoners of war" because of their support for striking miners, including an article detailing the criminal records of several guardsmen who were on active duty in the Cripple Creek–Victor mining district. Kicked out of town by the suppression of the newspaper, Emma Langdon relocated to Denver to work in the office of the Western Federation of Miners and help William D. Haywood and Charles Moyer organize the Industrial Workers of the World.

Ellis Meredith was not a pioneering Wobbly, but she was also a skilled political activist. A reporter for the *Rocky Mountain News*, she wrote romantic novels on the side and helped organize the Colorado Non-partisan Equal Suffrage Association in 1893. She corresponded with Susan B. Anthony and Carrie Chapman Catt and was a strategist behind Colorado's vote in favor of women's suffrage in 1893, making Denver the largest city where women could vote until California adopted women's suffrage in 1911. Meredith was a Democratic Party worker who became vice chair of the state party, a member of Denver's first charter review commission, and president of the Denver Election Commission from 1911 to 1915. According to one of her opponents, "She is a fine woman, of excellent ability, clever, reliable, patriotic and dependable, and knows too damn much about politics."[17]

When college students in the mid-1960s went to the Bay Area to check out a possible future, they were following a trail laid out by the nineteenth-century Europeans and East Coasters who went to Chicago for a preview of coming attractions. Some—we've mentioned Rudyard Kipling and James Bryce—ventured into the even newer West beyond the Great Lakes to marvel over Tacoma or Minneapolis. By the mid–twentieth century, the track had shifted to Los Angeles, a puzzle that elicited a variety of answers from Simone de Beauvoir, Umberto Eco, Christopher Isherwood, David Hockney, Tom Wolfe, Rayner Banham, and many others. Journalist Neil Morgan in 1963 restated the nineteenth-century idea that exuberantly growing western cities represented the national future, nominating Los Angeles as "the center of gravity in the westward tilt." Two years later, *Fortune* described Los Angeles as the "prototype of the super-city." Richard Austin Smith found "a scaled-down, speeded-up version of the process of urbanization" and concluded that Los Angeles "may now be emerging as the forerunner of the urban world of to-morrow." To other writers of the decade it was a "leading city" or even the "ultimate city." Journalist Richard Elman traveled to the Los Angeles suburb of Compton "with the thought in mind that this was the future . . . what lies in store for all the new suburbs of all the big cities of America."[18]

The 1970s and 1980s extended the California image to the newly named Sunbelt. Austin, Denver, Salt Lake City, Tucson, and other southwestern cities began to appear on lists of "centers of power" or "cities of great opportunity."[19] Houston was "the last word in American cities" and "*the* city of the second half of the twentieth century." It was "the place that scholars flock to for the purpose of seeing what modern civilization has wrought," said Ada Louise Huxtable.[20] So was Phoenix, "the quintessential Sun Belt boomtown." It was "the nation's best example of the shape of the new recreation-oriented, low-density settlement pattern beginning to emerge across the nation," said Richard Louv. It was America's most "super-American city," added geographer Pierce Lewis.[21]

To try the same exercise in the early twenty-first century requires a lot of fingers for counting off a dozen or a score of exemplars. For the continuing resource frontier we might head north to Fairbanks and Edmonton.

Edmonton has been the operational base for continued development of northern Canadian tar sands, with current and planned pipelines converging on the city before fanning out again into southern Canada and the United States. Fairbanks enjoyed boom times in the 1970s with the construction of the Alaska Pipeline and the opening of North Slope oil fields. It remains the equipment and supply center. We might also head south to McAllen and Brownsville in the Lower Rio Grande Valley, where irrigated agriculture remains a driving force much like its role in southern California three generations earlier.

As a converse to resource development, Vancouver, Portland, and Seattle offer models for reducing the impact of urbanization on the natural landscape and promoting social interaction in the process. Behind appealing rhetoric about the Northwest Coast as "Salmon Nation" and the great, green land of Cascadia are real accomplishments in regional planning and city building. Portland takes the lead in green building and incorporating principles of environmental sustainability into city policy. It is great for bicycling, ecofriendly buildings, and environmentally conscious investing. Seattleites think their town is equally green. Their Convention and Visitors Bureau in 2006 pasted its new catchword *metronatural* on the Space Needle in eighteen-foot letters (to considerable local derision, admittedly). Vancouverites are proud that they are prospering without destroying the surrounding farms and forests and in 2007 unveiled an Ecodensity Charter to make Vancouver the leading model of an environmentally sustainable city.[22]

For another contrast, this time between two cities driving hell-bent into the age of services, turn to Las Vegas and Colorado Springs. The new Nevada metropolis is a triumph of the leisure economy, for its central economic product is experience. It is not only a place that produces recreational experiences (as do Los Angeles, San Francisco, and Tokyo) but also a venue for consuming those experiences: "The ability of quench desire brings people, the chance to dream of more brings them back." A great hotel-building boom that began with the Mirage in 1988 and added another thirteen megahotels by 2000—places like Paris and New York–New York—gave the city 125,000 hotel rooms and transformed gambling into theme park gaming. Leisure is a subset of the vast personal services industries, whose customers include conventioneers and vacationers but also retirees, who make up 20 percent of Las Vegas: "In the transformation to entertainment as the basis of culture, Las Vegas leads all others."[23]

Colorado Springs is a politically and culturally conservative anti-Vegas, developing an economy heavily based on services that require and promote self-discipline rather than indulgence. It remains an important military center, with the Air Force Academy, Peterson Air Force Base, Fort Carson, and the relatively new Schriever Air Force Base to deal with missile defense and satellite control. In the 1980s, the city became the headquarters for the U.S.

Olympic Committee, which converted another decommissioned air base into the Olympic Training Center, and attracted many national federations for individual Olympic sports. Electronics manufacturing and information technology businesses boomed in the 1990s but declined after 2000 (from roughly 21,000 to 8,000 workers), but the well-educated and well-behaved labor force attracted call centers for high-end insurance and financial companies. Most remarkable has been an influx of Evangelical Christian churches and organizations like New Life Church, Focus on the Family, and the International Bible Society. They have benefited from a combination of affordability, local political conservatism, and networking opportunities in what journalists have dubbed a "Vatican for evangelical Christianity."

Western cities also represent the future as environments for new multiethnic cultures. El Paso, Los Angeles, Honolulu, and Vancouver offer a variety of previews of the multiethnic, international future of the North American West. Atlantic cities from the 1840s to the 1940s struggled with adapting the narrow culture of North Sea Protestantism to the full range of European languages, religions, and national loyalties. They forged various forms of American and Canadian identity from the 1850s to the 1950s. Newer western cities now have to incorporate a wider range of races and cultures with roots in Europe, Africa, Mexico, Middle America, East Asia, and South Asia—as well as peoples here long before the second-millennium migrations.

In taking on this task, they are also continuing one of the hidden themes of the American frontier. The West has always been the region of contact between native North Americans, westward-moving European Americans and African Americans, northward-moving Latin Americans, and eastward-moving immigrants from the Pacific islands and Asia. In the 1850s or the 1890s, Anglos, Mexicans, Chinese, and others met everywhere across the landscape—in railroad construction crews, in mining camps, and in the agricultural valleys of California, Colorado, Washington, and British Columbia. A century later, they mix primarily in the West's growing cities. World War II added western U.S. cities as the destination of African Americans fleeing the impoverished South. The war and national policies pushed Native Americans into Phoenix, Los Angeles, Seattle, Denver, Winnipeg, and other cities. After 1965 renewed northward and eastward migrations across international borders also targeted western cities, making them testing grounds for the multicultural North America of the next century.

Hal Rothman has suggested that Las Vegas (again) is one of the first "postintegration" cities in the United States, where nearly all growth has come since *Brown v. Board of Education of Topeka* and political battles have not had to center on the unmaking of segregationist institutions. Latinos and Asian Americans, at least in aspirations to home ownership and in family patterns, are the closest match with the two-parents-with-children norm of the baby boom years. Immigration has brought new people and vitality

PORTLAND, OREGON, AND ITS SURROUNDINGS, 1889.
ISSUED BY THE OREGON IMMIGRATION BOARD.

FIGURE 65. The older West: Portland, Oregon, in 1889. Portland in 1889 was poised for economic takeoff and explosive growth. This view looks south along the Willamette River, showing the heart of the original city on the west bank, the first bridges, and bustling waterfront with steamers and railroads reminiscent of Omaha two decades earlier. (Oregon Historical Society, Neg. 23627.)

to politically landlocked cities like Denver. It has also brought new life to public spaces. Southern California may have an inordinate number of gated upscale communities, but Asian and Latino newcomers are also transform-ing the streets and neighborhoods of Los Angeles with murals and festivals, Pico-Union sidewalk vendors, bustling business activity in the old down-town department store district, and mass marches with hundreds of thou-sands of people demonstrating for immigration rights around City Hall and along Wilshire Boulevard.[24]

I will inch toward a conclusion by contrasting Jonathan Franzen's novel *The Twenty-seventh City* (1988) with Leslie Marmon Silko's *Almanac of the Dead* (1991).[25] The two stories are set in St. Louis and Tucson, respectively. Both are about political corruption, real estate, and racial division. One obvi-ous difference is the character of the deals: urban renewal and redevelop-ment projects in the older city and new desert subdivisions in the newer. Racial conflict in St. Louis is deep but straightforward: black against white. In Tucson the mix swirls complexly among whites, American Indians, Mexican Indians, Hispanic Americans, Mexicans, Californians, and East Coasters. Franzen throws in one off-the-wall element in the person of a new police chief who is a woman from Bombay and then proceeds with a conventional

FIGURE 66. The newer West: Winnipeg circa 1990. In this promotional brochure, Winnipeg reaches back to its heritage as a gateway to the Prairie Provinces, adapts a slogan from Fort Worth ("Where the West begins"), and stakes a claim on the new high-tech and information economy of the coming century. (Author's collection.)

narrative of personal and political intrigue. Silko accepts no such constraints, introducing and dropping characters as her needs change, flipping among half a dozen settings, and shifting tone from down and dirty realism to something akin to the semifantastic imagination of Latin American fiction. The modern West, she implies, is too complex and too unformed to sit still for a traditional novelistic portrait.

This implication is a reminder to caution. A group of cities that stretch over thousands of miles of continent and ocean and now house tens of millions of people is hard to encompass in simple generalizations. In the six years since I started working systematically on this book, western cities have been the sites of well over 500,000,000 person-years of individual experience (or 182 billion person-days), raising a caution about picking any few experiences as typical.[26] Nevertheless, I want to end on a sweeping note by emphasizing change. In the era of preindustrial cities, the towns created in western North America by imperial reach were controlled from Europe and patterned after Europe. In the long century of industrial urbanization, from the 1820s through the 1930s, western cities were important but secondary participants in a globally transforming process. Over the last two generations, however, they have begun to nurture social and economic change that has been spinning off in some of the directions I've just summarized and perhaps many more. It will be fun to watch.

INTRODUCTION

1. Many of the cyberpunk writers have lived in the North American West—Texas for Sterling, British Columbia for Gibson, Washington for Stephenson, Oregon for John Shirley, and California for Rudy Rucker.

2. William Gibson, in Edo Van Belkom, *Northern Dreamers: Interviews with Famous Science Fiction, Fantasy, and Horror Writers* (Kingston, Ontario: Quarry Press, 1998), 89.

3. William Gibson, *Virtual Light* (New York: Bantam Spectra, 1994), 25, 62–63.

4. William Gilpin, *The Mission of the North American People: Geographical, Social and Political* (Philadelphia: Lippincott, 1874), 69, 77, 89, 108, 119–20, 127.

5. Geographers will see that my concept of centrality draws on James Vance's idea of "mercantile cities" and A. F. Burghardt's idea of "gateway cities," both of which emphasize the role of cities as organizers of extensive and often long-distance trading hinterlands and the role of city leaders in creating the necessary physical and commercial connections. At the same time, it also draws on the ideas of central place theory, which argues that nested trading areas naturally coalesce around a hierarchy of towns and cities. Nineteenth-century city builders were happy to conflate the two forms of centrality in arguing the advantages of their cities, and most important urban centers functioned in both ways. See James Vance, *The Merchant's World: The Geography of Wholesaling* (Englewood Cliffs, NJ: Prentice-Hall, 1970); A. F. Burghardt, "A Hypothesis about Gateway Cities," *Annals of the Association of American Geographers* 61 (1971): 269–85; and William Cronon, *Nature's Metropolis: Chicago and the Great West* (New York: Norton, 1991).

6. Linda W. Slaughter, *The New Northwest: A Pamphlet Stating Briefly the Advantages of Bismarck and Vicinity, Soil, Timber, Climate Settlements, Business &c., &c.* (Bismarck: Burleigh County Pioneers' Association, 1874), 12.

7. Boise City Board of Trade, *Boise City and Southwestern Idaho: Resources, Progress, and Prospects* (Boise: Boise City Board of Trade, 1887–88).

8. Katherine Morrissey, *Mental Territories: Mapping the Inland Empire* (Ithaca, NY: Cornell University Press, 1997).

9. *General Directory of Fresno County, California, for 1881* (Fresno: The Fresno Republican, 1881), 70; *Memorial and Biographical History of the Counties of Fresno, Tulare, and Kern, California* (Chicago: Lewis Publishing Company, 1890?), 107;

Imperial Fresno: Resources, Industries and Scenery Illustrated and Described. A Souvenir of the Fresno Republican (Fresno: The Fresno Republican Publishing Co., 1897), 44; Fresno County Chamber of Commerce, *Fruitful Fresno: The Superlative County of California* (Fresno: Fresno County Chamber of Commerce, 1917).

10. Slaughter, *The New Northwest*, 21.

11. Roderick D. McKenzie, "The Concept of Dominance and World-Organization," *American Journal of Sociology* 33 (July 1927): 39.

12. Josiah Strong, *Our Country: Its Possible Future and Its Present Crisis* (New York: Baker and Taylor, 1891), 39.

13. H. H. Bancroft, *The New Pacific* (New York: Bancroft, 1899); Neil Morgan, *Westward Tilt: The American West Today* (New York: Random House, 1963); Earl Pomeroy, *The Pacific Slope* (New York: Knopf, 1965); Thomas Bender, *A Nation among Nations: America's Place in World History* (New York: Hill and Wang, 2006).

14. In the early twentieth century, the U.S. Census began to develop a new "metropolitan" category to describe large cities and their closely associated suburban communities. The Census Bureau has tinkered with the criteria over the decades, but the basic concept has remained the same: large cities and their commuter zones. They have been called Metropolitan Districts from 1910 to 1940, Standard Metropolitan Areas in 1950, Standard Metropolitan Statistical Areas from 1960 to 1980, and Metropolitan Statistical Areas or Consolidated Metropolitan Statistical Areas in 1990 and 2000. Canada in 1951 introduced the label "Census Metropolitan Area" for a comparable but more tightly drawn category defined as "the main labour market area of a continuous built up area having 100,000 or more population."

15. The Canadian West as a whole accounts for 30 percent of the national population.

16. The Ontario CMAs of Toronto, Windsor, and Oshawa were close behind.

17. For 2001–5, the organization Science Watch ranked U.S. universities based on the number of high-impact papers published in twenty-one fields of science and social science. Half of the top twelve were western institutions (Stanford, the University of California [UC]–Berkeley, UC–San Diego, UC–San Francisco, Cal Tech, and the University of Washington). See *Science* 314 (November 11, 2006): 901.

18. The United States shifted from 46 percent urban to 51 percent between 1910 and 1920. Canada shifted from 49 percent urban in 1921 to 54 percent in 1931. Scholarship that disagrees with this effort to trace commonalities among western Canadian and U.S. urban experiences includes Norbert McDonald, *Distant Neighbors: A Comparative History of Seattle and Vancouver* (Lincoln: University of Nebraska Press, 1987); and Michael Goldberg and John Mercer, *The Myth of the North American City* (Vancouver: University of British Columbia Press, 1986).

19. Wallace Stegner, *Wolf Willow: A History, a Story, and a Memory of the Last Plains Frontier* (New York: Viking Press, 1962), 82–83.

20. Marcus Lee Hansen, *The Mingling of the Canadian and American Peoples, vol. 1: Historical*, completed by John Bartlett Brebner (New Haven: Yale University Press, 1940).

21. These suggestions are an update of Walter Sage's *Canada from Sea to Sea* (Toronto: University of Toronto Press, 1940), in which a British Columbia history professor

argues the dominance of continental economic connections running north–south over Canadian national connections running east–west.

22. The theoretical framework for this book traces back to economic historian Norman Scott Brian Gras, a Canadian who studied at Harvard University with Frederick Merk (himself a disciple of Frederick Jackson Turner). In *An Introduction to Economic History* (New York: Harper and Brothers, 1922), Gras outlines a development history for North America that revolves around the transformation of the continent into a series of resource hinterlands organized around commercial cities. Canadian historian Harold Innis built this idea into the "staple theory" of Canadian history, which describes the repeated development of resource regions and their connection to world markets through metropolitan centers—Montreal and Toronto most obviously but also western cities such as Winnipeg and Vancouver. In the United States, both Gras's metropolitan argument and Turner's interest in sectional differentiation, especially in *The Rise of the New West: 1819–1829* (New York: Harper and Brothers, 1906), influenced Richard C. Wade's path-breaking argument in *The Urban Frontier* (Cambridge, MA: Harvard University Press, 1959) that cities led rather than followed the nineteenth-century frontier. This comprehensive metropolitan/regional model of North American growth has more recently animated the work of geographer Donald W. Meinig and historian William Cronon. Among the many relevant historiographic essays, see J. M. S. Careless, "Frontierism, Metropolitanism, and Canadian History," *Canadian Historical Review* 35 (1954): 1–21; Carl Abbott, "Frontiers and Sections: Cities and Regions in American Growth," *American Quarterly* 37 (1985): 395–410; and Elizabeth Jameson and Jeremy Mouat, "Telling Differences: The Forty-ninth Parallel and Historiographies of the West and Nation," *Pacific Historical Review* 75 (May 2006): 183–230.

23. Leslie Marmon Silko, *Almanac of the Dead* (New York: Simon and Schuster, 1991).

CHAPTER ONE

1. Some Spanish towns were denominated as *villas* (Santa Fe, San Antonio), and others, as *pueblos* (El Pueblo de la Reina de Los Angeles). The terms were not precise, but a villa was usually larger or expected to be larger. *Ciudad* was used for larger and more substantial cities.

2. Eleanor D. Adams, ed., *Bishop Tamaron's Visitation of New Mexico* (Albuquerque: Historical Society of New Mexico, 1954), 47, quoted in John Reps, *Cities of the American West* (Princeton: Princeton University Press, 1979), 47–48; Francisco Dominguez, *The Missions of New Mexico, 1776*, trans. Eleanor D. Adams and Fray Angelico Chavez (Albuquerque: University of New Mexico Press, 1956), 39–40; and F. A. Wislizenus, *Memoir of a Tour to Northern Mexico, Connected with Col. Doniphan's Expedition, in 1846 and 1847* (Washington, DC: Tippin and Streeter, 1848). See also Leroy Hafen, ed., *Ruxton of the Rockies* (Norman: University of Oklahoma Press, 1950), 180.

3. These criteria are derived in part from the efforts of archaeologists and historians of early civilizations to define cities as distinct from large agricultural villages.

4. Darrett Rutman, *Winthrop's Boston: Portrait of a Puritan Town* (Chapel Hill: University of North Carolina Press, 1965).

5. None of these British coastal cities could rival Mexico City as the metropolis of the eighteenth-century Americas. With a population that passed 100,000 in the later 1700s, the capital of New Spain outshone Boston and Philadelphia in wealth, culture, and political reach.

6. The political settlement of Mississippi Valley borders involved the transfer of Louisiana from France to Spain in 1763, the establishment of the western border of the new United States in 1783, the transfer of Louisiana from Spain to France and its acquisition by the United States in 1803, the establishment of a boundary between the American Louisiana Territory and New Spain (meaning Texas and New Mexico) in 1818, the independence of Texas in 1836, its annexation by the United States with conflicting border claims in 1845, and American conquest of New Mexico and California in 1845–48, with a final tidying up of boundaries with the Gadsden Purchase of what is now southern Arizona.

7. Sonoma was where Anglo-Americans proclaimed Bear Flag Republic in 1846. The present northwest borders were not completely settled until the twentieth century. Russia agreed with the United States (1825) and Britain (1826) about the southern reach of Alaska. Spain agreed with Britain in 1790 on the forty-second parallel (the future Oregon–California border) as the northern limit of its claims. The United States and Britain bickered over the intermediate territory until they divided it in 1845, when the first waves of Oregon Trail pioneers had started Oregon City as a rival to Fort Vancouver. The United States then acquired California and its backcountry in 1848, purchased Alaska in 1867, and finally won agreement on the Alaska–Canada boundary in 1903.

8. The Laws of the Indies were not compiled and published as a complete set until 1681. Historians of city planning, however, use the term for the 1573 edicts, which would be folded into the 1681 codification.

9. The English colonists were somewhat less systematic, but they too set aside central spaces in the middle of new towns. New Haven was laid out on a three-by-three grid, with eight residential blocks surrounding a central common. The ambitious Philadelphia plan drawn up for William Penn in 1682 combined central squares with gridiron designed for growth and was ambitious in scale, as Penn extended it from the Delaware to Schuylkill.

10. Marc Simmons, "Governor Cuervo and the Beginnings of Albuquerque: Another Look," *New Mexico Historical Review* 55 (1980): 188–207.

11. The same physical pattern held true to a lesser extent in the English colonies. Boston was essentially unplanned, but it grew compactly because it was located on what was effectively an island. The same was true of New York, which spread steadily north from the southern tip of its island. Philadelphia's comprehensive plan envisioned a city that would grow compactly westward from the Delaware River, but many of its residents preferred to straggle north and south along the riverfront. The settlement fabric was even more attenuated at St. Mary's, the first capital of Maryland. In 1678, complained Charles Calvert, Lord Baltimore, himself: "It can hardly be called a town, it being in length by the water about five miles, and in breadth upwards toward the land at least one mile—in all which space,

there are not above thirty houses, and those at considerable distance from each other, and the buildings (as in all other parts of the Province), very mean, and little, and generally after the manner of the meanest farm-houses in England" (quoted in John Reps, *Tidewater Towns: City Planning in Colonial Virginia and Maryland* [Williamsburg: Colonial Williamsburg Foundation, 1972], 56).

12. Mary Ryan, "A Durable Center: The Los Angeles Plaza, 1781–1930," *Urban History* 33 (December 2006): 463.

13. John Walton, *This Storied Land: Community and Memory in Monterey* (Berkeley: University of California Press, 2001), 80.

14. Josiah Strong, *Our Country: Its Possible Future and Its Present Crisis* (New York: Baker and Taylor, 1891), 198.

TRANSITIONS

1. William Thayer, *The Marvels of the New West* (Norwich, CT: Henry Bill Publishing Co., 1887), 401; Charles Dudley Warner, "Studies of the Great West: A Far and Fair Country," *Harper's New Monthly Magazine* 76 (March 1988): 557.

2. The ninety-fifth meridian, at varying distances, divides Galveston from Houston, Fort Smith from Tulsa, St. Joseph from Topeka, Duluth from Grand Forks, and Thunder Bay from Winnipeg.

3. The third chapter in Eric Hobsbawm's *The Age of Capital, 1848–1875* (New York: Scribner's, 1975) is titled "The World Unified."

4. Julian Ralph, *Our Great West: A Study of the Present Conditions and Future Possibilities of the New Commonwealths and Capitals of the United States* (New York: Harper and Bros., 1893), 305.

5. David Landes, *The Unbound Prometheus: Technical Change and Industrial Development in Western Europe from 1750 to the Present* (London: Cambridge University Press, 1969).

6. Edward Ullman, "Regional Development and the Geography of Concentration," *Papers and Proceedings of the Regional Science Association* 4 (1958): 179–98.

7. Robert Perkin, *The First Hundred Years* (Garden City, NY: Doubleday, 1954), 571; John Gunther, *Inside U.S.A.* (New York: Harper and Brothers, 1947), 224.

8. *Salt Lake Herald*, 1871, quoted in Thomas K. Hafen, "City of Saints, City of Sinners: The Development of Salt Lake City as a Tourist Attraction, 1869–1900," *Western Historical Quarterly* 28 (Autumn 1997): 369.

CHAPTER TWO

1. Douglas Durkin, *The Magpie* (Toronto: Hodden and Stoughton, 1923), excerpted in David Arnason and Mhari Mackintosh, *The Imagined City: A Literary History of Winnipeg* (Winnipeg: Turnstone Press, 2005), 80.

2. Ella Sykes, quoted in Jim Blanchard, *Winnipeg 1912* (Winnipeg: University of Manitoba Press, 2005), 40. Novelist Laura Goodman Salverson in *The Viking Heart* (Toronto: McClelland and Stewart, 1923) borrowed a trope often used for Chicago, having her character Borga Lindal marvel over the city of the early twentieth century in contrast to her memories of the early 1880s.

3. The Kansas City and Twin Cities stories are variations on a theme: different rivers, different bridges, different railroads, different entrepreneurs—and similar results. By the later 1870s and 1880s, for example, St. Paul and Minneapolis wholesalers were getting goods directly from New York, bypassing Chicago. They also had locally controlled rail lines and a huge flour trade that made Minneapolis the largest primary wheat market in the United States and the country's largest manufacturer of flour by 1885. Wrote James Bryce in 1887, "St. Paul and Minneapolis have striven for the last twenty years for the title of Capital of the Northwest" (*The American Commonwealth* [3rd ed., 1941], 635, http://oll.libertyfund.org/Home3/EBook.php?recordID=0004.02). Charles Dudley Warner in 1888 stretched a metaphor by calling them "the two posts of the gateway to an empire" ("Studies of the Great West: A Far and Fair Country," *Harper's New Monthly Magazine* 76 [March 1888]: 561).

4. Bryce, *The American Commonwealth*, 635.

5. John C. Hudson, *Plains Country Towns* (Minneapolis: University of Minnesota Press, 1985), 48.

6. John Hudson in *Plains Country Towns* has described "inland towns" that preceded railroad construction as gambles on future rail routes. When the site lost out, speculators might sometimes skid buildings across the Dakota prairie to a more favored town.

7. William Least Heat-Moon, *PrairyErth* (Boston: Houghton Mifflin, 1991).

8. It excludes Rocky Mountain cities, among which I count El Paso.

9. The table also shows the way that the growth of Omaha and Kansas City in the heart of the continent truncated the growth of potential rivals such as Sioux City, St. Joseph, Topeka, and Lincoln, all of which are within 100 miles of one of the big cities. Wichita at 200 miles distance was less affected by the metropolitan shadow.

10. Kansas City, Missouri's, mythicized achievement was to convince the Chicago, Burlington and Quincy (CBQ) Railroad to bridge the Missouri River at Kansas City in 1867, but local entrepreneurs had helped to make their case by starting their own railroads to St. Joseph and St. Louis that the CBQ could utilize. Once the bridge was in operation, Kansas City was the low-cost point toward which other railroads converged. At the time of the Federal Reserve decision, Omaha and Kansas City had equal access to Chicago, with three rail companies each, but Kansas City could ship west on the Missouri Pacific, Rock Island, and Santa Fe lines, whereas Omaha had only the Union Pacific. These transportation connections, plus the preferences of local banks, played into this and the other choices of the twelve winners.

11. The major Montreal and Toronto banks placed their western branches in Winnipeg, and the Union Bank moved from Quebec to Winnipeg early in the twentieth century.

12. *Nathan Nirenstein's National Occupancy Maps: Preferred Real Estate Locations—Downtown Retail Shopping Districts, vol. 10: Atlas for the Central States* (Springfield, MA, 1953). By way of comparison, Dayton, Ohio, very close in size to Omaha, had sixteen tall buildings with a total of 193 floors.

13. Timothy Mahoney, "'The Best People in Town': Midwestern Boosters in the Development of the Urban West, 1850–1900," paper presented at the Western History Association meeting, San Diego, October 6, 2001.

14. Howard D. Berrett, *Who's Who in Topeka* (Topeka: Adams Brothers, 1905).

15. *Who's Who in Omaha, 1928: Biographical Sketches of Men and Women of Achievement* (Omaha: Robert M. Baldwin Corp., 1928).

16. Rudyard Kipling, quoted in Leonard Eaton, *Gateway Cities and Other Essays* (Ames: Iowa State University Press, 1989), 60.

17. Carl Jonas, *Jefferson Selleck* (Boston: Little, Brown and Co., 1951), 41, 146. In Gateway City, Boss Flynn maintained stable order and kept corruption carefully hidden, with prostitution restricted to the district just north of Union Station and no pickpockets west of Tenth Street.

18. Ed Kleiman, *The Immortals* (Edmonton, Alberta: NeWest Press, 1980), excerpted in Arnason and Mackintosh, *The Imagined City*, 125.

19. Dallas with 14 percent foreign born in 1920 and Kansas City, Missouri, at 26 percent (27 percent if both Kansas Cities are combined) were less popular immigrant destinations.

CHAPTER THREE

1. "Secoma," of course, is an amalgam of Seattle and Tacoma, but the port as described in the stories is clearly the latter city.

2. William Kelly, *An Excursion to California* (London: Chapman and Hall, 1851), vol. 2, 255; B. E. Lloyd, *Lights and Shades in San Francisco* (San Francisco: A. L. Bancroft, 1876), 78–79.

3. Leland Stanford was based in San Francisco; Charles Crocker, Colis P. Huntington, and Mark Hopkins, in Sacramento.

4. George Henderson, *California and the Fictions of Capital* (Philadelphia: Temple University Press, 1998), 22–23.

5. Edith Sparks, *Capital Intentions: Female Proprietors in San Francisco, 1850–1920* (Chapel Hill: University of North Carolina Press, 2006), 22. Mrs. Hudson's store was listed in the 1888 city directory. Sparks finds that women's small and undercapitalized businesses found it hard to compete by the early twentieth century with comprehensive department stores and nationally marketed goods, with women shifting instead to the growing number of office work positions available to them.

6. Samuel Bowles, *Our New West* (Hartford: Hartford Publishing Co., 1869), 334. Geographer Grey Brechin has given this regional influence a negative twist in *Imperial San Francisco* (Berkeley: University of California Press, 1999), seeing it reaching imperiously into North America and across the Pacific with a domineering pyramid of mining, mechanization, metallurgy, military expansion, and money power.

7. Henry J. Warre and M. Vavasour, "To the Right Honorable the Secretary of State for the Colonies" (October 26, 1845), ed. Joseph Schafer, *Oregon Historical Quarterly* 10 (March 1909): 76.

8. Oregon City, the first territorial capital, held its own until around 1850, when it had 933 residents and was still the focal point for early roads.

9. *Bend of the River* (1952), a two-star western starring Jimmy Stewart, starts with the Portland waterfront and a Columbia River steamer before moving to dry land.

10. Portland also stayed far ahead of other cities in the Columbia River system such as Salem and Astoria in Oregon and Walla Walla in Washington. In terms that geographers use for analyzing urbanization in developing economies, it was a primate city that far outstripped hinterland cities in size and economic resources.

11. The term embraces the waters historically used by the Salish-speaking peoples of the Northwest. It is a reminder of the natural region and historic culture area that was divided by the national boundary settlement.

12. In 1901, Victoria had 21,000 people and Vancouver had 27,000. The figures in 1911 were 32,000 and 101,000.

13. Ezra Meeker, *Seventy Years of Progress in Washington* (Seattle, 1921), 328; Murray Morgan, *Puget's Sound: A Narrative of Early Tacoma and the Southern Sound* (Seattle: University of Washington Press, 1979), 301.

14. Jonathan Raban, *Hunting Mr. Heartbreak: A Discovery of America* (New York: Edward Burlingame Books, 1991), 245.

15. In 1900, Chinese accounted for 3 percent of California's population and 2.5 percent of Oregonians but only 0.7 percent of Washington residents.

16. Charles Higgins, *To California and Back* (San Francisco: Santa Fe Railroad, 1893), quoted in Raymond Rast, "The Cultural Politics of Tourism in San Francisco's Chinatown, 1882–1917," *Pacific Historical Review* 76 (February 2007): 44; Frank Norris, "The Third Circle" (1897), in *The Complete Edition of Frank Norris* (Garden City, NY: Doubleday, Doran and Co., 1928), vol. 4, 1.

17. Americans also applied the discourse of dirt and disease to immigrants from eastern and southern Europe and from Mexico. When bubonic plague appeared in Los Angeles in 1924, as William Deverell has detailed, authorities quarantined the Mexican American neighborhood south of downtown and destroyed hundreds of homes in the pursuit of sanitation. He notes that "The destruction of these homes and shacks was part of the overall plan" in which they were first declared to be nuisances so that no compensation would need to be paid (*Whitewashed Adobe: The Rise of Los Angeles and the Remaking of Its Mexican Past* [Berkeley: University of California Press, 2004], 188). Not to be outdone by larger cities, Reno's Board of Health had razed most of Chinatown in 1908 in a "crusade of cleanliness and morality," conveniently making land available for a growing downtown.

18. Look Tin Eli, "Our New Oriental City—Veritable Fairy Palaces Filled with the Choicest Treasures of the Orient," in *San Francisco: The Metropolis of the West* (San Francisco: Western Press Association, 1910), quoted in Rast, "The Cultural Politics of Tourism in San Francisco's Chinatown," 54.

19. The fearful rhetoric that constructed nonwhites as sexually dangerous was shared across the American South, where the focus was African Americans, and the West, where the focus was Asians and Mexicans. Twelve years after the Gentlemen's Agreement, the *Los Angeles Times* editorialized that "the Jap boys are taught by

their elders to look upon American girls with a view to future relations. . . . An American who would not die fighting rather than yield to that infamy does not deserve the name" (quoted in Roger Daniels, *The Politics of Prejudice: The Anti-Japanese Movement in California and the Struggle for Japanese Exclusion* [Berkeley: University of California Press, 1962], 47).

20. Jean Heffer, *United States and the Pacific: History of a Frontier* (Notre Dame, IN: University of Notre Dame Press, 2002), 184–89; Mike Davis, in *The Ecology of Fear* (New York: Henry Holt, 1998), inventories many examples of yellow peril literature.

21. Hubert Howe Bancroft, *The New Pacific*, rev. ed. (New York: Bancroft, 1913), 8–9, 13 (originally published 1900).

22. Wolf von Schierbrand, "The Coming Supremacy of the Pacific," *Pacific Monthly* 14 (October 1905): 211–26.

23. H. P. Wood, *Home-Land: Being a Brief Description of the Many Attractions of the City and County of San Diego, California*, "Louisiana Purchase Exposition Edition" (San Diego: Chamber of Commerce, 1905), 9; John S. Mills, *San Diego California: A Country Rich in Resources with Superior Attractions for the People Who Want the Best* (San Diego: Board of Supervisors and the Chamber of Commerce of San Diego County, California, 1915), 9 and back cover for map (Huntington Library rare book 3172); T. D. Beasley, *Map of the City of San Diego, California* (San Diego: E. M. Burdeck, 1915).

24. Quoted in *Creating Our Region: Steps to a More Livable Future* (Vancouver: Greater Vancouver Regional District, 1990).

25. *The Panama Canal at San Francisco* (San Francisco: Panama Canal Exhibition Company, 1915). This Panama Canal display anticipated the far more famous General Motors diorama at the 1939 New York World's Fair.

26. Edward Hungerford, *The Personality of American Cities* (New York: McBride, Nast and Co., 1913), 295.

27. *San Francisco: Her Foreign Trade* (San Francisco: Chamber of Commerce, 1920); San Francisco Chamber of Commerce, *Newsletter*, May 16, 1939; trade data from Dudley F. Pegrum, *The Basis of the Los Angeles Metropolitan Economy* (Los Angeles: Chamber of Commerce, n.d. [1945]).

CHAPTER FOUR

1. Joseph Smith, "Explanation of the Plat of the City of Zion, sent to the Brethren in Zion, the 25th of June, 1833," quoted in John Reps, *Cities of the American West* (Princeton: Princeton University Press, 1979), 290.

2. Robert Flanders, *Nauvoo: Kingdom in the Mississippi* (Urbana: University of Illinois Press, 1965), 298.

3. Thomas Alexander and James Allen, *Mormons and Gentiles: A History of Salt Lake City* (Boulder: Pruett, 1984).

4. *Reminiscences of General William H. Larimer and of His Son William H. H. Larimer* (Pittsburgh: Press of the New Era Printing Co., 1918), 168.

5. W. R. Vickers, *History of the City of Denver, Arapahoe County, and the State of Colorado* (Chicago: O. J. Baskin and Co., 1880), 221–23.

6. John Chivington, quoted in Donald Berthrong, *The Southern Cheyennes* (Norman: University of Oklahoma Press, 1963), 203.

7. John White, *Sketches from America* (London: Sampson Low, Son, and Marston, 1870), 276.

8. *Cheyenne Daily Leader*, quoted in Gilbert Stelter, "The City and Westward Expansion: A Western Case Study," *Western Historical Quarterly* 4 (1973): 192.

9. William Vickers, "History of Colorado," in *History of the Arkansas Valley, Colorado* (Chicago: O. L. Baskin, 1881), 34–37.

10. Eugene Moehring, "The Comstock Urban System," *Pacific Historical Review* 66 (August 1997): 359.

11. William Jackson Palmer to Queen Mellen, January 17, 1870, quoted in John S. Fisher, *A Builder of the West: The Life of General William Jackson Palmer* (Caldwell, ID: Caxton Printers, 1939), 177–79.

12. William Jackson Palmer to Robert A. Cameron, December 1871, quoted in George L. Anderson, "General William Jackson Palmer: Man of Vision," *Colorado College Studies* 4 (Spring 1960): 15.

13. Julian Ralph, *Our Great West: A Study of the Present Conditions and Future Possibilities of the New Commonwealths and Capitals of the United States* (New York: Harper and Bros., 1893), 315.

14. This and the following quotes from Spokane boosterism are found in Katherine Morrissey, *Mental Territories: Mapping the Inland Empire* (Ithaca, NY: Cornell University Press, 1997), 133, 137, 140–41.

15. D. W. Meinig, *The Shaping of America: A Geographical Perspective on 500 Years of History, vol. 3: Transcontinental America, 1850–1915* (New Haven: Yale University Press, 1998), 155; *El Paso Times*, August 28, 1910, quoted in Bradford Luckingham, *The Urban Southwest: A Profile History of Albuquerque–El Paso–Phoenix–Tucson* (El Paso: Texas Western Press, 1982), 35.

16. See the depiction of Juarez in Cormac McCarthy, *Cities of the Plain* (New York: Knopf, 1998).

17. Spokane was also constricted by Vancouver and Calgary, a fact not shown on maps that stopped at the national border.

18. This discussion needs to take note of Alberta and the possibility of a far northern empire. As Table 4.1 indicates, both Calgary and Edmonton are really twentieth-century cities. Because of the character of the Canadian rail system with its two crossings of the Continental Divide, neither could monopolize the trade of Alberta, the northern Rockies, and the farther Northwest. Calgary got its railroad first and took the early lead. Edmonton caught up in the 1910s as it became the center for a more extensive set of radiating lines. Calgary identified itself with a farming and ranching hinterland (Calgary Stampede). Edmonton benefited more from mid-century petroleum production and development of far northern resources (its sports teams are Oilers and Eskimos), but Calgary had more convenient connections to the United States during the new wave of energy exploration after 1974. The distinctions are small, but Edmonton is a bit more "Canadian" (it hosted the Commonwealth Games), whereas Calgary is a bit more "western" and "international" (it hosted a winter Olympics).

1. William E. Pabor, *Colorado as an Agricultural State* (New York: Orange Judd, 1883), 33; "The Chicago–Colorado Colony," 1871 pamphlet, quoted in *Experiments in Colorado Colonization, 1869–1862*, vol. 3, ed. James F. Willard and Colin Goodykoontz, 1926, University of Colorado Historical Collections, Boulder, 141.

2. William F. Smythe, *The Conquest of Arid America* (New York: Harper and Brothers, 1900), 238.

3. Caldwell is beautifully described by J. Anthony Lukas in *Big Trouble: A Murder in a Small Town Sets Off a Struggle for the Soul of America* (New York: Simon and Schuster, 1997).

4. Kathleen Underwood, *Town Building on the Colorado Frontier* (Albuquerque: University of New Mexico Press, 1987).

5. City profile in Fresno County Chamber of Commerce, *Fruitful Fresno: The Superlative County of California* (Fresno: Fresno County Chamber of Commerce, 1917), 7, 23.

6. Chester Rowell to W. M. Griffin, December 19, 1909, quoted in David Vaught, "Factories in the Field Revisited," *Pacific Historical Review* 66 (May 1997): 149.

7. *Imperial Fresno: Resources, Industries and Scenery Illustrated and Described. A Souvenir of the Fresno Republican* (Fresno: The Fresno Republican Publishing Co., 1897).

8. Douglas Sackman, *Orange Empires: California and the Fruits of Eden* (Berkeley: University of California Press, 2005), 34.

9. George Henderson, *California and the Fictions of Capital* (Philadelphia: Temple University Press, 1998).

10. *The Inside Track*, quoted in Matt Garcia, *A World of Its Own: Race, Labor, and Citrus in the Making of Greater Los Angeles, 1900–1970* (Chapel Hill: University of North Carolina Press, 2001), 23; Ronald Tobey, *Technology and Freedom: The New Deal and the Electrical Modernization of the American Home* (Berkeley: University of California Press, 1996), 63, 83.

11. U.S. Home Owners Loan Corporation report, quoted in Becky Nicolaides, "'Where the Working Man Is Welcomed': Working-Class Suburbs in Los Angeles, 1900–1940," *Pacific Historical Review* 68 (November 1999): 546.

12. Gilbert G. Gonzalez, *Labor and Community: Mexican Citrus Worker Villages in a Southern California County, 1900–1950* (Urbana: University of Illinois Press, 1994), 13; Nicolaides, 'Where the Working Man Is Welcomed'; Garcia, *A World of Its Own*, 24–25; Rayner Banham, *Los Angeles: The Architecture of the Four Ecologies* (New York: Harper and Row, 1971).

13. Fresno and Madura counties had 44,526 people in 1900, while Mesa, Delta, and Montrose counties had 19,693, a ratio of 2.3 to 1. In 1920, the figures were 140,982 and 47,798, for a ratio of 2.95 to 1. In 1950 they were 313,479 and 71,559, or 4.4 to 1.

14. The sixty-mile stretch from Boise through Caldwell and Nampa to Nyssa and Ontario, Oregon, is a reminder of what the Salt River Valley might look like if air-conditioning had not allowed massive growth in the southern desert.

1. *Virginia City Territorial Enterprise,* August 7, 1866, quoted in Kelly Dixon, *Boomtown Saloons: Archeology and History in Virginia City* (Reno: University of Nevada Press, 2005), 30. The description of Virginia City as a working-class community draws from Dixon's book and from Julie M. Schablitsky's "The Other Side of the Tracks: The Archeology and History of a Virginia City, Nevada Neighborhood" (Ph.D. dissertation, Portland State University, 2002). Also see Ronald M. James, *The Roar and the Silence: A History of Virginia City and the Comstock Lode* (Reno: University of Nevada Press, 1998).

2. Clemens did have contact with the Boston Saloon in its first location. Dan DeQuille, writing for the *Territorial Enterprise,* briefly noted that Clemens frequented a B Street "dead-fall," and others accused him of stealing a coat and boots and trading at the saloon for a bottle of "vile" whiskey.

3. Josiah Strong, *Our Country: Its Possible Future and Its Present Crisis* (New York: Baker and Taylor, 1891), 182.

4. Frank Fossett, *Colorado: Its Gold and Silver Mines, Farms and Stock Ranges, and Health and Pleasure Resorts* (New York: C. G. Crawford, 1879), 415.

5. Robert Athearn, *Westward the Briton* (New York: Scribner's, 1953), 52; William W. Howard, "The Modern Leadville," *Harper's Weekly,* December 1, 1888: 928; Ernest Ingersoll, *The Crest of the Continent* (Chicago: R. R. Donnelley and Sons, 1885), 224.

6. Julian Ralph, *Our Great West: A Study of the Present Conditions and Future Possibilities of the New Commonwealths and Capitals of the United States* (New York: Harper and Brothers, 1893), 205–7.

7. An analysis of 616 lodge members and officers shows a mix of salaried workers, capitalists, professionals, small business owners, and miners. Fraternal benefit societies and Masons tended to have more middle-class members, whereas lodges had more working-class members, but "the most notable pattern is cross-class association" (Elizabeth Jameson, *All That Glitters: Class, Conflict, and Community in Cripple Creek* [Urbana: University of Illinois Press, 1998], 106–8).

8. Sherman Bell, quoted in Ray Stannard Baker, "The Reign of Lawlessness: Anarchy and Despotism in Colorado," *McClure's Magazine* 23 (May 1904): 48.

9. Norman H. Clark, *Mill Town: A Social History of Everett, Washington from Its Earliest Beginnings on the Shores of Puget Sound to the Tragic and Infamous Event Known as the Everett Massacre* (Seattle: University of Washington Press, 1970), 78.

10. *San Diego Union,* April 15, 1912, quoted in Davey Jones, "A Fight for Free Speech in San Diego," *San Diego Indymedia,* January 21, 2005, http://www.iww.org/culture/articles/DJones1.shtml.

11. Quoted in Adam Hodges, "Enemy Aliens and Silk Stocking Girls: The Class Politics of Internment in the Drive for Urban Order during World War I," *Journal of the Gilded Age and Progressive Era* 6 (October 2007): 444, 446.

12. Allan Levine, *The Bolshevik's Revenge: A Sam Klein Mystery* (Winnipeg: Great Plains Publications, 2002), 15.

13. Police chief, quoted in Irene Ledesma, "Texas Newspapers and Chicana Workers' Activism, 1919–1974," *Western Historical Quarterly* 26 (Autumn 1995): 321. The San

Antonio strikers won an empty victory, because the pecan-shelling companies replaced workers with machinery to avoid paying the wage rates set by the Fair Labor Standards Act.

14. See Vicki Ruiz, "*Una Mujer sin Fronteras*: Luisa Moreno and Latina Labor Activism," *Pacific Historical Review* 73 (February 2004): 1–20.

CHAPTER SEVEN

1. Bessie Post was my wife's great-aunt. Her comments are taken from letters in our possession.

2. John White, *Sketches from America* (London: Sampson Low, Son, and Marston, 1870); John M. White, *The Newer Northwest: A Description of the Health Resorts and Mining Camps of the Black Hills of South Dakota and Big Horn Mountains in Wyoming* (St. Louis, MO: Self-Culture Pub. Co., 1894). The Newberry Library copy of the latter has "Elliott Coues Sept. 1895" inked on the title page.

3. Los Angeles Chamber of Commerce stenographic report, October 28, 1926, quoted in Greg Hise and William Deverell, *Eden by Design: The 1930 Olmsted-Bartholomew Plan for the Los Angeles Region* (Berkeley: University of California Press, 2000), 33.

4. Edward Hungerford, *The Personality of American Cities* (New York: McBride, Nast and Co., 1913), 296.

5. Chamber of Commerce of the City of San Diego, *Information Relative to the City of San Diego, California, illustrated with twenty-two photographic views, Containing, also, a Business Directory of the City* (San Diego: Office of the San Diego Union, 1874), 11, 18.

6. H. P. Wood, *Home-Land: Being a Brief Description of the Many Attractions of the City and County of San Diego, California*, "Louisiana Purchase Exposition Edition" (San Diego: Chamber of Commerce of San Diego, California, 1904), 5, 9, 15.

7. *The United States, with Excursions to Mexico, Cuba, Puerto Rico, and Alaska* (Leipzig: Karl Baedecker, 1909), 489; Lewis Iddings, "Life in the Altitudes: The Colorado Health Plateau," *Scribner's* 19 (1896): 143.

8. *The Natural Resources of Colorado with a Map of the Denver and Rio Grande System, Presented with the Compliments of the Passenger Department* (Denver: Denver and Rio Grande Railroad, 1892) offered a systematic comparison of Colorado and Switzerland, demonstrating that the former had loftier peaks, higher towns, a drier climate, superior mineral springs, and a longer cog railway.

9. Samuel Bowles, *The Switzerland of America* (Springfield, MA: S. Bowles, 1869), 19.

10. Even Seattle got into the act when boosters recast the damp shores and wine-dark waters of Puget Sound as the Mediterranean of America, drizzly climate as "the zone of filtered sunshine," and cool summers as protection against the racially enervating effects of the tropics. See Erwin L. Weber, *In the Land of Filtered Sunshine: Why the Pacific Northwest Is Destined to Dominate the Commercial World* (Seattle: Chamber of Commerce, 1924), quoted in Matthew Klingle, *Emerald City: An Environmental History of Seattle and an Evolving Sense of Place* (New Haven: Yale University Press, 2007), 164.

11. Dick Hall, "Ointment of Love: Oliver E. Comstock and Tucson's Tent City," *Journal of Arizona History* 19 (Summer 1978), quoted in Michael Logan, *Desert Cities: An Environmental History of Phoenix and Tucson* (Pittsburgh: University of Pittsburgh Press, 2006), 91.

12. Jerome Smiley, *History of Denver, with Outlines of the Earlier History of the Rocky Mountain Country* (Denver: Denver Times, 1901), 977.

13. Quoted in Thomas Noel and Barbara Norgren, *Denver: The City Beautiful and Its Architects, 1893–1941* (Denver: Historical Denver, 1987), 26. The famous Mulholland Drive along the crest of the Santa Monica Mountains/Hollywood Hills served some of the same functions but dates to the later decade of the 1920s and was intended as much for land development as for tourism.

14. This discussion is drawn from an examination of highway maps in the cartography collections at the Newberry Library, Chicago. Most of the state and gas company maps were drawn by a few companies such as Chicago-based Gousha and Rand-McNally.

15. The mountain received its English-language name from British explorer George Vancouver, honoring another British naval officer. From the 1870s into the 1920s, Tacoma argued for renaming the peak as the Indian-derived Tahoma or Tacoma. The Northern Pacific Railroad, which terminated in the city of Tacoma, used the alternative name in much of its publicity material, for obvious reasons. Seattle, of course, resisted stoutly and successfully.

16. Kevin Starr, *Material Dreams: Southern California through the 1920s* (New York: Oxford University Press, 1990), 278; "Santa Barbara's Opportunity" (undated but probably mid-1920s), quoted in Lee M. A. Simpson, *Selling the City: Gender, Class, and the California Growth Machine* (Stanford: Stanford University Press, 2004), 158.

17. Chris Wilson, *The Myth of Santa Fe: Creating a Modern Regional Tradition* (Albuquerque: University of New Mexico Press, 1997), 8, 331.

18. Catherine Cocks, *Doing the Town: The Rise of Urban Tourism in the United States, 1850–1915* (Berkeley: University of California Press, 2001), 182.

19. Elizabeth Gray Potter and Mabel Thayer Gray, *The Lure of San Francisco: A Romance amid Old Landmarks* (San Francisco: Paul Elder and Co., 1915); Tirey L. Ford, *Dawn and the Dons: The Romance of Monterey* (San Francisco: A. M. Robertson, 1926).

20. The number of domestic revenue passengers boarding flights in the United States more than doubled for the decades 1955–65 and 1965–75 and nearly did so for 1975–85, going over the thirty-year span from 39,025,000 to 357,109,000.

CHAPTER EIGHT

1. This discussion relies on Janet LeCompte's meticulous and sensitive edition of the diary, published as Emily French, *Emily: The Diary of a Hard-Worked Woman*, ed. Janet LeCompte (Lincoln: University of Nebraska Press, 1987).

2. Herbert Croly, "Portland, Oregon: The Transformation of the City from an Architectural and Social Viewpoint," *Architectural Record* 31 (June 1912): 591–607.

3. Keith Bryant's *Culture in the American Southwest: The Earth, the Sky, the People* (College Station: Texas A&M University Press, 1901) also cites examples in Phoenix,

El Paso, and Oklahoma City. Art deco and art moderne were international styles that gained popularity just as architects and tycoons were deciding what southwestern downtowns should look like.

4. Charles A. Tracy, "The Police Function in Portland, Oregon, 1851–1874: Part II," *Oregon Historical Quarterly* 80 (Summer 1979): 159.

5. This paragraph and the quoted phrases are drawn from Becky Nicolaides, "Where the Working Man Is Welcome: Working Class Suburbs in Los Angeles," *Pacific Historical Review* 68 (November 1999): 517–59.

6. Quoted in Robert Fairbanks, *For the City as a Whole: Planning, Politics, and the Public Interest in Dallas, Texas, 1900–1965* (Columbus: Ohio State University Press, 1998), 40.

7. Mark Wild, *Street Meeting: Multiethnic Neighborhoods in Early Twentieth-Century Los Angeles* (Berkeley: University of California Press, 2005), 2, 13.

8. John Steinbeck, *Tortilla Flat* (New York: Modern Library, 1937), 10–11.

9. "Bungalow Belts" included other styles as well, such as Mediterranean revival models in the Southwest and "English cottage" styles in the Northwest. They all shared a modern open floor plan for the main level and a low one-story or one-and-a-half-story profile.

10. Walter Van Tilburg Clark, *City of Trembling Leaves* (New York: Random House, 1945), 5.

11. James M. Cain, *Mildred Pierce* (1941), in *Cain X 3* (New York: Knopf, 1969), 105–6.

12. Lionel Frost, *The New Urban Frontier: Urbanization and City Building in Australasia and the American West* (Kensington, Australia: New South Wales University Press, 1991). Frost draws his north–south dividing line in North America much as this study does. In Australia he finds a difference between Sydney (the oldest city and one with geographic constraints) and Melbourne, Adelaide, and Perth.·

13. Patricia Evridge Hill, *Dallas: The Making of a Modern City* (Austin: University of Texas Press, 1996), 72.

14. The phrase "radical middle class" comes from Robert Johnston, *The Radical Middle Class: Populist Democracy and the Question of Capitalism in Progressive Era Portland, Oregon* (Princeton: Princeton University Press, 2003). The phrase "for the city as a whole" comes from Fairbanks, *For the City as a Whole*.

15. Hill, *Dallas*, xxvii.

16. *Montclair Mirror*, September 26, 1903, quoted in Thomas J. Noel, *The City and the Saloon: Denver, 1858–1916* (Lincoln: University of Nebraska Press, 1982), 74.

17. *Oakland Enquirer*, February 27, 1911, quoted in Lee M. A. Simpson, *Selling the City: Gender, Class and the California Growth Machine* (Stanford: Stanford University Press, 2004), 107–8, see also 115.

18. Burnham was the country's best-known urban planner for his role in coordinating the development of the World's Columbian Exposition in Chicago in 1893 and his leadership in helping Washington, D.C., recover some of the civic spaces anticipated in its original plan.

19. Michael Logan, *Desert Cities: An Environmental History of Phoenix and Tucson* (Pittsburgh: University of Pittsburgh Press, 2006), 97.

20. Carl Jonas, *Jefferson Selleck* (Boston: Little, Brown and Co., 1951), 129–30.

21. Phoenix transformed its Cowboy and Indian Carnival into a more sober territorial fair in 1905.

22. Walter Hines Page, "The Larger West Coast Cities," *World's Work*, August 1905: 6501.

CHAPTER NINE

1. Rudolfo Anaya, *Alburquerque* (Albuquerque: University of New Mexico Press, 1992), 59, 114–15.

2. See http://www.venetian.com/attractions/gondola.cfm. An inventory of water features along the Las Vegas Strip has included "Lake Como" at the Bellagio, a miniature harbor for New York–New York, a beach pool with wave action at Mandalay Bay, room for a sea battle at Treasure Island, and a trip down the Nile at the Luxor. See Marienka Sokol, "Reclaiming the City: Water and the Urban Landscape in Phoenix and Las Vegas," *Journal of the West* 44 (Summer 2005): 52–61.

3. Marc Norman, *Bike Riding in Los Angeles* (New York: E. P. Dutton, 1972), in David L. Ulm, *Writing Los Angeles: A Literary Anthology* (New York: Library of America, 2002), 568.

4. For those with wide musical tastes, Venice was instrumental in launching the national careers of both Lawrence Welk, whose first locally televised show originated from the Aragon Ballroom in 1951, and Jim Morrison and the Doors, who emerged from the hip Venice scene in the 1960s.

5. Michael Sorkin, ed., *Variations on the Theme Park: The New American City and the End of Public Space* (New York: Hill and Wang, 1992).

6. Thomas Pynchon, *The Crying of Lot 49* (New York: HarperCollins, 1999), 20.

7. Leslie Marmon Silko, *Almanac of the Dead* (New York: Simon and Schuster, 1991), 376.

8. Roosevelt extended "national forest" designation over areas to be traversed by the aqueduct, despite the absence of many trees, in order to prevent speculators from driving up the cost of the right-of-way.

9. With the completion of the Colorado River Pipeline from Parker Dam, the regional water supply included roughly 100 second-feet (cubic feet of water per second) from the Los Angeles River, 400 from the Owens Valley, 200 from the Mono Basin, and 1,500 from the Colorado River.

10. It is difficult to measure, but Los Angeles, with iron pipes and water meters, may have used the water more efficiently than ranchers with open ditches and flood irrigation.

11. David Torres-Rouff, "Water Use, Ethnic Conflict, and Infrastructure in Nineteenth-Century Los Angeles," *Pacific Historical Review* 75 (February 2006): 120–21.

12. Robert Righter, *The Battle over Hetch Hetchy: America's Most Controversial Dam and the Birth of Modern Environmentalism* (New York: Oxford University Press, 2005), 244.

13. Abel Wolman, "The Metabolism of Cities," *Scientific American*, March 1965: 179–90.

14. Jessica Teisch, "Great Western Power, 'White Coal,' and Industrial Capitalism in the West," *Pacific Historical Review* 70 (May 2001): 240.

15. Also built in the 1930s were Fort Peck Dam on the Missouri River and Shasta Dam in northern California.

16. Edward Abbey, *The Monkey Wrench Gang* (New York: HarperPerennial, 2006), 173.

17. Righter, *The Battle over Hetch Hetchy*, 235.

TRANSITIONS TWO

1. Ivor Winters, *Selected Poems* (Athens: Swallow Press/Ohio University Press, 1999), 44–45.

2. Raymond Chandler, *The Little Sister* (London: Hamish Hamilton, 1949), 1.

3. Winters, *Selected Poems*, 46. The reference is likely to the Arroyo Seco Parkway from downtown Los Angeles to Pasadena, the first link in California's freeway system, but might apply as well to the Hollywood Freeway or San Diego Freeway, which climb from the Los Angeles Basin up and over into the San Fernando Valley.

4. William Thayer, *Marvels of the New West* (Norwich, CT: Henry Bill Co., 1887); Julian Ralph, *Our Great West* (New York: Harper Brothers, 1893); Edward Hungerford, *The Personality of American Cities* (New York: McBride, Nast and Co., 1913).

5. James Bryce, *The American Commonwealth* (New York: Macmillan and Co., 1888); Rudyard Kipling, *From Sea to Sea: Letters of Travels* (New York: Scribner's, 1899).

6. As a reminder, California came first; then Oregon, Nevada, Kansas, and Nebraska; and then six states in a burst of activity in 1889–90—Washington, Idaho, Montana, Wyoming, North Dakota, and South Dakota. Utah followed in 1896. The twentieth century brought Oklahoma in 1907, New Mexico and Arizona in 1912, and Alaska and Hawaii in 1959. Admission of Oklahoma, New Mexico, Arizona, and Hawaii was delayed by concerns that large nonwhite populations created barriers to assimilation and threatened the nation's delicate racial balance.

7. The U.S. numbers are taken from Census 2000 PHC-T-3, Table 3: Metropolitan Areas Ranked by Population 2000, released April 2, 2001. Since that time, the Census has redefined metropolitan area criteria. The 2000 data understate the increase in the number of metropolitan centers because a number of places that were counted separately in 1940, such as San Bernardino and San Jose, were included in Consolidated Metropolitan Statistical Areas in 2000.

8. Adam Rome in *The Bulldozer in the Countryside: Suburban Sprawl and the Rise of American Environmentalism* (New York: Cambridge University Press, 2001) has an excellent treatment of the changing visual imagery of suburbia.

9. Peter Blake, *God's Own Junkyard* (New York: Holt, Rinehart and Winston, 1964); Nathaniel Owings, *The American Aesthetic* (New York: Harper and Row, 1969).

10. William H. Whyte Jr., "Urban Sprawl," in *The Exploding Metropolis*, by the editors of *Fortune* (Garden City, NY: Doubleday and Co.), 133, 138.

1. For example, see the entry to Los Alamos as described in Bernice Brode, "Tales of Los Alamos," in *Reminiscences of Los Alamos, 1943–45*, by Lawrence Badash, Joseph Hirschfelter, and Herbert Broida (Boston: Kluwer, 1980), 134–35.

2. Laura Fermi, "The Fermis' Path to Los Alamos," in *Reminiscences of Los Alamos, 1943–45*, by Lawrence Badash, Joseph Hirschfelter, and Herbert Broida (Boston: Kluwer, 1980), 102; Phyllis Fisher, *Los Alamos Experience* (New York: Japan Publications, 1985), 59; Lenore Fine and Jesse A. Remington, *The Corps of Engineers: Construction in the United States* (Washington, DC: U.S. Army, Office of Military History, 1972), 695. Marie Kinzel describes Los Alamos residents of 1943 as "pioneers on a new frontier" ("The Town of Beginning Again," *Survey Graphic* 35 [October 1946]: 354).

3. Catherine Bauer, "War-Time Housing in Defense Areas," *Architect and Engineer* 151 (October 1942): 33.

4. David Farber and Beth Bailey, "Fighting Man as Tourist: The Politics of Tourist Culture in Hawaii during World War II," *Pacific Historical Review* 65 (November 1996): 647.

5. Amy Kesselman, *Fleeting Opportunities: Women Shipyard Workers in Portland and Vancouver during World War II* (Albany: State University of New York Press, 1990), 29.

6. Roger Lotchin, "The City and the Sword," in *Essays on Sunbelt Cities and Recent Urban America*, ed. Robert Fairbanks and Kathleen Underwood (College Station: Texas A&M University Press, 1990), 95.

7. Margaret Pugh O'Mara, *Cities of Knowledge: Cold War Science and the Search for the Next Silicon Valley* (Princeton: Princeton University Press, 2005).

8. Douglas Coupland, *Microserfs* (New York: HarperCollins, 1995), 219, 320.

9. "New Economy Cities" is a category developed by the Progressive Policy Institute, issued in 2001.

10. J. Frank Dobie, writing for *Holiday* magazine in 1948, quoted in Don Graham, ed., *Literary Austin* (Fort Worth: Texas Christian University Press, 2007), xiii.

11. San Francisco, at 45 percent, and Seattle, at 46 percent, were the only cities with higher proportions of college grads.

12. The Austin cityscape thus displays social distinctions similar to the contrast between Silicon Valley and San Francisco: In the one are technical specialists who design and create fantastically minute and complex physical systems that can support huge volumes of data processing; in the other are media manipulators who create oh-so-cool applications to run on the systems. Douglas Coupland in *Microserfs* tries to sum up the difference: "Karla says the relationship had to be somewhat serious because 'you *know* how hard it is to lure anybody down here from San Francisco.' She's right. You could offer San Franciscans a free Infiniti J30 and they'd *still* have some excuse not to drive 25 measly miles down to Silicon Valley. Actually, there's a slight back-and-forth snobbery between the Valley and the City. The Valley thinks the City is snobby and decadent, and the City thinks the Valley is techishly boring and uncreative" (*Microserfs*, 298).

13. Linda Scarbrough, *Road, River, and Ol' Boy Politics: A Texas County's Path from Farm to Supersuburb* (Austin: Texas State Historical Association, 2005), 334.

1. For baseball fans, Cincinnati beat Los Angeles 6–3, benefiting from a powerhouse outfield of Frank Robinson, Vada Pinson, and Wally Post, who combined for eight hits.

2. The redeveloped culture district included a symphony hall named for Dorothy Chandler and a theater named for real estate tycoon Mark Tapper.

3. Philip Trounstine and Terry Christensen, *Movers and Shakers: The Study of Community Power* (New York: St. Martin's Press, 1982), 87.

4. Trounstine and Christenson, *Movers and Shakers*, 89.

5. Charles A. Graham and Robert Perkin, "Denver: Reluctant Capital," in *Rocky Mountain Cities*, ed. Ray B. West (New York: Norton, 1949), 281.

6. Robert Lineberry, *Equality and Urban Policy: The Distribution of Municipal Services* (Beverly Hills: Sage, 1977), 55–56. Slating committees like the Good Government League also operated in Dallas, where the Citizens Charter Association (CCA) ran slates of council candidates until 1975, and Abilene, where the Citizens Charter Committee and Citizens for Better Government (CBG) ran slates from 1963 to 1982. The CCA won 86 percent of the seats it contested; the CBG, 92 percent; and the GGL, 96 percent. Their picks were overwhelmingly white business- and professional men with above-average incomes.

7. Texas law allows cities great freedom in annexing land within five miles of their boundaries. It also allows strip annexation, a technique that Houston used in 1977 to annex the Gulf Freeway corridor and the Clear Lake area twenty-two miles from downtown, gaining the Johnson Space Center and the right to be "Space City, U.S.A."

8. Edmonton's civic elite co-opted immigrant communities with token representation and attention. In Winnipeg, Mayor Stephen Juba (1954–77) won support from the heavily ethnic North Side by sounding like a populist even while acting like a neoprogressive.

9. Louise Erdrich, *Love Medicine: A Novel* (New York: Holt, Rinehart and Winston, 1984), 132.

10. Gordon Sinclair, *Cowboys and Indians: The Shooting of J. J. Harper* (Toronto: McClelland and Stewart, 1999), quoted in David Arnason and Mhari Mackintosh, *The Imagined City: A Literary History of Winnipeg* (Winnipeg: Turnstone Press, 2005), 168.

11. Scott Ellsworth, *Death in a Promised Land: The Tulsa Race Riot of 1921* (Baton Rouge: Louisiana State University Press, 1982).

12. W. E. B. Du Bois, *The Crisis* (July 1913), quoted in Josh Sides, *L.A. City Limits: African American Los Angeles from the Great Depression to the Present* (Berkeley: University of California Press, 2003), 11.

13. Douglas Flamming, *Bound for Freedom: Black Los Angeles in Jim Crow America* (Berkeley: University of California Press, 2005), 193.

14. Roybal was one of the first Mexican Americans to win a council seat in a southwestern city without the backing of the Anglo civic leadership; he entered Congress in 1963. The characterizations of Boyle Heights are in George Sanchez, "'What's

Good for Boyle Heights Is Good for the Jews': Creating Multiracialism in the Eastside during the 1950s," *American Quarterly* 56 (September 2004): 633, 637.

15. *Westminster School District of Orange County v. Gonzalo Mendez* was a class action suit brought in 1945 against the El Modena, Garden Grove, Santa Ana, and Westminster school systems. The suit successfully challenged a system of separate but equal schools for Anglos and Latinos. Mexican Americans in the 1940s posed a particular challenge for California courts because they did not fit neatly into the binary racial division of white and black.

16. Aircraft companies in World War II opened their factories to women and Mexican Americans in preference to blacks.

17. Jack Kerouac, *On the Road* (New York: Viking, 1957), in David R. Ulin, *Writing Los Angeles: A Literary Anthology* (New York: Library of America, 2002), 395.

18. Walter Moseley, *Little Scarlet* (Boston: Little, Brown, 2004), 51.

19. Native Americans mounted similar urban protests a few years later. Activists founded the American Indian Movement in Minneapolis in 1968 to fight police mistreatment. In 1969, a group of young activists took over Alcatraz Island and held it for two years in hope of creating a cultural and educational center. In March 1970, a hundred or so Indians occupied Fort Lawton in Seattle as the United Indians of All Tribes, hoping for a cultural center, university, and other unlikely outcomes. There was also organizing of pan-Indian culture and social service institutions in Los Angeles and Portland, Oregon.

CHAPTER TWELVE

1. "Interim Report on Journal, Building Site Use and Waterfront Development," *Portland City Club Bulletin* 50 (August 8, 1969): 33.

2. These generalizations are based on interviews with Beatriz Gallegos and Maury Maverick Jr.

3. Jane Jacobs, *The Death and Life of Great American Cities* (New York: Random House, 1961); Rachel Carson, *Silent Spring* (Boston: Houghton Mifflin, 1962); Michael Harrington, *The Other America: Poverty in America* (New York: Macmillan, 1962).

4. *Denver Post*, September 25, 1972.

5. Daniel Pope, "'We Can Wait. We Should Wait.' Eugene's Nuclear Power Controversy, 1968–1970," *Pacific Historical Review* 59 (August 1990): 357.

6. Some of the same impulses were at work in the 1960s and 1970s in the "Republic of Boulder" and would also come to light in small western cities like Missoula.

7. He would serve until he became secretary of transportation in the Carter administration in 1979, and he later served as governor of Oregon from 1987 through 1990.

8. Fort Worth district planning organizations also gave neighborhoods a regular role in land-use and development decisions.

9. Lloyd Axworthy, "The Politics of Urban Populism: A Decade of Reform," in *Urban and Regional Planning in a Federal State*, ed. William T. Perks and Ira M. Robinson (Stroudsburg, PA: Dowden, Hutchinson and Ross, 1979), 284.

10. David Ley, Daniel Hiebert, and Geraldine Pratt, "Time to Grow Up? From Urban Village to World City, 1966–91," in *Vancouver and Its Region*, by Graeme Wynn and Timothy Oke (Vancouver: University of British Columbia Press, 1992), 261.

11. Readers in the United States may need to be reminded that the federal and provincial governments in Canada often play a more active and interventionist role in municipal affairs that do the federal and state governments in the United States. In Vancouver, for example, the transformation of Granville Island on False Creek into a very successful restaurant, shopping, and market area was a federal project. Canada Place, the huge convention center that sits on the shore of Burrard Inlet like a beached cruise ship, was built by a federal crown corporation in time for Expo '86.

12. Janet Flammang, "Filling the Party Vacuum: Women at the Grassroots Level in Local Politics," in *Political Women*, ed. Janet Flammang (Beverly Hills: Sage Publications, 1984), 87–113.

13. The U.S. Commission on Civil Rights reported that Hispanics made up 6.3 percent of elected officials in Texas compared to 21 percent of the population. The figures were 5.5 percent compared to 11.7 percent in Colorado, 13.2 percent compared to 16.2 percent in Arizona, and 6.6 percent compared to 19.2 percent in California. The election of Mexican American Raymond Telles as mayor of El Paso for two terms (1957–61) was an exception to the pattern.

14. Section 5 applied to states and other political jurisdictions that used a literacy test for voter registration on November 1 in 1964, 1968, or 1972 and whose voter registration or turnout for any of the 1964, 1968, or 1972 presidential elections was less than 50 percent of the voting-age population. Originally aimed at the Deep South, the law was amended in 1974 to add Texas and other southwestern states. In the 1980s the measure applied to nine states and parts of thirteen others.

15. Frances FitzGerald, "The Castro," *New Yorker* 62 (July 28, 1986): 48; Neal Pierce, "San Francisco Face-Lift More Than Skin Deep," *Portland Oregonian*, June 17, 1984.

16. Ley, Hiebert, and Pratt, "Time to Grow Up?," 265.

17. Marc Simmons, *Albuquerque: A Narrative History* (Albuquerque: University of New Mexico Press, 1982), 378.

18. There were similarities in Dallas, where Annette Strauss in 1987 was described as her city's "first true coalition mayor of the modern age," elected with minority and liberal support. Her own opinion was that "a businessman had almost always done a wonderful job of leading this city, and I want to continue that." A product of affluent North Dallas and sister-in-law of Democratic Party power broker Robert Strauss, she might best be described as a Dallas millionaire with a sense of social obligation. See Dann Hulbert, "Shaking Things Up in Dallas," *Washington Post*, May 4, 1987.

19. Suzanne Weiss, "Denver Nuggets," *Planning* 56 (April 1990): 8; "Distinguished Leadership: Federico Pena," *Planning* 57 (March 1991): 16.

20. The following paragraphs use data from the 1980 and 2000 censuses, as analyzed at the census tract level by the Lewis Mumford Center, University at Albany, and available at http://mumford.albany.edu/census/. Segregation is measured by the

dissimilarity index, which captures the degree to which two groups are evenly or unevenly spread through a metro area as a whole. The higher the index, the higher the proportion of either group that would have to move to a different tract for the groups to become evenly distributed. The isolation index measures the racial/ethnic composition of the tract where the average member of a given group lives. An isolation score of 70 for Hispanics, for example, indicates that the average Hispanic lives in a neighborhood that is 70 percent Hispanic.

21. Peter Dreier, "Villaraigosa's Challenge: Governing Los Angeles in the Bush and Schwarzenegger Era," May 28, 2005, http://www.CommonDreams.org.

CHAPTER THIRTEEN

1. Robert Michael Pyle, *The Thunder Tree: Lessons from an Urban Wildland* (Boston: Houghton Mifflin, 1993), 3.

2. During the drought of the early 1950s, the Water Board drew a "blue line" on a regional map and refused to supply water to new development outside the line. The restriction was in effect from 1951 to 1960.

3. Pyle, *The Thunder Tree*, 98.

4. Pyle, *The Thunder Tree*, 127, 113.

5. Robert Adams, *White Churches of the Plains* (Boulder: Colorado Associated University Press, 1970); Robert Adams, *The New West: Landscapes along the Colorado Front Range* (Boulder: Colorado Associated University Press, 1974); Laurie Brown, Martha Ronk, and Charles E. Little, *Recent Terrains: Terraforming the American West* (Baltimore: Johns Hopkins University Press, 2000); Ann Wolfe, *Suburban Escape: The Art of California Sprawl* (Santa Fe: Center for American Places, 2006).

6. There are many ways to sort out fast-growing metropolitan areas. In the 1990s, for example, the West accounted for fourteen of the twenty-five fastest growing, and these included eight of the fastest ten: Las Vegas, Yuma, McAllen, Austin, Boise, Phoenix, Laredo, and Provo. Looking only at large metropolitan areas over 500,000, we find sixteen of the twenty-six that grew by 20 percent or more in the West (Las Vegas, McAllen, Austin, Phoenix, Denver, Colorado Springs, Dallas, Tucson, Portland, Houston, Salt Lake City, Fresno, Bakersfield, Albuquerque, Sacramento, and San Antonio).

7. James Q. Wilson, "Los Angeles Is—and Is Not—Different," in *Los Angeles: Viability and Prospects for Municipal Leadership*, ed. Werner Hirsch (New York: Praeger, 1971), 119–32.

8. Charles Bukowski, "Waiting," in *The Last Night of the Earth: Poems* (Santa Barbara: Black Sparrow Press, 1992), in David R. Ulin, *Writing Los Angeles: A Literary Anthology* (New York: Library of American, 2002), 510.

9. Rayner Banham, *Los Angeles: The Architecture of Four Ecologies* (New York: Harper and Row, 1971); Tom Wolfe, "The Kandy-Kolored Tangerine-Flake Streamline Baby," in *The Kandy-Kolored Tangerine-Flake Streamline Baby*, by Tom Wolfe (New York: Farrar, Straus and Giroux, 1965); Joan Didion, *Play It as It Lays* (New York: Farrar, Straus and Giroux, 1970).

10. Donald Waldie, quoted in Joan Didion, "Trouble in Lakewood," *New Yorker*, July 26, 1993: 47.

11. Alida Brill, "Lakewood, California: 'Tomorrowland' at Forty," in *Rethinking Los Angeles*, ed. Michael Dear, E. Eric Schockman, and Greg Hise (Thousand Oaks, CA: Sage, 1996), 107.

12. These are data from the 2000 census. New York, of course, is far ahead of any other city in transit use. The cities with the highest tendency for workers to commute alone by automobile were in a mid-American corridor running through Michigan, Ohio, Kentucky, Tennessee, and Alabama.

13. There is much overlap between supersuburbs and what Robert Lang calls "boomburbs," which he defines as municipalities that had at least 100,000 residents in 2000, were not the largest city in their metropolitan area, and have grown rapidly at double-digit rates in every decade since the 1950s. His definition produces fifty-three boomburbs: twenty-five in California, seven each around Phoenix and Dallas, three around Denver, two adjacent to Las Vegas, and one each for Salt Lake City, Seattle, and Portland. Only six of the fifty-three are outside the West, which he attributes to large-scale planned development and large-scale water provision in arid regions. The list includes the well-known examples like Bellevue (Washington) and Irving and less prominent places like West Valley City (Utah) and North Las Vegas. Robert Lang and Jennifer LeFurgy, *Boomburbs: The Rise of America's Accidental Cities* (Washington, DC: Brookings Institution, 2007).

14. The John Wayne Airport area that straddles Costa Mesa, Newport Beach, and Irvine includes the South Coast Plaza with over two million square feet of retail space and 25 million square feet of office space.

15. Bradford Luckingham, *Phoenix: The History of a Southwestern Metropolis* (Tucson: University of Arizona Press, 1989), 267.

16. Anne Vernez Moudon and Paul Mitchell Hess, "Suburban Clusters: The Nucleation of Multifamily Housing in Suburban Areas of the Central Puget Sound," *Journal of the American Planning Association* 66 (Summer 2000): 243–64. Bellevue, Washington, lies across from Seattle on the east side of Lake Washington. Only two bridges link the fast-growing suburbs east of Lake Washington to Seattle, giving Bellevue an enormous advantage in accessibility. Beginning in the late 1970s, Bellevue faced a proposed freeway shopping mall and a volley of scattershot office parks. City officials responded by zoning for a high-rise core where new office towers had to pass design review and must build to the sidewalk rather than cower behind parking lots. Now flush with Microsoft millionaires and tens of thousands of information technology jobs in high-tech industrial parks, Bellevue is a substantial city in its own right.

17. Lisa McGirr, *Suburban Warriors: The Origins of the New American Right* (Princeton: Princeton University Press, 2001).

18. The outliers as low-density regions are Oklahoma City and Denver.

19. *New York Times*, March 14, 1978; Brendan Gill, "Reflections: Los Angeles Architecture," *New Yorker* 56 (September 15, 1980): 109; Alison Lurie, *The Nowhere City* (New York: Coward-McCann, 1965), 25.

20. Tom Wolfe, *A Man in Full* (New York: Farrar, Straus and Giroux, 1998), 63.

21. The northern plains are Montana, Wyoming, and the Dakotas. The central mountains are Utah, Colorado, Nevada, Arizona, and New Mexico. The Northwest is Oregon, Washington, and Idaho.

22. The Randstadt cities are Amsterdam, Haarlem, Leiden, The Hague, Rotterdam, Dordrecht, and Utrecht, which ring the "green heart" of reclaimed farmland.

23. Christopher Leo, quoted in Jeffrey Cohen, "MetroVisions: In Winnipeg, 'Unicity' Comprises City and 11 Suburban Communities," *Pittsburgh Post-Gazette*, September 19, 2004, http://www.post-gazette.com/pg/04263/381606.stm.

24. *Creating Our Future: Steps to a More Livable Region* (Vancouver: Greater Vancouver Regional District, 1990).

25. See http://www.sos.state.or.us/archives/governors/McCall/legis1973.html.

26. Urban Growth Boundaries are required to include a twenty-year supply of developable land and are periodically expanded as a city grows. If effect, the growth boundary is like a skin that grows with the city but keeps it contained.

27. Hal Rothman, "How Do We Get to Bedford Falls," *Las Vegas Sun*, October 16, 2005; Hal Rothman, personal communication, July 13, 2006.

28. The problem with Calgary and Edmonton is that both cities are growing northward rather than growing toward each other, according to maps of 1996–2001 population change from Statistics Canada.

CHAPTER FOURTEEN

1. John Hamer and Bruce Chapman, *International Seattle: Creating a Globally Competitive Economy* (Seattle: Discovery Institute, 1993).

2. U.S. Department of Commerce, Office of Area Development, *Future Development of the San Francisco Bay Area, 1960–2020* (San Francisco: U.S. Department of Commerce, Office of Area Development, 1959), 34.

3. Statistics Canada uses the category "Visible Minorities," defined as persons "who are identified under the Employment Equity Act as being non-Caucasian in race or non-white in colour" but excluding First Nations peoples.

4. Robert Stone, *Dog Soldiers* (Boston: Houghton Mifflin, 1974).

5. John Keeble, *Yellowfish* (New York: Harper and Row, 1980).

6. Won Moo Hurh and Kwang Chung Kim, *Korean Immigrants in America* (Rutherford, NJ: Farleigh Dickinson University Press, 1984), 63.

7. Timothy Fong, *The First Suburban Chinatown: The Remaking of Monterey Park, California* (Philadelphia: Temple University Press, 1994), 72.

8. W. H. Timmons, *El Paso: A Borderlands History* (El Paso: Texas Western Press, 1990), 307.

9. Data are from U.S. Census estimates for 2005 and the Mexican 2005 Census, the latter reported at http://www.inegi.gob.mx.

10. On the Mexican side, the effects have been most pronounced in the growth of Tijuana, Mexicali, and Juarez.

11. Mexican and Central American immigrants accounted for one-third of the 12,000 arrests. Rodney King was a black motorist who was beaten by police officers while being arrested, which was captured on videotape. The four officers stood trial and

were found not guilty, stirring deep anger that escalated into four days of rioting that resulted in fifty-eight deaths.

12. The insight about the demonstration comes from Christopher Hawthorne, "The City Rediscovers the Street," *Los Angeles Times*, December 31, 2006. The Bonaventure Hotel is the prime exhibit in Frederic Jameson's influential essay "Post-modernism, of the Cultural Logic of Late Capitalism," *New Left Review* 146 (July–August 1984): 53–93.

13. Kristin Hill Maher, "Borders and Social Distinction in the Global Suburb," *American Quarterly*, September 2004: 781–806. The rationalizations in Irvine reproduce some of the cultural patterns of the American South, where many cities in the early twentieth century had black neighborhoods interspersed with affluent white neighborhoods. The black residents provided convenient sources of domestic workers, while the caste system substituted social distance for physical separation.

14. Another indicator of long-term change is the proportion of people aged five and older who speak a language other than English: Forty-two of the fifty metro areas with the highest percentages in 2000 were in the West. The list starts with Laredo at 92 percent and runs through Phoenix at 24 percent. In addition to Texas and California cities, the top fifty also included perhaps less expected places such as Honolulu, Yakima, and Flagstaff.

15. AnnaLee Saxenian, "Brain Drain or Brain Circulation: The Silicon Valley–Asia Connection," at http://www.ischool.berkeley.edu/research/publications/2000/136/6.

16. One measure of international connection is the value of overseas sales of manufactured goods per manufacturing worker (as compiled in the New Economy Index). Five western electronics cities ranked close to the top among U.S. metro areas at the end of the 1990s: San Francisco/San Jose was fourth with $80,000 per worker, San Diego was sixth with $62,000, Portland was eleventh with $48,000, Austin was twelfth with $47,000, and Phoenix was thirteenth with $46,000.

17. W. Eugene Hollon, *The Great American Desert* (New York: Oxford University Press, 1966).

18. Four more were in Florida. Data from the U.S. Department of Commerce, International Trade Administration, *Statistical Abstract of the United States 2002* (Washington, DC: U.S. Department of Commerce, 2002), Table 1241.

19. Edward Soja, Rebecca Morales, and Goetz Wolff, "Urban Restructuring: An Analysis of Social and Spatial Change in Los Angeles," *Economic Geography* 59 (April 1983): 211.

20. Information on the assets of the fifty largest commercial banks; headquarters of the 200 largest industrial corporations, the fifty largest service companies, commercial banking and financial companies, and advertising agencies; and the twenty-five largest retailers, transportation companies, utilities, and life insurance companies is from *Rand McNally Commercial Atlas and Marketing Guide, 1986* (Chicago: Rand McNally, 1986); information on airline passengers is from *Origin and Destination Survey of Airline Passenger Traffic* (Washington, DC: Air Transport Association of America, 1982).

21. The list includes nineteen firms in accounting, fifteen in advertising, twenty-three in banking and finance, eleven in insurance, sixteen in law, and seventeen in management consulting. See P. J. Taylor, G. Catalano, and D. R. F. Walker, "Exploratory Analysis of the World City Network," Virginia Tech Institute for Metropolitan Research, at http://www.mi.vt.edu/research/WorldCities/USasWorld.asp.

22. Data from http://skyscraperpage.com.

CHAPTER FIFTEEN

1. Archer County reached a peak population of 9,684 in 1930, dropped steadily to 5,759 in 1970, and has since recovered with exurbanites from Wichita Falls. Archer City had 1,901 people in 1950 and 1,848 in 2000.

2. Larry McMurtry, *Some Can Whistle* (New York: Simon and Schuster, 1982), 13.

3. David Wrobel, *Promised Lands: Promotion, Memory, and the Creation of the American West* (Lawrence: University Press of Kansas, 2002), 58.

4. Thomas Andrews, "'Made by Toile'? Tourism, Labor, and the Construction of the Colorado Landscape, 1858–1917," *Journal of American History* 92 (December 2005): 837–63.

5. James Shortridge, *Cities of the Plains: The Evolution of Urban Kansas* (Lawrence: University Press of Kansas, 2004), 377.

6. Marian Goldfein and Willima Casey, "Trade Centers of the Upper Midwest," *CURA Reporter* (University of Minnesota) 21 (February 1991): 1. The study covered Wisconsin, Minnesota, Iowa, Nebraska, the Dakotas, and Montana.

7. Strongly influenced municipalities sent 30 percent or more of their labor force to jobs in Census Metropolitan Areas and Census Agglomerations. Moderately influenced municipalities sent 5 to 30 percent.

8. Robin Cody's novel *Ricochet River* (Portland, OR: Blue Heron Press, 1992) offers a sensitive portrait of a fictionalized Estacada in the late 1950s.

9. Chilton Williamson Jr., *Roughnecking It; or, Life in the Overthrust* (New York: Simon and Schuster, 1982), 13.

10. The prison-building boom of the 1990s added another development prize that brought some towns full circle to the asylum/prison/university competitions of the nineteenth century.

11. Richard White, *Land Use, Environment and Social Change: The Shaping of Island County, Washington* (Seattle: University of Washington Press, 1980).

12. The coastal counties are Clatsop, Lincoln, and Tillamook (where the figure was 45 percent). Deschutes County includes the booming city of Bend.

13. Jeri Porter, quoted in *The Oregonian*, December 26, 2006.

14. In the Four Corners/Colorado Plateau region, for example, the *Atlas of the New West* (New York: W. W. Norton, 1997) documents scheduled service to Farmington, Cortez, Durango, Telluride, Gunnison, Montrose, and Grand Junction. For western Wyoming it identifies Jackson, Cody, Sheridan, Riverton, and Worland.

15. The "micropolitan statistical area" was defined for the first time in 2003 on the basis of 2000 Census data. Most micropolitan areas are traditional subregional centers like Pocatello, Idaho; Roseburg, Oregon; Grand Island, Nebraska; and Manhattan, Kansas. They occupy a third or fourth level in the urban hierarchy but

lack a single city with the necessary size to pass the metropolitan threshold, even though the total population included in the census definition may be equivalent. The statistical area populations of Fairbanks, Cheyenne, Great Falls, Pendleton, Twin Falls, and Lufkin all fell between 80,000 and 83,000 in 2000, but the first three are metropolitan and the latter three are micropolitan.

16. By one calculation, Rocky Mountain and Pacific state counties where more than 60 percent of the land is in federal ownership saw real personal income grow 60 percent faster than counties with no more than 10 percent federal ownership between 1970 and 2000. Sonoran Institute, "You've Come a Long Way, Cowboy: Ten Truths and Trends in the New American West," September 29, 2006, at http://www.sonoran.org/cowboy/index.html.

17. Hal Rothman, *Devil's Bargains: Tourism in the Twentieth Century West* (Lawrence: University Press of Kansas, 1998). Thomas Michael Power, in *Lost Landscapes and Failed Economies: The Search for a Value of Place* (Washington, DC: Island Press, 1996), argues to the contrary that tourism can be a positive economic transition.

18. Economic Research Service, U.S. Department of Agriculture, "Measuring Rurality: 2004 County Typology Codes," at http://www.ers.usda.gov/briefing/rurality/. There are a few oddities in the USDA results (Ogallala, Nebraska, and the Standing Rock Reservation of North Dakota as recreation centers), but the general pattern matches common perceptions. Mining counties had 15 percent or more of total earned income from mining during 1998–2000, and farming-dependent counties had 15 percent or more of total earned income from farming for 1998–2000 or 15 percent or more of workers in farm occupations. Nonmetro recreation counties were defined complexly on seasonal housing units and employment and income from hotels, motels, restaurants, and entertainment. Another measure uses metropolitan area data on the percent of change in Social Security program beneficiaries from 2000 to 2004 as reported in the *State and Metropolitan Area Data Book: 2006* (Washington, DC: U.S. Department of Commerce, Bureau of the Census, 2006). The national figure was 5 percent, but a number of small, attractive western metro areas grew by 10 percent or more, suggestive of an influx of retirees. The cities include Bellingham, Bend, Boise and Coeur d'Alene, St. George, Reno, Yuma and Prescott, Fairbanks and Anchorage, Killeen, and Santa Fe, along with another cluster in the retirement zone along the South Atlantic coast.

19. Frances Fuller Victor, *Atlantis Arisen, or Talks of a Tourist about Oregon and Washington* (Philadelphia: J. P. Lippincott Co., 1891), 54.

20. "Hatfield Makes Gorge Stop," *Gorge Weekly*, June 9, 1995.

21. See http://www.gorgecommission.org/act_section3.cfm.

22. Thomas McGuane, *Keep the Change* (Boston: Houghton Mifflin, 1989); Thomas McGuane, *Something to Be Desired* (New York: Vintage Books, 1985), 51.

23. Land used to be valued on its ability to support cattle, each of which requires several acres of pasture, with no premium for aesthetics. From the mid-1970s to the mid-1990s, however, the base value of Ouray ranch land on the market increased four times (and in some cases by as much as forty times), but the value of cattle, scarcely at all.

24. Peter Decker, *Old Fences, New Neighbors* (Albuquerque: University of New Mexico Press, 1998), 96–97.

25. Clarence Matson, "The Los Angeles of Tomorrow," *Southern California Business*, November 1924: 37, quoted in Clark Davis, "The View from Spring Street," in *Metropolis in the Making: Los Angeles in the 1920s*, by Tom Sitton and William Deverell (Berkeley: University of California Press, 2001), 183.

26. Los Angeles in the same years provided powerful but less focused cultural leadership, ranging from Central Avenue jazz clubs, to a set of innovative painters who made Venice Beach an artists' center in the 1950s and 1960s, to the skilled writers who reflected on the vagaries of modern life while trying to earn a living with film scripts.

27. Harry W. Fritz, "The Origins of Twenty-first Century Montana," *Montana* 42 (Winter 1992): 78.

28. Elliott Coues, ed., *History of the Expedition under the Command of Lewis and Clark* (New York: Dover, 1965), vol. 2, 664; Alexander Ross, *Adventures of the First Settlers on the Oregon or Columbia River* (London: Smith and Elder, 1849), 118.

29. Katrine Barber, *Death of Celilo Falls* (Seattle: University of Washington Press, 2005), 93.

CONCLUSION

1. Christopher Rand, *Los Angeles: The Ultimate City* (New York: Oxford University Press, 1967), 95.

2. Jean-Paul Sartre, "American Cities," in *Literary and Philosophical Essays* (London: Rider and Co., 1955), 166.

3. Richard F. Burton, *The City of the Saints, and across the Rocky Mountains to California*, ed. Fawn Brodie (New York: Knopf, 1963), 218.

4. Walter Van Tilburg Clark, *The City of Trembling Leaves* (New York: Random House, 1945), 3–12.

5. Alison Lurie, *The Nowhere City* (New York: Coward-McCann, 1965), 4, 14.

6. Herbert Croly, "The Transformation of the City from an Architectural and Social Viewpoint," *Architectural Record* 31 (June 1912): 592, 607; Walter Hines Page, "The Larger West Coast Cities," *World's Work*, August 1905: 6501.

7. Thomas Pynchon, *Vineland* (Boston: Little, Brown, 1990), 266–67.

8. Don DeLillo, *Underworld* (New York: Scribner's, 2003), 89–90.

9. Robert Venturi, Denise Scott Brown, and Steven Izenour famously saw Las Vegas as the epitome of horizontal form. In *Learning from Las Vegas* (Cambridge, MA: MIT Press, 1972) they see the city as a natural expression of American culture, a new Florence to the new Rome of Los Angeles. Its central component was the commercial strip, a new main street made up of separate nodes of activity that are separated by parking lots and connected by automobiles. Like Los Angeles, it seemed a city designed around high speed, with spaces created by billboards and traffic signals rather than buildings.

10. Walt Disney, quoted in John Findlay, *Magic Lands: Western Cityscapes and American Culture after 1940* (Berkeley: University of California Press, 1992), 67.

11. Larry McMurtry, *In a Narrow Grave: Essays on Texas* (Albuquerque: University of New Mexico Press, 1986), 119; Martin V. Melosi, "Dallas–Fort Worth: Marketing the Metroplex," in *Sunbelt Cities: Politics and Growth since World War II*, ed. Richard Bernard and Bradley Rice (Austin: University of Texas Press, 1983), 173; Kenneth Labich, "The Best Cities for Business," *Fortune*, October 23, 1989: 79.

12. *A Vision for the Future: Highlights of the Neal Pierce Study Commissioned by the Arizona Republic and the Phoenix Gazette* (Phoenix: Phoenix Newspapers Inc., 1988), 3; Peter Wiley and Robert Gottlieb, *Empires in the Sun: The Rise of the New American West* (New York: Putnam, 1982), 189–90.

13. John Anson Ford, *Thirty Explosive Years in Los Angeles County* (San Marino, CA: Huntington Library, 1961), 58.

14. Some of the same characteristics made Winnipeg a city that mingled "eastern" and "western" patterns of class relations.

15. Gary Snyder, quoted in Dennis McNally, "Prophets on the Burning Shore: Jack Kerouac, Gary Snyder, and San Francisco," in *A Literary History of the American West*, ed. J. Golden Taylor (Fort Worth: Texas Christian University Press, 1987), 483; Lacey Fosburgh, "San Francisco: Unconventional City for the Democratic Convention," *New York Times Magazine*, July 1, 1984.

16. William Rorabaugh, *Berkeley at War: The 1960s* (New York: Oxford University Press, 1989), 90.

17. Unidentified to Norman Mack, December 8, 1917, in the Ellis Meredith Papers, Colorado Historical Society, Denver. Meredith had a Portland counterpart in Abigail Scott Duniway, who published the suffrage newspaper *New Northwest* out of an office in downtown Portland and battled her hidebound brother and *Oregonian* editor Harvey Scott word for word over four decades.

18. Neil Morgan, *Westward Tilt: The American West Today* (New York: Random House, 1963), 136–37; Richard Austin Smith, "Los Angeles: Prototype of Supercity," *Fortune* 71 (March 1965): 99–100; Werner Hirsch, "Los Angeles: A Leading City?" in *Los Angeles: Viability and Prospects for Metropolitan Leadership*, ed. Werner Hirsch (New York: Praeger, 1971), 237–41; Richard Elman, *Ill-at-Ease in Compton* (New York: Pantheon, 1967), 4.

19. Wiley and Gottlieb, *Empires in the Sun*; John Naisbitt, *Megatrends* (New York: Warner Books, 1984).

20. Lynn Ashby, "The Supercities: Houston," *Saturday Review* 3 n.s. (September 4, 1976): 16–19; Ada Louise Huxtable, "Deep in the Heart of Nowhere," *New York Times*, February 15, 1976.

21. Wiley and Gottlieb, *Empires in the Sun*, 76; Richard Louv, *America II* (New York: Penguin Books, 1983), 49–51; Pierce Lewis, "Axioms for Reading the Landscape," in *The Interpretation of Ordinary Landscapes*, ed. D. W. Meinig (New York: Oxford University Press, 1979), 16.

22. In 2006 Seattle and Portland ranked first and second in the United States in the number of "green buildings" certified by Leadership in Energy and Environmental Design. Boulder and perhaps Eugene are examples of environmentally conscious cities where progressive initiatives in the 1960s and 1970s have evolved into what might be called cities of progressive consumption, where the middle class

supports the cause by eating, driving, and dressing right. Something of Boulder's reputation in its innovative heyday can be seen in Stephen King's decision to make it the rallying place for the forces of light as they prepare to battle embodied evil (which resides in Las Vegas) in the postapocalyptic novel *The Stand* (Garden City, NY: Doubleday, 1978).

23. Hal Rothman, *Neon Metropolis: How Las Vegas Started the Twenty-first Century* (New York: Routledge, 2002), xiii, xxiii.

24. Christopher Hawthorne, "The City Rediscovers the Street," *Los Angeles Times,* December 31, 2006.

25. Jonathan Franzen, *The Twenty-seventh City* (New York: Farrar, Straus and Giroux, 1988); Leslie Marmon Silko, *Almanac of the Dead* (New York: Simon and Schuster, 1991).

26. Adding the metropolitan populations of the U.S. West in 2000 (77,901,000) and the Canadian West in 2001 (5,425,000) gives 83,326,000. Multiplying that total by six gives 499,956,000.

BIBLIOGRAPHICAL ESSAY

INTRODUCTION: ALL ROADS LEAD TO FRESNO

Historians who have taken booster rhetoric as worthy of serious analysis include Carl Abbott, *Boosters and Businessmen: Popular Economic Thought and Urban Growth in the Antebellum Middle West* (Westport, CT: Greenwood, 1983); David Hamer, *New Towns in the New World: Images and Perceptions of the Nineteenth Century Urban Frontier* (New York: Columbia University Press, 1990); and David Wrobel, *Promised Lands: Promotion, Memory and the Creation of the American West* (Lawrence: University Press of Kansas, 2002).

On Canadian urbanization generally, see Warren Magnuson and Andrew Sancton, eds., *City Politics in Canada* (Toronto: University of Toronto Press, 1983); George A. Nader, *Cities of Canada*, 2 vols. (Toronto: Macmillan of Canada, 1975–76); and Gilbert Stelter and Alan Artibise, eds., *The Canadian City: Essays in Urban History* (Toronto: McClelland and Stewart, 1977).

The permeability of the U.S.–Canadian border is discussed in Marcus Lee Hansen, *The Mingling of the Canadian and American Peoples, vol. 1: Historical*, completed by John Bartlett Brebner (New Haven: Yale University Press, 1940); Marcus Lee Hansen, *The Atlantic Migration, 1607–1860* (Cambridge, MA: Harvard University Press, 1941); Beth LeDow, *The Medicine Line: Life and Death on a North American Borderland* (New York: Routledge, 2000); and John Lutz, "Work, Sex and Death on the Great Thoroughfare: Annual Migrations of 'Canadian Indians' to the American Pacific Northwest," Patricia Wood, "Borders and Identities among Italian Immigrants in the Pacific Northwest, 1880–1938," Jeremy Mouat, "Nationalist Narratives and Regional Realities: The Political Economy of Railway Development in Southwestern British Columbia, 1895–1905," and Daniel Marshall, "No Parallel: American Settler-Soldiers at War with the Nlaka'pamux of the Canadian West," all in *Parallel Destinies: Canadians, Americans, and the Western Frontier*, ed. John M. Findlay and Ken Coates (Seattle: University of Washington Press, 2002).

An extraordinarily rich study that does not fit neatly with the organization of this book is D. W. Meinig's magisterial four-volume exploration of the historical geography of North America in *The Shaping of America* (New Haven: Yale University Press, 1986–2004), consisting of *Atlantic America, 1482–1800, Continental America, 1800–1867, Transcontinental America, 1850–1915*, and *Global America, 1915–2000*. Also crossing chapter boundaries is Lawrence Larsen, *The Urban West at the End of the Frontier* (Lawrence: University Press of Kansas, 1978).

| 321

CHAPTER ONE. OUTPOSTS OF EMPIRES

John Reps, *Cities in the American West: A History of Frontier Urban Planning* (Princeton: Princeton University Press, 1979); Dora Crouch, Daniel T. Garr, and Axel I. Mindigo, *Spanish City Planning in North America* (Cambridge, MA: MIT Press, 1982); and Oakah L. Jones Jr., *Los Paisanos: Spanish Settlers on the Northern Frontier of New Spain* (Norman: University of Oklahoma Press, 1979) are essential sources on towns at the northern end of the Spanish–American frontier. David Weber, *The Spanish Frontier in North America* (New Haven: Yale University Press, 1992) provides an essential framework.

The histories of early Spanish and Mexican communities are discussed in Marc Simmons, "Governor Cuervo and the Beginnings of Albuquerque: Another Look," *New Mexico Historical Review* 55 (1980): 188–207; Michael Gonzalez, *This Small City Will Be a Mexican Paradise: Exploring the Origins of Mexican Culture in Los Angeles, 1821–1846* (Albuquerque: University of New Mexico Press, 2005); Kenneth T. Wheeler, *To Wear a City's Crown: The Beginnings of Urban Growth in Texas, 1836–1865* (Cambridge, MA: Harvard University Press, 1968); Jess de la Teja and John Wheat, "Bexar: Profile of a Tejano Community, 1820–1832," *Southwestern Historical Quarterly* 89 (1985): 5–34; and Jesús de la Teja, "A Spanish Borderlands Community: San Antonio," *Magazine of History* 14 (2000): 25–28. For Russian town building, see James R. Gibson, "Sitka versus Kodiak: Countering the Tlinget Threat and Situating the Colonial Capital in Russian America," *Pacific Historical Review* 67 (February 1998): 67–98.

The historical literature on the cities of England's North American colonies is voluminous. For points made in this brief discussion, refer to Darrett Rutman, *Winthrop's Boston: Portrait of a Puritan Town* (Chapel Hill: University of North Carolina Press, 1965); Joseph Ernst and H. Roy Merrens, "Camden's Turrets Pierce the Skies: The Urban Process in the Southern Colonies during the Eighteenth Century," *William and Mary Quarterly* 30 (1973): 548–74; John Reps, *Tidewater Towns: City Planning in Colonial Virginia and Maryland* (Charlottesville: University Press of Virginia, 1972); and Gary Nash, *The Urban Crucible: Northern Seaports and the Origins of the American Revolution* (Cambridge, MA: Harvard University Press, 1986). Carl Bridenbaugh, *Cities in the Wilderness: The First Century of Urban Life in America* (New York: Ronald Press, 1938); and Carl Bridenbaugh, *Cities in Revolt: Urban Life in America, 1743–1776* (New York: Knopf, 1955) are dated in methodology but still valuable for information.

CHAPTER TWO. ACROSS THE WIDE MISSISSIPPI

Stephen Aron, *American Confluence: The Missouri Frontier from Borderland to Border State* (Bloomington: Indiana University Press, 2006) is now the starting place for understanding the role of St. Louis in continental development. The rise of Chicago and relative decline of St. Louis are explored in Wyatt W. Belcher, *The Economic Rivalry between Chicago and St. Louis, 1850–1880* (New York: Columbia University Press, 1947); Jeffrey S. Adler, *Yankee Merchants and the Making of the Urban West: The Rise and Fall of Antebellum St. Louis* (New York: Cambridge University Press, 1991); and William Cronon, *Nature's Metropolis: Chicago and the Great West* (New York: Norton, 1991). Also see Richard Wade, *The Urban Frontier: The Rise of Western Cities, 1790–1830* (Cambridge, MA: Harvard University Press, 1959).

Small towns of the Upper Mississippi and Missouri valleys are discussed in Timothy Mahoney, *Provincial Lives: Middle Class Experience in the Antebellum Middle West* (New

York: Cambridge University Press, 1999); Catherine Stock, *Main Street in Crisis* (Chapel Hill: University of North Carolina Press, 1992); and John C. Hudson, *Plains Country Towns* (Minneapolis: University of Minnesota Press, 1985).

The economic development of prominent gateway cities is the subject of Jocelyn Wills, *Boosters, Hustlers, and Speculators: Entrepreneurial Culture and the Rise of Minneapolis and St. Paul, 1849–1883* (St. Paul: Minnesota Historical Society, 2005); Mildred Hartsough, *The Development of the Twin Cities as a Metropolitan Market* (Minneapolis: University of Minnesota Press, 1925); Lawrence Larsen and Barbara J. Cottrell, *Gate City: A History of Omaha*, 2nd ed. (Lincoln: University of Nebraska Press, 1992); A. Theodore Brown, *Frontier Community: Kansas City* (Columbia: University of Missouri Press, 1963); Charles Glaab, *Kansas City and the Railroads: Community Policy in the Growth of a Regional Metropolis* (Madison: State Historical Society of Wisconsin, 1962); H. Craig Miner, *Wichita: The Early Years, 1865–1880* (Lincoln: University of Nebraska Press, 1982); and Alan Artibise, *Winnipeg: A Social History of Urban Growth, 1874–1914* (Montreal: McGill-Queens University Press, 1975). Leonard Eaton, *Gateway Cities and Other Essays* (Ames: Iowa State University Press, 1989) examines their distinct physical form. James Shortridge, *Cities on the Plains: The Evolution of Urban Kansas* (Lawrence: University Press of Kansas, 2004) treats cities large and small in fascinating detail. John Borchert, *America's Northern Heartland* (Minneapolis: University of Minnesota Press, 1987) is another comprehensive look at the spatial evolution of the northern plains and the changing patterns of urbanization.

CHAPTER THREE. THE FIRST PACIFIC CENTURY

David Igler, "Diseased Goods: Global Exchanges in the Eastern Pacific Basin, 1770–1850," *American Historical Review* 109 (June 2004): 693–719, places the rise of West Coast trading ports in a broad framework. It supplements Jean Heffer, *The United States and the Pacific: History of a Frontier* (Notre Dame, IN: University of Notre Dame Press, 2002); Arthur Dudden, *The American Pacific from the Early China Trade to the Present* (New York: Oxford University Press, 1992); Walter McDougall, *Let the Sea Make a Noise: A History of the North Pacific from Magellan to MacArthur* (New York: Basic Books, 1993); and Arrell M. Gibson and John S. Whitehead, *Yankees in Paradise: The Pacific Basin Frontier* (Albuquerque: University of New Mexico Press, 1993).

The initial years of American San Francisco are analyzed in Gunther Barth, *Instant Cities: Urbanization and the Rise of San Francisco and Denver* (New York: Oxford University Press, 1975); and Roger Lotchin, *San Francisco, 1846–1856: From Hamlet to City* (New York: Oxford University Press, 1974). The city's economic roles and economic opportunities are explored in Gray Brechin, *Imperial San Francisco: Urban Power, Earthly Ruin* (Berkeley: University of California Press, 1999); Peter Decker, *Fortunes and Failure: White Collar Mobility in Nineteenth Century San Francisco* (Cambridge, MA: Harvard University Press, 1978); Jeffrey Hayda, *Citizen Employees: Business Communities and Labor in Cincinnati and San Francisco, 1870–1916* (Ithaca, NY: Cornell University Press, 2008); and Edith Sparks, *Capital Intentions: Female Proprietors in San Francisco, 1850–1920* (Chapel Hill: University of North Carolina Press, 2006). The city's nineteenth-century political life is the subject of Terrence McDonald, *The Parameters of Urban Fiscal Policy: Socioeconomic Change and Political Culture in San Francisco, 1860–1906* (Berkeley: University of California Press, 1986);

Philip Ethington, *The Public City: The Political Construction of Urban Life in San Francisco, 1850–1900* (Cambridge, MA: Harvard University Press, 1994); Mary Ryan, *Civic Wars: Democracy and Public Life in the American City during the Nineteenth Century* (Berkeley: University of California Press, 1997); and Robert Cherny and William Issel, *San Francisco, 1865–1932: Politics, Power and Urban Development* (Berkeley: University of California Press, 1986). Barbara Berglund, *Making San Francisco American: Cultural Frontiers in the Urban West, 1846–1906* (Lawrence: University Press of Kansas, 2007) examines social and cultural change.

James Mohr, *Plague and Fire: Battling Black Death and the 1900 Burning of Honolulu's Chinatown* (New York: Oxford University Press, 2005); Nayan Shah, *Contagious Divides: Epidemics and Race in San Francisco's Chinatown* (Berkeley: University of California Press, 2001); and Natalia Molina, *Fit to Be Citizens? Public Health and Race in Los Angeles, 1879–1939* (Berkeley: University of California Press, 2006) discuss the ways in which white society dealt with disease among Asian and Mexican immigrants.

Aspects of the Chinese American experience are in Judy Yung, *Unbound Feet: A Social History of Chinese Women in San Francisco* (Berkeley: University of California Press, 1995); Yong Chen, *Chinese San Francisco: A TransPacific Community, 1850–1943* (Stanford: Stanford University Press, 2000); Diana Ahmad, *The Opium Debate and Chinese Exclusion Laws in the Nineteenth-Century American West* (Reno: University of Nevada Press, 2007); and Marie Rose Wong, *Sweet Cakes, Long Journey: The Chinatowns of Portland, Oregon* (Seattle: University of Washington Press, 2004).

Immigrants to American cities from elsewhere in Asia are discussed in Yen le Espiritu, *Home Bound: Filipino American Lives across Cultures, Communities and Countries* (Berkeley: University of California Press, 2003); Dorothy Fujita-Rony, *American Workers: Colonial Power: Philippine Seattle and the Transpacific West, 1919–1941* (Berkeley: University of California Press, 2003); Linda Espana-Maran, *Creating Masculinity in Los Angeles's Little Manila* (New York: Columbia University Press, 2006); John Modell, *The Economics and Politics of Racial Accommodation: The Japanese in Los Angeles, 1900–1942* (Urbana: University of Illinois Press, 1977); and Joan Jensen, *Passage from India: Asian Indian Immigrants in North America* (New Haven: Yale University Press, 1988).

Alexander Saxton, *The Indispensable Enemy: Labor and the Anti-Chinese Movement in California* (Berkeley: University of California Press, 1971); Erika Lee, *At America's Gates: Chinese Immigration during the Exclusion Era, 1882–1943* (Chapel Hill: University of North Carolina Press, 2003); and Patricia Roy, *A White Man's Province: British Columbia Politicians and Chinese and Japanese Immigrants, 1858–1914* (Vancouver: University of British Columbia Press, 1990) deal with the politics of prejudice, to use the term from Roger Daniels, *The Politics of Prejudice: The Anti-Japanese Movement in California and the Struggle for Japanese Exclusion* (Berkeley: University of California Press, 1962).

CHAPTER FOUR. INLAND EMPIRE CITIES

The structure for this chapter draws extensively on D. W. Meinig, *The Shaping of America: A Geographical Perspective on 500 Years of History, vol. 3: Transcontinental America, 1850–1915* (New Haven: Yale University Press, 1998).

Essential sources on Salt Lake City and its region are Thomas G. Alexander and James B. Allen, *Mormons and Gentiles: A History of Salt Lake City* (Boulder: Pruitt Publishing, 1984); and Leonard Arrington, *Great Basin Kingdom: An Economic History of the Latter-Day Saints* (Cambridge, MA: Harvard University Press, 1958). Spatial perspectives are offered in D. W. Meinig, "The Mormon Culture Region: Strategies and Patterns in the Geography of the American West," *Annals of the Association of American Geographers* 55 (June 1965): 191–220; and Chauncey D. Harris, *Salt Lake City: A Regional Capital* (Chicago: University of Chicago Department of Geography, 1940). Also see Robert Flanders, *Nauvoo: Kingdom on the Mississippi* (Urbana: University of Illinois Press, 1965); Howard Lamar, *The Far Southwest, 1846–1912: A Territorial History* (New York: Norton, 1970).

Kathleen Brosnan, *Uniting Mountain and Plain: Cities, Law, and Environmental Change along the Front Range* (Albuquerque: University of New Mexico Press, 2002); and William Wyckoff, *Creating Colorado: The Making of a Western Landscape, 1860–1940* (New Haven: Yale University Press, 1999) are two recent and excellent studies of the relationships between Denver and its region. They complement Gunther Barth, *Instant Cities: Urbanization and the Rise of San Francisco and Denver* (New York: Oxford University Press, 1975). Carl Abbott, Stephen Leonard, and Thomas Noel, *Colorado: A History of the Centennial State* (Boulder: University Press of Colorado, 2005) organizes the history of the state around metropolitan growth. The up-to-date and comprehensive history of Denver is Stephen Leonard and Thomas Noel, *Denver: Mining Camp to Metropolis* (Niwot: University Press of Colorado, 1990). Also see Robert Athearn, *Rebel of the Rockies: The Denver and Rio Grande Western Railroad* (New Haven: Yale University Press, 1962); Gunther Barth, *Instant Cities: Urbanization and the Rise of San Francisco and Denver* (New York: Oxford University Press, 1975); Thomas Karnes, *William Gilpin: Western Nationalist* (Austin: University of Texas Press, 1970); and Harry E. Kelsey Jr., *Frontier Capitalist: The Life of John Evans* (Denver: State Historical Society of Colorado, 1969). The Cheyenne episode is examined in Gilbert Stelter, "The City and Westward Expansion: A Western Case Study," *Western Historical Quarterly* 4, no. 2: 187–202.

Discussions of other cities as focal points for assaults on native peoples include Chip Colwell-Chanthaphonh, *Massacre at Camp Grant: Forgetting and Remembering Apache History* (Tucson: University of Arizona Press, 2007); Eugene Moehring, "The Comstock Urban System," *Pacific Historical Review* 66 (August 1997): 337–62; and Eugene Moehring, *Urbanism and Empire in the Far West, 1840–1890* (Reno: University of Nevada Press, 2004).

The authoritative and imaginative treatment of Spokane is Katherine Morrissey, *Mental Territories: Mapping the Inland Empire* (Ithaca, NY: Cornell University Press, 1997). Also John Fahey, *The Inland Empire: The Unfolding Years, 1879–1929* (Seattle: University of Washington Press, 1986); D. W. Meinig, *The Great Columbia Plain: A Historical Geography, 1805–1910* (Seattle: University of Washington Press, 1968); W. Hudson Kensel, "Inland Empire Mining and the Growth of Spokane, 1883–1905," *Pacific Northwest Quarterly* 60, no. 2: 84–97.

For the partly unrealized region of the southwestern borderlands, see Bradford Luckingham, *The Urban Southwest: A Profile History of Albuquerque, El Paso, Phoenix, Tucson* (El Paso: Texas Western Press, 1982); and Samuel Truett, *Fugitive Landscapes* (New Haven: Yale University Press, 2006).

CHAPTER FIVE. GARDEN CITIES

Historians in recent years have been fruitfully examining the citrus cities of southern California: Matt Garcia, *A World of Its Own: Race, Labor, and Citrus in the Making of Greater Los Angeles, 1900–1970* (Berkeley: University of California Press, 2001); Douglas Sackman, *Orange Empires: California and the Fruits of Eden* (Berkeley: University of California Press, 2005); Douglas Monroy, *Rebirth: Mexican Los Angeles from the Great Migration to the Great Depression* (Berkeley: University of California Press, 1999); Gilbert G. Gonzalez, *Labor and Community: Mexican Citrus Worker Villages in a Southern California County, 1900–1950* (Urbana: University of Illinois Press, 1994); and Jose Alamillo, *Making Lemonade out of Lemons: Mexican American Labor and Leisure in a California Town, 1880–1960* (Urbana: University of Illinois Press, 2006).

Michael Logan is the expert on Arizona's irrigation-dependent cities: *The Lessening Stream: An Environmental History of the Santa Cruz River* (Tucson: University of Arizona Press, 2002) and *Desert Cities: An Environmental History of Phoenix and Tucson* (Pittsburgh: University of Pittsburgh Press, 2006). For Snake River cities, see Carol Lynn MacGregor, *Boise, Idaho: Prosperity in Isolation, 1882–1910* (Missoula: Mountain Press Publishing, 2006); and J. Anthony Lukas, *Big Trouble: A Murder in a Small Town Sets Off a Struggle for the Soul of America* (New York: Simon and Schuster, 1997).

Irrigation cities on Colorado's West Slope are discussed in Kathleen Underwood, *Town Building on the Colorado Frontier* (Albuquerque: University of New Mexico Press, 1987); and William Wycoff, *Creating Colorado: The Making of a Western American Landscape, 1860–1940* (New Haven: Yale University Press, 1999).

CHAPTER SIX. SMOKESTACK FRONTIERS

Rodman Paul, *Mining Frontiers of the Far West: 1848–1890* (New York: Holt, Rinehart, and Winston, 1963) pioneered in offering an urban interpretation of western mining development, soon followed by Duane Smith, *Rocky Mountain Mining Camps* (Bloomington: Indiana University Press, 1967).

There are a number of excellent studies of community life and labor activism in mining and mill towns, including Elizabeth Jameson, *All That Glitters: Class, Conflict, and Community in Cripple Creek* (Urbana: University of Illinois Press, 1998); David Emmons, *The Butte Irish: Class and Ethnicity in an American Mining Town* (Urbana: University of Illinois Press, 1989); Jerry Calvert, *The Gibralter: Socialism and Labor in Butte, Montana, 1895–1920* (Helena: Montana State Historical Society, 1989); Mary Murphy, *Mining Cultures: Men, Women and Leisure in Butte, 1914–41* (Urbana: University of Illinois Press, 1997); Norman H. Clark, *Mill Town: A Social History of Everett, Washington from Its Earliest Beginnings on the Shores of Puget Sound to the Tragic and Infamous Event Known as the Everett Massacre* (Seattle: University of Washington Press, 1970); Laurie Mercier, *Anaconda: Labor, Community and Culture in Montana's Smelter City* (Urbana: University of Illinois Press, 2001); and Chris Friday, *Organizing Asian American Labor: The Pacific Coast Canned-Salmon Industry, 1870–1942* (Philadelphia: Temple University Press, 1994).

On industrial labor in larger western cities, begin with Vicki Ruiz, *Cannery Women, Cannery Lives: Mexican Women, Urbanization, and the California Food Processing Industry, 1930–1950* (Albuquerque: University of New Mexico Press, 1987);

and Zaragoza Vargas, *Labor Rights Are Civil Rights: Mexican American Workers in Twentieth Century America* (Princeton: Princeton University Press, 2005).

The climax of labor-management conflict after World War I is treated in David Jay Bercuson, *Confrontation at Winnipeg: Labour, Industrial Relations, and the General Strike* (Montreal: McGill-Queens University Press, 1990); and Dana Frank, *Purchasing Power: Consumer Organization, Gender, and the Seattle Labor Movement, 1919–1929* (New York: Cambridge University Press, 1994). Also see Bruce Nelson, *Workers on the Waterfront: Seaman, Longshoremen, and Unionism in the 1930s* (Urbana: University of Illinois Press, 1988).

CHAPTER SEVEN. MONEY IN THE AIR

The pioneering study of tourism in western North America is Earl Pomeroy, *In Search of the Golden West: The Tourist in Western America* (New York: Knopf, 1957), which can be supplemented by Robert Athearn, *Westward the Briton* (New York: Scribner's, 1953). Catherine Cocks, *Doing the Town: The Rise of Urban Tourism in the United States, 1850–1915* (Berkeley: University of California Press, 2001) takes a specifically urban viewpoint.

Lee M. A. Simpson, *Selling the City: Gender, Class and the California Growth Machine, 1880–1940* (Stanford: Stanford University Press, 2004) discusses tourism in Santa Barbara. For San Francisco, see Catherine Cocks, *Doing the Town: The Rise of Urban Tourism in the United States, 1850–1915* (Berkeley: University of California Press, 2001); and Raymond Rast, "The Cultural Politics of Tourism in San Francisco's Chinatown, 1882–1917," *Pacific Historical Review* 76 (February 2007): 29–60. For Monterey, see John Walton, *Storied Land: Community and Memory in Monterey* (Berkeley: University of California Press, 2001); Connie Chiang, "Monterey-by-the-Smell: Odors and Social Conflict on the California Coastline," *Pacific Historical Review* 73 (May 2004): 183–214; and Connie Chiang, "Novel Tourism: Nature, Industry and Literature on Monterey's Cannery Row," *Western Historical Quarterly* 35 (Autumn 2004), 309–30.

The evolution and effects of tourism and leisure on other well-known destinations are the subject of Chris Wilson, *The Myth of Santa Fe: Creating a Modern Regional Tradition* (Albuquerque: University of New Mexico Press, 1997); Victoria Dye, *All Aboard for Santa Fe: Railway Promotion in the Southwest* (Albuquerque: University of New Mexico Press, 2007); Susan Wiley Hardwick, *Mythic Galveston: Reinventing America's Third Coast* (Baltimore: Johns Hopkins University Press, 2002); Lewis F. Fisher, *Saving San Antonio: The Precarious Preservation of a Heritage* (Lubbock: Texas Tech University Press, 1996); Thomas Bremer, *Blessed with Tourists: The Borderlands of Religion and Tourism in San Antonio* (Chapel Hill: University of North Carolina Press, 2004); and William David Estrada, *The Los Angeles Plaza: Sacred and Contested Space* (Austin: University of Texas Press, 2008). Judith Mattivi Morley, *Historic Preservation and the Imagined West: Albuquerque, Denver, and Seattle* (Lawrence: University Press of Kansas, 2006) examines the rise of preservation programs in larger cities in the second half of the twentieth century.

For the relationship between urban business and recreational interests and national park development, see Theodore R. Catton, *National Park, City Playground: Mount Rainier in the Twentieth Century* (Seattle: University of Washington Press, 2006); and

Hal Rothman, *The New Urban Park: Golden Gate National Recreation Area* (Lawrence: University Press of Kansas, 2004).

CHAPTER EIGHT. CITIES OF HOMES

The abundance of scholarship makes the pull of Los Angeles especially strong when dealing with downtown, neighborhood development, and planning. Key books on the metropolis include Becky Nicolaides, *My Blue Heaven: Life and Politics in the Working Class Suburbs of Los Angeles, 1920–1965* (Chicago: University of Chicago Press, 2002); Clark Davis, *Company Men: White Collar Life and Corporate Culture in Los Angeles, 1880–1940* (Baltimore: Johns Hopkins University Press, 2000); Mark Wild, *Street Meeting: Multiethnic Neighborhoods in Early Twentieth-Century Los Angeles* (Berkeley: University of California Press, 2005); Greg Hise, *Magnetic Los Angeles: Planning the Twentieth-Century Metropolis* (Baltimore: Johns Hopkins University Press, 1997); Richard Longstreth, *City Center to Regional Mall: Architecture, the Automobile, and Retailing in Los Angeles, 1920–1950* (Cambridge, MA: MIT Press, 1997); and Richard Longstreth, *The Drive-In, the Supermarket, and the Transformation of Commercial Space in Los Angeles, 1914–1941* (Cambridge, MA: MIT Press, 1999).

Middle-class efforts to tame and shape western cities are treated in a number of studies. Robert Johnston, *The Radical Middle Class: Populist Democracy and the Question of Capitalism in Progressive Era Portland, Oregon* (Princeton: Princeton University Press, 2003) is a pioneering argument about the existence of progressive coalitions across class lines that can be compared with William Toll, *The Making of an Ethnic Middle Class: Portland's Jewry over Four Generations* (Albany: State University of New York Press, 1982). Thomas J. Noel, *The City and the Saloon: Denver, 1858–1916* (Lincoln: University of Nebraska Press, 1982) discusses the spatial politics of prohibition. For political life more generally, Amy Bridges, *Morning Glories: Municipal Reform in the Southwest* (Princeton: Princeton University Press, 1997) is a prize-winning comparative examination of politics in the urban Southwest. Also see Robert Fairbanks, *For the City as a Whole: Planning, Politics, and the Public Interest in Dallas, Texas, 1900–1965* (Columbus: Ohio State University Press, 1998); and Patricia Evridge Hill, *Dallas: The Making of a Modern City* (Austin: University of Texas Press, 1996). Lee M. A. Simpson, *Selling the City: Gender, Class and the California Growth Machine, 1880–1940* (Stanford: Stanford University Press, 2004) makes a contrary argument about the power of the bourgeois values and goals.

Formal planning before 1940 is discussed in William H. Wilson, *The City Beautiful Movement* (Baltimore: Johns Hopkins University Press, 1989); Mansel Blackford, *The Lost Dream: Businessmen and Planning on the Pacific Coast* (Columbus: Ohio State University Press, 1993); Judd Kahn, *Imperial San Francisco* (Lincoln: University of Nebraska Press, 1979); Carl Abbott, *Portland: Planning, Politics, and Growth in a Twentieth Century City* (Lincoln: University of Nebraska Press, 1983); and Greg Hise and William Deverell, *Eden by Design: The 1930 Olmsted-Bartholomew Plan for the Los Angeles Region* (Berkeley: University of California Press, 2000).

Keith Bryant, *Culture in the American Southwest: The Earth, the Sky, the People* (College Station: Texas A&M University Press, 1901) inventories the development of cultural institutions, literature, and the visual arts in four southwestern states. The economic and cultural functions of festivals and world's fairs are treated in William

Deverell, *Whitewashed Adobe: The Rise of Los Angeles and the Remaking of Its Mexican Past* (Berkeley: University of California Press, 2004); Robert Rydell, *All the World's a Fair: Visions of Empire in American International Expositions* (Chicago: University of Chicago Press, 1984); and Matthew Bokovoy, *The San Diego World's Fairs and Southwestern Memory, 1880–1940* (Albuquerque: University of New Mexico Press, 2005). An insightful discussion of the development of the typical residential landscape is Janet Ore, *The Seattle Bungalow: People and Houses, 1900–1940* (Seattle: University of Washington Press, 2006). Ronald Tobey, *Technology as Freedom: The New Deal and the Electrical Modernization of the American Home* (Berkeley: University of California Press, 1996) uses Riverside, California, to study the coming of domestic electricity.

CHAPTER NINE. WATER, POWER, PROGRESS

There is a vast literature on the urban reach for water supplies. Studies of cities in rainy regions tend to emphasize technical and institutional innovation in positive terms, such as Nelson Blake, *Water for the Cities: A History of Urban Water Supply Problems* (Syracuse, NY: Syracuse University Press, 1958); and Rick Harmon, "The Bull Run Watershed: Portland's Enduring Jewel," *Oregon Historical Quarterly* 96 (Summer–Fall 1995): 242–70. Studies of the search for water by cities in the arid West tend to treat the importation of supplies as dubious at best, as thievery at worst. For example, see William L. Kahrl, *Water and Power: The Conflict over Los Angeles' Water Supply in the Owens Valley* (Berkeley: University of California Press, 1982); John Walton, *Western Times and Water Wars: State, Culture and Rebellion in California* (Berkeley: University of California Press, 1991); Mark Reisner, *Cadillac Desert: The American West and Its Disappearing Water* (New York: Penguin Books, 1987); and Blake Gumprecht, *The Los Angeles River: Its Life, Death and Possible Rebirth* (Baltimore: Johns Hopkins University Press, 1999). Sarah Elkind, *Bay Cities and Water Politics: The Battle for Resources in Boston and Oakland* (Lawrence: University Press of Kansas, 1998) places the efforts of a western city in comparative context, whereas Grey Brechin, *Imperial San Francisco: Urban Power, Earthly Ruin* (Berkeley: University of California Press, 1999) places that city's environmental claims in the framework of grasping capitalism. Norris Hundley, *The Great Thirst: Californians and Water, a History* (Berkeley: University of California Press, 2001) is the most balanced treatment of the topic.

Jared Orsi, *Hazardous Metropolis: Flooding and Urban Ecology in Los Angeles* (Berkeley: University of California Press, 2004); and Mike Davis, *The Ecology of Fear* (New York: Metropolitan Books, 1998) explore the negative effects of metropolitan growth on the underlying physical environment and the relative intractability of the southern California landscape.

Char Miller, *On the Border: An Environmental History of San Antonio* (Pittsburgh: University of Pittsburgh Press, 2001); Michael Logan, *Desert Cities: An Environmental History of Phoenix and Tucson* (Pittsburgh: University of Pittsburgh Press, 2006); and Matt Klingle, *Emerald City: An Environmental History of Seattle* (New Haven: Yale University Press, 2007) are comprehensive discussions of the interactions of city and landscape, with Klingle's book in particular offering new frameworks for analysis.

CHAPTER TEN. WARS AND RUMORS OF WAR

The starting points for assessing the effects of World War II on western U.S. cities are a pair of books by Gerald Nash: *The American West Transformed: The Impact of the Second World War* (Bloomington: Indiana University Press, 1985) and *World War II and the West: Reshaping the Economy* (Lincoln: University of Nebraska Press, 1990).

More specifically on the wartime experience of western cities are Roger Lotchin, *The Bad City in the Good War: San Francisco, Los Angeles, Oakland, and San Diego* (Bloomington: Indiana University Press, 2003); Marilynn Johnson, *The Second Gold Rush: Oakland and the East Bay in World War II* (Berkeley: University of California Press, 1993); Charles Wollenberg, *Marinship at War: Shipbuilding and Social Change in Wartime Sausalito* (Oakland: Western Heritage Press, 1990); Beth Bailey and David Farber, *The First Strange Place: The Alchemy of Race and Sex in World War II Hawaii* (New York: Free Press, 1992); Carl Abbott, *The New Urban America: Growth and Politics in Sunbelt Cities* (Chapel Hill: University of North Carolina Press, 1981); and Jon Hunner, *Inventing Los Alamos: The Growth of an Atomic Community* (Norman: University of Oklahoma Press, 2004). Philip Funigello, *The Challenge to Urban Liberalism: Federal–City Relations during World War II* (Knoxville: University of Tennessee Press, 1978) places western cities in national context. Roger Lotchin, *Fortress California, 1910–1960: From Warfare to Welfare* (New York: Oxford University Press, 1992) places these military roles in longer historical context, as does Peter Hall and Ann Markusen, *The Rise of the Gunbelt: The Military Reshaping of Industrial America* (New York: Oxford University Press, 1991).

Women as war workers are the topic of Karin Anderson, *Wartime Women: Sex Roles, Family Relations, and the Status of Women in World War II* (Westport, CT: Greenwood Press, 1981); and Amy Kesselman, *Fleeting Opportunities: Women Shipyard Workers in Portland and Vancouver during World War II and Reconversion* (Albany: State University of New York Press, 1990).

For different angles on the rise of the electronics industry and its urban effects, see Peter Hall and Manuel Castells, *Technopoles of the World: The Making of Twenty-first Century Industrial Complexes* (New York: Routledge, 1994); Ann Markusen, Peter Hall, and Amy Glasmeier, *High Tech America: The What, How, When, and Why of the Sunrise Industries* (Boston: Allen and Unwin, 1986); AnnaLee Saxenian, *Regional Advantage: Culture and Competition in Silicon Valley and Route 128* (Cambridge, MA: Harvard University Press, 1994); Allen J. Scott, *Technopolis: The Geography of High Tech in Southern California* (Berkeley: University of California Press, 1993); Glenna Mathews, *Silicon Valley, Women, and the California Dream* (Stanford: Stanford University Press, 2003); Margaret O'Mara, *Cities of Knowledge: Cold War Science and the Search for the Next Silicon Valley* (Princeton: Princeton University Press, 2005); Christophe Lecuyer, *Making Silicon Valley: Innovation and the Growth of High Tech, 1930–1970* (Cambridge, MA: MIT Press, 2006); and Linda Scarbrough, *Road, River, and Ol' Boy Politics: A Texas County's Path from Farm to Supersuburb* (Austin: Texas State Historical Association, 2005). Mansel Blackford, *Pathways to the Present: United States Development and Its Consequences in the Pacific* (Honolulu: University of Hawaii Press, 2007) places economic and environmental changes on the West Coast and the Pacific in the context of Cold War politics and military policy.

The scholarship on the Latino and African American experience in early-twentieth-century Los Angeles is now abundant: Albert Camarillo, *Chicanos in a Changing Society: From Mexican Pueblos to American Barrios in Santa Barbara and Southern California, 1948–1930* (Cambridge, MA: Harvard University Press, 1979); Ricardo Romo, *East Los Angeles: History of a Barrio* (Austin: University of Texas Press, 1983); Douglas Monroy, *Rebirth: Mexican Los Angeles from the Great Migration to the Great Depression* (Berkeley: University of California Press, 1999); Mark Wild, *Street Meeting: Multiethnic Neighborhoods in the Early Twentieth Century Los Angeles* (Berkeley: University of California Press); Douglas Flamming, *Bound for Freedom: Black Los Angeles in Jim Crow America* (Berkeley: University of California Press, 2005); George Sanchez, *Becoming Mexican American: Ethnicity, Culture, and Identity in Chicano Los Angeles, 1900–1945* (New York: Oxford University Press, 1993); Edward Escobar, *Race, Police, and the Making of a Political Identity: Mexican Americans and the Los Angeles Police Department, 1900–1945* (Berkeley: University of California Press, 1999); Eduardo Obregón Pagán, *Murder at the Sleepy Lagoon: Zoot Suits, Race, and Riot in Wartime Los Angeles* (Chapel Hill: University of North Carolina Press, 2003).

For southern California in the years from World War II, see Josh Sides, *L.A. City Limits: African American Los Angeles from the Great Depression to the Present* (Berkeley: University of California Press, 2003); Laura Pulido, *Black, Brown, Yellow, and Left: Radical Activism in Los Angeles* (Berkeley: University of California Press, 2006); Raphael Sonenshein, *Politics in Black and White: Race and Power in Los Angeles* (Princeton: Princeton University Press, 1993); Eric Avila, *Popular Culture in the Age of White Flight: Fear and Fantasy in Suburban Los Angeles* (Berkeley: University of California Press, 2004); Kevin Leonard, *The Battle for Los Angeles: Racial Ideology and World War II* (Albuquerque: University of New Mexico Press, 2006); Gerald Horne, *Fire Next Time: The Watts Uprising and the 1960s* (Charlottesville: University Press of Virginia, 1995); and Allison Varzally, *Making a Non-white California: Californians Coloring outside Ethnic Lines, 1925–1955* (Berkeley: University of California Press, 2008).

On racial minorities and race relations in the Bay Area in the first half of the twentieth century, important sources are Albert Broussard, *Black San Francisco: The Struggle for Racial Equality, 1900–1954* (Lawrence: University Press of Kansas, 1993); Shirley Ann Wilson Moore, *To Place Our Deeds: The African American Community in Richmond, California, 1910–1963* (Berkeley: University of California Press, 2000); Robert Self, *American Babylon: Race and the Struggle for Postwar Oakland* (Princeton: Princeton University Press, 2003); Chris Rhomberg, *No There There: Race, Class and Political Community in Oakland* (Berkeley: University of California Press, 2004); Gretchen Lemke-Santanagelo, *Abiding Courage: African American Women and the East Bay Community* (Chapel Hill: University of North Carolina Press, 1996); and Steve Pitti, *The Devil in Silicon Valley: Northern California, Race, and Mexican Americans* (Princeton: Princeton University Press, 2003).

For the same issues outside California, see Wing Chung Ng, *The Chinese in Vancouver, 1945–1980: The Pursuit of Identity and Power* (Vancouver: University of British Columbia Press, 1999); Quintard Taylor, *The Forging of a Black Community: Seattle's Central District from 1870 to the Civil Rights Era* (Seattle: University of Washington

Press, 1994); Matthew Whitaker, *Race Work: The Rise of Civil Rights in the Urban West* (Lincoln: University of Nebraska Press, 2005); and Mario Garcia, *Desert Immigrants: The Mexicans of El Paso, 1880–1920* (New Haven: Yale University Press, 1981).

Political reform and reactions in the Bay Area are discussed in Frederick Wirt, *Power in the City* (Berkeley: University of California Press, 1975); John H. Mollenkopf, *The Contested City* (Princeton: Princeton University Press, 1983); Stephen McGovern, *The Politics of Downtown Development: Dynamic Political Culture in San Francisco and Washington, D.C.* (Lexington: University of Kentucky Press, 1998); Joseph Rodriguez, *City against Suburb: The Culture Wars in an American Metropolis* (Westport, CT: Praeger, 1999); Richard DeLeon, *Left Coast City: Progressive Politics in San Francisco, 1975–91* (Lawrence: University Press of Kansas, 1992); and Chester Hartman, *The Transformation of San Francisco* (Totowa, NJ: Rowman and Allenheld, 1984).

City and metropolitan politics in Los Angeles and its environs are treated in Tom Sitton, *Los Angeles Transformed: Fletcher Bowron's Urban Reform Revival, 1938–53* (Albuquerque: University of New Mexico Press, 2005); Lisa McGirr, *Suburban Warriors: The Origins of the New American Right* (Princeton: Princeton University Press, 2001); and Spencer Olin Jr., Rob Kling, and Mark Poster, eds., *Post-suburban California: The Transformation of Orange County since World War II* (Berkeley: University of California Press, 1991). Mike Davis, *City of Quartz: Excavating the Future in Los Angeles* (New York: Vintage Books, 1992) ranges widely and incisively over politics and culture.

For Portland's experiments in city and regional planning, see Paul Lewis, *Shaping Suburbia: How Political Institutions Organize Urban Development* (Pittsburgh: University of Pittsburgh Press, 1996); Carl Abbott, *Portland: Planning, Politics and Growth in a Twentieth Century City* (Lincoln: University of Nebraska Press, 1983); and Carl Abbott, *Greater Portland: Urban Life and Landscape in the Pacific Northwest* (Philadelphia: University of Pennsylvania Press, 2001).

On Houston, see Joe Feagin, *Free Enterprise City: Houston in Political-Economic Perspective* (New Brunswick, NJ: Rutgers University Press, 1988); Chandler Davidson, *Bi-racial Politics: Conflict and Coalition in the Metropolitan South* (Baton Rouge: Louisiana State University Press, 1972); Robert Bullard, *Invisible Houston: The Black Experience in Boom and Bust* (College Station: Texas A&M University Press, 1987); Beth Anne Shelton, Joe R. Feagin, Robert Bullard, Nestor Rodriguez, and Robert D. Thomas, *Houston: Growth and Decline in a Sunbelt Boomtown* (Philadelphia: Temple University Press, 1989); and David McComb, *Houston: A History* (Austin: University of Texas Press, 1981).

Political change in other cities is treated in Amy Bridges, *Morning Glories: Municipal Reform in the Southwest* (Princeton: Princeton University Press, 1997); Robert Fairbanks, *For the City as a Whole: Planning, Politics, and the Public Interest in Dallas, Texas, 1900–1965* (Columbus: Ohio State University Press, 1998); Michael Logan, *Fighting Sprawl and City Hall: Resistance to Urban Growth in the Southwest* (Tucson: University of Arizona Press, 1995); Mario Garcia, *The Making of a Mexican American Mayor: Raymond L. Telles of El Paso* (El Paso: Texas Western Press, 1998); Bradford Luckingham, *Phoenix: The History of a Southwestern Metropolis* (Tucson: University of Arizona Press, 1989); Janet Daly-Bednarik, *The Changing Image of the City: Planning for Downtown Omaha, 1945–73* (Lincoln: University of Nebraska Press, 1992); David R. Johnson, John A. Booth, and Richard J. Harris, *The Politics of San*

Antonio (Lincoln: University of Nebraska Press, 1983); and Anthony Orum, *Power, Money and the People* (Austin: Texas Monthly Press, 1987).

CHAPTER THIRTEEN. RESHAPING THE METROPOLIS

Larry Ford, *Metropolitan San Diego: How Geography and Lifestyle Shape a New Urban Environment* (Philadelphia: University of Pennsylvania Press, 2005); Carl Abbott, *Greater Portland: Urban Life and Landscape in the Pacific Northwest* (Philadelphia: University of Pennsylvania Press, 2001); and Patricia Gober, *Metropolitan Phoenix: Place Making and Community Building in the Desert* (Philadelphia: University of Pennsylvania Press, 2006) are entries in a Metropolitan Portraits series that tries to place contemporary cities in historical and spatial perspective. John Findley, *Magic Lands: Western Cityscapes and American Culture after 1940* (Berkeley: University of California Press, 1992) is a creative effort to understand the cultural impulses behind western cityscapes, the topic also of Scott Bottles, *Los Angeles and the Automobile* (Berkeley: University of California Press, 1987).

Multiple aspects of growth and culture in Los Angeles are probed in several anthologies: Michael J. Dear, E. Eric Schockman, and Greg Hise, eds., *Rethinking Los Angeles* (Thousand Oaks, CA: Sage Publications, 1996); Allen J. Scott and Edward Soja, eds., *The City: Los Angeles and Urban Theory at the End of the Twentieth Century* (Berkeley: University of California Press, 1996); Michael J. Dear, ed., *From Chicago to L.A.: Making Sense of Urban Theory* (Thousand Oaks, CA: Sage Publications, 2002); and a special Los Angeles issue of *American Quarterly* 56 (September 2004), with articles by George Sanchez, Josh Sides, Regina Freer, Sarah Schrank, and many others.

Early efforts to regulate urban and regional growth are summarized in Peter Bosselman and David Callies, *The Quiet Revolution in Land Use Control* (Washington, DC: Council on Environmental Quality, 1972). The Oregon experience is discussed in Gerrit Knaap and Arthur C. Nelson, *The Regulated Landscape: Lessons on State Planning from Oregon* (Cambridge, MA: Lincoln Institute of Land Policy, 1992); Connie Ozawa, ed., *The Portland Edge: Challenges and Opportunities in Growing Communities* (Washington, DC: Island Press, 2005); and Jerry Weitz, *Sprawl Busting: State Programs to Guide Growth* (Chicago: American Planning Association, 1999). The Northwest can be compared with William Fulton, *The Reluctant Metropolis: The Politics of Urban Growth in Los Angeles* (Point Arena, CA: Solana Press Books, 1997).

For the West's fastest-growing city, see Hal Rothman, *Neon Metropolis: How Las Vegas Started the Twenty-first Century* (New York: Routledge, 2002); Hal Rothman and Mike Davis, *The Grit beneath the Glitter: Tales from the Real Las Vegas* (Berkeley: University of California Press, 2002); Mark Gottdiener, Claudia Collins, and David Dickens, *Las Vegas: The Social Production of an All American City* (Malden, MA: Blackwell, 1999); and Eugene Moehring, *Resort City in the Sunbelt: Las Vegas, 1930–1970* (Reno: University of Nevada Press, 1989).

CHAPTER FOURTEEN. TRANSNATIONAL URBANISM

As a counterpoint to WTO-era Seattle, see Timothy Gibson, *Securing the Spectacular City: The Politics of Revitalization and Homelessness in Downtown Seattle* (Lanham, MD: Lexington Books, 2004); Stephen Erie, *Globalizing L.A.: Trade, Infrastructure and*

Regional Development (Stanford: Stanford University Press, 2004); Lawrence Herzog, *From Aztec to High Tech: Architecture and Landscape across the Mexico–U.S. Border* (Baltimore: Johns Hopkins University Press, 1999).

For twentieth-century immigration more generally, see Elliott Barkan, *From All Points: America's Immigrant West, 1870s–1952* (Bloomington: Indiana University Press, 2007).

Timothy Fong, *The First Suburban Chinatown: The Remaking of Monterey Park, California* (Philadelphia: Temple University Press, 1994); Leland T. Saito, *Race and Politics: Asian Americans, Latinos, and Whites in a Los Angeles Suburb* (Urbana: University of Illinois Press, 1998); John Horton, *The Politics of Diversity: Immigration, Resistance, and Change in Monterey Park, California* (Philadelphia: Temple University Press, 1995); and Bernard Wong, *The Chinese in Silicon Valley: Globalization, Social Networks, and Ethnic Identity* (New York: Rowman and Littlefield, 2006).

Theoretical frameworks for understanding changing economic roles are found in Saskia Sassen, *The Global City: New York, London, Tokyo* (Princeton: Princeton University Press, 2001); Manuel Castells, *The Informational City* (Oxford: Blackwell, 1991); and Manuel Castells, *End of Millennium* (Malden, MA: Blackwell, 1998).

CHAPTER FIFTEEN. THE LONG ARM OF THE METROPOLITAN WEST

William Riebsame and James D. Robb, eds., *Atlas of the New West* (New York: Norton, 1997); and William [Riebsame] Travis, *New Geographies of the American West* (Washington, DC: Island Press, 2007) examine the redistribution of activity in the age of aviation and e-mail.

Peter Decker, *Old Fences, New Neighbors* (Albuquerque: University of New Mexico Press, 1998); Hal Rothman, *Devil's Bargains: Tourism in the Twentieth Century American West* (Lawrence: University Press of Kansas, 1998); and Thomas Power, *Lost Landscapes and Failed Economies: The Search for a Value of Place* (Washington, DC: Island Press, 1996) explore the transition to a postresource economy.

Katrine Barber, *The Death of Celilo* (Seattle: University of Washington Press, 2005); Art Gomez, *The Quest for the Golden Circle: The Four Corners and the Metropolitan West, 1945–1970* (Albuquerque: University of New Mexico Press, 1994); Andrew Gulliford, *Boomtown Blues: Colorado Oil Shale, 1885–1915* (Boulder: University Press of Colorado, 1989); Mim Dixon, *What Happened to Fairbanks: The Effects of the Trans-Alaska Pipeline on the Community of Fairbanks, Alaska* (Boulder: Westview Press, 1978); and William Robbins, *Hard Times in Paradise: Coos Bay, Oregon* (Seattle: University of Washington Press, 2006) are case studies of economic and social change in small western cities.

Regional resource and conservation planning in the metropolitan shadow are discussed in Timothy Duane, *Shaping the Sierra: Nature, Culture and Conflict in the Changing West* (Berkeley: University of California Press, 2000); Elizabeth Hamin, *Mojave Lands: Interpretive Planning and the National Preserve* (Baltimore: Johns Hopkins University Press, 2003); Hal Rothman, *The New Urban Park: The Golden Gate National Recreation Area and Civic Environmentalism* (Lawrence: University Press of Kansas, 2004); and Carl Abbott, Sy Adler, and Margery Post Abbott, *Planning a New West: The Columbia River Gorge National Scenic Area* (Corvallis: Oregon State University Press, 1994).

segregation in, 218; tourism and, 250, 262–63; war economy in, 172

Dalles, The (Ore.), 271–72

dams, 85, 91, 150–61; water management and, 89–91, 150–61, 172, 271, 306n9, 307n15

Decker, Peter, 266–67

density: urban, 138–41, *167*, 229–35, 294n11, 314n26

Denver: boosterism, 1, 3–4, 74, 116, 148–49, 257; discrimination in, 79–81, 270; as economic center, 4, 10, 34, 36, 75–84, 99, 108–10, 135, 182, 183, 285; education in, 183; as gateway, 4, 39, 45; growth of, 224, 225, 231, 232, 248, 250, 253, 270, 313n13; housing in, 132–33, 136–37, 139–40, 189; immigration to, 287–88; landscape and, 276–77; politics in, 143–49 passim, 206, 284; population growth of, 9, 35, 99, 220–21, 228, 230–31, 247, 312n6; the railroad and, 4, 33, 82–84; reform in, 188, 189, 192, *193*, *194*, 199, 213, 216; segregation in, 218; tourism in, 116, 121–23; war economy in, 176, 177, 180, 181, 277; water management in, 90–91, 157, 220; women in, 284–85

depressions, financial, 48, 83, 109, 122, 135, 144, 146–47, 153, 157

discrimination, 64–69, 79–82, 154, 176, 217–18, 298n19

disease: health resorts and, 116–22, 277; immigration and, 56, 66–67; plague, 66–67, 298n17

diversity, political, 203–18

divorce: Reno and, 115, 129–31

downtown. *See* centers; commercial districts

economy: interior West development of, 41–54, 100–14; international, 237–55; military influence on, 170–85, 239–40, 286–87; national, 46, 52, 258–59, 296n3; Pacific Rim, 55–73, 84, 134–36, 165; Pacific Rim as center, 1–2, 55–64, 69;

Pacific vs. Atlantic, 9, 21–22, 70, 165; Southwest and cross-border, 244–46, 314n10; urban development and, 4, 39–40, 74–87, 100–114 passim, 228–36, *268*; urban growth and consolidation of, 32–34, 36; West as part of global, 164–68, 237–55, 275; Western development of, 10–11, 26–27

edge cities, 227–29

Edmonton: early settlement of, 24; as economic center, 34, 166, 255; energy industry in, 12, 248–50, 285–86; population growth of, 10, 225, 234, 300n18, 314n28; reform in, 191, 208, 309n8; war economy in, 172

education, 28, 35, 68, 90, 94, 103–4, 106, 138, 141–44, 160, 175, 182–84, 198–201, 205–6, 207–13 passim, 224, 226–27, 238, 242–43, 246, 251, 260–63 passim, 280, 285, 287, 308n11, 310n15

electricity, 54, 72, 72–73, 84–85, 93–95, 106, 111, 120, 133, 152–61, 165–67, 172, 177–79, 188, 190, 271–72

El Paso: boosterism, 86; as economic center, 34, 85–87, 245, *245*, 267; growth of, 125, 134, 228, 232, 304n3; immigration to, 244–45, 247, 311n13; labor agitation in, 108–9; reform in, 213; segregation in, 218

environment: tourism and, 115–26, 150–52, 257–65; urban development vs., 100–114, 150–61, 203–11, 220–36, 237–39, 262–66, 286–87, 310n6, 314n26, 319n22; urban green spaces, 52, 118, 130, 141–45, 234

ethnicity: Asian, on Pacific coast, 55–73, 135, 241–44; as commodity, 126–29; eastern Europeans, 53–54, 137; enclaves in Southwest, 96–98, 201–2, 217–18, 244–48

Evans, John, 79–80

Everett (Wash.): growth of, 63, 105, 231, 270; labor unrest in, 107–8

138–41, 205n9; military, 170–71,
174–76, 220–33, *222*, 226, 228, 230

Houston: architecture in, 280; boosterism, 239, 255; as economic/energy
center, 12, 248–50, 253, 281–82;
education in, 183; as gateway, 50,
295n2; immigration to, 242, 247;
oil industry in, 34; politics in, 41,
309n7; population growth of, 9,
32, 224, 228, 231, 259, 277, 312n6;
reform in, 191, 192, 212–15; segregation in, 218; settlement of, 29;
war economy in, 171, 181

Hudson's Bay Company, 24, 55–56, 60,
62–63

Hugo, Richard, 138

immigration: Asian, 2, 9, 65–69,
240–44; between the United
States and Canada, 11–12, 102–3;
to California, 95–98; European,
29, 52–54, 102, 104, 135, 169–70;
Hispanic, 9, 82, 86–87, 96–98,
244–47, 314n11; to interior West,
47, 52, 100–114 passim, 133; labor
and, 55–58, 64–73, 94–99, 100–114
passim, 167, 275, 287–90; Pacific
Rim, 55–58, 64–73, 239–48, 287;
politics of, 9, 65–69, 143, 309n8;
to urban areas, 228, 277–78

Independence (Mo.), 44

industry, 29, 56–64; aerospace, 73, 159,
165, 171–72, 174, 177–82, 188, 199,
216, 224, 226, 260, 262, 304n20,
310n16, 316n14; Boeing, 108, 172,
174, 177, 199; copper, 94, 103–5,
110, 123; electronics and communication, 180–85, 238, 247–52, 262,
287; energy, 12, 152–61, 169–85
passim, 206–7, 210, 235, 270,
280; manufacturing, 54–62 passim, 83–85, 103–14 passim, 171–81,
244–45, 296n3, 315n16; mining,
12, 48, 58–59, 63–65, 75–87 passim, 90, 94, 100–106, 110–14, 123,
159–61, 257–59, 261, 263, 284,
297n6, 317n18; oil, 34, 46, 54, 73,
134, 155, 165, 190, 197, 224, 248–50,
255, 259–60, 278, 285–86;

ranching, 27, 45, 54, 80–89 passim, 97, 153, 256–59 passim,
264–67; service, 165, 167, 243,
262–63, 286; shipping, 55–64;
timber, 12, 62, 84–85, 105, 107–8,
257, 259, 261, 270

information technology, 2, 14, 169,
182–85, 287

innovation: the West and, 10, 100–114,
150–61, 169–71, 180–85, 203–11,
223, 226, 238, 247–52, 262,
278–82, 286–87, 308n12. *See also*
maturing

intellectuals, 169–71, 175, 183–84, 205,
260, 273

interior West: growth of, 29, *43*, 44–46,
177; rural tourism in, 256–72

irrigation, the building of the West and,
88–99, *98*, 150–61

Japan: economic and labor influence
of, 67–69, 73, 94, 96, 126, 138,
176, 198, 239–43, 251

Kansas City: boosterism, 3; growth of,
44, 46, 49–50; immigration to,
297n19; reform in, 192

Ku Klux Klan, 142–43, 280

labor, migration of workers, 11, 55–56,
64–73, 93–97, 100–114 passim,
132–33, 175–78, 195, 244, 247

labor unions, 104–14, 224, 302n13

Lakewood (Calif.), 223–24

landscape, importance of, 29, 35, 40,
45, 48, 78, 89–99 passim, 152–60
passim, 166, 220–22, 258–67 passim, 275–77, 286, 307n8, 317n23.
See also health; leisure; nature;
tourism

Langdon, Emma, 284

Laramie (Wyo.), 48

Las Vegas: consumption and, *167*,
319n22; population growth of,
9–10, 164, 166, 228, 230, 231, 247,
267, 277, 287, 312n6, 313n13; segregation in, 218; tourism in, 121,

151, 250, 270, 280, 286; as urban
growth prototype, 10, 235, 280,
318n8; war economy in, 172; water
systems and, 159, 235, 306n2

Latin America: emigration from, 18, 65,
217, 244, 246, 247, 287, 314n11

Leadville (Colo.), 82–83, 103, 126

leisure: in western cities, 38, 115–31,
151–52, 165, 257–67, 286

Lincoln (Nebr.), 49–50, 258, 296n9

literature, 4, 24, 39, 84, 230, 260; fiction, 2, 96, 102, 115, 130, 147, 150–51,
152, 161, 242, 247, 256–57, 260,
266; nature, 11–12, 48, 150, 166,
205–7, 220–224, 316n8; nostalgic,
17, 55, 102, 164; promotional, 5–10,
31, 32, 40, 70, 72–73, 85, 103, 115,
116–28 passim, 144, 147, 163, 277;
race-related, 68–69, 169, 186, 196,
200–201, 203, 243, 247; technology, 2, 169, 182, 185, 273, 275, 288;
travel writings, 103–4, 115–16, 164,
174; western rural, 51, 160, 196, 257,
266, 267; western urban, 53, 54,
55, 100, 132, 138, 152, 219–23, 230,
237, 273, 278, 288

Los Alamos (N. Mex.), 170–71, 175, 179,
185

Los Angeles: boosterism, 70, 73, 116,
137, 269; development of, 145–47,
153–55, 161, 186–87, 225, 273, 280;
economic growth of, 10, 109, 134,
135, 164, 181, 252–55, 253, 282; establishment of, 23, 26–27; housing
in, 136–38, 198, 222; immigration
to, 241, 243, 246–47, 287–88; landscape of, 276–77; nostalgia about,
163–64; oil industry in, 34; population growth of, 9, 32, 229–30,
275–76; race relations in, 197–201,
213, 217–18, 228, 264, 269, 298n17,
314n11; the railroad and, 33, 95; as
resource center, 5, 270; suburbs in,
222–23; tourism and, 116–18, 121,
146–48, 250, 262–63, 285–86; war
economy in, 171, 176

maturing: of Western cities, 8–10, 28,
33–37, 46–50, 53–54, 62–64, 70,
85–85, 103, 134, 164–65, 234–36,
275, 277–83. See also innovation

McMurtry, Larry, 256–57

Medford (Ore.), 12

megalopolis. See urbanization

Meredith, Ellis, 284–85

Mesa (Ariz.), 91, 225, 227, 230

Mexico: migration between United
States and, 42, 68, 86–87, 96–97,
104–14 passim, 119, 136, 199,
226–37, 244–47, 269, 275; northern settlements in, 18–28 passim,
42, 86–87

Mexico City: U.S. connections with, 15,
19, 42, 82, 85, 87, 239, 275, 294n5

migration: labor, 135; urban, 51–52,
102–3. See also immigration

military influence on economy, 163–85,
239–40, 286–87; Air Force,
171–72, 178, 246, 286; Army,
81–82, 110, 171, 179, 246; empire-
building and, 19–21, 55–56; housing, 170–72, 174–82; Navy, 72–73,
171, 188; war in, 9, 41, 69–70,
79–82, 92, 104, 109–10, 114, 141–43,
147, 167, 169–85, 187, 220, 239,
283; western presence, 169–85,
220, 239–40

Minneapolis: as gateway, 42, 50;
growth of, 49, 135, 136; manufacturing growth of, 46, 296n3;
protests in, 310n19

minorities: urbanization and, 228–29,
280, 287; working-class communities and, 101–14 passim, 133, 135,
137–38, 186–202, 228

Mississippi River: urban growth along,
23, 24, 28–29, 39–54, 75, 136, 175

Missoula (Mont.): environmentalism
in, 310n6; growth of, 263, 271;
labor agitation in, 109

Montana, 50, 103–4, 257–72 passim

Monterey: as economic center, 26,
27, 105; tourism in, 119, 123, 126,
261–62

196, 269; reform in, 188, 189, 192, 212, 287; segregation in, 218; tourism in, 116–25 passim, 146; water in, 91, 158–60

Pikes Peak, 51, 103, 106, 120, 123

politics: conservative, 155, 186, 192, 213–15, 229, 282, 287; immigration and, 309n8, 309n14; liberalism, 78, 168, 187, 202–33, 283, 305n14; populism, 106, 129, 141–43, 207; progressivism, 155, 187–88, 190–92, 202, 205–18, radical, 54, 110–12, 141–42, 198, 207–8, 211, 283, 305n14; reform in, 309n6, 311n14; socialism, 106–11 passim, 141–43, 192; women and, 142, 146, 210–11, 214, 229, 284–85, 319n17

population: growth in metropolitan areas, 9–10, 30, 32, 35, 55–73 passim, 84–87, 166, 220–36, 298n12, 311n20, 312n6; shift from rural to urban, 9, 29, 31–33, 51–52, 166, 292n18, 301n13, 314n26; shift to the West, 8–9, 48–49, 163–69, 177–81, 221, 275, 292n15, 317n18

Portland: activism in, 203–4, 207–8, 270; boosterism, 36, 62, 70, 144, 148–49, 278; environmentalism in, 191–92, 264–65, 286, 319n22; as gateway city, 4, 115–16, 259, 298n10; growth of, 224–25, 231–33, 288, 315n16; housing in, 134–40 passim, 196; immigration to, 65–67, 66, 70, 144, 175–76, 195, 243, 247; industry in, 108–10, 135; information industry in, 182, 248; politics in, 141–42, 144–45; population growth of, 35, 62, 65–67, 70, 230, 233, 312n6, 313n13; as port, 58, 60–63; reform in, 191–92; tourism in, 123; war economy in, 171–77 passim; water systems of, 156–57; women leaders in, 210

ports: economic opportunities for, 21–24, 41–46, 55–73, 172, 276, 298n10

Port Townsend (Wash.), 63, 63

poverty, urban, 58–59, 132, 186–202 passim

Prairie Provinces: growth of, 48–49, 53–54, 231, 263–64

Provo (Utah): as cultural center, 271; growth of, 90, 99, 172, 231, 312n6; immigration to, 12

Pueblo (Colo.), 82–83, 157

Puget Sound: economy and shipping in, 55–64, 237–39; growth of, 231–37 passim, 260–61; immigration to, 64–73 passim; labor in, 11, 104, 107–12 passim

Pyle, Robert Michael, 219–21

Pynchon, Thomas, 152, 278

race: city image and, 146–49; class and, 96–99, 100–114, 246–48; discrimination and, 64–69, 79–82, 154, 176, 186–202, 217–18, 307n6; identity and, 269; interracial settlement, 23, 55–73, 100–14 passim, 204–18, 239–48, 287–90; labor and, 169, 175–76; suburbanization and, 224, 228

railroads: building of, 4–5, 33–35, 42, 46–48, 59, 62–65, 78–87, 95, 106, 108, 269, 296n3; city-building and the, 4, 31, 33–35, 37, 42–48, 59, 63, 92, 133, 135, 257, 260, 296n6; projected, in Boise, 5, 6; promotion, 116–19, 121–23, 304n15; transcontinental, 13, 14, 31, 33, 37, 42, 44–45, 62–63, 118, 121

recreation. See leisure

Redding (Calif.), 12

reform, 35, 38, 106, 141–44, 187–90, 302n13, 309n6, 319n17

Regina (Sask.), 48–49

regulation, urban, 52, 89–91, 100–114, 118, 130, 138–45, 150–61, 203–11, 229–39, 264, 286–87, 294n11, 310n6, 314n26

religion: churches, 102, 104, 260, 287; class and, 133; early European settlement, 20–23; Mormons, 75–78

Reno: divorce and, 115, 129–31; growth of, 139–40, 261–62, 276, 317n18; race relations in, 298n17

174, 189, 297n17; as sign of urban permanence, 28, 36, 102, 260; traveling, 115–16; working-class, 102, 132–33, 245, 310n16

Woodlands, the (Tex.), 225–26

world's fairs, 70–73, 72, 109, 119, 145–49, 193, 210, 241, 299n25, 306n21, 311n11

writers, western, 267, 270, 271, 283–84, 295n2, 316n8, 318n26

Wyoming: discrimination in, 80–81; energy and, 160; growth of, 50, 80–81

Young, Brigham, 75–76